TORTURE, PSYCHOANALYSIS AND HUMAN RIGHTS

Torture, Psychoanalysis and Human Rights contributes to the development of that field of study referred to as 'psycho-social' that is presently more and more committed to providing understanding of social phenomena, making use of the explicative perspective of psychoanalysis. The book seeks to develop a concise and integrated framework of understanding of torture as a socio-political phenomenon based on psychoanalytic thinking, through which different dimensions of the subject of study become more comprehensible.

Monica Luci argues that torture performs a covert emotional function in society. In order to identify what this function might be, a profile of 'torturous societies' and the main psychological dynamics of social actors involved – torturers, victims, and bystanders – are drawn from literature. Accordingly, a wide-ranging description of the phenomenology of torture is provided, detecting an inclusive and recurring pattern of key elements. Relying on psychoanalytic concepts derived from different theoretical traditions, including British object relations theories, American relational psychoanalysis and analytical psychology, the study provides an advanced line of conceptual research, shaping a model, whose aim is to grasp the deep meaning of key intrapsychic, interpersonal and group dynamics involved in torture.

Once a sufficiently coherent understanding has been reached, Luci proposes using it as a groundwork tool in the human rights field to re-think the best strategies for prevention and recovery from post-torture psychological and social suffering. The book initiates a dialogue between psychoanalysis and human rights, showing that the proposed psychoanalytic understanding is a viable conceptualization for expanding the thinking of crucial issues regarding torture, which might be relevant to human rights and legal doctrine, such as the responsibility of perpetrators, the reparation for victims and the question of 'truth'.

Torture, Psychoanalysis and Human Rights is the first book to build a psychoanalytic theory of torture from which psychological, social and legal reflections, as well as practical aspects of treatment, can be mutually derived and understood. It will appeal to psychoanalysts, psychoanalytic psychotherapists and Jungians, as well as scholars of politics, social work and justice, and human rights and postgraduate students studying across these fields.

Monica Luci, PhD, is an analytical psychologist and relational psychoanalyst, with extensive experience in the psycho-social assistance and psychotherapeutic work with asylum seekers and refugee survivors of torture. On the topics of survivors of torture and post-traumatic states in psychological assessment, psychotherapy and research, she has contributed to a number of international conferences and taught in several professional and academic contexts. She is also an author, translator and editor of publications on the themes of trauma, collective violence, cultural studies, transcultural psychology, sexuality and ethical issues.

TORTURE, PSYCHOANALYSIS AND HUMAN RIGHTS

Monica Luci

LONDON AND NEW YORK

First published 2017
by Routledge
2 Park Square, Milton Park, Abingdon, Oxon OX14 4RN

and by Routledge
711 Third Avenue, New York, NY 10017

Routledge is an imprint of the Taylor & Francis Group, an informa business

© 2017 Monica Luci

The right of Monica Luci to be identified as author of this work has been asserted by her in accordance with sections 77 and 78 of the Copyright, Designs and Patents Act 1988.

All rights reserved. No part of this book may be reprinted or reproduced or utilised in any form or by any electronic, mechanical, or other means, now known or hereafter invented, including photocopying and recording, or in any information storage or retrieval system, without permission in writing from the publishers.

Trademark notice: Product or corporate names may be trademarks or registered trademarks, and are used only for identification and explanation without intent to infringe.

British Library Cataloguing-in-Publication Data
A catalogue record for this book is available from the British Library

Library of Congress Cataloging-in-Publication Data
Names: Luci, Monica, 1972–, author.
Title: Torture, psychoanalysis, and human rights / Monica Luci.
Description: New York : Routledge, 2017. | Includes bibliographical references and index.
Identifiers: LCCN 2016042612| ISBN 9781138908598 (hardback : alk. paper) | ISBN 9781138908604 (pbk. : alk. paper) | ISBN 9781315694320 (e-book)
Subjects: LCSH: Psychoanalysis. | Torture—Psychological aspects. | Torture victims. | Human rights.
Classification: LCC BF173 .L783 2017 | DDC 150.19/5—dc23
LC record available at https://lccn.loc.gov/2016042612

ISBN: 978-1-138-90859-8 (hbk)
ISBN: 978-1-138-90860-4 (pbk)
ISBN: 978-1-315-69432-0 (ebk)

Typeset in Bembo and Stone Sans
by Florence Production Ltd. Stoodleigh, Devon, UK

To Leonardo with love

CONTENTS

Acknowledgments ix
Introduction xi

PART 1
The phenomenon of torture   1

1   Torture: what is it? A definition of the field of inquiry   3

Torture in international law   3
Torture in literature   8
References   13

2   Torturous societies   15

Torture: a power relationship between two embodied social realities   15
The basic features of a torturous society   20
References   27

3   Social actors of torture   31

Perpetrators   31
Victims of torture   51
Bystanders   63
References   75

PART 2
A psychoanalytic understanding of torture   91

4   Paradoxical Multiple Self States and Monolithic Self States: destinies of the Reflective Triangle   93

A theoretical premise   94
The paradox of the multiple self: multiplicity as unity and dissociation as continuity   96

The in-between space: *an investigation into the phenomenology of states of* twoness *and* states of thirdness   100
Paradoxical multiple self-states *and* monolithic self-states: *destinies of the Reflective Triangle*   121
References   128

5   The emotional life of torturous societies: Monolithic Societal States   135

Freud: what kind of group psychology?   137
Application to torturous societies   139
The shape of a Monolithic Societal State   143
Torture   156
References   158

6   The Splintered Reflective Triangle in bystanders, perpetrators and victims of torture   161

Me–You and You–Me: bystanders and the phenomenon of the 'missing witness'   162
Other–Me and Me–Other: the objectification of perpetrators   167
Other–You and You–Other: de-subjectification of the victims   176
References   185

PART 3
Implications for human rights   193

7   The permissibility of torture   195

Arguments for torture   195
Arguments against torture   200
Emotional undercurrents of rational arguments   206
References   208

8   Three fields of application in human rights: responsibility of perpetrators, reparation for victims and the problem of truth   211

Responsibility of perpetrators of torture   211
Reparation for survivors of torture   219
The question of 'truth'   227
References   237

Index   245

ACKNOWLEDGEMENTS

The research that led to this book would not have been possible without the contribution of many people in the academic and clinical fields and in my private life.

I am grateful to all the staff I met at the Centre for Psychoanalytic Studies of University of Essex for the interesting and stimulating academic environment in which my research started and developed. First and foremost, I would like to express my sincere and warm gratitude to Renos Papadopoulos, Professor of Analytical Psychology, who provided insight and expertise that greatly assisted the research that led to this book and made it possible. Our discussions and different perspectives on the topic were immensely thought-provoking and enriching. Particularly special and affectionate thanks to Andrew Samuels, Professor of Analytical Psychology, whose tremendously interesting work, and research spirit inspired this book, and without his knowledge and valuable critique, this study would not have been as far-reaching.

I would like to acknowledge Professor John Packer, former Director of the Human Rights Center of University of Essex and now Professor of Law and Director of the Human Rights Research and Education Centre at the University of Ottawa, for sharing his ideas during the earlier phases of this research and for his trust and enthusiastic encouragement in the dialogue between psychoanalysis and human rights.

Particularly warm thoughts go to my patients who inspired my work and without whom this study would never have started, and to my colleagues at the Italian Council for Refugees in Rome, with particular mention of Fiorella Rathaus and Massimo Germani, that enabled me to work in the field of care of survivors of torture and who exchange daily their views on issues of clinical rehabilitation with me.

Finally, a tender mention goes to my family and friends for their continuous understanding and support. Among them, my special loving and particular thanks go to Leonardo, to whom I am indebted for almost everything, and whose love, stimulating intelligence, encouragement, copious criticism, material, moral and spiritual care enabled me to complete this work.

Excerpts from *Nineteen Eighty-Four* by George Orwell. Copyright 1949 by Houghton Mifflin Harcourt Publishing Company and renewed 1977, by Sonia Brownell Orwell, Reprinted by permission of Houghton Mifflin Harcourt Publishing Company. All rights reserved.

Also excerpts from *Nineteen Eighty-Four* by George Orwell (Martin Secker & Warburg 1949, Penguin Books 1954, 1989, 2000). Copyright 1949 by Eric Blair. This edition copyright © the Estate of the late Sonia Brownell Orwell, 1987. Introduction © copyright Ben Pimlott, 1989. Notes on the Text © copyright Peter Davison, 1989. Reproduced by permission of Penguin Books Ltd.

Disclaimer: Throughout the book, gender-specific terms *may* be used in order to ease the text flow. Whenever a gender-specific term is used, it should be understood as referring to both genders, unless explicitly stated. This is done solely for the purpose of making the text easier to read, and no offense or sexism is intended.

INTRODUCTION

> Indifference is the deadweight of history . . . it numbly operates, but still operates . . . it is the raw matter that obstructs intelligence . . . Between absenteeism and indifference a few unattended hands, out of any control, weave the canvas of collective life.[1]
>
> (Antonio Gramsci, *The Indifferent*, 1 February 1917)

Many years before the research that led to this book, then during the process of writing, I initiated working as a clinical psychologist and, then, as Jungian analyst with asylum seekers and refugees who had survived torture. That experience was one of the most problematic, demanding and challenging in my life, but it was and still is a great source of knowledge, nurturance and relational richness.

Especially during the earliest years, I felt that the work with my patients who had survived extremely disruptive experiences and their moving life stories 'at the mind's limits' (from Améry, 1980) had a powerful uprooting, alienating effect on me. Thanks to them, I did become aware of something that could not be easily communicated to others – even very qualified friends and esteemed colleagues – and could not be easily integrated into my life.

First, I became aware 'first hand' about the existence and wide spread of torture in the contemporary world, which was something I prejudicially relegated to a gloomy obscurantist past. Second, being exposed to the survivors' live narratives and physical marks reproduced in my mind a compulsive repetitive thinking of the disturbing material of my patients in therapy. For all their powerful and dreadful content, these thoughts possessed an essential quality of 'secrecy', that I could not fully understand. In this regard, Marcel Viñar writes:

> nobody wants to know anything or believe anything about the horrors of torture, which, as a consequence, are actively ignored – a reaction which

extreme horror provokes, [this is] because no optimum distance [to fear] is possible, only avoidance or fascination. The person who watches is either too close – involved and captivate – or too far – an outsider, and maybe cannot feel anything.

(Viñar, 2005: 315)

My reaction was one of fascination and captivation. Indeed, in a separate room of my mind a repetitive and haunting question never ceased to torment me about it: '*Why torture?*'

At the time, I had the impression that our knowledge of torture was at the same point of Winston's in George Orwell's *Nineteen Eighty Four*, when, at the beginning of his attempt to enfranchise himself from the external and internal domination of the Party, he writes in his diary: 'I do understand *HOW*, but I do not understand *WHY*' (1949: 83). Similarly, we know how torture works and to what extent in the world, but we are far from reaching an understanding of its deep psychological rationale. What is the reason for continuing a cruel practice that is inaccurate in producing intelligence, ineffective as punishment, useless and illegal as war making tech-nique and, in addition, has deep destructive effects on victims' private life and in the life of communities? Beyond ethical and health concerns, if humanity still continues to use torture there must be a motivation, though distorted and morally wrong.

In fact, despite the relevant number of international declarations and conventions prohibiting human rights violations, nowadays torture is still a highly pervasive practice. When the Second World War was about to end, the United Nations was created and, as early as 1948, the General Assembly adopted the Universal Decla-ration of Human Rights. Article 5 of this declaration reads: 'No one shall be subjected to torture or to cruel, inhuman or degrading treatment or punishment', phrasing which can be found reproduced, almost or wholly word for word, until now in regional declarations on human rights and subsequent conventions. Nevertheless, it was recognized that torture in the world was continuing and practiced to a great and frequent extent. In 2004, the authors of the Istanbul Proto-col were still able to note: 'The striking disparity between the absolute prohibition of torture and its prevalence in the world today demonstrates the need for states to identify and implement effective measures to protect individuals from torture and ill-treatment' (OHCHR, 2004:1). Amnesty International reports every year on breaches of human rights, indicating that torture invariably takes place in a signi-ficant number of countries. For example, between January 2009 and May 2013, Amnesty International received reports of torture and other ill-treatment committed by state officials in 141 countries, and from every world region. The 2014 report was significantly titled *Torture in 2014: 30 Years of Broken Promises*.

In his *Understanding Torture* Wisnewski writes:

> There has never been a time when the world was without torture. It has emerged in many ways, and has been supported in many institutional venues,

but it has never been far from civilization.... Our changing relations to torture are one of the most interesting features of its history. We have at once thought torture absolutely necessary to secure a just trial, and through it utterly incompatible with any kind of justice. We have both abhorred it and demanded it.... Unfortunately, torture doesn't seem to be going anywhere. This painful and lamentable fact – that torture is both in our past and on our horizon – demands our scrutiny.

(Wisnewski, 2010: 3–4)

Reflecting on the overall phenomenon of torture today necessitates an effort to gain a deeper and wider interdisciplinary understanding in terms of the primary deep reason for its use and the conditions that lead to its emergence. Torture is a complex, multifaceted phenomenon with political, social, economic, psychological, legal, philosophical aspects, and, because of this complexity, it requires a complex analytical perspective. This book is intended as a psycho-social study aimed at developing an integrated framework for the understanding of torture, which might address this socio-political phenomenon from a psychoanalytic perspective. However, it also engages controversial issues of the legal theory and practice of the protection of human rights and the fight against torture. Approaching torture in this way is not accidental: as Elaine Scarry argues, torture is the inversion of both justice and health (1985: 41–2).

Psychoanalytic investigation is not usually associated with the phenomena of legal justice. The traditional reluctance of psychoanalysis to comment upon the domain of jurisprudence has arisen out of the predominant interest of psychoanalysis in psychological and clinical enquiry rather than cultural or social processes. But this has been changing slowly. Nowadays, psychoanalysis is more interested in the social processes, while increasingly recognizing its ethical foundations as both theory and practice. In particular, it is worth noticing the attention given in the last two decades by American relational psychoanalysis to social issues (Altman, 2008, 2009; Grand, 2008, 2013; Hollander, 2006, 2009; Layton et al., 2006; Summers, 2006, 2009, among many others), in a few cases in direct connection with human rights (Harris and Botticelli, 2010; Thomas, 2009), along with the interesting debate that is currently developing within analytic psychology about social and political themes (Beebe, 2003; Papadopoulos, 2002, 2005; Samuels, 2001, 2015a, 2015b; Singer, 2000, 2012; Zoja, 2009, among many others).

At first glance, torture does not seem to be a uniform phenomenon. It can be used in a number of different socio-political contexts and for different conscious reasons: it may be used by regimes to fight opposition; in counterinsurgency wars to silence 'subversion' and/or to fight (so called) 'state enemies'; in the context of intelligence gathering by secret services; in the context of the 'war on terror' to fight 'terrorists', etc. Despite such a variety in its manifestations, the phenomenon of torture is here investigated in order to detect a possible unifying unconscious pattern, which may go beyond this apparent multiplicity. The effort is to identify a 'core structure' of torture that might offer an understanding and organize its key themes in a coherent and inclusive view, while also leaving space in terms of the variability of the phenomenon.

A particular emphasis will be on the continuum of intrapsychic, interpersonal, group and socio-political aspects of torture, in order to stress that, beyond this multiplicity and complexity, from a psychological perspective, there is continuity among these different levels.

The method and structure of the book

The method of this study consists in: 1) critically reviewing the literature on torture addressing both its socio-political aspects and key issues of the social actors involved; 2) developing a framework of understanding of the phenomenon of torture based on psychoanalysis and analytical psychology, which might give reasons for the essential intrapsychic, interpersonal, groupal/institutional dynamics described in the previous part; 3) connecting such a model to the human rights field, exploring a possible dialogue between these two disciplines – psychoanalysis and human rights – on some essential questions with mutual benefit.

The aim of Part 1 is to delineate the subject matter of the book: the phenomenon of contemporary state torture with consideration to its social, groupal and individual aspects.

Chapter 1 is intended to define the research area, detecting some core features and giving a concise definition of the phenomenon of state torture. In order to do this, this chapter investigates the 'what', 'who' and 'why' of torture according to both contemporary international law and relevant literature that analyzes the topic from different perspectives. The aim is to arrive at a definition of torture that grasps the 'general profile' of the phenomenon beyond its relative variations.

Chapter 2 provides an overview of the main socio-political features characterizing 'torturous societies' (i.e. societies where torture is systematically used) in terms of their socio-political dynamics and narratives. An argument is developed indicating that torture appears in certain societies, in which the conditions for torture to emerge are created. These conditions are outlined in order to demonstrate a 'typical recurring pattern': 1) a power relationship between two embodied social realities: the torturous power and the sub-human; 2) an emotional situation characterized by a state of terror in the face of a perceived threat; 3) the double bind between torture and terror; 4) the presence of an invisible enemy; 5) the need for separations; and 6) the establishment of a better world ideology, which aims to recreate society.

The aim of Chapter 3 is to present a concise picture of the main key issues concerning social actors involved in torture. In the wake of leading authors' works on this theme, this phenomenological analysis looks at the fundamental social and psychological issues characterizing the experience of social actors of torture, i.e. perpetrators, victims and bystanders. The considerable amount of existing literature on perpetrators is organized into three main problem areas: 1) 'the problem of evil', which describes social processes that make evil and torture more likely to occur in society; 2) 'the making of torturers', which outlines the most common methods employed to create torturers out of ordinary people; and 3) 'the future of torturers', which depicts what happens to torturers after the collapse of torturous powers. In the section dedicated to victims, a portrait of victims of torture is delineated: their somatic and psychological suffering; the way this is described in psychological and psychiatric narratives; the traumatic bonding and the intergenerational transmission of trauma; and possible positive responses to the experience of torture. As far as the population of bystanders is concerned, the paragraph addresses the complex picture of different bystanders' attitudes, including internal and external bystanders. Attitudes towards torture are placed along a continuum of responses of denial: from an attitude of passive support (the continuum between perpetrators and bystanders) to passive opposition (the continuum between bystanders and victims). Rescuers and political opponents are included in this analysis.

The aim of Part 2 is to develop a psychoanalytic framework of understanding of the phenomenon of torture outlined in Part 1. Psychoanalytic concepts from different psychoanalytic traditions (British object relations theories, American relational psychoanalysis and analytical psychology) are selected in order to grasp key intrapsychic, interpersonal and group dynamics involved in torture. This blend of theories (especially the combination of analytic psychology and relational psychoanalysis) has some legitimacy, which is briefly addressed at this point. Also in this part, large and small group dynamics, as well as the interpersonal and intrapsychic mechanisms described in Part 1 are analyzed and understood in light of the proposed paradigm of understanding.

In Chapter 4 a range of psychoanalytic concepts are presented and discussed to give conceptual underpinnings to the central concept of the *Reflective Triangle*. This concept relies on the image of a triangle to represent a state of mind, which makes use of three (real or phantasized) poles – i.e. Me, You and Other – to process emotions and to shape thinking. The modes of using these three poles are critical to the mode of processing issues of identity and difference in relationships, which is at the core of crucial reflective skills and symbolizing functions. Several psychoanalytic theories seem to suggest, in different theoretical languages, that a healthy self works as a paradoxical multiplicity of self states, that is in *states of thirdness* (or through *Reflective Triangles*). The possibility of maintaining such a state of mind is at the core of the *Paradoxical Multiple Self States* dynamics, where identity and difference can be processed simultaneously. On the contrary, a *Splintered Reflective Triangle*, and in turn *Monolithic Self States* are at the origin of *states of twoness*, in which identity and difference cannot be processed at the same time, while the reflective function of self is compromised.

The aim of Chapter 5 is to reconsider large group dynamics in torturous societies, as outlined in Chapter 2, in light of the psychoanalytic concepts of the concepts of *Monolithic Societal States* and *states of twoness*, as discussed in Chapter 4. The groundwork for such an interpretation is offered by Freud's *Group Psychology and the Analysis of the Ego* and Foucault's description of the Bentam's Panopticon. The latter provides the ideal political geometry of a *Monolithic Societal State*, where the social dynamics result from a system of multiple splintered triangles. Torture is understood as the manifestation of a *Splintered Reflective Triangle* at a social level, which shapes, on one hand, monolithic group identities based on an overemphasized sameness *versus* another group whose difference is overemphasized as well. The space of the *Reflective Triangle* is not available, with the resulting one-dimensional connections based on identity *or* on difference prompting individuals to work in a bi-dimensional way within their roles of perpetrators, victims and bystanders. This is meant to explain the typical pattern of social relations established in torturous societies and the dehumanizing logics of torture.

Chapter 6 illustrates how the phenomena of bystanders, perpetrators and victims of torture, as described in Chapter 3, could be understood in greater depth by making use of the concept of the *Splintered Reflective Triangle* (Chapters 4 and 5). For each category of social actor, we can find, to a certain extent, the repetition of the same pattern: an extensive use of *states of twoness* that generates, on the one hand, 'psychotic' (horizontal) phenomena of identity (among those who perceive themselves as peers and belonging to the same group) and, on the other hand, 'perverse' (vertical) phenomena of difference (among those in conditions of social inequality and/or in hierarchical contexts). In such a state of mind, the in-between spaces of individual self are progressively 'sequestered', and individuals tend to behave as perpetrators, victims or bystanders, depending on their group and social identity.

Part 3 focuses on the main debates in human rights literature on torture, in light of the previous understanding of the phenomenon. The general aim is to initiate a dialogue between the fields of psychoanalysis and human rights on the topic of torture as well as to show that the proposed psychoanalytic framework is a viable conceptualization for expanding the understanding of crucial issues that might be relevant to the legal doctrine.

Chapter 7 contains a critical review of the main 'for' and 'against' arguments of the debate on the permissibility of torture. From this review, it appears that most pro-torture arguments are shaped according to a pattern of oversimplified thinking based on polarizations, terrifying phantasies of annihilation, omnipotent phantasies of defences and protection combined with the logic of self-sacrifice. It becomes clearer that the subject of rational philosophical or moral arguments, on the basis of which political or legal decisions are taken, has its internal emotional rationale. On the other hand, arguments 'against' torture take into consideration more complex perspectives on the issue.

Chapter 8 suggests three major themes on torture in human rights debate as a line of development for further research:

1 The issue of responsibility of perpetrators: torture poses a delicate question of allocation of criminal liability. The problem in the legal field is often defined in terms of whether the abuse perpetrated by ordinary soldiers can be imputed, and to what extent, to the higher military echelons, to the top-level policy makers and legal officers, or even to the political leaders. The important question of *mens rea* in a superior-subordinate relationship in military and civil contexts is discussed as a crucial point when allocating criminal responsibility in torture.

2   The question of the reparation of victims: the problem essentially deals with the dilemma 'how to redress?' The combination of measures of redressing is a very delicate matter, with some element of risk about re-victimization or inadequate remedy. Under international law the standard is '*restitutio in integrum*'. This ideal, as well as being impossible to implement, may be deceptive and risky after torture, given the complexity and wide spectrum of social, physical and psychological consequences for the victim's life. Weaknesses and strengths in the range of remedies and the importance of a participatory process are discussed.

3   The problem of 'truth', which concerns the entire population, bystanders included. Torture implies dehumanization of all parties involved and society overall. Therefore, all these parties require some repair, some healing, some renewal of their humanity and some truth. This question is often addressed in post-conflict societies under the chapter of Truth and Reconciliation Commissions. One of the most controversial points for such commissions concerns the balance they can find between what we might call the 'truth of perpetrators' and the 'truth of victims', between amnesties to perpetrators and reparation for victims they can recommend. The main question seems to be concerned with the potential to construct 'shared truths'.

In each of these closely interconnected sections, the proposed model aims to provide a new perspective to reframe these key problems by offering new insights and possible paths to be further explored in human rights terms.

The struggle against torture imposes interdisciplinary joint efforts: first, to understand the phenomenon as profoundly as possible and, second, to implement more and more adequate approaches for intervention and prevention. The latter point is beyond the scope of this book, although it will hopefully suggest some areas of inquiry and some lines of development for further research.

Note

1   Translated by author

References

Altman, N. (2008) 'The psychodynamics of torture'. *Psychoanalytic Dialogues*, 18: 658–70. doi:10.1080/10481880802297681

Altman, N. (2009) *The Analyst in the Inner City: Race, Class, and Culture through a Psychoanalytic Lens*. New York: Routledge.

Améry, J. (1980) *At the Mind's Limits*. Bloomington, IN: Indiana University Press.

Amnesty International (2014) *Torture in 2014: 30 Years of Broken Promises*. 13 May 2014, Index number: ACT 40/004/2014. Available at: www.amnestyusa.org/research/reports/torture-in-2014-30-years-of-broken-promises.

Beebe, J. (Ed.) (2003) *Terror, Violence and the Impulse to Destroy: Perspectives from Analytical Psychology*. Einsiedeln: Daimon Verlag.

Gramsci, A. (1917) 'Gli indifferenti'. In D'Orsi, A. (Ed.), *La nostra città futura. Scritti torinesi (1911–1922)*. Roma: Carocci, 2004, pp. 134–5.

Grand, S. (2008) 'Sacrificial bodies: Terrorism, counter-terrorism, torture'. *Psychoanalytic Dialogues*, 8: 671–89. doi:10.1080/10481880802297699

Grand, S. (2013) *The Reproduction of Evil: A Clinical and Cultural Perspective*. New York: Routledge.

Harris, A. and Botticelli, S. (Eds.) (2010) *First Do No Harm: The Paradoxical Encounters of Psychoanalysis, Warmaking, and Resistance*. New York, London: Routledge.

Hollander, N.C. (2006) 'Trauma, ideology, and the future of democracy'. *International Journal of Applied Psychoanalytic Studies*, 3: 156–67. doi:10.1002/aps.97

Hollander, N.C. (2009) 'A psychoanalytic perspective on the paradox of prejudice: Understanding US policy toward Israel and the Palestinians'. *International Journal of Applied Psychoanalytic Studies*, 6: 167–77. doi:10.1002/aps.205

Layton, L., Hollander, N.C., Gutwill, S. (2006) *Psychoanalysis, Class and Politics: Encounters in the Clinical Setting*. London and New York: Routledge.

Office of the United Nations High Commissioner for Human Rights (2004) Istanbul Protocol: Manual of the Effective Investigation and Documentation of Torture and Other Cruel, Inhuman and Degrading Treatment or Punishment, Professional Training Series no. 8/Rev. 1, New York, Geneva.

Orwell, G. (1949) *Nineteen Eighty-Four*, London: Penguin, 2008.

Papadopoulos, R.K. (Ed.) (2002) *Therapeutic Care for Refugees. No Place Like Home*. London: Karnac, Tavistock Clinic Series.

Papadopoulos, R.K. 'Political violence, trauma and mental health interventions'. In Kalmanowitz, D. and Lloyd, B. (Eds.), *Art Therapy and Political Violence: With Art Without Illusion*, London: Brunner-Routledge, pp. 35–59

Samuels, A. (2001) *Politics on the Couch: Citizenship and the Internal Life*, London: Profile Books.

Samuels, A. (2015a) *A New Therapy for Politics?* London: Karnac.

Samuels, A. (2015b) *Passions, Persons, Psychotherapy, Politics. The Selected Works of Andrew Samuels*. London/New York: Routledge.

Scarry, E. (1985) *The Body in Pain: The Making and Unmaking of the World*, New York, Oxford: Oxford University Press.

Singer, T. (Ed.) (2000) *The Vision Thing: Myth, Politics and Psyche in the World*. London and New York: Routledge.

Singer, T. (Ed.) (2012) *Psyche and the City: A Soul's Guide to the Modern Metropolis*. New Orleans: Spring Journal Books.

Summers, F. (2006) 'Fundamentalism, psychoanalysis, and psychoanalytic theories'. *Psychoanalytic Review*, 93: 329–52. doi:10.1521/prev.2006.93.2.329

Summers, F. (2009) 'Violence in American foreign policy: a psychoanalytic approach'. *International Journal of Applied Psychoanalytic Studies*, 6: 300–20. doi:10.1002/aps.202

Thomas, N.K. (2009) 'Obliterating the other: What can be repaired by "truth" and testimony?'. *International Journal of Applied Psychoanalytic Studies*, 6: 321–38. doi:10.1002/aps.203

Viñar, M.N. (2005) 'The specificity of torture as trauma: the human wilderness when words fail'. *The International Journal of Psychoanalysis*, 86(2) (April): 311–33. doi:10.1516/HTXE-6E9W-7BPE-BECD

United Nations, Universal Declaration of Human Rights. Adopted by the General Assembly of the United Nations on 10 December 1948. Available at: www.un.org/en/universal-declaration-human-rights/ (accessed 5 November 2015).

Wisnewski, J.J. (2010) *Understanding Torture*. Edinburgh: Edinburgh University Press.

Zoja, L. (2009) *Violence in History, Culture, and the Psyche: Essays*. New Orleans: Spring Journal Books.

PART 1
The phenomenon of torture

1

TORTURE: WHAT IS IT?

A definition of the field of inquiry

Torture seems to be an elusive subject of knowledge: its nature seems to be multi-faceted, its aims manifold, and the contexts and forms of its practice diverse in space and time (Innes, 1998). Legal, philosophical and historical languages may all attribute different meanings to the same word, addressing a range of different related issues. However, the persistence of torture in the world and the impossibility so far of eradicating it make it important to recognize the necessity of narrowing a definition in order to gain a deep insight into the phenomenon (Matthews, 2008: 31).

With this purpose in mind, we need to position ourselves at intermediate distance from our subject of study, neither too close nor too far, not being distracted by the details of a too deep analysis but remaining sensitive to core distinctions. In this chapter, the attempt will be to define the field of inquiry, looking at the 'what', 'who' and 'why' of torture in contemporary legal definitions and in other essays on contemporary state torture. The aim is to draft a definition of the phenomenon, which will be further investigated into in the following chapters.

Torture in international law

The prohibition of torture is absolutely and fundamentally embedded within international law. It is deemed a peremptory norm or *jus cogens*, meaning that it cannot be abrogated by treaty law or other rules of international law, pursuant to the Vienna Convention on the Law of Treaties.[1] However, what we mean by 'torture' may be controversial, because there is no single definition existing under international law.

The international legislation about human rights defines the notion of torture in three main international conventions. The first instrument providing a comprehensive and clear definition of torture was the 1975 UN Declaration on the

Protection of All Persons from Being Subjected to Torture and Other Cruel, Inhuman or Degrading Treatment or Punishment. Article 1 Point 1 of this Declaration states:

> torture means any act by which severe pain or suffering, whether physical or mental, is intentionally inflicted by or at the instigation of a public official on a person for such purposes as obtaining from him or a third person information or confession, punishing him for an act he has committed or is suspected of having committed, or intimidating him or other persons. It does not include pain or suffering arising only from, inherent in or incidental to, lawful sanctions to the extent consistent with the Standard Minimum Rules for the Treatment of Prisoners.

In Point 2,

> Torture constitutes an aggravated and deliberate form of cruel, inhuman or degrading treatment or punishment.

In 1984, the UN General Assembly adopted the Convention Against Torture and Other Cruel, Inhuman or Degrading Treatment or Punishment that entered into force in June 1987. Its definition of torture has become customary in international law. In Article 1 torture is defined as,

> any act by which severe pain or suffering, whether physical or mental, is intentionally inflicted on a person for such purposes as obtaining from him or a third person information or a confession, punishing him for an act he or a third person has committed or is suspected of having committed, or intimidating or coercing him or a third person, or for any reason based on discrimination of any kind, when such pain or suffering is inflicted by or at the instigation of or with the consent or acquiescence of a public official or other person acting in an official capacity. It does not include pain or suffering arising only from, inherent in or incidental to lawful sanctions.

Another relevant definition of torture is the one contained in the 1985 Inter-American Convention to Prevent and Punish Torture. Article 2 reads:

> For the purposes of this Convention, torture shall be understood to be any act intentionally performed whereby physical or mental pain or suffering is inflicted on a person for purposes of criminal investigation, as a means of intimidation, as personal punishment, as a preventive measure, as a penalty, or for any other purpose. Torture shall also be understood to be the use of methods upon a person intended to obliterate the personality of the victim or to diminish his physical or mental capacities, even if they do not cause physical pain or mental anguish.

The concept of torture shall not include physical or mental pain or suffering that is inherent in or solely the consequence of lawful measures, provided that they do not include the performance of the acts or use of the methods referred to in this article.

Comparing conceptions of torture in international human rights law and international criminal law, both in doctrine and case law, Sir Nigel Rodley detects three props as central in our modern legal understanding of the concept of torture: 1) the intensity of pain or suffering inflicted; 2) the status of the perpetrator; 3) the question of purpose (Rodley, 2002). Similarly, in Interpretation of Torture in the Light of the Practice and Jurisprudence of International Bodies, the Office of the High Commissioner for Human Rights (OHCHR) detects four elements to be taken into account when qualifying an act as torture: 1) the nature of the act; 2) the intention of the perpetrator; 3) the purpose; 4) the involvement of public officials or assimilated (OHCHR, 2011: 3).

The 'what': the pain or suffering inflicted

The issue of what constitutes torture refers to the kinds of practice used and the degree of pain or suffering caused. The OHCHR's reference to the 'nature of the act' (the 'what'), finds that the 'legal definition of torture encompasses both acts and omissions that inflict severe pain or suffering', and that this pain can be either physical or mental (2011: 3–4). Thus, the threat of torture or mock executions is comprised within this concept of mental suffering.[2]

Even if, for most legal instruments, pain and suffering must be 'severe', the distinction between torture and cruel, inhuman, or degrading treatment is not always clear. While the authorities suggest that pain intensity is not determinative in distinguishing between torture and other forms of ill-treatment, the intensity of force is still a substantial factor in certain situations. In case the force is used legally for a lawful purpose, and it is proportional and not excessive, it will generally not amount to cruel, inhuman or degrading treatment. The threshold for acceptable force is much lower in situations of powerlessness, such as in detention, or in other situations of direct control that similarly amount to deprivation of liberty. It is accepted that, in such a cindition, any form of physical or mental pressure or coercion constitutes at least cruel, inhuman or degrading treatment, regardless of the proportionality test (Nowak and McArthur, 2006).

Judicial attempts to interpret these concepts or to make clear distinctions have proved difficult. Rodley (2002) illustrates cases where the term 'torture' was referenced and others where this category was not used, although the treatment in question could have been similar, or even the same. To simply limit the discourse to the three conventions mentioned, in the 1984 United Nations Convention against Torture and Other Cruel, Inhuman or Degrading Treatment or Punishment (UNCAT) the reference to torture as an aggravated form of other ill-treatment is dropped and this Convention acknowledges that 'there may be other understandings of torture that are *wider* than narrower' (Rodley, emphasis in original, 2002: 476). No reference to the aggravated intensity of pain or suffering, nor to severity can be found in the Inter-American Convention to Prevent and Punish Torture (1985). No pain or suffering needs to be demonstrated where the methods used are 'intended to obliterate the personality of the victim or to diminish his physical or mental capacities' (Article 2). The international criminal tribunals (the International Criminal Tribunal for Rwanda and the International Criminal Tribunal for the former Yugoslavia) and the Rome Statute of the International Criminal Court dealt in several different ways with the issue of the requirement of aggravated intensity of pain or suffering to regard a crime as torture. Few cases address this distinction in the same way (see Rodley, 2002).

Despite the sometimes blurry, yet persistent, distinction between torture and other forms of ill treatment, it is clear that the UN Committee Against Torture (UNCAT) aims to guarantee the same safeguards and protection for both categories of ill-treatment: 'Experience demonstrates that the conditions that give rise to ill-treatment frequently facilitate torture and therefore the measures required to prevent torture must be applied to prevent ill-treatment'.[3] This proclamation by the UNCAT, represents a clear shift in the torture/CIDT distinction. States are now obligated to prevent torture and other forms of ill-treatment by applying the same UNCAT measures to all forms of ill-treatment, irrespective of varying levels of severity. Given this development and interpretation in international law, the choice of the word 'severe' must not be apprehended in a way that allows a dichotomous justification for ill-treatment in certain circumstances, while the prohibition of torture is absolute.

Ultimately, we can derive from the point debated that the 'what' of torture, is indisputably the *pain or suffering inflicted*.

The 'who': a public agent as perpetrator

In Article 1 of both the UNCAT and the UN Declaration on the Protection of All Persons, the perpetrator is identified in a 'public official'. So, the typical torturer will be a law-enforcement official or member of the security or intelligence services, precisely seeking to obtain, in the course and in furtherance of his or her duties, information or confession. This is to exclude private acts for purely personal ends.

While the question of the involvement of a public official is usually straightforward, the recognition of the 'other person acting in an official capacity' (UNCAT) may be more problematic and delicate (OHCHR, 2011: 4). As such, the perpetrator may also be someone with no official status acting in collusion with, and to advance the purposes of public officialdom, often to shroud the responsibility of members of that officialdom. Conversely, the direct perpetrator of the torture may be acting in collusion with, and to advance the purposes of, civilian political authorities who prefer to turn a blind eye to the 'excesses' of law-enforcement or security officials. Since torture is normally committed in the dark and secret reaches of state power, it is likely that those involved may be able to conceal their responsibility, particularly in the light of their public functions. The UNCAT asserts that a state 'bears international responsibility' for the acts and omissions of individuals 'acting in [an] official capacity or acting on behalf of the State'[4] and is 'obligated to adopt effective measures to prevent . . . other persons acting in an official capacity from directly committing, instigating, inciting, encouraging, acquiescing in or otherwise participating or being complicit in acts of torture as defined in the Convention.'[5]

Therefore, a *public official* has to be the perpetrator, directly or indirectly, for the violation of torture to be established.

The 'why': the purposive element

There is virtually uniform treatment of the factor of *purpose* as a, if not *the*, central component of the concept of torture. Rodley states:

> Except in respect of crimes against humanity, as defined in Article 7 of the Rome Statute for the International Criminal Court . . . Every other instrument defining torture contains a reference to a purposive element: Article 1 of the UN Declaration and Convention against Torture, Article 2 of the Inter-American Torture Convention, and the Elements of Crimes concerning the war crime of torture under the ICC Statute in respect of international armed conflict (Article 8(2)(a)(ii).1) and of non-international armed conflict (Article 8(2)(c)(i).4).
>
> (Rodley, 2002: 481)

In particular, the UNCAT (1984) does highlight very effectively the purposeful use of torture when inflicted as a means of obtaining information or confession, or as a punishment for a person's purported act, or for intimidating or coercing a person, or due to discrimination of any kind. The OHCHR (2011) identifies the UNCAT list of different purposes for the commission of torture as a guideline, but noticing it is not exhaustive. Similarly, Koru and Hofstadter (2015) observe that, even though the purpose of torture can be categorized under headings, the content of these categories is not complete, and can be interpreted in a flexible manner. For example, an act that is inflicted on a person for the purpose of punishment can appear in various forms, such as beating, violent shaking, prolonged isolation, rape and sexual assault (Nowak and McArthur, 2008: 75).

Rodley comments (2002: 481–2) that even more explicit is the intention of the Inter-American Convention to target the purpose (to 'obliterate the personality of the victim', or 'diminish his . . . mental capacities', even in the absence of physical pain or mental anguish), as a characterizing feature of torture.

Torture in literature

The 'what': the torment

Torment, both physical and psychological, seems to be the essential concern of torture (Améry, 1980; Foucault, 1975; Innes, 1998; Korovessis, 1970; Millet, 1994; Peters, 1996; Scarry, 1985).

However, the relation between torture and pain is less obvious than it appears. Pain and stress generate reactions in humans that are better understood in terms of combinations of mental and physical processes. The body-mind dichotomy should be dropped in order to properly understand the experience of human pain. Améry (1980), who experienced torture, movingly describes the essence of pain:

> The pain was what it was. Beyond that there is nothing to say. Qualities of feeling are as incomparable as they are indescribable. They mark the limit of the capacity of language to communicate.
>
> (Améry, 1980: 33)

In torture, the elaborate and highly articulate sensory system is assaulted with the deliberate intention of triggering pain mechanisms. As Melzack and Wall (1983: 32) observed, pain has a complex structure, subjectively perceived and psychologically conditioned. In torture, conditions are specifically designed to enhance the experience of pain, to block the operation of natural pain inhibitors, to prevent optimal conditions for recovery from pain, and to increase the pain in as many ways as possible. In order to maximize pain, 'technical' personnel, such as doctors and psychologists, are often enrolled as collaborators (Allhoff, 2006; Bloche and Marks, 2005a, 2005b, 2005c; Gordon and Marton, 1995; Harper and Roberts, 2007; on this topic see Chapter 3).

The manipulation of pain and stress in torture suggests that it is a violent attack on the foundation of the human being, the body, although the final targets may be their mind and/or social identity. Methods of torture are oriented to penetrate, beat and perforate the body, to shatter the mind, to humiliate, to disrupt biological rhythms, and to destroy relationships and social bonds, human dignity and self-respect (Sironi and Branche, 2002). In their assault on the victim's body, torturers seek to produce the illusion that the body is the source of harm to the mind. One's own body is perceived as the origin and cause of the suffering, such as in stress positions, where torture does not even require the immediate presence of torturers, who can come and go at their pleasure.

As Millet (1994) effectively summarizes,

> The practice of torture is an imposition of the body upon the mind. So that the mind (self, idea, will) is put at the mercy of the body's capacity to withstand pain. Physical torture implies all that we mean as psychological torture, plus a great deal. For one suffers here the frustration of insult and ill will, the hurt of being hurt on purpose, the realization that one is deliberately

made to suffer physical pain – the body's pain compounded by the injury of injustice and contempt; psychic wounds. If insult is the psychological equivalent of a blow, torture aims at the organization of insult so general and overwhelming as to destroy: through helplessness, the shame of helplessness, an exhaustion and impotence directed toward a final surrender of the self.

(Millet, 1994: 92)

Incontestably, torture deals with physical and psychological torment and is accurate at targeting vital human needs (physiological needs, the need for physical and mental boundaries, the need for intimate relations, the need to maintain a good image of oneself, the need for a sense of agency, the need to trust humanity and retain hope, etc.). Meanwhile, knowledge about techniques to inflict pain through torture is a subject of secret communication among the military and secret services of diverse countries, and there exists a shameful commerce of such a skill as conducting torture sessions (McCoy, 2006; Robin, 2005).

The 'who': the public character of torture

Torture is not private violence. Though currently secret, it belongs to a *public* discourse and practice, pertaining to the state and its agencies.

Peters (1985) detects this essential aspect of twentieth-century torture: 'torture stands in the same relation to such private offences as trespass, battery or aggravated assault as a state execution stands in relation to murder. Torture is thus something that public authority does or condones' (1985: 3).

Torture is, in our times, the 'sub-legal' and 'paralegal' physical coercion of individuals deemed dangerous to the 'state's notion of order' (1985). In the same way, writing on the modern state, Millet (1994) agrees that, on the ground of torture, *permission* is crucial. To indulge fancy without permission is criminal and to be punished, a merely individual act without meaning, self-indulgent, aberrant and forbidden. However, with permission it might become patriotism, laudable, salaried and professional services. Everything depends upon permission, which belongs to the state (Millet, 1994: 36). Torture is something a state does or condones.

Similarly, writing on the social context of torture, Kelman pinpoints that,

> the essential phenomenon of torture . . . is that it is not an ordinary crime, but a crime of obedience, a crime that takes place, not in opposition to the authorities, but under explicit instructions from the authorities to engage in acts of torture, or in an environment in which such acts are implicitly sponsored, expected, or at least tolerated by the authorities.
>
> (Kelman, 1993: 23)

Parry, in his book *Understanding Torture* (2010), explains that torture is a normal part of the state coercive apparatus. Torture is about dominating the victim for a variety of purposes, including public order, control of racial, ethnic and religious minorities, and domination for the sake of domination, and it fits within the practice and beliefs of the modern state. Torture is employed to create – and to destroy and re-create – political identities in a political system. Its violence is secretly at the service of the state.

The public character of torture is also evident in its use by non-state social actors. For example, if a rebel group controls a certain area and has the capacity to capture and confine people, and then harms those captives for a purpose that serves the interest of the group, legally, this would fit with the meaning of torture (Hajjar, 2013). A clear contemporary example is that of ISIS, which uses other torture followed by horrible executions of prisoners to send intimidating messages to other states, and tries, by these means, to reach recognition as a power at the service of the creation of an Islamic State.

The 'why': a question of 'truth'

Although torment is indisputably the essential ingredient of torture, according to Quiroga and Jaranson (2008), the most important criteria in the definition of the phenomenon is the intention and purpose of torturers and their cooperators, i.e. the reason for its use (the 'why').

The distinction between the judicial torture of the past and political torture of our time is relevant in terms of historical and legal perspectives. However, whether torture be judicial or political, past or present, it has the following features: 1) it happens between social actors with a different endowment of power and/or citizenship; 2) it goes always along with a *question of 'truth'*.

In *Torture and Truth*, Page DuBois writes that torture performed at least two functions in ancient Greece:

> As an instrument of demarcation, it delineates the boundary between slave and free, between the untouchable bodies of free citizens and the torturable bodies of slaves. . . . In the work of the wheel, the rack, and the whip, the torturer carries out the work of the *polis*; citizen is made distinct from non-citizen, Greek from barbarian, slave from free.
> (DuBois, 1991: 63, in Schulz, 2007: 13)

The citizen cannot be tortured. The non-citizen may be. Again and again, speakers in the courts describe the *basanos* as a *search for truth*. A claim is made that truth resides in the slave's body. But what kind of truth is the slave's truth? Aristotle says: 'The slave is a part of the master – he is, as it were, *a part of the body, alive but yet separated from it*' (DuBois, 1991: 63, in Schulz, 2007: 14, emphasis added). The master can conceal the truth, since he possesses reason and can chose between truth and lie, and consequently can choose the penalty associated with false testimony. His own point of vulnerability is his slave's body, which can be forced to produce the truth.

Since very early times, torment, imbalanced power and 'truth' were the main components of torture. Peters quotes a third-century jurist's definition, Ulpian, who declared: 'By *quaestio* [torture] we are to understand the torment and suffering of the body in order to elicit the *truth*'. In the thirteenth century, the Roman lawyer, Azo, gave his definition: 'Torture is the inquiry after *truth* by means of torment'. Meanwhile, in the seventeenth century, the civil lawyer Bocer said that: 'Torture is interrogation by torment of the body, concerning a crime known to have occurred, legitimately ordered by a judge for the purpose of eliciting the *truth* about the said crime' (Peters, 1985: 1, emphasis added).

Michel Foucault, who investigated the relationship between power and knowledge in *Discipline and Punish*, understands interrogational torture of the past as '*torture of the truth*' (Foucault, 1975: 40, emphasis added), a strict judicial game, where, through a regulated practice, obeying a well-defined procedure (various stages, certain duration, certain instruments used, the length of ropes and heaviness of the weights used, the number of interventions made by the interrogating magistrates, all were carefully codified), a physical challenge determined the truth of the defendant's culpability (Foucault, 1975: 39–40). In the practice of torture, pain, confrontation and truth were bound together; they worked together on the person's body. The search for truth through judicial torture was certainly a way of obtaining evidence, but it was also the battle that 'produced' the *truth* – or a decision between guilty and innocent – according to a ritual. The *confession* had, to a certain extent, priority over any other kind of evidence. It was also the act by which the accused accepted the charge. This process transformed an investigation into a voluntary affirmation of the accuser's truth.

Scarry writes on the paradoxical relationship between physical pain and interrogation that aims at gaining the 'truth'. Central to Scarry's definition of torture is the idea that interrogation (i.e. language) and the body in pain function both against one another and together in torture. Indeed, pain is world-destroying: while feeling pain, all the psychological and mental contents that constitute both one's self and one's world, which give rise to language and in turn are made possible by language, cease to exist. The torturer wants to 'deconstruct the prisoner's voice' (Scarry, 1985: 20). She asserts that the prisoner's conscious presence in the world is *unmade* by intense pain: the world, the self, and the voice are lost through intense pain as the prisoner's self shrinks to the size of his body. The reality of this pain implicitly confers reality upon the power of the torturer, while the prisoner's shrinking self concedes more territory to the torturer (Scarry, 1985: 4, 35, 27).

Crelinsten (1993) reports that, according to the *S 21 Interrogator's Manual* from the central prison-execution facility of the Khmer Rouge, the purpose of torturing is to elicit responses from prisoners. 'It's not something we do for the fun of it. ... we must make them hurt so that they will respond quickly' (1993: 39–40). Crelinsten comments that information, confessions and ultimately broken people are the end products of the torturer's work (1993: 40). While torture appears to revolve around interrogation, it is more complex than that:

'making them talk' implies more than just making them talk about something in particular. 'Making them talk' is also about power, about imposing one's will on another. One party is absolutely powerful, the other, coerced party is totally powerless and defenseless. One party can ask and answer, act and react, while the other party can only react verbally, never knowing whether the verbal reaction will trigger renewed violence or death.

(Crelinsten, 1993: 42)

Sartre, in the preface to the memoir of a torture victim, Henri Alleg, grasps something crucial about the relationship between truth and power in torture.

The purpose of it [torture] is to force from one tongue, amid its screams and its vomiting up of blood, the secret of everything [i.e. the truth]. Senseless violence: whether the victim talks or whether he dies under his agony, the secret that he cannot tell is always somewhere else and out of reach. It is the executioner who becomes Sisyphus. If he puts the question at all, he will have to continue forever.

(Sartre, 1958: xxxix)

John T. Parry (2004) notes that any attempt at resistance by a torture victim entails the possibility of an escalation of the violence. Whether victims acquiesce early in the torture or resist, they are tortured, and torture does not cease because of any act of theirs. It is a decision solely at the behest of the torturer. Even compliance with the wishes of the interrogator is not causally relevant to determining when the torture will end.

The truth produced by torture has a peculiar nature, it can be equally used to oppose or to defend. It is the opposite of what is ordinarily regarded as truth: an unambiguous, definitive and definite meaning. Moreover, systems relying on torture as a suitable technique to gather information about subversive acts or plans do not generally ask whether torture produces accurate outcomes: they already know results are accurate. These aspects suggest that knowledge and truth have a special ambiguous status in torture.

On the groundwork of this first analysis of law and literature, it seems that the phenomenon of 'torture' emerges as a peculiar link established in public discourse and practice (the 'who') between the prisoner's physical and psychological torment (the 'what') and truth in the context of heavily unbalanced power relations (the 'why').

This obscure definition will hopefully acquire some meaning as our framework of understanding develops further.

Notes

1 Vienna Convention on the Law of Treaties. Adopted in Vienna on 22 May 1969, entered into force 27 January 1980. 1155 UNTS 331, Article 53.

2 Committee against Torture, A/45/44 para. 190.
3 UN Committee Against Torture (UNCAT), General Comment No. 2: Implementation of Article 2 by States Parties, 24 January 2008, CAT/C/GC/2, para. 3
4 Ibid., para. 15
5 Ibid., para.17.

References

Allhoff, F. (2006) 'Physician involvement in hostile interrogations'. *Cambridge Quarterly of Healthcare Ethics*, 15(4): 392–402. doi:10.1017/S0963180106060506

Améry, J. (1980) *At the Mind's Limits*. Bloomington, IN: Indiana University Press.

Bloche, M.G. and Marks, J.H. (2005a) 'Doctors and interrogations'. *New England Journal of Medicine*, 352: 1633–4. doi:10.1056/NEJMc051947

Bloche, M.G. and Marks, J.H. (2005b) 'Doctors and interrogators at Guantanamo Bay'. *New England Journal of Medicine*, 353(1): 6–8. doi:10.1056/NEJMp058145

Bloche M.G. and Marks, J.H. (2005c) 'When doctors go to war'. *New England Journal of Medicine*, 352: 3–6. doi:10.1056/NEJMp048346

Crelinsten, R.D. (1993) 'In their own words: the world of the torturer'. In Crelinsten, R.D. and Schmid, A.P. (Eds.), *The Politics of Pain: Torturers and Their Masters*. Centrum voor Onderzoek van Maatschappelijke Tegenstellingen/Center for the Study of Social Conflicts, AK Leiden, Netherlands: Leiden University, pp. 39–72.

DuBois, P. (1991) *Torture and Truth*. London: Routledge.

Foucault, M. (1975) *Discipline and Punish: The Birth of the Prison*. New York: Random House, 1979.

Gordon, N. and Marton, R. (1995) *Torture: Human Rights, Medical Ethics and the Case of Israel*. London and New Jersey: Zed Books.

Hajjar, L. (2013) *A Sociology of Violence and Human Rights*. London, New York: Routledge.

Harper, D. and Roberts, R. (2007) 'The complicity of psychology in the security state'. In Roberts, R. (Ed.), *Just War: Psychology, Terrorism and Iraq*. Ross-on-Wye: PCCS Books, pp. 15–45.

Innes, B. (1998) *The History of Torture*. London: Brown Books.

Kelman, H.C. (1993) 'The social context of torture: policy process and authority structure'. In Crelinsten, R.D. and Schmid, A.P. (Eds.), *The Politics of Pain: Torturers and their Masters*. Centrum voor Onderzoek van Maatschappelijke Tegenstellingen/Center for the Study of Social Conflicts, AK Leiden, Netherlands: Leiden University, pp. 21–38.

Korovessis, P. (1970) *The Method: Personal Account of the Tortures in Greece*. London: Allison and Busby.

Koru, F.E. and Hofstadter, N. (2015) 'By the rules: comparative study on the legal framework of torture in Turkey and Israel'. Available at: http://stoptorture.org.il/by-the-rules-executive-summary/?lang=en (accessed 18 September 2015).

Matthews, R. (2008) *The Absolute Violation. Why Torture Must Be Prohibited*. Montreal and Kingston, London, Ithaca: McGill-Queen's University Press.

McCoy, A. (2006) *A Question of Torture: CIA Interrogation, from the Cold War to the War on Terror (American Empire Project)*. New York: Metropolitan Books/Henry Holt.

Melzack, R. and Wall, P.D. (1983) *The Challenge of Pain*. London: Penguin Books, 1988.

Millet, K. (1994) *The Politics of Cruelty: An Essay on the Literature of Political Imprisonment*. London: Penguin Books.

Nowak, M. and McArthur, E. (2006) 'The distinction between torture and cruel, inhuman or degrading treatment'. *Torture*, 16(3): 147–51.

Nowak, M. and McArthur, E. (2008) *The United Nations Convention Against Torture: A Commentary*. Oxford: Oxford University Press.

Office of the High Commissioner for Human Rights, Interpretation of Torture in the Light of the Practice and Jurisprudence of International Bodies, 2011. Available at: www.ohchr.org/Documents/Issues/Torture/UNVFVT/Interpretation_torture_2011_EN.pdf (accessed 7 November 2015).

Organization of American States, Inter-American Convention to Prevent and Punish Torture, adopted at Cartagena de Indias, Colombia, on, 9 December 1985, entered into force 28 February 1987, OAS Treaty Series, No. 67. Available at: www.oas.org/juridico/english/treaties/a-51.html (accessed 14 September 2014).

Parry, J.T. (2004) 'Escalation and necessity: defining torture at home and abroad'. In Levinson S. (Ed.), *Torture: A Collection*. Oxford: Oxford University Press, pp. 145–64.

Parry, J.T. (2010) *Understanding Torture: Law, Violence and Political Identity*. Ann Arbor, MI: University of Michigan Press.

Peters, E. (1985) *Torture*. Expanded Edition, Philadelphia: University of Pennsylvania Press, 1996.

Quiroga, J. and Jaranson, J. (2008) 'Torture'. In Reyes, G., Elhai, J.D. and Ford, J.D. (Eds.), *The Encyclopedia of Psychological Trauma*. John Wiley, pp. 654–7.

Robin, M. (2005) 'Counterinsurgency and torture: exporting torture tactics from Indochina and Algeria to Latin America'. In Roth, K. and Worden, M. (Eds.), *Torture: Does It Make Us Safer? A Human Rights Perspective*. New York: New Press, pp. 44–54.

Rodley, N. (2002) 'The definition(s) of torture in international law'. *Current Legal Problems*, 55: 465–93. doi:10.1093/clp/55.1.467

Scarry, E. (1985) *The Body in Pain. The Making and Unmaking of the World*. New York, Oxford: Oxford University Press.

Sartre, J.P. (1958) 'Preface'. In Alleg, H. *The Question*, London: John Calder Publishers, 2006.

Schulz, W.F. (Ed.) (2007) *The Phenomenon of Torture: Readings and Commentary*. Philadelphia, PA: University of Pennsylvania Press.

Sironi, F. and Branche, R. (2002) 'Torture and the borders of humanity'. *International Social Science Journal*, 54: 539–48. doi:10.1111/1468-2451.00408

United Nations, Convention against Torture and Other Cruel, Inhuman or Degrading Treatment or Punishment. Adopted and opened for signature, ratification and accession by General Assembly resolution 39/46 of 10 December 1984, entered into force 26 June 1987. Available at: www.ohchr.org/EN/ProfessionalInterest/Pages/CAT.aspx (accessed 14 September 2014).

United Nations, Convention on the Law of Treaties. Signed at Vienna on 23 May 1969, entered into force 27 January 1980. Available at: https://treaties.un.org/doc/Publication/UNTS/Volume%201155/volume-1155-I-18232-English.pdf (accessed 11 January 2014).

United Nations, Declaration on the Protection of All Persons from Being Subjected to Torture or Other Cruel, Inhuman and Degrading Treatment or Punishment. Adopted by General Assembly resolution 3452 (XXX) of 9 December 1975. Available at: www.ohchr.org/EN/ProfessionalInterest/Pages/DeclarationTorture.aspx (accessed 14 September 2014).

2
TORTUROUS SOCIETIES

This chapter intends to provide an overview of the main characteristic features of societies in which torture appears, in terms of their socio-political dynamics and narratives. The focus here will be on state torture.

Recently non-state actors are increasingly engaged in conduct that violates human rights, including torture, as one of the integral coercive means used to gain or exercise power. In this case, the term 'non-state actor' covers a wide spectrum of subjects, such as *de facto* regimes, armed opposition groups, or groups with close links to the state. Other entities which have reportedly been responsible for human rights violations include private security companies, multinational corporations and military components of missions operated by intergovernmental operations.

Although we live in a complex world characterized by multiple centers of power and non-state actors, the Westphalian sovereignty principle means that the state still has substantial power to influence events within its borders and in other states. Individual and cultural factors may be important determinants of torture but they always interact with the policy process and the authority structure that ultimately give rise to the practice (Kelman, 2005). Torture is something state power carries out or secretly admits (Jackson, 2005; Jongman, 1991; Rejali, 1991).

Torture: a power relationship between two embodied social realities

It is quite evident that torture is the quintessence of a power relation: it always develops between two social parties in an asymmetrical relation, the *powerful* and the *powerless*. Lazreg invites us to read the phenomenon of torture as 'a genuine battle between two *embodied realities*' (2008: 6, emphasis added). Millet writes, 'The authorities generally win; it is not a game, after all, . . . one party has every resource in force and numbers and time and the other has nothing but willpower'

(1994: 34). Vidal-Naquet similarly writes, 'The essential feature of the practice of torture . . . is that one man or one class of society claims absolute power over another man or another class of society' (Vidal-Naquet, 1963, in Schulz, 2007: 195).

I will designate these two embodied realities as the *torturous power* and the *sub-human*.

The torturous power

The torturous power proves a set of characteristic features (further analyzed in Chapter 5). A first essential characteristic is its being *monolithic* rather than pluralistic. The term 'monolithic' is used by Staub (1993) to characterize a society in which there is a small range of predominant values, while the legitimacy of the rulers rests on the basis of a unitary unchallengeable ideology, whether political or religious. It may also be the case of states that are run by a ruling clique with an extremely narrow population base but have the support of military forces or external allies. Often the government in question represents very limited economic interests and potentates, with its legitimacy reliant on military or religious institutions, an economically or militarily powerful fragment of the people it rules. Pierre Vidal-Naquet makes a similar argument about France and its use of torture in Algeria:

> The use of torture in Algeria was to a great extent the defensive reaction of a minority whose privileged position was threatened, of an army which had been ordered to protect this minority and which could find no other means of action, and of a government which, with the support of the majority of the nation, did all it could over a period of years to ensure that this minority retained its privileged position.
> (Vidal-Naquet 1963, in Schulz, 2007: 195)

Berto Jongman (1991) shows that human rights violations, including torture, are much more likely to occur in non-democratic than they are in democratic societies because of the nature of the policy process and the authority structure characterizing such societies. In his study, the probability of torture seems to decrease significantly in societies in which a democratic ethos prevails (25 per cent vs. 84 per cent) and at high level of development (31 per cent vs. 84 per cent) (Jongman, 1991). However, a *monolithic mode of governance* may be pursued not only in totalitarian political systems but also in democratic countries whereas they are ruled by powerful elites that legitimate themselves on a religious or military base. One glaring example of democracy turning toward a 'monolithic' mode is that of the United States of George W. Bush, a president elected with a narrow majority of votes (and a controversial electoral result) and widely reliant on the support of religious lobbies and the arms industry both for his election and administration (Milbank, 2001:A02; Keller, 2003; Hartung and Ciarrocca, 2004).

Pluralism can be either a matter of culture or a matter of political arrangements, or both. In pluralistic societies, values are varied and conflicts are supposed to be worked out in the public domain. There is, or there should be, discussion, exploration, a process of political debate and even conflict among groups with different values. Nonetheless, there are social conditions under which democratic cultures drastically reduce these opportunities for pluralistic debate and even sanction the use of torture, just as there are social conditions under which ordinary, decent individuals may be induced to take part in such activity. As Kelman (2005: 128) suggests, torture in democratic societies is most likely to occur in the context of counter-terrorist activities or armed conflict. For instance, the United States has adopted torture in different historical circumstances: in the mid-1990s, the US government revealed that, for much of the previous decade, the US Army's School of Americas had used training manuals which advocated practices such as torture, extortion, kidnapping and execution (Amnesty International, 2002). In the context of counterinsurgency programmes in Central America, the US provided training and transfer of skills to those appointed to torture (Blum, 2004; Chomsky and Herman, 1979: 272; Langguth, 1978; McCoy, 2005; Otterman, 2007, 80–6; Peters, 1985: 163; Soldz, 2008: 594; Weschler, 1990). After the 9/11 attacks, they employed systematic torture as a part of the so-called 'war on terror', and attempted to legitimize it as an almost-legal measure within the context of a national security discourse (Lansford *et al.*, 2009; McCoy, 2006). Other charges of torture against democratic countries have been brought against Israeli authorities for their treatment of Palestinians involved in or accused of terrorist activities (Cohen and Golan, 1991; Gordon and Marton, 1995; Imseis, 2001) and against British authorities for their treatment of Irish Republican Army members caught in or suspected of acts of terrorism (Jackson, 2007).

Another crucial point of torturous powers is their *belief in their own cultural/ economic/moral superiority*, while their communities are experiencing *difficult life conditions*. The cluster of attitudes commonly associated with this belief includes a sense of specialness, deservingness and entitlement, making one perceive certain societal rules as irrelevant because one's experience, feelings, thoughts are deemed to merit privileged status (Eidelson and Eidelson, 2003: 184). This superiority core belief tends to create difficulty when getting along with others, in part because of a lack of empathy and inclination to understand others' experiences and viewpoints. This belief is also inconsistent with a willingness to compromise. Additional problems are created by the tendency to judge others harshly, especially when they fail to act in accordance with one's inflated self-image. Being choosy appears to be an especially important component of this collective superiority worldview. Evidence of choosiness and entitlement is often found in the selective recounting of a group's history. Volkan used the term *chosen glories* to describe 'ritualistic recollections of events and heroes whose mental representations include a shared feeling of success and triumph among group members' (1999: 45). This mythical and heroic past, which often demonizes other groups, is available for political entrepreneurs to call on in their efforts to mobilize support for a nationalist agenda (Brown, 1997; Crawford, 1998). The development of Hitler's ideology of Aryans as a master race destined to achieve their deservedly rightful rule over other peoples of the world is a chilling example (Gonen, 2000). The Germans during Nazism saw themselves as superior in character, competence, honor, loyalty, devotion to family, civic organization and cultural achievements.

However, this sense of a cultural superiority seems to be often accompanied by some sense of internal or external vulnerability. Paradoxically, the belief in cultural or economic superiority often goes hand in hand with difficult life conditions: economic hardships, persistent and intense political conflict, and rapid, substantial social change and/or traumatic historical events. Regarding Nazi Germany, Staub (2003) notices that, partly as a result of the tremendous devastation in past wars (Craig, 1982; Mayer, 1955) and the lack of unity and statehood until 1871, there was a deep feeling of vulnerability and shaky self-esteem in the country. Following unification, a brief period of strength, the loss of World War I and the intense life problems that followed were a great blow to cultural and societal self-concept. Such conditions powerfully affect individuals and give rise to basic psychological needs among many members of the society: the need for security, freedom from physical danger and at least minimal fulfilment of material necessities; the need for a sense of positive identity, which means being regarded as a valuable person/people, with the capacity to act effectively in the world; and the need for a meaningful comprehension of reality, a sense of how the world is ordered and one's place in it.

The same pattern of self-inflated representation and the need to regain some self-esteem can be found in Lazreg's analysis (2008: 3) of the *guerre révolutionnaire* (revolutionary-war), which was fought in Algeria by France. The theory of this kind of war, which made significant use of systematic torture, was developed in the 1950s by a group of veterans of colonial wars. Many had also fought in World War II and were men who had suffered a loss of honor and relevance in the fast-changing society of post-war France. The Algerian War offered them the opportunity to recoup both. For the civil and military establishment, it crystallized the memory of a vast and long-unchallenged imperial venture with its entanglement in cultural and political identity, combined with the fear of the loss of relevance in the Cold War era, when the European colonial empires were crumbling (Lazreg, 2008: 19).

Another example is that of Argentina between 1976 and 1983 (the years of the military junta), in which the culture, literature and the strong voices of intellectuals and leaders identified Argentina as a superior country, partly because of the European origin of its population, and partly because of its great natural resources. But progressively, this sense of superiority was in stark contrast with the actual conditions of life, such as tremendous inflation, a decline in production, and intense political conflict and violence.

The sub-human

Staub (1993: 113; 2003: 297) points out that a belief in cultural superiority without safety measures for the protection of outsiders makes it easier and more likely that democratic societies will use force against outside groups. From the point of view of the torturous power, the torturable are generally those who, as a matter of fact, are already out of the domain of civil rights and do not deserve the same respect to be decent human beings as others.

We have seen that, among the ancient Greeks and Romans, who regulated torture by attaching it to the person, torture delineated the boundary between the slave and the free, between the untouchable bodies of free citizens and the torturable bodies of slaves (Forrest, 1996; Innes, 1998).

Nowadays, a basic pre-condition for torture remains the existence of a group of devalued people, who are considered less than human (Dolan, 2009: 11; Gordon and Marton, 1995: 121; Staub, 1993: 112). A contributing factor to the dehumanization of torture victims is the fact that, even when they are citizens, they often do not belong to the same ethnic or religious community as the torturers. The subhuman is someone that already has a minority status within society, the colonized, the inferior, the poor (e.g. 'the black' in the apartheid system, Palestinians to the Israelis, Algerians to the French colonizers, Kurds to the Turks, etc.) or, alternatively, such sub-humanity is created (the 'subversives' – a label that included heterogeneous categories of population in Argentina, Chile, and other Latin American countries, the 'terrorists' for the Western countries under attack from 'Islamic terrorism').

In our recent past, there are plenty of examples of this vertical distribution of rights, worth and humanity. In Staub's analysis (1989), a history of devaluation of a group of people, such as the Jews in Germany or the Armenians in Turkey, or a history of splits between groups, favours the social process of scapegoating or ideological persecution, which pre-selects the group as a victim. As Sartre observes, the victims' status as 'sub-human' – the colonized – is central to the paradigm of torture:

> colonialism ends by the annihilation of the colonized. They own nothing, they are nothing. . . Under the constant pressure of their masters, their standard of living has been reduced year by year. . . . For most Europeans in Algeria, there are two complementary and inseparable truths: that they have the divine right, and that the natives are subhuman. This is a mythical interpretation of reality, since the riches of the one are built on the poverty of the other.
>
> (Sartre, 1958: xi–xii)

Torture settles on an already well established power asymmetry in society. Kelman (2005: 133) shows that within torturous systems there is a social need to distinguish 'the innocents' from 'the guilty', who often match with the politically 'uncommitted' and the political opponents of a regime. For this reason, a discourse about 'subversion' and 'enemies of the state' is generally created, reinforcing or creating anew a category of deplorable 'sub-humans'. They are described as 'terrorists', 'insurgents', or 'dissidents' who endanger the state and undermine the law, non-citizens who are not entitled to community protection. Rather, they are considered dangerous elements against whom the community has the right to protect itself. A central assumption of torture is that victims are guilty. Thus, torture becomes at the same time punishment of the guilty, while serving as a warning to their accomplices, and a means to elicit information that is necessary for state protection.

With such a redundancy of reasons, the process of dehumanization of the victims of torture (Heinz, 1993: 81–4; Kelman, 1993: 36), whether it is already inscribed in the social processes or artificially created by the propaganda, becomes legitimate and favours a vertical alignment of human dignity. To be excluded from the state – to be denied the rights of citizenship – is tantamount to becoming a non-person, vulnerable to arbitrary treatment and torture.

The basic features of a torturous society

The defence from threat: the exceptional emergency narrative and extraordinary powers

An important condition, which makes torture appear to be a legitimate and necessary political instrument in the eyes of relevant authorities, is the presence of an emotional situation characterized by a state of terror in the face of a perceived threat or an actual state of vulnerability. To what extent this terror is a genuine emotional state spontaneously arising out of the population or fabricated through a fear-inducing propaganda, which exploits themes of state enemies, exceptionally dangerous circumstances and the consequent need for protection depends on the specific socio-political conditions.

This emotional situation tends to facilitate the creation of narratives about 'an emergency state' (see Chapter 7) and provides reasons to reorganize society in a more vertical way, with a strong leadership as a protecting 'superpower', asking for and obtaining identification from people, and an out-group, which becomes a marginalized less-than-human target of social violence.

According to Kelman's analysis (Kelman, 1993, 2005) the *perceived threat* to the security of the state provides the rationale for a policy of torture, and enables the state to implement that policy, while establishing the purpose and justification, recruiting the agents or perpetrators, and defining the targets of torture. However, the perceived threat can be either internal or external, and the actual source of threat is not always the one identified by propagandistic discourse. Mostly, it is very far from it (Kelman, 2005: 128–9).

Edward Peters (1985) also emphasizes that the purpose and justification of torture is the protection of the state against *perceived internal or external* threats to its security – which often means the maintenance in power of those elements of the population that have gained control of the state apparatus. The practice of torture is justified by reference to the particular doctrine of the state's legitimization: maintaining law and order or stability, or the rule of 'the people' whom the state claims to embody, or the rule of God, or the survival of Western civilization, or the integrity of national institutions.

Richard Jackson (2005), employing the Critical Discourse Analysis, demonstrates how, during the 'war on terror' following the 11 September attacks in the USA, the American administration's public language of counter-terrorism came to infuse administration security policies, normalizing the practices of cruel, inhuman and degrading treatment of terrorist suspects, as well as their torture and murder. A good part of these sub narratives were about the suffering, as is evident in expressions such as 'national tragedy', a 'calamity', a 'wound to the nation', and 'a day that would never be forgotten'. The exceptional nature of the event – the attack and collapse of the Twin Towers – placed the event itself outside the realm of normal political discourse, in a state of exception (see Chapter 7). A second aspect of this discourse was re-constructing the event as an 'act of war', which conferred on the state powers usually reserved for supreme emergencies, as well as justification for military-based self-defence.

With a similar logic about threat and 'necessity defence', in 1987 the Landau Commission Report on the General Security Service in Israel and Occupied Territories authorized the use of 'moderate physical pressure' (i.e. torture) as a method of interrogation of Palestinian detainees suspected of terrorism (Cohen and Golan, 1991). The importance of the argument of the threat is confirmed by Heinz's interviews (1993: 100–4) with Latin American military officers involved in torture in Argentina, Brazil, Chile and Uruguay. Heinz detects seven main themes in their interviews, among which a transversal one is that of the threat and the consequent necessity to fight an internal/external war.

Thus, the perceived threat sets the rationale for the creation of special state powers. After such a pattern is set and precedents are created, however, the destruction of traditional guarantees can be put in place with one simple piece of legislation which suspends all that came before: an overall 'emergencies' or 'special powers' act was invoked routinely in the Southern American hemisphere, but also by the United States in the 'war on terror,' or by Great Britain that has long depended on extraordinary powers and emergency legislation regarding Northern Ireland or by any state where the military has taken precedence over civilian legal agency (Millet, 1994: 52).

Salvatore Senese (2006) explains how this emotional and cultural climate results in specific political-institutional conditions where torture can develop and spread. His teaching comes from the sessions of the Russell Tribunal II on Latin America, which were not limited to the documentation and acknowledgment of the many and terrible cases of torture, but dealt with an examination of the institutional features characterizing the torture-powers of many Latin American countries during the 1960s, 1970s and 1980s (beyond the type of power and its conceptualization or pretended legitimization). The peculiar institutional feature of these countries was a national security legislation characterized by: 1) the juridical possibility of intervention by the central power, sometimes at the hands of military forces or under their safeguard, on the constitutional guarantees of the country with power of dissolution, suspension, veto, etc.; 2) the absolute indeterminacy of the concept of 'insurgency' and 'national security', which prompted this legislation; 3) the removal of the jurisdiction to investigate and judge on infractions to the national security from ordinary tribunals, and the attribution of such jurisdiction to special military tribunals; 4) the proscription of *habeas corpus* for those alleged of national security violations.

Kelman (1993, 2005) notices that, within the logic of an 'internal war' or an 'emergency situation', the paradigm of security reasons is based on an abstract idea of the state as something needing protection. It is not an obligation of the state to provide safety and protection to its citizens, but there is a reversal of these roles. Thus the ideology of national security splits a people into the logics of 'us *vs.* them', thereby magically transforming offenders into defenders of the state (or persecutors on behalf of the state) and the threatened into enemies of the state (or victims of persecution and eventually torture). If the conflict is acted out against an external enemy, the task of dehumanization is easier because enemies are already *aliens*, that is people excluded by the recognition of internal law and national and community bonds. When the threat is internal and less clearly detectable, the alien sub-human is not so easily found, and *ipso facto* a category of 'subversives' and 'enemies of the state' needs to be created.

The double bind of terror and torture

Terror and torture seem to have a circular relation: torture needs a widespread terror to be justified and terror is magnified and supported by the spectacle of torture, which is secret but shown (Foucault, 1975; Graziano, 1992; Scarry, 1985: 28). One could argue that torture and terror have a mutual supporting function. On the one hand, a serious threat to survival may trigger a collective terror and induce a power to make use of torture as a political way to deal with it; on the other hand, the ruling power may also use torture to sustain terror, in order to give continuation to its rule and to be legitimized by public consent.

In the 'war on terror', Marks (2007: 2) notes that a traumatic event, such as the vivid and devastating collapse of the Twin Towers provided evidence to a 'terrorscopic' vision of the world in which we are constantly under threat from Islamic fundamentalism. The impact of basic emotions, such as anger or fear, whether evoked by terrorism or other risks, is felt beyond the sphere of individual behaviour and becomes amplified across groups and populations. This sets the ground for a legitimization of a torture policy of people potentially responsible for such terror. In this regard, Lazreg writes, 'The colonial state in Algeria engaged in five related acts of terror: torture, rape, disappearances, summary executions, and reprisals. Terror and torture worked together like Jekyll and Hyde, feeding on each other, supporting each other, filling in for each other' (2008: 7). Robin (2005) emphasized the fact that torture was 're-invented' as a strategy in counter-insurgency warfare, to face the 'terrifying' prospect that enemies could be anywhere and not easily identified among the civil population: a terrorizing perception of being continuously under siege at the hand of unknown and potentially disproportionate forces.

In the years 1974–1983, something similar happened in Argentina where kidnapping and disappearances operated alongside torture in urban locations (garages) according to the logic of 'secret display', which often characterizes torture with the aim of spreading and sustaining terror. Hollander (2008: 698) describes this use of terror during the Dirty War by the military junta. She remembers people watching individuals being spirited away from an apartment building, a university classroom, a theatre or a restaurant. The only way to protect themselves was to deny the arbitrary repression of the innocents by thinking that the victims must have been up to something to merit the reasonable actions of the state.

Some authors emphasize that torture also has the function to display government power, be it authoritarian or democratic, and to have an impact on population. As Foucault (1975: 46) points out, the public character of torture of the past was also expressed in the implicit receiver of the message of torture. People were the target of the spectacle of ceremonies of agony. The powerful effect of terror, the scandal and the fear elicited by the images of torture was at the same time sought out and denied. The purpose of spectacular torture was to make the assembled crowds witness to the punishment and aware of the supreme power of the sovereign. According to Foucault, spectacular torture embodies a form of power that was 'exalted and strengthened by its visible manifestations' (Foucault, 1975: 57) in order to demonstrate who are the enemies.

Similarly, Kanan Makiya describes how torture worked in Saddam Hussein's Iraq. He writes,

> The range of cruel institutional practices in contemporary Iraq – confession rituals, public hangings, corpse displays, executions, and finally torture – are designed to breed and sustain widespread fear. But these practices are also visible and invisible manifestations of power, extensions of, for example, the state's right to wage war on the nation's enemies. . . . The increased power of the re-emerging sovereignty was visible in the splendour of the ceremony and confirmed by the numbers of people who came to participate in the occasion.
> (Makiya, 1989, in Schulz, 2007: 201).

Scarry (1985) offers an incredibly poignant analysis of this function of torture. She agrees with the point that the intensification of pain in torture is the language with which the torturer's power expresses itself. Although real pain is inflicted on a real person, torture is also a demonstration and magnification of the felt-experience of pain. Torture then goes on to deny and to falsify the reality of the very thing it has itself objectified by a perceptual shift, which converts the vision of suffering into the wholly illusory but, to the torturers and the regime they represent, wholly convincing 'spectacle of power'. In her analysis, torture is the invariable and simultaneous occurrence of three phenomena: 1) pain is inflicted on a person in ever-intensifying ways; 2) the pain, continually amplified within the person's body, is also amplified in the sense that it is objectified, made visible to those outside the person's body; and 3) the objectified pain is denied as pain and read as power (1985: 27). What assists the conversion of absolute pain into the fiction of absolute power is an obsessive, self-conscious display of agency (1985: 56–8). Thus, the torturer's power is possible thanks to terror, and feeds into terror as well. And terror needs torture to magnify its impact.

An invisible enemy and the need of separations

When torture is used state enemy is usually *invisible*. He is someone not immediately recognizable and for this reason, or this excuse, often arbitrary. In fact, torture has been massively employed, for example, in battles against nationalist guerrilla forces, such as in Indochina and Algeria (Robin, 2005), where French soldiers found themselves embroiled in what they called a 'rotten war', a war in which the enemy was not easily identifiable through a uniform. In this struggle against an 'invisible' enemy, the French 'revolutionary war' doctrine was later elaborated in Algeria as counterinsurgency warfare, in which torture was a main weapon (Galula, 1964). The genesis of this new kind of warfare is the idea that the enemy takes the form of an invisible political organization hidden among the civilian population. One can know its leaders and its structure only by waging a war of information: by arresting masses of civilian 'suspects', interrogating them and if necessary, torturing them. Among the fathers of this French doctrine was Colonel Roger Trinquier, the author of *La Guerre Moderne* [Modern Warfare], published in 1961, which become a reference for the United States during its entanglements in Vietnam and Latin America. According to Robin (2005), Operation Condor was the ultimate expression of the lessons Americans learned from the French. Established in 1975 by the autocratic governments of South America, Operation Condor coordinated intelligence activity between the military dictatorships of Chile, Argentina, Uruguay, Brazil, Paraguay and Bolivia. Its ostensible purpose was to exchange information on the activities of government opponents and exiles. The network was required to destroy the 'invisible enemy', rid the world of subversive forces (intellectuals, writers, trade unionists, psychologists, journalists, etc.) and impose a world of military order. The only way to identify this occult enemy was apparently through information obtained under torture (Feitlowitz, 1998: 8).

Something similar happened in the 'war on terror', in which the enemy was invisible, hidden among the population, its soldiers were ordinary men supporting Islam, with the line between common Muslims and more or less active opponents of the political hegemony and 'true terrorists' significantly blurred. It is now quite notorious that, on this basis, some people were kidnapped by the CIA (and eventually other secret agencies) and transferred to secret prisons all over the world to be tortured and others were detained in prisons under direct American administration (Abu Ghraib in Iraq, Guantanamo Bay in Cuba and Bagram in Afghanistan) where torture was routinely practiced (Amnesty International, 2006; Satterthwaite, 2006; Silverstein, 2005). In this sense, torture seems to perform the function of drawing a line dividing good and bad, friends and enemies, innocents and guilty, in order to create a bigger distance between these groups.

Torturous society is the realm of multiple separations and arbitrary splits, apparently undertaken in order to detect the 'state enemies'. A question of dividing society into the good part, the protector, and the bad part, those to persecute, is at stake. This is carried out splitting the whole into us and them, patriots and 'subversives', superhuman and sub-human, a common trait of societies where torture appears (Crelinsten, 2003; Staub, 1990; Zimbardo, 2004).

Blass (2000) notices that the Third Reich, for example, employed a two-pronged approach to propaganda: first, there was propaganda that likened Hitler to a god (the maximum good), while the second type of propaganda was virulently anti-Semitic (the maximum evil). Jews were variously depicted as exploitative usurers, power-seeking capitalists, godless communists, sexually perverse threats to Aryan women and children and demons bent on destroying Germany (2000: 133) This double reality is also described by Danielian (2010) with regard to Turkish chauvinism before and after the Armenian genocide, as well as in the treatment of Greeks, Armenians, Jews and Christians who were subject to humiliating practices. Turks ridiculed the victims for lining up submissively for slaughter like 'sheep'. This was coupled with a Turkish self-image as the glorious aggressor who identified with the 'wolf'. However, such a self-image stood in direct contrast to the picture of the Turks who were described as 'obsequious', even 'cringing' and 'nerveless', and as servile to authority. Danielian makes the hypothesis that you can find the 'sheep' of the Turkish psyche hidden within this underlying dynamic of shameful obsequiousness and servility to authority. For Turks at that time, wolves and sheep, the victor and the vanquished, were mutually exclusive experiences and could not be reconciled. One deserved an extreme measure of glory, the other an extreme measure of degradation.

Sometimes this need to separate is so deeply felt that it ends up functioning as a bulwark to a sense of internal physical illness or corruption. Lifton (1986) documented the biomedical ideology of Nazism that diagnosed a deadly racial disease of the Aryan race in the presence of the Jews, who 'were agents of "racial pollution" and "racial tuberculosis", as well as parasites and bacteria causing sickness, deterioration, and death in the host people they infested. They were the "eternal blood sucker", "vampire", "germ carrier", "people's parasite" and "maggot in a rotting corpse"' (1989: 16); 'the Jews were a lower species of life, a kind of vermin, which upon contact infected the German people with deadly diseases' (1989: 16). In this case, the need for the purity of the race led toward genocide, starting with deportation and torture, going through sadistic experiments and ending with extermination.

A better world: establishing ideology and re-creating society

Another distinguishing feature of a torturous society is the adoption of a *better world* ideology. Communism was an example of this. Also a *nationalistic ideology* is one where the focus is on the welfare, wellbeing and future of one's own nation. These ideologies usually provide a positive image of the nation or society to be created, of how things can be, thereby offering a new comprehension of reality and hope.

They also offer people a chance for achieving significance in difficult times, by participating in the fulfilment of the respective ideology (Koenigsberg, 2007; Staub, 1990, 1996, 1999).

The project of renewal and transformation of society was very concrete in Argentina under General Videla: it included not only a very organized system of kidnappings, torture and disappearances but also the adoption of the disappeared subversives' children by new families, who had the task to raise a new generation (Avery, 2004). Similarly, in Germany, as the Nazi party rose to power in 1933, no target within Nazification took a higher priority than the re-education of German youth (Miller, 2005: 37).

Some authors suggest that torture works by renewing society (Crelinsten, 2003). Indeed, the targets of torture are not criminals, but morally incomplete individuals whose deviancy lies in the subjective realm, rather than in concrete transgressions. As Orwell (1949) describes: 'The object of persecution … [becomes] persecution. The object of torture … [becomes] torture. The object of power … [becomes] power' (1949: 276). Crelinsten (2003) very clearly illustrates that the torture system relies on an ideological construction of a reality, which is reshaped according to a new template: laws are rewritten or reinterpreted, a new language and vocabulary devised, social relations redefined and all these processes of transformation channelled through and amplified by the mass media. What is observable is a broad process of *transformation of society*. An essential part of this system is a constant stream of propaganda creating a powerful and dangerous enemy that threatens the social fabric. Laws are directed against this enemy, labels to describe this enemy are promulgated and disseminated via the mass media, people are divided into us and them, for us and against us. If target groups happen to include violent insurgents or separatists at their radical fringe, so much the better, since the threat will be more easily depicted as real. But this is not always necessary in the business of constructing reality (Crelinsten, 2003).

In conclusion, our analysis and reorganization of the literature shows the following characteristics of the torturous societies: 1) a sense of internal vulnerability, widespread terror in the face of an imminent and dangerous threat, 2) the splitting into two social embodied realities: a superpower representing or claiming to represent the dominant segment of society and a sub-human minority intended for persecution; 3) the creation of narratives about exceptional emergency situations and extraordinary powers; 4) the search for invisible state enemies, whom you need to torture in order to protect the state, and against whom you consequently need to impose multiple separations/distinctions; 5) the establishment of a circular relation between terror and torture; and 6) a better world ideology that becomes a self-referential system tightened in itself, in which illusion informs reality, and torture is a constitutive part of the system.

The project of a 'new man' is part of many totalitarian ideologies. Torture goes about fashioning them anew. Orwell (1949) describes very effectively how terror works to reconstruct society and to create the 'new man'. This project requires that the system become absolute, self-referential and tightened in itself in a paradoxical closure.

References

Amnesty International (2002) *Unmatched Power, Unmet Principles: The Human Rights Dimensions of US Training of Foreign Military and Police Forces*. New York: Amnesty International USA Publications. Available at: www.amnestyusa.org/pdfs/msp.pdf (accessed 15 March 2015)

Amnesty International (2006) *United States of America: Below the Radar: Secret Flights to Torture and Disappearance*. Index: AMR 51/051/2006, 5 April 2006.

Avery, L. (2004) 'A return to life: the right to identity and the right to identify Argentina's "living disappeared"'. *Harvard Women's Law Journal*, 27 (Spring): 235–72.

Blass, T. (Ed.), (2000) *Obedience to Authority: Current Perspectives on the Milgram Paradigm*. Mahwah, NJ: Lawrence Erlbaum Associates.

Blum, W. (2004) *Killing Hope: US Military and CIA Interventions Since World War II*. Monroe, ME: Common Courage.

Brown, M.E. (1997) 'Ethnicity and violence'. In Guibernau, M. and Rex, J. (Eds.), *The Ethnicity Reader: Nationalism, Multiculturalism and Migration*. Malden, MA: Blackwell, pp. 80–100.

Chomsky, N. and Herman, E. (1979) *The Washington Connection and Third World Fascism*. Boston, MA: South End Press.

Cohen, S. and Golan, D. (1991) *The Interrogation of Palestinians During the Intifada: Ill-treatment, 'Moderate Physical Pressure' or Torture?* Jerusalem: B'tselem – The Israeli Information Center for Human Rights in the Occupied Territories.

Craig, G.A. (1982) *The Germans*. New York: New American Library.

Crawford, B. (1998) 'The causes of cultural conflict: an institutional approach'. In Crawford, B. and Lipschutz, R.D. (Eds.), *The Myth of 'Ethnic Conflict': Politics, Economics and 'Cultural' Violence*. Berkeley, CA: University of California Press, pp. 3–43.

Crelinsten, R.D. (2003) 'The world of torture: a constructed reality'. *Theoretical Criminology*, 7: 293–318. doi:10.1177/13624806030073003

Danielian, A. (2010) 'A century of silence'. *The American Journal of Psychoanalysis*, 70 (September): 245–64. doi:10.1057/ajp.2010.12

Dolan, C. (2009) *Social Torture: The Case of Northern Uganda, 1986–2006*. New York: Berghahn Books.

Galula, D. (1964) *Counterinsurgency Warfare: Theory and Practice*. Westport, CT: Praeger Security International, 2006.

Gordon, N. and Marton, R. (1995) *Torture: Human Rights, Medical Ethics and the Case of Israel*. London and New Jersey: Zed Books.

Eidelson, R.J. and Eidelson, J.I. (2003) 'Dangerous ideas: five beliefs that propel groups toward conflict'. *American Psychologist*, 58(3): 182–92. doi:10.1037/0003-066X.58.3.182

Feitlowitz, M. (1998) *A Lexicon of Terror: Argentina and the Legacies of Torture*. New York: Oxford University Press.

Forrest, D. (1996) 'The methods of torture and its effects'. In Forrest, D. (Ed.), *A Glimpse of Hell: Reports on Torture Worldwide*. London: Cassell and Amnesty International, pp. 104–21.

Foucault, M. (1975) *Discipline and Punish: The Birth of the Prison*. New York: Random House, 1979.

Gonen, J.Y. (2000) *The Roots of Nazi Psychology: Hitler's Utopian Barbarism*. Lexington, KY: University Press of Kentucky.

Gordon, N. and Marton, R. (1995) *Torture: Human Rights, Medical Ethics and the Case of Israel*. London and New Jersey: Zed Books.

Graziano, F. (1992) *Divine Violence: Spectacle, Psychosexuality, and Radical Christianity in the Argentine 'Dirty War'*. Boulder, San Francisco, Oxford: Westview Press.

Hartung, W.D. and Ciarrocca, M. (2004) *The Ties that Bind: Arms Industry Influence in the Bush Administration and Beyond*. World Policy Institute (Special report), October.

Heinz, W.S. (1993) 'The military, torture and human rights: experiences from Argentina, Brazil, Chile and Uruguay'. In Crelinsten, R.D. and Schmid, A.P. (Eds.), *The Politics of Pain: Torturers and their Masters*. Centrum voor Onderzoek van Maatschappelijke Tegenstellingen/Center for the Study of Social Conflicts, AK Leiden, Netherlands: Leiden University, pp. 73–108.

Hollander, N.C. (2008) 'Living danger: on not knowing what we know'. *Psychoanalytic Dialogues*, 18: 690–709. doi:10.1080/10481880802297707

Imseis, A. (2001) 'Moderate torture on trial: critical reflections on the Israeli Supreme Court Judgement concerning the legality of general security service interrogation methods'. *Berkeley Journal of International Law*, 19(2): 328–49. doi:10.15779/Z381P9P

Innes, B. (1998) *The History of Torture*. London: Brown Books.

Jackson, R. (2005) *Writing the War on Terrorism: Language, Politics and Counter-Terrorism*. Manchester: Manchester University Press.

Jackson, B.A. (2007) 'Counterinsurgency intelligence in a 'long war': the British experience in Northern Ireland'. *Military Review*. (January–February). Available at: www.rand.org/content/dam/rand/pubs/reprints/2007/RAND_RP1247.pdf (accessed 8 November 2016).

Jongman, B. (1991) 'Why some states kill and torture while others do not', *PIOOM Newsletter*, 3(1): 8–11.

Keller, B. (2003) 'God and George W. Bush.' *New York Times*, 17 May.

Kelman, H.C. (1993) 'The social context of torture: policy process and authority structure'. In Crelinsten, R.D. and Schmid, A.P. (Eds.), *The Politics of Pain: Torturers and their Masters*. Centrum voor Onderzoek van Maatschappelijke Tegenstellingen/Center for the Study of Social Conflicts, AK Leiden, Netherlands: Leiden University, pp. 21–38.

Kelman, H.C. (2005) 'The policy context of torture: a social-psychological analysis'. *International Review of the Red Cross*, 87(857) (March): 123–34. doi:10.1017/S1816383100181214

Koenigsberg, R.A. (2007) *Hitler's Ideology: Embodied Metaphor, Fantasy and History*. Charlotte, NC: Information Age Publishing.

Langguth, A.J. (1978) *Hidden Terrors: The Truth About US Police Operations in Latin America*. New York: Pantheon Books.

Lansford, T., Watson, R.P. and Covarrubias, J. (Eds.) (2009) *America's War on Terror*. Second Edition, Burlington, VT: Ashgate.

Lazreg, M. (2008) *Torture and the Twilight of the Empire*. Princeton, NJ: Princeton University Press.

Lifton, R.J. (1986) *The Nazi Doctors: Medical Killing and the Psychology of Genocide*. New York: Basic Books, 1986.

Makiya, K. (1989) 'Republic of fear: the politics of modern Iraq'. In Schulz, W.F. (Ed.), *The Phenomenon of Torture. Readings and Commentary*. Philadelphia, PA: University of Pennsylvania Press, 2007, pp. 201–3.

Marks, J.H. (2007) 'The language and logic of torture'. CLCWeb: *Comparative Literature and Culture*, 9(1). Available at: http://docs.lib.purdue.edu/clcweb/vol9/iss1/11/ (accessed 10 May 2015).

Mayer, M. (1955) *They Thought They Were Free: The Germans, 1933–45*. Chicago, IL: University of Chicago Press.

McCoy, A. (2005) 'Cruel science: CIA torture and US foreign policy'. *New England Journal of Public Policy*, 19(2), 15: 209–62. Available at: http://scholarworks.umb.edu/nejpp/vol19/iss2/15 (accessed 3 January 2017)

McCoy, A. (2006) *A Question of Torture: CIA Interrogation, from the Cold War to the War on Terror (American Empire Project)*. New York: Metropolitan Books/Henry Holt.
Milbank, D. 'Religious Right Finds Its Center in Oval Office'. *Washington Post*, 24 December 2001, p. A02.
Miller, A.G. (Ed.) (2005) *The Social Psychology of Good and Evil*. New York: Guilford Press.
Millet, K. (1994) *The Politics of Cruelty: An Essay on the Literature of Political Imprisonment*. London: Penguin Books.
Orwell, G. (1949) *Nineteen Eighty-Four*. London: Penguin, 2008.
Otterman, M. (2007) *American Torture: From the Cold War to Abu Ghraib and Beyond*. Melbourne: Melbourne University Press.
Peters, E. (1985) *Torture*. Expanded Edition, Philadelphia, PA: University of Pennsylvania Press, 1996.
Rejali, D. (1991) 'How not to talk about torture: violence, theory and the problems of explanation'. In Huggins, M. K. (Ed.), *Vigilantism and the State in Modern Latin America: Essays on Extralegal Violence*. Westport, CT: Praeger, pp. 127–44.
Robin, M. (2005) 'Counterinsurgency and torture: exporting torture tactics from Indochina and Algeria to Latin America'. In Roth, K. and Worden, M. (Eds.), *Torture: Does It Make Us Safer? A Human Rights Perspective*. New York: New Press, pp. 44–54.
Sartre, J.P. (1958) 'Preface'. In Alleg, H., *The Question*. London: John Calder Publishers, 2006.
Satterthwaite, M. (2006) 'Extraordinary rendition and disappearances in the "War on Terror"'. *Gonzaga Journal of International Law*, 10: 70–5. Available at: www.law.gonzaga.edu/gjil/2006/08/extraordinary-rendition-and-disappearances-in-the-war-on-terror/
Scarry, E. (1985) *The Body in Pain: The Making and Unmaking of the World*. New York, Oxford: Oxford University Press.
Senese, S. (2006) 'Argentina. Tortura e dittature militari in American Latina negli anni '70: la dottrina della sicurezza nazionale'. In Bimbi, L. and Tognoni, G. (Eds.), *La Tortura Oggi nel Mondo*. Roma: Fondazione Internazionale Lelio Basso, pp. 63–72.
Silverstein, K. (2005) 'Pentagon memo on torture-motivated transfer. *Los Angeles Times*, 8 December. Available at: http://articles.latimes.com/2005/dec/08/nation/na-torture8 (accessed 29 March 2010).
Soldz, S. (2008) 'Healers or interrogators: psychology and the United States torture regime'. *Psychoanalytic Dialogues*, 18(5): 592–613. doi:10.1080/10481880802297624
Staub, E. (1989) *The Roots of Evil: The Origins of Genocide and Other Group Violence*. Cambridge: Cambridge University Press.
Staub, E. (1990) 'The psychology and culture of torture and tortures'. In Suefeld, P. (Ed.), *Psychology and Torture*. Washington, DC: Hemisphere, pp. 49–77.
Staub, E. (1993) 'Torture: psychological and cultural origins'. In Crelinsten, R.D. and Schmid, A.P. (Eds.), *The Politics of Pain: Torturers and Their Masters*. Leiden, The Netherlands, COMT, pp. 109–23.
Staub, E. (1996) 'Breaking the cycle of violence: helping victims of genocidal violence heal'. *Journal of Personal and Interpersonal Loss*, 1(2): 191–7.
Staub, E. (1999) 'The origins and prevention of genocide, mass killing and other collective violence'. *Peace and Conflict: Journal of Peace Psychology*, 5: 303–7.
Staub, E. (2003) *The Psychology of Good and Evil: Why Children, Adults, Groups Help and Harm Others*. New York: Cambridge.
Vidal-Naquet, P. (1963) 'Torture: cancer of democracy, France and Algeria 1954–62'. In Schulz, W.F. (Ed.), *The Phenomenon of Torture: Readings and Commentaries*. Philadelphia, PA: University of Pennsylvania Press, 2007, p. 195.

Volkan, V. (1999) 'Psychoanalysis and diplomacy: Part I. Individual and large group identity'. *Journal of Applied Psychoanalytic Studies*, 1: 29–55. doi:10.1023/A:1023026107157

Weschler, L. (1990) *A Miracle, A Universe: Settling Accounts with Torturers*. Chicago, IL: University of Chicago Press, 1998.

Zimbardo, P.G. (2004) 'A situationist perspective on the psychology of evil: understanding how good people are transformed into perpetrators'. In Miller, A.G. (Ed.), *The Social Psychology of Good and Evil*. New York: Guilford, pp. 21–50.

3
SOCIAL ACTORS OF TORTURE

This chapter intends to review the main key issues of social actors involved in torture as they arise from literature. In the wake of lead authors on this theme (Cohen, 2001; Crelinsten, 2003; Ehrenreich and Cole, 2005; Staub, 1989, 1990, 1993, 1997, 1999, 2003; among others), the analysis is here organized in a three-parted classification, looking for the fundamental social and psychological dynamics characterizing *perpetrators*, *victims* and *bystanders*. Some authors refer to these actors as composing what they call an 'atrocity triangle' (Cohen, 2001; Hilberg, 1992; Staub, 2003). Naturally, this tripartite categorization is an ideal grouping of more complex and blurred subjective realities. However, it proves effective, in conveying the range of phenomena observed in social actors in times of atrocities, to study the main dilemmas characterizing these three roles.

Perpetrators

In recent decades, a considerable amount of literature has been written about the phenomenology of perpetrators in witness literature, philosophy, sociology, social psychology, and psychoanalysis, in an effort to account for their behaviour (Arendt, 1963; Blass, 2000; Crelinsten, 2003; Crelinsten and Schmid, 1993; Kelman, 1993, 2005; Kelman and Hamilton, 1989; Huggins, 2012; Huggins *et al.*, 2002; Lifton, 1986; Milgram, 1963, 1974; Miller, 2005; Staub, 1989; Todorov, 1991; Zimbardo, 1972, 2004, 2007, among others).

My proposal is to approach such literature on torturers in a double perspective: adresing, on the one hand, *the problem of evil*, whereby the psychosocial dynamics that make evil and torture possible in society are examined, while looking at the intersection between individual and social spheres; on the other hand, *the making of torturers*, digging for the actual methods used to create torturers out of ordinary men.[1]

The problem of evil

There is consensus within the literature that torturers are likely to be quite ordinary people. This disturbing observation is particularly clear when examining Holocaust studies (for example, Browning, 1993; Christie, 1991; Lifton, 1986; Todorov, 1991; among others).

Camp survivors' stories seem to agree on the following point: only a small minority of Nazi guards could legitimately be called sadists (Bettelheim, 1952; Levi, 1986). Primo Levi writes, 'They were made of the same cloth as we, they were average human beings, averagely intelligent, averagely wicked: save the exceptions, they were not monsters, they had our faces' (1986: 202).

One of the most clear and astonishing evidence of the 'good mental health' of people carrying out atrocities came out of the study of the Nuremberg defendants, which was commissioned after the defeat of Nazi Germany by the World Federation of Mental Health. Social scientists in charge of studying the phenomenon of a social structure organized around abuse and torture, hoped to find out who the torturers were and how they differed from normal individuals. As part of the project, Rorschach test data were gathered and evaluated, and that was expected to reveal a peculiar psychopathology. But that was not the case.

With equal dismay, while observing Adolph Eichmann sitting at his trial in Jerusalem, Hannah Arendt had to acknowledge that, despite the prosecutor's efforts to demonize him, this man, who was responsible for one of the most devastating evils in the history of humanity stood before the court as a profoundly mediocre, indeed ordinary, human being. 'The trouble with Eichmann' Arendt writes, 'was precisely that so many were like him, and that the many were neither perverted nor sadistic, that they were, and still are, terribly and terrifyingly normal' (Arendt, 1963: 276).

What does make evil more likely in society? From the literature on social violence, it seems that a pattern of four psychosocial dynamics must be put into place in order to create a situation where torture is possible: a) *the internalization of an ideology,* b) *the obedience to authority,* c) the systematic use of *compartmentalizations at social, institutional, and psychological levels* and d) the use of *action as involvement.*

The internalization of an ideology

In Chapter 2, the term ideology is used as a synonym for a rigid pattern of beliefs, generally proposed by those in power, which provides an understanding of what is happening or about to happen in an 'emergency state'. Some authors suggest that an ideology must be internalized as a preparatory stage for what logically follows in terms of actions. The social philosopher Sam Keen (1986), in his analysis of national propaganda images from around the world, makes clear that before a soldier can kill, he must internalize an image of a hated or feared enemy. Heinz interviewed military officers who tortured in Argentina, Brazil, Chile and Uruguay finding that among the most recurring themes there were a) 'the communist threat' –

a genuine sense of the magnitude of an immediate threat to the state by an imminent take over by Marxism and guerrilla movement; b) 'there was a war' – in all four countries, officers stressed that they fought a war, which they had to win and that war implied a number of important justifications and explanations (1993: 101–3). These images were rehearsed by the national rhetoric, which projected the widespread presence of secretive enemies to justify repressive actions by the government for the good of law-abiding citizens. In Huggins and Haritos-Fatouros's research (1998) on Brazil, a similar imagery was found to be fostered via the media and within military and police academies. Both militarized and civil police were informally taught through work socialization to recognize and guard against the ever-present pervasive danger that had put Brazil in the midst of a national security emergency. According to this propaganda, their lives could be jeopardized by a peer who was too interested in saving his own skin, too insensitive to threats, too slow to react, or simply unprepared to act violently when violence was called for (Heinz, 1993; Huggins et al., 2002).

Kelman (1993: 31–2) explains that the ideology concerning the threat to the state security provides a definition of the situation and the rationale for a policy of torture. It does it by: 1) establishing the *purpose* and *justification* of torture: the protection of the state against internal and external threats to its security; 2) recruiting the *agents* or perpetrators of torture: agents of a professional force with a significant role in protecting the state against internal threats to its security; 3) defining the *targets* of torture: the so-called state enemies who constitute serious threats to the state's security and survival. For that, as well as for other reasons, such as their ethnicity or ideology, they are placed outside the protection of the state, thus becoming a non-person, vulnerable to arbitrary treatment, torture and, sometimes, even extermination.

The obedience to authority

Kelman and Hamilton define a crime of obedience as 'an act performed in response to orders from authority that is considered illegal or immoral by the larger community' (1989: 46). The fact that a criminal action serves various personal motives or is carried out with a high degree of initiative and personal involvement, does not necessarily remove it from the category of crimes of obedience, as long as the action is supported by the authority structure, and as long as the perpetrators have good reasons to believe that their actions are authorized, expected, or at least tolerated and probably approved by the authorities (1989: 50).

The phenomenon of 'blind obedience' to authority will be outlined as it exists at individual, groupal/institutional and institutional/societal levels, with the use of three classic studies. The aim is to show that, given certain conditions, individuals find themselves in a 'field of forces' – be that dual, groupal or institutional – that very strictly orientate and structure their behaviour and thinking in a definite direction. Resisting this powerful 'field of social forces' can be very difficult, painful or, in certain conditions, even dangerous for one's own survival.

Individual level: Stanley Milgram

One of the classic and most astonishing studies demonstrating the dynamics of blind obedience is Stanley Milgram's *Obedience to Authority* (1974). First published in the same year as the daring capture of Adolf Eichmann by Israeli agents (Milgram, 1963) as Hannah Arendt's *Eichmann in Jerusalem*, Milgram's work on obedience has been associated with the Holocaust from the beginning. His findings were indeed shocking because it revealed that a variety of ordinary American citizens could so readily be led to engage in 'electrocuting a nice stranger' just because they were ordered to do so by a researcher. Milgram created a laboratory scenario described to research subjects as being concerned with punishment and learning. Participants, who were volunteers with different ages and backgrounds (primarily male), arrived at the Yale University laboratory and encountered a white-coated experimenter with stern demeanour and another apparent volunteer (an accomplice). An elaborate staging then occurred in which another participant, in the role of 'learner', was to receive electric shocks for mistakes that he would make during a word-association task. The device which the 'teacher' (the actual participant) would use to administer the shocks was a realistic 'shock generator', labelled as delivering shocks from 15 to 450 volts. Participants were instructed to administer increasingly severe shocks for each error made on a series of memory trials. No actual shocks were delivered, although the learner acted as if he were receiving the punishment. Located in an adjoining room, he emitted audible sounds of pain, which could be clearly heard by the participant. Pounding on the wall, the learner also mentioned a recently diagnosed 'heart problem' and, ultimately, demanded to be released on a repeated basis. Milgram's intent was to produce an intense moral conflict for the participant in terms of whether to obey the experimenter, but at the cost of continuing to harm a protesting victim, or to side with the learner but, in so doing disobeying the experimenter. Milgram (1974) reported startling findings: a) 65 per cent of the participants obeyed orders until the end of the shock series, in terms of inflicting electric shocks of the maximum voltage, even when the silence of the learner was suggesting that he might have died; b) various groups (e.g. psychiatrist, undergraduate students, etc.) could not predict the obedience rate, instead invariably underestimating the obtained results by extremely wide margins. A complex debate developed on the possibility of using these research findings to understand the behaviour of people involved directly and indirectly in torture or other atrocities, particularly the Holocaust (on this topic see Blass, 2000; Fenigstain, 1998; Mastroianni, 2002; Mandel, 1998; Miller, 1986, 2004). Milgram himself recognized many conceptual limits to his research, but, despite these drawbacks, obedience studies have much to tell us about the reason why people in subordinate-superordinate relationships cede personal autonomy in favour of meeting higher order needs, even if this entails violating their own moral beliefs. By doing so, they relinquish responsibility for their actions and become agents of someone else's will, that is, they enter what Milgram refers to as an 'agentic state'.

Since Milgram's results were so unexpected, he and other authors (Kilham and Mann, 1974; Meeus and Raaijmakers, 1986, 1995; Smith and Bond, 1993) carried out a number of variations to better understand the conditions under which obedience and disobedience are more likely. For the development of my argument, the following results are worthy of notice:

1   The required actions caused Milgram's participants (who were not suffering any personality disorders) a great deal of *distress*. Participants were observed sweating, wavering, biting their lips and moaning as they struggled through the experiment (Elms, 1995; Elms and Milgram, 1966).
2   In follow-up studies, Milgram (1974) found that some factors influence obedience: a) the proximity/immediacy of the authority figure: obedience decreases as the distance to the experimenter increases; b) the immediacy/proximity of the victim to the participants: in a series of experiments, results indicate that the closer the teacher was to the learner, the lower the level of obedience; c) group pressure: open defiance of confederates breaks the social consensus of the situation and reduces the strength of the experimenter's social power producing a sharp drop in obedience.

Milgram seems to be aware that his experiments work in the context of a cultural belief in the trustworthiness of science, but does not emphasize enough the extent to which this might function as an ideological context. He defines 'ideology' as: 'a set of beliefs and attitudes that legitimates the authority of the person in charge and justifies following his or her directives' (1974: 189). I would like to emphasize that in his experiment the ideology of science was crucial in explaining the legitimacy of the experimenter's authority. Even in this kind of ideological stand, a great deal of suffering can be inflicted on a human being to achieve a 'superior goal'.

Groupal and institutional levels: Philip Zimbardo

Focusing on group dynamics from a situational perspective, in 1971 Philip Zimbardo designed a dramatic experiment to study the dynamics of a prison (Zimbardo, 1975; 2007; Zimbardo *et al.*, 1999). The experiment was carried out in the basement of Stanford University, which was opportunely organized to simulate a real prison. Participants were supposed to live in the prison day and night, if prisoners, or to work there for 8-hour long shifts, if guards. The designed duration of the experiment was a 2-week period, in order to allow sufficient time for the situation norms to develop and patterns of social interaction to emerge, change and crystallize. The study was thought to ensure that all research participants would initially be as normal as possible, with good physical and mental health, and without any history of involvement in drugs or crime or violence, so as to exclude dispositional knots. Another important feature of the experiment was the novelty of the prisoner and guards' roles: participants had no prior training in how to play the randomly assigned roles. The student-prisoners underwent a realistic surprise arrest by officers of Palo

Alto Police Department, who cooperated with the researchers, and were taken to the police station for booking, after which each prisoner was brought to the 'prison' (the basement of Stanford University). Each of the prisoners' uniform had an ID number, while the cutting of hair was simulated with stockings placed on their heads. The guards wore military-style uniforms and silver-reflecting sunglasses to enhance anonymity. Data were collected via systematic video recordings, secret audio-video recordings of conversations of prisoners in their cells, interviews and tests at various times during the study, post-experiment reports and direct, concealed observations.[2] The projected 2-week experiment had to be terminated after only 6 days because of the level of cruelty that had been reached and the suffering provoked within the dynamics between guards and prisoners: pacifist young men were behaving sadistically in their role as guards, inflicting humiliation and pain and suffering on other young men, on whom the inferior status of prisoner had been 'imposed'. Some 'guards' even reported enjoying behaving sadistically. Some of the intelligent, healthy college students who were occupying the role of prisoner showed signs of 'emotional breakdown'. The prisoners who adapted better to the situation were those who mindlessly followed orders and who allowed the guards to dehumanize and degrade them ever more with each passing day and night. The only personality variable that had any significant predictive value was the F-scale of authoritarianism: the higher the score, the more days the prisoner survived in this totally authoritarian environment.

Zimbardo declared that he terminated the experiment not only because of the escalating level of violence and degradation by the guards against the prisoners, but also because he was made aware by his assistant of the transformation he was undergoing personally, behaving like a rigid institutional authority figure more concerned about the security of his prison than as a psychological researcher (Zimbardo, 2004; Zimbardo *et al.*, 1999; Zimbardo *et al.*, 2000). He considered his transformation to represent the most profound measure of the power of the experimental situation.

Zimbardo offers a 'situationalist' interpretation of the experiment: the intrinsically pathological situation in which normal young people were placed could distort and 're-channel' their behaviour. The abnormality there resided in the psychological nature of the situation and not in those who passed through it. He observed how the use of power was self-aggrandizing and self-perpetuating: whenever there was any perceived threat by the prisoners, this new level subsequently became the baseline from which further hostility and harassment would begin (Zimbardo, 2004). In this regard, Milgram's observation that there is a link between the experimenter and the space of experiment is extremely interesting. He writes,

> Authority systems are frequently limited by a physical context [in Zimbardo's experiment the simulated prison in the basement of university] and often come under the influence of the authority when we cross the physical threshold into his domain. . . . There is a feeling that the experimenter 'owns' the space and that the subject must conduct himself fittingly. . . . Even

more important ... is the fact that entry into the experimenter's realm of authority is voluntary, undertaken through the free will of the participants.

(Milgram, 1974: 140)

This creates the sense of commitment and obligation, which will play a part in binding the subject to his role.

Institutional and societal level: John Conroy

In *Unspeakable Acts, Ordinary People* (2000), John Conroy focuses in great detail on three instances of extreme cruelty committed by respectable institutions:

1. *The interrogation of Irish subjects by the British police in Northern Ireland.* In the summer 1971, 14 Irishmen were picked up by the police after a period of escalating violence in Northern Ireland and arrested because they were believed to have connections with the Irish Republican Army. Upon arrest, these men were beaten severely by members of the local police and military, with hoods placed over their heads, then handcuffed and transported by helicopter to an interrogation site. There, they were subjected to the so-called 'five techniques', a combination of tortures consisting of hooding, noise bombardment, food deprivation, sleep deprivation and forced standing for days, with beatings administered at random intervals. The extreme pain, disorientation, fear and physical deprivation regularly resulted in the onset of a psychotic state, with vivid hallucinations and delusions. After some weeks, the men were transferred to another center for recuperation. Years later, when interviewed by Conroy, the victims still exhibited symptoms of their ordeal, in fact some had already died prematurely. Despite a prolonged investigation after which the victims were offered financial compensation (but which did not brand the five techniques as torture), those who administered the five techniques showed no guilt or remorse when interviewed. They believed they were fighting a war against the IRA and protecting British interests.

2. *The premeditated beating of Palestinians by the Israeli Army.* Conroy calls the Israeli incident the 'night of the broken-clubs', as it depicts the intentional fracturing of the arm and leg bones of Palestinians by Israeli soldiers at the end of January 1988. This punitive action occurred after a speech by Israeli Army officials asking Palestinians to end a period of insurrection, which was greeted with stone throwing, tyre burning, and the barricading of roads. On two occasions, two small groups of Palestinian men were rounded up at night and taken to a field where they were gagged and bound, and then beaten with clubs to break the bones in their arms and legs. Their hands then were untied and gags removed – the victims were unconscious at this point – with one Palestinian who had not been beaten allowed to go for help after the soldiers left. One of the officers who had taken part in these actions later found them reprehensible and reported the incidents to his superiors. After a number of

attempts to cover up the beatings, a trial was held in which the commanding colonel was charged. The focus of the trial was on whether an illegal order should be followed when the person instructed knows it to be illegal. Those in higher office insisted that they had stated that arms and legs could be 'beaten' but not 'broken'. The colonel was found guilty and demoted to the rank of private, causing him to lose a substantial portion of his pension. After a period of unemployment, however, he founded a very successful private security service. When Conroy interviewed the soldiers who took part in these incidents, many felt guilty and uneasy about what they had done. One officer who was interviewed justified the beating of individuals who showed no resistance by referring to the Palestinians as a 'different population', 'a different kind of citizen'.

3   *The torture of a suspect by the Chicago police.* The third incident concerns the torture, in 1982, by the Chicago police of an individual who was suspected of killing two officers. The murders had followed the shooting of five police officers, four fatally, in little more than a month in the same law enforcement area of jurisdiction. Seven years after being convicted of the killing of the officers, the defendant filed a civil suit against those who held him in custody awaiting arraignment, stating that he had been tortured after his arrest. He claimed that various police officials beat him, put a plastic bag over his head so that he could not breathe, burned him with cigarettes, and administered electric shocks to parts of his body. When a inquiry was finally launched into the events, dozen of other prisoners and ordinary individuals – mostly minority males – came forward to testify that they, too, had been beaten and shocked in police custody. These allegations were followed by the usual investigations, trials and re-trials. The end result was that the accused were ostensibly cleared of any wrong doing.

These three cases are paradigmatic of how obedience to authority in the context of an institution designated to administer violence can make of torture a legitimate action and grant impunity to its perpetrators. These three incidents lead Conroy to conclude, 'It seems a very small leap to argue that torture is the perfect crime. There are exceptions, yes, but in the vast majority of cases, only the victim pays' (2000: 256). The reason for this injustice, at least in the incidents reported, may be that public sentiment resided more with the torturers than with the victims. Even in those cases where secret torture comes to light in liberal democracies, Conroy observes that a series of official rationalizations is put forward in order to excuse the use of such methods. The first is a complete denial. When the evidence is overwhelming, the abuse is minimized. Then the victims are disparaged, followed by a justification of the treatment on the grounds that it was necessary under the circumstances. The officials may also label those who take up the cause of the victims as state enemies. Another defence is that the torture is no longer taking place and that there is nothing to be gained in dredging up the past. Governments will also allocate the blame to a few bad apples, rather than the entire institution.

The compartmentalizations at social, institutional and psychological levels

As Todorov (1991) notices, the authority principle deals with different levels of *separations*, which are used as defence from evil. However, these separations are in turn what makes evil possible and simple. In a totalitarian system, the division of life into impermeable compartments – a kind of social schizophrenia – is a defence mechanism for anyone with some moral principles left to preserve. Todorov detects three levels of separation which are especially characteristic of totalitarian countries. The first separation is in the definition of good and evil provided by that party or state which takes charge of all social goals. (see Chapter 2). The second separation is fulfilled when each profession sets itself apart from others: in such a case, the restriction of responsibility towards one's own field is explicitly demanded. Everyone must keep to his own group of professionals. This creates a shift in people's mind within the isolated chambers of their technical and functional roles. The third separation takes place within people's mind. It is the operating principle of an internal dissociating device typical of atrocity producing situations. In 1961, Eichmann's attention is focused not on the horrendous acts of which he stands accused but on the possibility that his accusers may be running roughshod over the neat delineation of responsibilities among the various divisions of the Third Reich. In his mind, the separations were watertight and remained so. His department was responsible only for organizing the transfer of people, for finding trains and selecting stations; in other words, limited and specific tasks (Arendt, 1963).

Compartimentalization and the bureaucratic specialization to which it gives rise are at the root of the absence of feelings of responsibility. Todorov illustrates how this compartmentalization works in a hierarchical organization, as far as it extends. At one end of the organizational chain, there are people whose sleep is never disturbed by the consequences that take place on their orders. Only at the other end of the chain must there be someone to deliver the final blow, someone who will know no peace of mind until the day he dies but who nevertheless is not really guilty of anything. Those who made all this possible – the countless other intermediaries – can always shift their responsibility onto the next link in the chain. We have before us an entirely new kind of responsibility that cannot be considered the same as that of the ordinary criminal (see Chapter 8).

Moving the focus from a social to a psychological perspective, Lifton's work highlights the internal fragmentation such a social context produced in Nazi doctors (1986). He devotes a great deal of attention to the transformation of their inner world and calls this process '*doubling* of the self'. He describes the countless means by which the compromised individual manages to maintain a positive self-image: by agreeing to do one thing but not another, by isolating the private from the public, by trying to make up for public vice with private virtue. Lifton sees in *doubling* a means of adaptation to extremity. This adaptation requires a dissolving of 'psychic glue' as an alternative to a radical breakdown of the self. In Auschwitz, the pattern was established under the duress of the individual doctor's transition period. If an environment is sufficiently extreme and one chooses to remain in it, they may be able to do so only by means of *doubling*, as a defence from the fear of inner disintegration. However, doubling remains problematic, since it does not include the radical dissociation and sustained separateness characteristic of multiple personality, in which the two selves are more profoundly distinct and autonomous and tend either not to know about each other or else to see each other as *alien*. Doubling is more focused and temporary and occurs as part of a larger institutional structure, which encourages or even demands it.

Action as involvement

Ideological movements and totalitarian systems induce members to participate. Members must follow special rituals and rules; they must join in educational or work activities for building the new society (Orwell, 1949). The more they participate, the more difficult it becomes for them to distance themselves from the system's goals and deviate from its norms of conduct, not only publicly and overtly, but also internally. Moreover, action makes you focus on the details of the job, on its requirements and not on its meaning. Involvement in action is a method of binding one's thinking and behaviour to the system. The actions promoted are those that fit into the framework of ideology. Bruno Bettelheim described the inner struggle of a man who was against the Nazis but had to use the obligatory greeting 'Heil Hitler'. Even such a limited participation can result in substantial psychological reorganization (Bettelheim, 1952). Hannah Arendt (1963) describes such a turning point for Eichmann. When he was first exposed to the bodies of massacred Jews, he reacted with revulsion. But then 'higher ideals' (that is powerful motives) such as Nazi ideology and loyalty to the Führer, as well as a desire to advance his career, led him to ignore his distress and continue with his 'work'. Distress eventually disappeared. We can suppose that first participation contributed to bind him to Nazism. What one chooses to do at such crucial 'turning points' where the nature of facts is no longer deniable, is fundamental to the active involvement in the logics of the torturous system.

Those institutions that traditionally exercise the state's monopoly on legitimized violence, i.e. the police and the military, become specialized units at the service of such a process of promotion of 'action'.

The making of torturers

Who are they?

Most torturers are soldiers and police officers. In Argentina during the period of the Dirty War regime, concentration camp guards and torturers were recruited from the ranks of the police force and from the penal system (Feitlowitz, 1998); during the repressive years of the Greek Colonels, military policemen were selected for specialized torture units (Amnesty International, 1977); in Turkey, it was the Jandarma (military police) (HRFT, 2004); and, in Israel, it was agents of the General Security Services (Imseis, 2001). Military and police training, based as they are on hierarchical models of authority and obedience, lend themselves to 'ordered' violence.

Looking closer at the specific issue of torture, what emerges from literature is that torturers are made and not born (Browning, 1993; Conroy, 2000; Haritos-Fatouros, 2003; Huggins et al., 2002). They are typically ordinary human beings who perform violent and abhorrent acts under particular socio-political situations and work circumstances.

The production of a profession

Not every torturer has undergone a specialist training, but it is clear from the literature that, for the most part, a specific technology of 'production' can be recognized, especially in those institutions authorized to use violence (army, police, secret services, etc.). There is little difference between the training of soldiers in general and the training of torturers in particular. More often than not, the second one is a by-product of the first one, with torture becoming an integral part of one's duty, a duty that is often expressed in terms of hyper-masculinity – you have 'to be a man'[3] (Crelinsten, 1993; Haritos-Fatouros, 1993; Heinz, 1993; Wolfendale, 2006).

The making of torturers consists mostly of a systematized programme of 'traumatizing' and 'perverting' treatments consisting of beatings, insults and threats designed specifically to humiliate and brutalize recruits. This traumatic training is aimed at favouring submission in the context of an irrational, unpredictable world, where the only escape is to obey orders blindly. This treatment is functional to the initiation to a new ideology, new values and a system of rewards. Crelinsten (2003) notices that torture training usually includes techniques designed to supplant normal moral restraints about harming (innocent) others and to replace them with cognitive and ideological constructs that justify torture and victimization and neutralize any factor that might lead to pangs of conscience or disobedience to authority. Far from being soldiers who fail to live up to military ideals or crack under pressure, torturers are usually soldiers trained using the most sophisticated military techniques, aimed at cultivating a moral psychology which makes the occurrence of torture more likely (Wolfendale, 2006: 63).

The characteristic features of the moral psychology of military torture are not rage, hatred and sadism, but detachment and desensitization – ironically, the very traits that stoicism can also encourage. In other words, torturers' capacities for empathy and respect are suppressed as part of the training that leads to torture (Sherman, 2005:178).

From literature, it is possible to derive a set of different stages of this training: a) *recruitment and selection*, b) *initiation*, c) *training and reshaping of identity*, d) *techniques to overcome difficulties in performing evil*.

For descriptive reasons, the phases of the making of a torturer are here clear cut but, in fact, a certain variability can be found in different institutional and social contexts.

Recruitment and selection

Soldiers or policemen who become torturers can be quite ordinary in terms of personal and social backgrounds (Conroy, 2000; Haney et al., 1973; Haritos-Fatouros, 1993; Lifton, 1986; Milgram, 1963, 1974; Staub, 1989). However, some authors emphasize that, in certain circumstances, a pre-existing ideological persuasion or specific personality traits may be important at the stage of selection. Those who demonstrate a strong obedience to authority, as well as being fiercely against someone or something or attracted to some ideology are more likely to be pre-selected as torturers (Gibson, 1990; Haritos-Fatouros, 1993; Lifton, 1986; Staub, 1989, 1993). Torturers are usually the most loyal, patriotic, and obedient of soldiers (Staub, 1993: 106). In many cases, the majority of the servicemen transformed into torturers belong to a low socio-economic class. In the Greek case, a fair percentage were village boys. The sense of belonging to a highly esteemed, highly feared, and all-powerful army corp was the strongest long-term positive reward of all because these boys enjoyed many standing privileges and rights during and after completing their military service (Allodi, 1993; Crelinsten and Schmid, 1993: 52; Haritos-Fatuoros, 2003; Huggins et al. 2002).

Staub summarizes his findings on the recruitment and selection of perpetrators as follows:

> the personalities of people who, in the course of the evolution of group violence become perpetrators, are likely to be primarily the expression of the culture. . . . People who have developed strong respect for authority usually like to be part of a hierarchical system. They enjoy being led as well as having authority over others lower in the hierarchy. They prefer order and predictability. Their preference for and reliance on authority, hierarchy and structure make social conditions under which effective leadership and the protective role of the leaders break down, and when uncertainty about the future and about how to deal with the present is great . . . especially difficult for them.
>
> People whose basic needs in childhood were frustrated to a greater extent may also be especially affected by social conditions and group conflict that frustrate basic needs. Individuals with personal wounds, and/or with hostility towards other people that is kept in check under normal conditions, may be activated by conditions that instigate group violence. All such persons may find a clear and well-defined ideology and involvement with an ideological movement highly appealing. . . . Personality appears to be a source of selection of people by those in authority for perpetrator roles. It also seems to be a source of 'self-selection' not initially for destroying others but for roles that later may become violent. Need for identity and connection, low self-esteem . . . the desire to find leaders and the need for clear-cut ideological vision, may all lead people to 'join'.
>
> (Staub, 1999: 187)

In his interviews of sixteen ex-military policemen who had served during the military dictatorship in Greece and had been trained to administer torture, Mika Haritos-Fatouros (1993: 148–9) identified a three-phase selection procedure among Greek torturers. The first selection took place at the time when they were drafted at the age of 18. The main criterion for their selection to be a Greek Military Police (ESA)[4] candidate was their own and their families' political beliefs and attitudes concerning the military regime, and their anti-communist feelings and actions. The second major selection occurred following the first three months of hard training at the KESA camp (the Center for Military Police Training), on the basis of the general behaviour of the recruits during their training in terms of the ability to endure beatings of all kinds and exercises to exhaustion, the obedience to the demands of authority, even the most illogical and degrading kind. The third and final selection took place inside EAT-ESA camp (the Special Interrogation Section of ESA), or other similar camps, after approximately two months of further training, testing and screening of the servicemen.

Similarly, Crelinsten and Schmid (1993: 51–2) identify four routes to becoming a torturer:

1. a career advancement route whereby an individual within a military or a police organization is promoted or assigned after basic training to a special force or unit that engages in torture;
2. direct conscription, either into the armed forces in general or directly into a specialized unit, especially for young boys, poorly eductaed and coming from lower class and authoritarian families;
3. in the context of counterinsurgency and antiterrorist campaigns, captured insurgents, guerrillas or terrorists can be persuaded to work for their captors;
4. a forth route to torture is serendipitous and not easily categorized.

Initiation

Beyond and despite the ideological conviction, coercion is very often implied and crucial to initiation to the group of torturers during the phase of recruitment. What authors seem to suggest is that exposure to initial traumatic experiences implies a reorganization of mind, with a reshaping of social bonds, the establishment of new loyalties to peers and a recognized authority, and a change in world view and ethical principles (see Chapter 6). This is a silent mental reorganization, that may occur also to bureaucratic perpetrators. Characteristically, actual torturers usually undergo a more blatant and violent initiation that works as binding factor to authority and the subgroup of torturers.

Mika Haritos-Fatouros (1993) writes,

> The elaboration of factors binding the recruits to the authority of violence that they had to obey was both explicitly and implicitly carried out. . . . It started with an initiation ceremony on the first day of arrival at the KESA

training camp. After an initiation beating inside the cars taking the recruits to the camp and upon entering the camp, the recruits were asked to swear allegiance to the totemic-like symbol of authority used by the junta, promising on their knees, faith to the commander-in-chief and to the revolution.

(Haritos-Fatouros, 1993: 150)

Similarly, Aronson and Mills (1959) have shown that the more difficult the initiation process, the greater is the emotional attachment to the group that the individual is about to join. During the first week in camp, the initiation procedures, which also involved harsh treatment and restriction of satisfaction of their primary needs (restrictions on eating, drinking, toilet facilities, etc.) produced high levels of stress in the new cadets. The apparent aim of the officials in command was to crush, right from the start, any will for resistance and to facilitate the changing of attitudes and beliefs (Haritos-Fatouros, 1993: 154).

This is part of a de-individuation strategy to degrade and strip away a trainee's previous identity in order to reshape it as part of a new role within a controlled group identity (see also Zimbardo's Stanford University experiment). Trainees often undergo such a violent 'initiation rite', which marks the passage from one life to another.

Lifton (1986) notices that relevant to carrying out atrocities is the principle that 'once baptized', that is named or confirmed by someone in authority, a particular self is likely to become more clear and definite (a self that is compliant to someone in authority). What he called the 'Auschwitz self', a splitting of personality which enables a person to distance himself from his usual moral perceptions and behaviour, underwent a similar baptism when the Nazi doctor conducted his first selections. Torturers undergo similar processes of spiritual merging into the values of a new community, with a consequent re-birth. Doubling, as described by Lifton, is temporary and occurs as part of a larger institutional structure, which encourages or even demands it and is infused with transcendence, the sense of entering a religious order and of being 'reborn' (1986: 425). Françoise Sironi also recognizes the importance of the application of traumatic techniques to the 'trainee' as initiation (Sironi, 1999). Traumatic initiation is aimed at inducting the torturer into an affinity group with a strong sense of belonging (army unit, paramilitary cell, etc.). Sometimes, this initiation is organized in a such a way that the first thing the new recruits must do, once they get back from an evening on the town to confirm they are above the common rules is to torture a prisoner (Sironi and Branche, 2002).

Huggins *et al.* (2002) detect this process of traumatic reshaping of the trainees' identity occurred when the Brazilian police workers were first transported to the Militarized Police Academy on the back of a flatbed truck, 'like cattle being taken to slaughter' (2002:145).

According to Huggins *et al.* (2002) other mechanisms included the use of abusive name calling, physically exhausting drills and punishments, inconsistent commands and divide-and-rule orders. The very essence of this treatment was its inconsistency aimed at creating 'learned helplessness', which promoted a trainee's obedience to authority by making him totally dependent on those who judged his performance and rewarded him for being a 'good little boy'. Any trainee who failed to become sufficiently helpless by resisting being stripped of his individuality was a threat to organizational integrity and thus someone to be isolated and excluded.

Training and the reshaping of identity

Training represents an important part of the acculturation of torturers. Gibson and Haritos-Fatouros (1986), Gibson (1990), Conroy (2000), Crelinsten and Schmid (1993) among others have all documented the brutalizing and humiliating training that many torturers have received.

> Basic training is a programme, applied to soldiers, aiming to 'empty' them of habits, their own character and individuality. . . . The method of disruption is used. By training in the sense of near physical torture, strict rules on hygiene and equipment, no freedom, irregular hours, hard physical activity, not too much contact with family or girlfriends. Additives in food to diminish the sex drive so as to break down all 'negative' elements and defences. Nothing must guard them against indoctrination: therefore, strict rules and isolation are applied and enforced.
> (Crelinsten and Schmid, 1993: 54)

The basic idea is to break down the former, civilian identity of the new recruit and to build up a new identity based upon identification with the military subculture, its ideology, internal structure and worldview, hence the isolation from family and friends who represent the old worldview of the civilian, and constitute relational underpinnings for the recruit's previous identity.

This treatment is combined with an exaltation of the qualities of the group they are joining, often referred to as a 'special unit'. Ronald Crelinsten describes these units as having 'exalted reputations within the military or police command structure. If their existence is known to the public, they are often highly respected and/or highly feared' (Crelinsten and Schmid, 1993: 45). As a soldier describes,

> Because they have enforced on you this inferiority complex, it's not so strange that you want to please them [commanding officers], because . . . they break you down, they've made you feel that you are nothing, and all of a sudden they say you've got great qualities, you can do that, we very much want you to do that. It will be super. You can do it . . . It's not an objective decision that I want to do it or not.
> (Crelinsten and Schmid, 1993: 51)

These units' rhetoric and their formidable reputations appeal directly to soldiers' professional pride in two ways: 1) through an emphasis on the most important of the military virtues such as self-sacrifice, courage, loyalty and patriotism; and 2) the appeal to the military goals of protecting national security and peace. Only those who truly embody the military virtues deserve to join these units. However, this prestige is enhanced and maintained by the intense and often brutal training process that those who are selected or wish to join must undergo.

Beyond abuse, future torturers are provided with specialized training that is aimed at refining and systematizing the skills of numbed policemen and recruits. Millet writes,

> Torture has a budget and staff, training procedure, study and teaching methods, is regarded as a science. There are classes, classrooms, visual aids, technical terms, and apparatus: slide photographs of torture are followed with practical demonstrations on prisoners. The classes are described in the testimony of the prisoners who were used as live subjects in classes where acknowledged experts like Lieutenant Hayton would instruct large groups of eighty or one hundred army personnel, the lecture and photographs followed with practical 'hands-on' exercises.
>
> (Millet, 1994: 246–7)

Conroy (2000) found that, in some instances, the torturers did not go through a period of rigorous training but merely attended a course on counter-intelligence work in which methods of interrogation were demonstrated. One individual who attended such a course told Conroy that the subject of torture was introduced in a casual relaxed manner, as if it were an everyday matter. Then one day a prisoner was brought in and the teacher began demonstrating extremely painful methods of obtaining information (for more on this double entrance – harsh and soft – to 'snapping' mental functioning see Chapter 6). Soon the teacher asked the students to participate; eventually every student took turns submerging the hooded victim's head in water until he was near drowning. No information was obtained and the instructor commented they had not been tough enough. Later, this man told Conroy,

> It was unreal because I never thought I could participate in anything like this and accept it. It was kind of like being brainwashed because for these two weeks we had been hearing all the evil things these people were going to do us, that they would sell our country to the Soviet Union and to Cuba. You had the feeling that you did the right thing, that many people would be grateful for the things you were doing.
>
> (Conroy, 2000: 704)

The training also very likely strengthens a torturer's commitment to his specialized social control organization and its violent mission. Once torturers have been 'created', there frequently follows a social-psychological process in which 'perpetrators develop an intense, fanatical commitment to some higher good and supposed higher morality in the name of which they commit atrocities' (Staub, 1989: 64). This ideological commitment couples with the development of an orientation which differentially excludes certain groups from one's own 'moral universe', making gross harm upon them much easier.

Overcoming difficulties in performing evil

Other or complementary strategies contribute to overcoming the recruit's resistance to act violently during his training:

- *Internalization of ideology within an authority structure*: Milgram's experiments on obedience to authority showed that obedience dropped as the suffering of the victim became more apparent (1974). Yet, even though torturers are directly faced with their victims' suffering, they still usually obey. During their training, they are desensitized first to their own pain, suffering and humiliation and then to others'. This provides the necessary aggression and facilitates the internalization of that ideology that justifies the use of pain against someone who is perceived as evil. In this process that implies harsh mistreatments, future torturers come to share their authority's ideology. Milgram thinks that 'every [obedience] situation . . . possesses a kind of ideology, which we call the 'definition of the situation', and which is the interpretation of the meaning of social' (1974: 145). To come to share such a definition of the situation, pain and suffering are essential elements. Through them they come to share the view of the authorities that the task they are engaged in serves a high purpose that transcends any moral scruples they might bring to the situation. They come to see themselves as playing an important part in an effort to protect the state: to ensure its security and integrity, to maintain law and order, or to keep alive the fundamental values of the state, which are being subjected to a merciless onslaught by ruthless enemies who are intent to destroying it. The way repugnance to torture is won in the organizational field is through the fragmentation of roles and responsibility: hierarchy and obedience to authority allow for the chain of command to bear the unbearable moral weight of atrocities. As Milgram (1974) puts it, 'an authority system . . . consists of a minimum of two persons sharing the expectation that one of them has the right to prescribe behaviour for the other' (1974: 143–3).
- *Systematic dehumanization of the victim*: The dehumanization of the victim through language, detention conditions and torture not only reduces the victim to a contemptible object in the eyes of the torturer, it also encourages the torturer to feel less morally responsible for harming them. The victims' suffering and humiliation (caused solely by the torture) come to be seen as evidence of their sub-human qualities (Crelinsten and Schmid, 1993: 41; Glover, 2001:36; Sussman, 2005: 4).
- *Routinization of the work*: According to some authors (Crelinsten, 2003; Crelinsten and Schmid, 1993; Haritos-Fatouros, 2003; Hilberg, 1961; Huggins, 2002; Huggins *et al.*, 2002; Kelman, 1993, 2005, 2010; Lifton, 1986) *routinization* accomplishes two functions. First, it reduces the necessity of making

decision, minimizing the occasions in which moral questions may arise. Second, it makes it easier to avoid the implications of the action, since the actor focuses on the details of the job rather than on its meaning. In particular, Kelman (2010) points out that *routinization* operates at the level of the individual actor and at the organizational level. Individual job performance is broken down into a series of discrete steps, most of which are carried out in automatic, regularized fashion. Proceeding in a routine fashion – processing papers, exchanging memos, diligently carrying out assigned tasks – mutually reinforces the view that what is going on must be perfectly normal, correct and legitimate. The shared illusion of being engaged in a legitimate enterprise helps the participants to assimilate their activities to other purposes, such as the efficiency of their performance, the productivity of their unit, or the cohesiveness of their group. Thus, when these actions cause harm to others, people acting them can feel relatively free of guilt, as in the case of Eichmann, who declared himself at his trial, 'Not guilty in the sense of indictment' (Arendt, 1963: 21). Hilberg has suggested that Holocaust functionaries coped 'by not varying their routine and not restructuring their organization, not changing a thing in their correspondence or mode of communication' (Hilberg, 1961: 274).

- *Piecemeal involvement*: Routinization of the process helps the *piecemeal* involvement through which ordinary people are engaged in cooperating with a torturous system. The gradual involvement is enhanced by the fact that tasks are so structured that their final purpose is disconnected from the different intermediate enactments it needs to be accomplished. Milgram describes how once people have accepted to have taken the initial step, they are in a new psychological and social situation in which the pressures to continue are powerful. In order to disengage oneself from the destructive enterprise once the 'big picture' is realized, respondents need to justify their previous actions. Unable to find that justification, they remain bound to the situation (1974: 149).

- *Professionalism:* The language of professionalism, together with the narrow role focus that it promotes, routinize and normalize torture (Crelinsten and Schmid, 1993; Conroy, 2000; Gibson and Haritos-Fatouros, 1986; Huggins, 2000, 2002; Kelman, 1993; Lifton, 1986; Wolfendale, 2006). The discourse of professionalism instils a narrow moral vision within torturers so that they focus solely on the task they are performing and not the larger moral import of what they are doing. Martha K. Huggins points out that the language of professionalism removes all reference to the infliction of violence on an actual human body. It effectively 'disembodies' violence (Huggins, 2000: 61; 2002). Torture is no longer a brutal act of violence against another human being, rather, as the sociologist Herbert Kelman puts it, the 'routine application of specialized knowledge and skills' (Kelman, 1993: 31). It becomes part of a routine job that is subject to role-specific professional standards and justifications (Kelman, 1993: 30). This is evident in the fact that torture is almost never called by that name; it is always 'interrogation' (Crelinsten, 1993: 40). Thus, professionalization of torture serves the purpose of abdicating moral responsibility for one's

actions and enables the torturer to create a distance between his personal moral self and professional activities (Huggins, 2000: 63).
- *Progressive features* of training mark the gradual movement from one worldview (human, civilian, empathic, caring) to another (inhuman, torturous, cruel, detached). The subject (the conscript/recruit/torturer-to-be) is progressively desensitized while the object (the subversive/communist/terrorist/victim-to-be) is progressively dehumanized, objectified, and stripped of any identity except for the demonizing labels of the dangerous enemy who will take your life if you do not protect yourself (Crelinsten and Schmid, 1993: 56). These processes of 'ideologization', and desensitization of the torturer and dehumanization of the victim take place at the same time (Haritos-Fatouros, 1993, 2003).

The future of a torturer

Once reintegrated into civil life, many torturers – though not all of them – experience burnout or post-traumatic stress symptoms. Their couple relationships often suffer, as do those with their children and friends (Lifton, 1989b; Verbitsky, 1996).

Sherman points out that the torturer himself becomes dehumanized by the process of his 'production' (Sherman, 2005: 178). Some former torturers, when interviewed, were found to have given up so much of their personal and professionals lives to their needlessly demanding jobs without adequate recognition and reward (Allodi, 1993; Fanon, 1963; Huggins *et al.*, 2002; Verbitsky, 1996). They are often left with pockets of guilt and shame or numbed forms of quiet self condemnation or a strange compulsion, at the same time, to speak and not to speak, to blame and to cover up for one's superiors. Allodi found that,

> Many years later, ... [they] still deny they knew abuses were taking place or that they participated in them in any way. Exceptionally, those who said they knew affirmed they were disgusted, depressed or ashamed of it. They have as a group little capacity to develop moral judgement, in keeping with their deprived background, little education, stunted moral and intellectual growth. ... In prison, over seven years later, they remained anxious and depressed, with multiple psychosomatic manifestations of their psychological distress. They feel neglected and separated from their relatives and financially pressed.
>
> (Allodi, 1993: 138–9)

In his interview with Horacio Verbitsky, Adolfo Scilingo tells his memories about what happened during the flights of the Escuela de Mecànica de la Armada (ESMA).[5] As an ESMA officer he personally murdered thirty political prisoners, throwing them alive from the aeroplane into the ocean. Every Wednesday for two years these routine flights took place: the prisoners were placed in a room with soothing music, injected with sedatives by a doctor, driven to the airport and stripped naked, and then placed on the plane for dumping. Catholic Church leaders, Scilingo claims, had been consulted and approved the murders 'as a Christian form of death'. He remembers that after these 'flights' he felt very distressed and took sleeping-pills and excessive amounts of alcohol to calm down. At times during the interview, he is aware of having destroyed his family and himself. However, he seems to be struggling against the knowledge of what happened and his awareness of his superiors' 'treason'. He provides alternate narratives of events, while his mind seems busy struggling with an irresolvable double reading of events, one provided by the official authorities during the Dirty War, and another, more sceptical, he elaborated later. He looks at the ideological explanations of the 'internal state of war' as an explicative paradigm for his and his superiors' behaviour. However, as the social context has changed, this argument appears to offer an embarrassingly small fig leaf to cover up significant shame. Nonetheless, he seems to be more upset by the lack of responses from military commanders than by his murders of people thrown alive into the sea during the 'death flights'.

Measures of psychological distress indicate that torturers are generally a highly distressed group, sometimes with organic lesions or disorders (bronchitis, osteo-arthritis, skin lesions). However, this is not always the case. Lifton, for example, documented a variety of attitudes among Nazi doctors towards their past (1986). Some of them looked very fixed in their effective defences still at work to prevent them from gaining a complete awareness of their crimes and enabling them to have a decent life. Others suffered from a clearer sense of guilt, and their suffering and the partial relief of being able to tell their story was much more overt. Even in those who had powerful resistances towards recalling memories or expressing judgement on their deeds and events, Lifton (1986) perceives that a part of their self had become alien to them. He writes,

> I had the impression that many of the former Nazi doctors retained pockets of guilt and shame, to which they did not have access ... Those unacknowledged feelings were consistent with a need to talk. But their way of dealing with those feelings was frequently the opposite of self-confrontation: rather, the dominant tendency among these Nazi doctors was to present themselves as decent people who tried to make the best of a bad situation. And they wanted a confirmation from me of this view of themselves ... Yet none of them – not a single former Nazi doctor I spoke to – arrived at a clear ethical evaluation of what he had done, and of what he had been part of. They could examine events in considerable detail, even look at feelings and speak generally with surprising candour – but almost in the manner of a third person. The narrator, morally speaking, was not quite present.
> (Lifton, 1986: 9)

Huggins *et al.* (2002) write that, after interviews some Brazilian police officials, thanked the interviewer, explaining that it had been like 'a strange catharsis' in which they felt torn between wanting to talk about their former work and feeling 'strangely forbidden' to do so (2002: 60).

The problem is not only in what torturers do to others but also in what they do to themselves. As Yawar put it 'Inhumanity cannot be inflicted without being internalized' (2004: 370). The question was dramatically expressed by Alexander Lavranos, father of one of the Greek torture trial defendants, 'We are a poor but decent family ... and now I see him [the son] in the dock as a torturer. I want to ask the court to examine how a boy whom everyone said was a 'diamond' became a torturer. *Who* morally destroyed my home and my family?' (Amnesty International, 1977: 41).

Victims of torture

Who are they?

Victims of torture are not a homogenous group of people. However, they can be associated with the political opposition of a regime and/or tend to come from marginalized, criminalized and impoverished sections of society, a minority group, or a group with a minority status (an already discriminated ethnic or religious group, sexual minorities, drug users, asylum seekers, women), who are considered as 'subversive' to the political order, sometimes simply for what they are and sometimes for what they think or represent (Amnesty International, 2000). Criminal suspects are frequently victims of torture. Members of armed groups, those suspected of terror-related offences, or otherwise deemed to constitute a threat to national security, are particularly at risk. Some are tortured simply because they are in the wrong place at the wrong time, because of mistaken identity or because they have incurred the displeasure of those in power, conflicting with their interests, whether financial or political (Amnesty International, 2014). They can be highly educated political activists, or aware students working for a political party or fighting for a cause. In any case, they are perceived as outsiders, dissident voices.

Often, after years of persecution targeting them and their families or sometimes with unexpected kidnapping, detention and torture, survivors are faced with the immediate task of coping with the physical pain and psychological suffering associated with the abusive treatment they experienced. They must overcome shock and numbness produced after emerging from torture. They often must come to grips with a burden of guilt and shame they feel for having survived their experiences when others did not (Ortiz, 2001; Price, 1995). Through torture, a metamorphosis takes place: an individual may change dramatically. Personal trust in oneself, in others, in God (or in others' possible benevolence) is shattered. The person may feel more akin to the dead than to the living.

In addition, survivors who are forced to relocate away from their homeland face the complex process of exile, in which they must adapt to a new culture and society (Luci, 2916; Montgomery, 2011; Papadopoulos, 2002). The flight, the process of asylum-seeking and settlement in a new country are additional events that aggravate the social and economic consequences of political persecution and torture. Separation from family, loss of social and occupational status, deprivation of social support networks, uncertainty about the future, problems settling in a new country and adapting to a new culture, the anti-immigrant bias and racism in the host country, housing and economic problems are among the many issues faced by refugee survivors of torture (Basoğlu et al., 2001; Peters, 1996; Somnier et al., 1992; Witterholt and Jaranson, 1998). Those who have escaped without proper documentation may face the risk of being summarily deported back to their home country or placed in detention. Sometimes it takes years to find and put together the missing pieces of their broken biographies, undertaking a new direction for their lives. As part of this process, some survivors will become ill and their physical or psychological condition will necessitate professional evaluation, care and rehabilitation (Basoğlu, 1999; Gerrity et al., 2001; Price, 1995; Williams, 2001; Wilson and Drožđek, 2004).

Physical and psychological consequences of torture

The body speaks

For torture survivors, the body is the place where the mark of power is imprinted (Cunningham and Cunningham, 1997) and it often offers powerful testimony of the survivor's terrible experience (Amris and Williams, 2007; Kira et al., 2006; Varvin and Stajner-Popovic, 2002; Vorbrüggen and Baer, 2007). The somatic sequelae of torture are generally related to the type of torture the person endured and/or indirect results of their psychological condition (Amris and Williams, 2007; Amris et al., 2009; Basoğlu, 1992; Goldfeld et al., 1988). For those who flee from their country and seek asylum abroad, being able to report their experience and get help for their condition may be crucial to obtaining a residence permit (Fassin and d'Halluin, 2005; Freedom from Torture, 2011; Tower, 2013). The body become the place that displays the evidence of torture. The *Istanbul Protocol* (OHCHR, 2004) offers guidelines to physicians to examine in particular the skin, face, chest and abdomen, the musculoskeletal system, the genito-urinary system, the central and peripheral nervous systems for medical evaluation to document torture. In consideration of the most common forms of torture, it provides a reference framework of the most common lesions that are reported.

Beyond specific injuries and losses in the function of some organs produced by specific torture methods, the medical literature reports that survivors often experience a change from the intense and acute pain of torture into a chronic pain once they are free (Amris and Prip, 2000a, 2000b; Amris, 2005; Amris and Williams 2007; McCulley, 2014; Olsen et al., 2006; Williams, 2003; Williams and Amris, 2007). Pain is experienced in multiple sites, is long-lasting and chronic and may be the only presenting complaint. It may shift in location and vary in intensity. Pain in torture victims can be nociceptive (a condition caused by tissue damage where the pain has been elicited by nociceptors), neurogenic (a condition caused by a lesion or a dysfunction of the nervous system), secondary to trauma or other causes, such as vascular, infectious, toxic, metabolic, or degenerative conditions

(Amris, 2005; Amris and Prip, 2003). Pain may sometimes be also the expression of distress, which may be sustained by Post-Traumatic Stress Disorder (PTSD) (Teodorescu et al., 2015). Therefore chronic pain in torture survivors is a complex problem and it needs a multidisciplinary therapeutic approach and careful consideration of certain cultural expressions (Amris and Prip, 2000a; Amris, 2005; Roche, 1992; Thomsen et al., 1997). It reminds the person of the loss of control over one's body during torture, and provokes attention deficits and insomnia. This is often exacerbated by the disbelief that many patients encounter when they try to share their experiences. On the subject of pain, Spitz makes the following observation:

> Pain is also unshareable in that it is resistant to language . . . All our interior states of consciousness: emotional, perceptual, cognitive and somatic can be described as having an object in the external world . . . But when we explore the interior state of physical pain we find that there is no object 'out there' – no external, referential content. Pain is not of, or for, anything. Pain is. And it draws us away from the space of interaction, the sharable world, inwards.
>
> (Spitz, 1989, quoted in Vaknin, 2005: 250)

George calls the experience of destruction and loss of self in intense bodily pain 'enigmatic' (2016: 52), but it is uncontrovertibly documented in studies in sociology, anthropology, psychology, psychoanalysis and literature. The damage that totally aversive pain inflicts upon the self may be often short-lived, nonetheless it can sometimes be enduring, self-diminishing, permanent and even terminal.

Psychological and psychiatric narratives on survivors

It goes without saying that being a survivor of torture *per se* does not automatically imply being affected by a mental disorder. However, psychological symptoms were found to be from two to three times more common among torture survivors when compared to non-tortured refugees (Masmas et al., 2008). The presentation of survivors' mental health is similarly depicted across a number of different studies, with the most common conditions reported including post-traumatic stress, depression and anxiety symptoms and/or disorders[6] (Basoğlu, 1992; Basoğlu et al., 2001; McCulley, 2014; Roncevic-Grzeta et al., 2001; Saraceno et al., 2002; Wenzel et al., 2000). Victims frequently report symptoms of chronic low mood, lack of interest and sleep disturbance not amounting to a specific syndrome. They may also report classic post-traumatic symptoms such as flashbacks, recurrent nightmares, reduced interest in life and relations, memory and concentration impairment, irritability/aggressiveness, anxiety, emotional liability/self isolation, social withdrawal, sexual dysfunctions and generally impaired functioning; some of them report of schizophrenia-like states (Basoğlu et al., 1994; Mollica, 2004).

The most common psychological responses to torture are summarized in the *Istanbul Protocol* (OHCHR, 2004). They include: 1) *re-experiencing the trauma* through flashbacks or intrusive memories; recurrent frightening dreams or nightmares that include elements of torture and other related traumatic event(s) in either their original or symbolic form; physiological or psychological stress reactions at exposure to cues that symbolize or resemble torture or some element of the traumatic situation. 2) *Avoidance and emotional numbing* such as profound emotional constriction; profound personal detachment and social withdrawal; inability to recall important aspects of trauma; avoidance of any thoughts, conversations, activities, places or people that arouse the recollection of trauma. 3) *Hyperarousal*, i.e. exaggerated startle response; difficulty falling or staying asleep; hypervigilance; irritability or outbursts of anger; difficulty concentrating; generalized anxiety; shortness of breath, sweating, dry mouth, dizziness; gastrointestinal distress. 4) *Symptoms of depression* such as depressed mood; markedly diminished interest or pleasure in activities; appetite disturbance and resulting weight loss, or weight gain; insomnia or hypersomnia; psychomotor agitation or retardation; fatigue and loss of energy; difficulty in attention, concentration and memory; feelings and thoughts of worthlessness, guilt and hopelessness; thoughts of death and dying, suicidal ideation and attempts. 5) *Damaged self-concept and foreshortened future:* a subjective feeling of having been irreparably damaged and of having undergone an irreversible personality change; sense of foreshortened future: not expecting to have a career, marriage, children or a normal life span. 6) *Dissociation and depersonalization:* dissociation is meant as a disruption in the integration of consciousness, self-perception, memory and actions; the person may be cut off or unaware of certain actions or may feel split in two and feeling as if observing him or herself from a distance; depersonalization manifest itself through feeling detached from oneself or one's body; impulse control problems, resulting in behaviours that the survivor considers highly atypical with respect to his or her pre-trauma personality.

Torture appears to be such an extreme stressor that many cultural differences in the expression of distress reduce, with some findings seeming to confirm the cross-cultural validity of some symptoms associated with Post-Traumatic Stress Disorder (PTSD) (Jaranson and Popkin, 1998: 20; Hinton and Lewis-Fernàndez, 2011). However, the lack of understanding of the socio-cultural context has been criticized both by clinicians and culturally-informed epidemiologists for several reasons: 1) the category fallacy of Western psycho-diagnostic categories as defined by the DSM and the ICD, not appropriate in non-Western cultures; 2) differences in the way people perceive or express their plight or illnesses; 3) the actual partial diversity of trauma reactions (Hinton and Lewis-Fernandez, 2011; Marsella *et al.*, 1996; Mattar, 2012); 4) the need to adapt diagnostic instruments across cultures (Shoeb *et al.*, 2007; Wilson and So-Kum Tang, 2007); 5) the possible cultural flaws of psychiatric epidemiological instruments, in which decision rules produce diagnoses bound by the aforementioned category fallacy; 6) the amplification of the PTSD paradigm without evidence that this category is the most relevant way to describe local survivors' mental health problems (de Jong, 2005). All these factors indicate the need for more research on culture-bound disorders and idioms of psychological suffering. One of the challenges in the coming decades will be to produce a worldwide inventory of traumatic stress reactions by using a phenomenological approach employing a combination of qualitative and quantitative research methods (de Jong and van Ommeren, 2002). It is expected that this will yield a neurobiological and universal core of post-traumatic reactions with a large variety of culturally related manifestations connected with this core (de Jong, 2004).

PTSD and Complex-PTSD

A relevant debate developed in literature about the suitability of the psychiatric label of PTSD to describe the psychological after-effects of torture and much has been written about its advantages/disadvantages and the limitations of its applicability (Bracken, 1998; Friedman and Jaranson, 1994; Summerfield, 2001; Young, 1997; Zarowsky and Pedersen, 2000, among many others).

Torture certainly qualifies as an extreme traumatic stressor and many of its victims meet diagnostic criteria for PTSD (American Psychiatric Association, 2013). However, there has been a continual narrowing of the diagnosis for medico-legal purposes. Simply to label survivors as having PTSD is inadequate in terms of describing the magnitude and complexity of torture's effects (Hermann, 1992; Quiroga and Jaranson, 2005).

Some have stressed the importance of making a diagnosis of PTSD (e.g. Allodi, 1991; Turner, 2000) and of establishing treatment programs for this condition. However, for a complex trauma such as torture, limitations in the use of PTSD have to be accepted with equal force. A meta-analysis of 181 surveys on tortured populations from 40 countries found that rates of PTSD and depression showed a large degree of variability (0 per cent to 99 per cent for PTSD and 3 per cent to 85.5 per cent for depression) (Steel *et al.*, 2009). Opponents of the PTSD formulation have stated that torture survivors are experiencing a normal reaction to an abnormal stressor or societal pathology, (Papadopoulos, 2002; Summerfield, 2001). Papadopoulos warns against the risk of a pathologizing discourse:

> one of the main dilemmas facing clinicians working with traumatized individuals as a result of political oppression and violence is that the psychological reactions are part of a wider response to these socio-political events and taking the pathological sounding symptoms out of their context may distort the unique position individuals adopt in relation to these violations.
> (Papadopoulos, 2002: 15)

The preoccupation is that, in the process of medical assessment and treatment, the victim might become more victimized and powerless (Summerfield, 2001; Young, 1997). Another meta-analysis (Johnson and Thompson, 2008) concluded that most epidemiologically-sound studies found relatively low rates of PTSD following torture. However, Steel and colleagues' meta-analysis found that reported torture emerged as the strongest factor associated with PTSD, followed by cumulative exposure to potentially traumatic events (Steel *et al.*, 2009). Most studies on the effects of torture have not been controlled with regard to the potentially confounding effects of other life traumas that happened before and after torture, while there is good evidence supporting a dose-response relationship between cumulative trauma and development and maintenance of PTSD in torture survivors (e.g., Johnson and Thompson, 2008).

Increasingly, researchers have suggested that responses to torture are best understood as a spectrum of conditions rather than as a single disorder (Kira, 2002) and a number of researchers and clinicians have argued that the diagnosis of PTSD is not a perfect fit for those populations where traumatization occurred repeatedly and extensively (Briere and Spinazzola, 2005; Herman, 1992a, 1992b; Taylor et al., 2006; van der Kolk *et al.*, 2005). Individuals exposed to trauma over a variety of time spans and developmental periods suffer from a variety of psychological problems not included in the diagnosis of PTSD, including depression, anxiety, self-hatred, dissociation, substance abuse, self-destructive and risk-taking behaviours, re-victimization, problems with interpersonal and intimate relationships (including parenting), medical and somatic concerns and despair, all of which are very similar to those experienced by survivors of torture (Courtois, 2004; Pearlman, 2001). In the frame of this attempt to give a name to torture survivors' suffering, concepts have been proposed to classify the longer-term effects in personality and world view, such as Complex PTSD (C-PTSD), Continuous Traumatic Stress Response, Disorders of Extreme Stress Not Otherwise Specified, Enduring Personality Change after Catastrophic Experience (Herman, 1992a; van der Kolk, 2001; van der Kolk et al., 1996; WHO, 1992). The most significant diagnostic conceptualization seems to be that of C-PTSD (Kissan *et al.*, 2014; Teegen and Vogt, 2002; Teegen and Schriefer, 2002), although this syndrome is not specific to torture victims as it is also highly prevalent in victims of other complex and prolonged traumas (see Kissan *et al.*, 2014). C-PTSD consists of seven different problem areas (Herman, 1992a, 1992b):

1 *Alterations in the regulation of affective impulses*, with symptoms such as persistent sadness, suicidal preoccupation, difficulty with modulation of anger and self-destructiveness, difficulty modulating sexual involvement;
2 *Alterations in attention and consciousness*, leading to amnesias and dissociative episodes and depersonalization. This category includes an emphasis on dissociative responses, which are different to those found in the criteria for PTSD, including those in which one feels removed from one's mental processes or body;
3 *Alterations in self-perception*, such as a chronic sense of guilt and on-going intense shame. Chronically abused individuals often incorporate the lessons of abuse into their sense of self and self-worth, thereby acquiring a sense of helplessness and of being completely different from other human beings;

4   *Alterations in perception of the perpetrator,* including incorporating their belief system, attributing total power to the perpetrator or becoming preoccupied by the relationship to the perpetrator, including preoccupation with the re-enactment of trauma;
5   *Alterations in relationship with others,* such as not being able to trust and not being able to feel intimate with others, belief that people are venal and self-serving, and out to get what they can, by whatever means, including using/abusing others;
6   *Somatization and/or medical problems,* these somatic reactions and medical conditions may relate directly to the type of abuse suffered and any physical damage that was caused or they may be more diffuse;
7   *Alterations in systems of meaning,* whereby chronically abused individuals often feel hopeless about finding anyone to understand them or their suffering. They despair of ever being able to recover from their psychic anguish.

Especially when torture is prolonged, over many years or when the survivor is young, many other changes may occur. Long-term sequelae often include a multiplicity of symptoms, emotional lability, difficulty with relationships, inability to trust, changes in the way one looks at oneself or the world, the repetition of harm, trauma-congruent hallucinations, depression, impaired memory, personality changes, suicidal ideation, identity disorders, conduct or substance abuse problems, physical impairments, disturbances in the value-processing system, and the intensification of pre-trauma disorders or conditions (Carlsson, *et al.*, 2006; McCulley, 2014).

Traumatic bonding

According to attachment theory (Bowlby, 1969), human beings are born with a psychobiological system (the attachment behavioural system) that motivates them to seek proximity to supportive others (i.e. attachment figures) in times of need for the sake of gaining a sense of safety and security. Although attachment orientations are initially formed in relationships with primary caregivers (usually parents) during infancy and early childhood, Bowlby (1988) also argued that relationships formed later on in life (i.e. with friends, romantic partners, etc.) can alter the sense of security. The attachment style can change subtly or dramatically depending on these relational experiences (Mikulincer and Shaver, 2007).

An important feature of the attachment system is that it is more readily activated in times of stress and danger: people under threat have a greater need to be cared for and more easily attach to others. Any attachment is better than no attachment, a fact that is evidenced by the reality of relationships which, otherwise, would be incomprehensible. Traumatic bonding is thought to occur among hostages, abused children and abused spouses (Dutton and Painter, 1993; Finkelhor, 2007), and it is one of the most pernicious effects of torture. Dutton and Painter (1993) define *traumatic bonding* as 'powerful emotional attachments . . . seen to develop from two specific features of abusive relationships: power imbalances and intermittent good-bad treatment' (1993: 105). Van der Kolk (1989) illustrates that in torture the traumatic bonding between the victim and the torturer(s) is created through:

1. *Intimacy*: there is hardly any situation involving torture that is without the propinquity of something very familiar, without the intimacy of a room, a neighbour, a friend or a lover.
2. *An asymmetrical relationship*: being together in a closed place over a relatively long period of time, the torturer and the victim become emotionally engaged with each other in an unbalanced distribution of power.
3. *Attention paid to the individuality of the victim*: torture is personal and requires close attention to the way a victim sits and stands, breathes and shouts, is looking at and listening to.
4. *A remaking of loyalties*: torture uses severe bodily and mental pain to get its victims to say, think, believe, or do things that will violate whom they have become in life, to break down old loyalties and build up new ones in their place.
5. *The isolation of the victim and the promise of a return to communication and community*: within torture this represents a false promise, which offers only a false return 'home', as it was, to the realm of culture and its cooperative systems of shared values and appropriate meanings. [7]

In the attempt to maintain attachment bonds, victims turn to the nearest source of hope to regain a state of psychological and physiological calmness. In situations of captivity and sensory and emotional deprivation, prisoners may develop strong emotional ties to their tormentors (Bettelheim, 1943; Bowlby, 1969; Finkelhor and Brown, 1985). The need to stay attached contributes to the denial and dissociation of the traumatic experience; in order to preserve an image of safety and to avoid losing the hope of the existence of a protector, victims may then begin to organize their lives around maintaining a bond with their captors placating themselves. Under the heading of a power differential is the situation wherein the abused person experiences social isolation. Allen observes that 'the continually overpowered person feels increasingly incompetent and helpless, ever more reliant on the person with power' (Allen, 1993: 4).

This type of attachment may also be experienced during infancy and early childhood. Children, and later adults, who have lived in fear of their caregiver, will maintain their bond to their desperately needed attachment figure by resorting excessively to dissociation in order to save the continuity of the attachment bond, by splitting off their terrifying memories of being abused. According to research (de Zulueta, 2006b), these are the individuals most vulnerable to suffer from PTSD after a traumatic experience in adulthood. The resulting working models are those of an idealized attachment relation, as well as a 'dysregulated self in interaction with a mis-attuning and frightening other' (Schore, 2001: 240 quoted in de Zulueta 2006a: 98). However, as Herman warns, the intensity of the pathological bond is also actively searched for by the victim, because an ordinary relationship cannot offer the same degree of emotional intensity (1992a: 92). In other words, the traumatic character of the relationship is responsible for that special compulsion to search for and repeat the same pattern of relationship.

We know that a trauma response occurs when all escape routes are cut off. The inability to escape or control the stress contributes to the cascade of terror and physiological arousal, which is often described (de Zulueta, 2006a). The final common pathway for events that are incomprehensible and terrifying is a reaction of extreme physiological arousal, a basic biological response of fight, flight, or freeze. Severe or prolonged stress may then lead to chronic inability to modulate basic biological safety and alarm mechanisms (van der Kolk, 1989). As early as 1899, Pierre Janet described how traumatized people become 'attached' to the trauma. Freud (Breuer and Freud, 1895) was confounded by patients' compulsive tendency to re-experience and re-enact the trauma in a variety of ways. Vivid recollections, flashbacks and nightmares repeatedly intrude into the consciousness. Behavioural re-enactments can take the form of stereotypic motoric acts associated with the trauma (automatisms), which occur without the subject's awareness of their significance. Re-enactment behaviours can also be very complex (van der Kolk, 1989, 2015).

In the experience of torture, such trauma is mediated by a relationship with the torturers: an attachment bond. Torturers seek to sever the prisoner's other bonds to family, community and society precisely to maximize the impact of torture and weaken individual identity and resistance. They seek to replace healthy social connections and ties with a perverted bond to the torturer, creating a state of dependence for the torture victim, via confounding and intermittent good–bad treatments, and pain to reinforce such an attachment.

As Sussman describes:

> What the torturer does is to take his victim's pain, and through it his victim's body, and make it begin to express the torturer's will. The resisting victim is committed to remaining silent, but he now experiences within himself something quite intimate and familiar that speaks for the torturer, . . . My suffering is experienced as not just something the torturer inflicts on me, but as something I do to myself, as a kind of self-betrayal worked through my body and its feelings. . . . The victim of torture finds within herself a surrogate of the torturer . . .
>
> (Sussman, 2005: 29)

The core of torture is the experience of the victim of a part of himself to be in collusion with their tormentor. It is not only the experience of a loss of control of themselves in the presence of others, but to be transformed in what Sussman (2005) calls a 'truly heteronymous will' (someone expressing the will of another, the will of a hated and feared enemy). This is the very torment of every victim of torture and the true meaning of the expression 'breaking the prisoner'. Even if the victim does not break, they will still characteristically discover within themselves a host of traitorous temptations. This treachery is to be found not only in the wayward physiological responses of their body, but in those feelings and desires in which they find their will to be already incipiently invested.

This is also a major reason of shame in torture. It is essential for human beings to possess a sense of independent agency, to be recognized by others as being capable of rationality, and to have the ability to choose which of their feelings, desires and emotions to present to others. Rather, after torture doubt is cast on their personal ability to have cares and commitments, which are more immediately and authentically their own instead of those of another agent. According to Sussman, torture aims to make each of its victims a natural slave (Sussman, 2005: 29).

The trauma of torture through generations

The crime of torture also creates victims well beyond the tortured person (Schwab, 2010). Many studies have documented the transmission of the psychological effects of torture to the second and even third generation (Daud *et al.*, 2005; Auerhahn and Laub, 1998; Danieli, 1998; Daud *et al.*, 2005; Prager, 2003; Schwab, 2010; van der Kolk *et al.*, 2005; Yordanova, 2015). In such cases, we can concur with William Faulkner that, 'The past is never dead. It's not even past' (1951: 80). PTSD, once set, compromises the ability of caring offspring and conveys the transmission of some traumatic mental states to them (de Zulueta, 2006a; Palosaari *et al.*, 2013; van Ijzendoorn and Bakerman-Kranenbers, 1997; Yehuda *et al.*, 2001, 2005). This transgenerational effect has been observed in children of concentration camp survivors, Hiroshima victims, war veterans and other categories of survivors (Daud *et al.*, 2005; Dekel and Goldblatt, 2008; DeVoe *et al.*, 2011; Yehuda *et al.*, 2005, among many others). Children of tortured parents are reported to suffer from a range of reactive symptoms including recurrent nightmares, increased states of anxiety, emotional, sleeping and eating disorders, developmental delays, problems with the regulation of aggression and inability to develop basic trust (Daud *et al.*, 2005; Harkness, 1993; Montgomery *et al.*, 1992; Schore, 2001; Yehuda *et al.*, 2001). Children of torture victims often feel personally responsible or guilty for what occurred to their parent. According to several studies, they were found to be more anxious and exhibit more depressive-like symptoms than the control. They also display an array of behaviour problems, both at school and at home (Daud *et al.*, 2005), show signs of regression, and suffer from psychosomatic symptoms.

De Zulueta (2006a) highlights the interconnections between attachment systems and PTSD. She presents the attachment system as a mediator between the traumatic experience and possible symptoms: 'it is not always the event *per se* that precipitates the symptoms of PTSD, but how people respond to the traumatised individual's needs and how that mirrors earlier attachment experiences' (de Zulueta, 2006a: 198). It is now accepted that traumatised individuals need to be re-attached or re-integrated within their community and family as part of their treatment (Gorst-

Unsworth, 1992). Research on neurobiology confirms that this has a tremendous impact on their recovery. (Henry, 1997; Yehuda *et al.*, 2002). Unfortunately, in the case of torture survivors this reintegration into the net of affective meaningful relationships and social bonds may be complicated both for situational factors (often the flight from one's own country after torture and the consequent rift from family and community) and for emotional difficulties. This attachment approach at post-traumatic states opens an important perspective on how torture may have an impact both on the internal world of working models and the external matrix of family and community relations. In this sense, torture can be understood as an act of cultural transformation, capable of reshaping individuals' character and whole societies, creating in its wake dislocated, apathetic and fearful populations who withdraw from public life or re-enact cruelties on other human beings (de Zulueta, 2006a).

A range of positive responses to torture

In recent decades authors, have wondered if they had underestimated the human capacity to thrive after extremely aversive events (Bonanno, 2004; Bonanno and Mancini, 2008; Cicchetti and Luthar, 2003; Clarke and Clarke, 2003). Indeed, a significant number of people manage to endure the temporary upheaval of loss or potentially traumatic events remarkably well, with no apparent disruption in their ability to function at work or in intimate relationships, and seem to move on to new challenges with apparent ease (Galea *et al.*, 2002; Mancini and Bonanno, 2006; Suedfeld, 2002).

Although psychological impairment commonly flows from the experience of torture, some authors suggests that the stripping away of habit and security and the exposure to human limits deriving from adversity, sometimes leads to a gain in wisdom and compassion and to a sense of psychological renewal (Papadopoulos, 2002, 2007). Some of these authors refer to these positive responses as resilience, while others make sharper distinctions with reference to concepts regarding positive consequences of trauma.

Resilience and protective factors

The concept of resilience was originally formulated by the 'positive psychology' movement that focuses on identifying strengths of individuals when faced with adversity. Although a universal definition does not exist, some authors agree that resilience is a multidimensional, dynamic construct made up of a variety of factors, which can be categorized as: a) psychological and dispositional attributes; b) family support and cohesion; and c) external support systems (Campbell-Sills *et al.*, 2006; Conner and Davidson, 2003; Friborg *et al.*, 2006; White *et al.*, 2008).

Resilience reflects the ability to maintain a stable equilibrium. Papadopoulos (2007) refers to the original meaning of the term *resilience* which is derived from the physics of materials to indicate the ability of a body not to alter after being subjected to pressure or deformation (i.e. adverse conditions). Then, metaphorically, people are resilient when they withstand pressure and do not alter their basic values, skills or abilities.

There is paucity of studies on the prevalence of resilience among torture survivors, while there is some research on the coping mechanisms that moderate the relationship between resilience variables and psychological symptoms (Basoğlu et al., 1994; Hooberman, 2007).

A positive response to torture

Some studies emphasize post-traumatic growth after trauma and even torture. Kira et al. (2006) studied torture survivors to explore how persons who have undergone torture differ from persons who have undergone only general trauma, comparing the effects of torture to those of other kinds of traumas. Contrary to the initial hypotheses, this research found that although tortured individuals have a significantly higher trauma dose, they are more resilient, and more socio-culturally adjusted, as well as showing more post-traumatic growth. They are more tolerant of differences in religion, race and culture, and feel more supported. However, they are physically less healthy than individuals in the community who were not tortured.

Suedfeld (1990) reports that, after repatriation, 21 per cent of former POWs in the Korean war said that they had benefited from the experience of having undergone brainwashing. There are even more striking data on American POWs in the Vietnam War, many of whom underwent years of torture. In one interview study, an amazing 61 per cent of former Vietnam POWs reported salutogenic effects of captivity. In both groups of former POWs, positive long-term outcomes included increased optimism, better social and family relationships, firm commitment to a cause or a post-captivity life plan, and, perhaps most commonly, a sense of personal self-realization.

Lifton (1961) reports that Western missionaries, teachers and businessmen who underwent brainwashing in the early decades of communist China, after returning home, 'consistently reported a sense of having been benefited and emotionally strengthened, of having become more sensitive to their own and others' inner feelings, and more flexible and confident in human relationships. Each had thus gone further than ever before in realizing his human potential' (Lifton, 1961: 238).

Suedfeld (1997, 2002) mentions survivors of the Holocaust who built exceptional and admirable works upon their experiences, from the logotherapy of Viktor Frankl to the literature Nobel Prize winner Elie Wiesel. Other lesser-known survivors have worked productively, established families, and contributed to their communities through charitable and educational activities. Some consider that the Holocaust experience made them stronger and more sensitive to others, more aware of what is important in life and more dedicated to the common good. The one exception to this positive pattern is a consistently higher score for mistrust than for trust.

One of the primary questions, often debated, is whether self-enhancers might evidence genuinely favourable rather than superficial adjustment in the context of such extreme adversity (Bonanno, 2004; Shalev, 2002, 2004).

The question that naturally follows concerns the conditions under which people succeed in carrying on generally happy lives even though they also experience some adverse symptoms. More research is needed to understand the social and psychological conditions that are crucial to post-traumatic growth.

However, it cannot be ignored that some torture survivors derive a great deal of meaning from their experience and are able to transform their own and their companions' suffering into a higher opportunity of social and individual liberation meaning. In this regard, Papadopoulos develops the idea of an Adversity Activated Development (AAD) (2004; 2007) as 'positive developments that are the direct result of being exposed to adversity' (2007: 306). He pinpoints that, 'There are endless accounts of individuals and groups who found meaning in their suffering and were able to transmute their negative experiences in a positive way, finding new strength and experiencing transformative renewal' (2007: 306).

This links to the positive meaning within the etymology of the word 'trauma'. Exploring such an etymology, Papadopoulos (2002, 2005, 2007) notices that it derives not only from the Greek word *titrosko*, 'to rub in', but from the verb *teiro*, 'to rub off' or 'to rub away'. Insofar as the rubbing is of two kinds, the effect of trauma is not only the injury or wound, but also a cleaning of the surface where previous marks were found (Papadopoulos, 2002, 2004, 2005, 2007). The AAD refers to this second effect of trauma, to the experience of a sense of regeneration, rebirth and revitalization, in which the powerful and potential injurious experiences erase previous values, routines and life styles. Apparently, acknowledging this paradoxical outcome may create very powerful and justified moral dilemmas, whereas, in the case of torture, people have been victims of despicable acts of social or political violence.

However, countering a reductive discourse on trauma, Papadopoulos proposes a Trauma Grid that comprises a range of different effects of trauma – *negative, neutral and positive* – at different levels – on the individual, the family, the community and the social/cultural environment (Papadopoulos, 2004, 2007). In this sense, the tool is a path-breaking instrument that takes into consideration the complexity of contexts and responses, which may be in a mutual relationship.

Bystanders

Todorov writes,

> in any human collectivity, there is a convinced, resolute minority who act, and a passive, indecisive majority who prefer to follow, and that minority almost always prevails. Those who passionately despise and hate, . . . who openly enjoy the suffering of others, are few in number, yet they set the tone for everyone.
>
> (Todorov, 2007: 23)

Bystander is the term most widely used in literature on collective violence to describe those who are neither victims nor perpetrators (Cohen, 2001; Hilberg, 1992; Staub, 1989, 1997, 2003, 2011, 2012). Unlike other similar terms (audiences, passers-by, onlookers, observers, spectators) and since the laboratory studies on the diffusion of responsibility by Darley and Latané (1968), the word bystander has acquired a pejorative meaning of passivity and indifference. Here, the term is used to mean all those people who share a range of mental states of denial that torture is happening. Some authors suggest that the bystander role is crucial to the maintenance of the 'world of torture' (Cohen, 2001; Crelinsten, 2003; Hollander, 1992, 2008). Crelinsten (2003) thinks that the world of torture is one where social reality is reconstructed according to new rules. Inherent and central to the construction of a torture regime is the build-up of a combination of political apathy, tolerance towards the scapegoating of other groups which contributes to the spread of us/them thinking throughout society, even when the bystander does not necessarily believe in the promulgated ideology of hate. A variety of cognitive neutralization techniques, such as 'just world thinking' ('The victim must have done something to deserve it'), denial ('This cannot happen to me') and repression, largely encouraged or imposed by regimes ('silence is health', became a cynical commentary on everyday life in Argentina during the 'Dirty War') (Keiser, 2005: 65), are also necessary ingredients. This passivity or silent acquiescence on the part of the wider society allows for the construction of an authoritarian reality, which ends permeating more and more spheres of political and social life until it is sufficiently anchored in law, custom and discourse to define what is right and what is wrong, what is permissible and what is not.

As described in Chapter 2, an essential feature of the bystander's psychology is the internalization of the ideology of the 'social emergency state'. Such internalization is partially accomplished with the consent of the individual and through participation in activities promoted by the torturous power through rituals and rules. The totalitarian state of Orwell's *Nineteen Eighty-Four* is the perfect torturous society, which is permeated by denial but demands that people participate in order to keep the system functioning. In the novel, this state of mind is called *doublethink*, an essential feature of the Big Brother society: 'the power of holding two contradictory beliefs in one's mind simultaneously, and accepting both of them' (1949: 223).

> To tell deliberate lies while genuinely believing in them, to forget any fact that has become inconvenient, and then, when it becomes necessary again, to draw it back from oblivion for just so long as it is needed, to deny the existence of objective reality and all the while to take account of the reality which one denies.
>
> (Orwell, 1949: 223)

Cohen's detailed analysis of denial (2001) underscores the diverse ways in which individuals who do not directly perpetrate torture or are not directly victimized by torture, actively select what they perceive and what they refuse to acknowledge. In this sense, bystanders are not merely passive. For Cohen, there are different degrees of social denial:

1   *Nothing is happening*: a complete and literal denial of the facts. All allegations and evidence are dismissed as lies, fabrications, fantasies or deliberate disinformation.
2   *What is happening is really something else*: the facts are admitted (something is indeed happening) but their meaning is denied, reinterpreted or reallocated. This is often a question of semantics or word games: torture becomes 'moderate physical pressure' (as referred to in the Landau Commission case [Weill, 2014: 135]), 'special procedure' (as used by the French used to call it in Algeria [Parry, 2010:100]) or 'enhanced interrogation techniques' (as used in the 'war on terror' [McCoy, 2012]).
3   *What is happening is completely justified*: the procedures followed by the state are defended on the basis of extraordinary circumstance. Harsh procedures are deemed necessary to fight the war against terrorism (or communism, crime, fundamentalism or whatever); to preserve national security, to assist in the gathering of intelligence, etc.

The paradox of denial is that those who choose to turn 'a blind eye' are aware to some extent of what they are choosing to ignore. Geras captures the subtleties of this form of not-knowing:

> There are the people who affect not to know, or who do not care to know and so do not find out; or who do know or do not care anyway, who are indifferent; or who are afraid for themselves or for others, or who feel powerless; or who are weighed down, distracted or just occupied (as most of us) in pursuing the aims of their own lives.
>
> (Geras, 1998: 96)

There are many ways to sustain this inner/outer split: by not watching television news or reading newspapers, not talking about politics with friends, and pursuing an intense, almost caricatured immersion in private diversions. If protracted, this 'innerism', which is an adaptive strategy, may create a pathological alienation from self and society, or an exaggerated defensiveness about one's own country's record, or even a literal rather than simulated blindness to what is happening (Cohen, 2001).

Writing about genocide and group conflict, Staub (2012: 293) notices that bystanders not only have the potential influence to inhibit the evolution of destructiveness, but do so in a particular way. Bystanders' decisions about whether to be silent or to speak out and above all the timing of their decision changes their own attitudes, as if they were on a gradient between participation and taking action against the construction of the atrocity regime. Research indicates that, when bystanders remain passive, not only do they substantially reduce the likelihood that other bystanders will respond (Latané and Darley, 1970; Staub, 1978), but their own capacity to feel empathy for the victims reduces, while they are more likely to adopt 'just world' thinking[8] (Staub, 1978).

However, though valuable, an extensive use of the concept of the 'bystander state' may risk obscuring the differences in people's attitudes within society. Bystanders in different contexts have different motives and different opportunities to intervene. It is also quite misleading to say that a bystander always remains in the same bystander position. In history, there are many examples of bystanders who have turned into rescuers or, more tragically, became perpetrators.

In order to understand such subtler differentiations, we need to differentiate between *internal* and *external* bystanders, and within these categories, *passive* and *active support* or *opposition*.

To really comprehend why people become bystanders, and not helpers, we need to problematize and contextualize the bystander's knowledge, motivation and opportunities to act in every single situation.

Internal bystanders

In some sections of society, bystanders' denial is a more active attitude of complicity with and in support of perpetrators, while in other contexts bystanders are more passive and become the target of regime propaganda and victimization.

Cohen (2001) and Staub (2012: 307) who make similar distinctions between two possible bystander states: a) *passive (and active) support*; and b) *passive (and active) opposition*. In this vein, I propose that there is a continuum *between perpetrators' and bystanders' states* (already partially addressed) on the one hand, and *between bystanders' and victims' states*, on the other hand with different positions and degree of collaboration with perpetrators or victims (Figure 3.1).

Perpetrators   (active/passive support)   *Bystanders*   (passive/active opposition)   *Victims*

FIGURE 3.1 The continuum between perpetrators, bystanders and victims in population

Passive support: between perpetrators' and bystanders' states

Cohen (2001) emphasizes that in many societies that inflict cruelties on their own citizens, ethnic minorities, occupied or colonized populations, there is little difference between perpetrators and bystanders: bystanders belong to the same ethnic group of perpetrators, they are exposed to the same ideology and stereotypes, and they are prone to beliefs such as 'just world thinking' and blaming victims. Bystanders like perpetrators are gradually drawn into accepting as normal actions which are initially repugnant; they deny the significance of what they see by avoiding or minimizing information about victims' suffering. A glaring example is that of Nazi Germany, in which some ignored the regime's euthanasia programmes, especially in the beginning. Others were passive and not concerned about the fate of the victims. In other contexts, there were semi-active participants boycotting Jewish stores and breaking intimate relationships and friendships with Jews. Many benefited in some way from the Jews' fate, by assuming their jobs and buying their businesses (Hilberg, 1961). As a consequence, the majority came to accept and even support the persecution of Jews. Others became perpetrators (Staub, 1989: 305).

For example, Cohen (2001) agrees that, since an early stage of Nazism, the majority of the German people knew the general outline of the extermination policy, although not all the details. Large sections of the population either knew or suspected what was happening in the East. The operation of the *Einsatzgruppen* in Ukraine, Lithuania, the Baltic Countries and Eastern Galicia became known to millions of Germans almost immediately and the spectacles there generated curiosity, knowledge about and even participation in the violence. Laqueur (1980) writes that from June 1941 onwards, although only a handful of Germans knew everything, very few knew nothing. Rumours about the death camps came from soldiers on leave and spread widely; by 1943, the use of gas was discussed by Germans and even by foreigners; in January 1944, SS men were mailing photographs of the Auschwitz crematoria and ovens with corpses. Despite secrecy and disinformation, the Final Solution was an 'open secret'. However, 'to know' and 'to believe' were not the same thing. This is the type of logical inconsistency accepted in wartime, reflecting a disintegration of rationality. A mental (and political) state of denial means not giving the information much thought; it is simply disregarded.

Horwitz describes this state in his fine study on the people living around Mauthausen during the last phase of the camp's existence (1944 to May 1945). Living around the concentration camps entailed passive and prolonged observation of the crematoria smoke and the odour of burning flesh, which wafted over the surrounding community: residents sealed their windows at night to shut out the smell. But how did they interpret what they saw and smelled? The cumulative exposure to brutalities disturbed some nearby residents, whose complaints about being involuntary witnesses of atrocities were responded to by Nazi authorities with invites to ignore what they could otherwise not help but notice (Horwitz, 1991: 53).

In some circumstances, the pressure from a totalitarian state is so hard to endure that it is impossible, without risking one's own life, to be more than a passive bystander at best. In some cases, people who do not cooperate with the perpetrators are even killed. That was the case of Rwanda in 1994, where an enormous number of Hutus (including women and children) participated in the murders of Tutsis. These accomplices did not literally murder, but they were helpful in conducting surveillance and in reporting the hiding places of Tutsis. On similar occasions, it is almost impossible to refer to the bystander concept at all, since there is only room for victims and perpetrators (Staub, 2003).

There are also examples of 'democratic culture(s) of denial', in which the population adopts an attitude of passive support. Cohen refers to the example of

Israel during Intifada (2001: 157), claiming that the Israeli public's assent to official propaganda, myth and self-righteousness simply resulted from a willing identification – not a fear of arbitrary imprisonment or punishment. No one believed the official denials about specific allegations, such as torture, death squads and killing unarmed demonstrators, but there was self-imposed silence and internal inhibitions, which prevented people from openly speaking about what they knew. For liberals, there was a dissonance between their professed universal values and events. One possible resolution was to break ranks and step out of the bystander role into dissent and activism. Another was to return into the safe arms of the consensus: you publicly deny what you privately know, or you pretend to believe that dirty work is done by others, or you live avoiding any more information or confrontation.

Crelinsten (2003: 304) thinks that, when acquiescent bystanders find their way into the social institutions where torture is practiced, they become torturers themselves.

Passive support within institutions: the case of health professionals

In a grey area between bystanders and perpetrators – or eventually more on the side of the perpetrators – are those professionals who lend their professional knowledge and skills to institutions that practice torture. What is most disturbing is the presence among them of doctors and psychologists, whose professions are expected to enhance people's well-being and human dignity. These examples (but we can also think of lawyers working for torturous governments, who try to come up with legal justifications for the practice of torture – see Chapter 7) are powerful and impressive illustrations of how collective states of mind can inform well-educated persons and supposedly ethical workers and their institutions, and how problematic it is to resist the slippery slope of a torturous system, particularly if you are working in secret and segregated places.

Medicine has always played a pivotal role in torture and its complicity persists (Archdiocese of São Paulo, 1998; Bloche and Marks, 2005a, 2005b; Gordon and Marton, 1995; Lifton, 1986, 2004; Maio, 2001; Marks, 2005, 2007; Vesti and Lavil, 1995). According to Stephen H. Miles, somewhere between 20 per cent and 50 per cent of torture survivors report 'seeing physicians serving as active accomplices during the abuse' (Miles, 2006: 24).

Circumstances of medical involvement or participation in torture may be many and difficult to prove: immediately before torture (diagnosis and treatment), during torture (diagnosis, treatment, and direct and indirect participation) or after torture (diagnosis, treatment, falsification of journals, certificates or reports); without the free consent of the prisoner; with either the prisoner or the doctor not being free to identify themselves (or with the doctor refusing to be identified); and with the doctor acting in the interests of persons other than the prisoner (Sonntag, 2008). The Chilean Medical Association has reported on the participation of doctors in torture in terms of: a) evaluating the victim's capacity to withstand torture; b) supervising torture through the provision of medical treatment if complications occur; c) providing professional knowledge and skills to the torturer; d) falsifying or deliberately omitting medical information when issuing health certificates or autopsy reports; e) providing medical assistance within the torture system without either denouncing torture or resigning from such work; f) administering torture by directly participating in it; and g) remaining silent in spite of the knowledge that abuses have taken place (British Medical Association, 1992: 34–5).

A principal factor reported in the literature concerning the medical professional's passive support for torture is known as *dual loyalty* (Allhoff, 2008; Mostad and Moati, 2008; Sonntag, 2008). Dual loyalty is a 'Clinical role conflict between professional duties to a patient and obligations, express or implied, real or perceived to the interest of a third party such as an employer, insurer or the state' (Physicians for Human Rights and University of Cape Town, 2006: 12). A physician who is too fully 'integrated' into the system may not be able to impose his views to counter security measures that may be detrimental to prisoners' health (Pont et al., 2012: 475). The dilemma of medical independence is taken a step further when physicians are actually incorporated into military, police or security forces, or salaried by a prison administration. In such situations, when conflicts of interest arise, physicians are caught between their loyalty to 'the service' and their own ethical obligations as physicians. The effect is that a doctor turns a blind eye to a criminal offence, such as torture, and by doing so, they become an integral part of the process (Mostad and Moati, 2008).

Doctors implicated in torture are primarily very ordinary people, incapable of resisting unjust orders, ready to justify the means by the end, and quick to take refuge in a straightjacket of professionalism (not very different from torturers, in fact). Something seems to block their awareness and prevent them from taking a clear look at what they are doing. In some cases, the testimony given by prisoners suggests reluctance on the part of the doctor to play the role assigned to him or perhaps an attempt to offer some small assistance to the prisoner (Amnesty International, 1990: 16). In other cases, the doctor is reported to play a consistent and malevolent role.

Lifton (2004) explains, from his perspective, the reason why there is a risk in being a military prison doctor, highlighting how 'atrocity-producing situations' can be created: situations that are 'so structured, psychologically and militarily, that ordinary people can readily engage in atrocities' (Lifton, 2004: 351). With reference to Abu Ghraib, he states: 'doctors and other medical personnel were part of the command structure that permitted, encouraged and sometimes orchestrated torture to a degree that it became the norm – with which they were expected to comply – in the immediate prison environment' (2004: 415–16).

Apart from extreme cases, where physicians participate actively in applying torture or even in devising it, experience has shown that medical participation often comes about in an oblique way. Although there may often be some degree of coercion (fear of losing position, rank, or other benefits or, in extreme cases, even their freedom or life), many doctors convince themselves that their actions may actually be beneficial 'within the circumstance to the victims' (Reyes, 1995: 46).

The division of labour between doctors and torturers, the fact of fitting into a hierarchy, and the technical nature of their involvement, all serve to dilute responsibility and exonerate those who commit the violations.

The legitimizing role of physicians in interrogation was clearly demonstrated by the fact that during 'in-depth interrogations' in Northern Ireland in the early 1970s, there was the recommendation that a doctor should be present at all times at the interrogation center and should be able to observe the course of the oral interrogation of prisoners. The medical opposition to this role was subsequently codified in the World Medical Association's Declaration of Tokyo in 1975, which condemns all actions that could passively or actively harm a patient.

Today, despite the regrettable position of a few medical organizations, many others have created guidelines concerned with how medical professionals are somehow implicated in torture. These guidelines and policies address what is expected of medical professionals, as well as what the medical professionals expect of the international community. In the Hamburg Declaration (1997), the World Medical Association (WMA) details the rights and duties that can be expected from a medical doctor in a torture-related situation. It is also reaffirmed that there is never any excuse for violating human rights. In a 2002 resolution, the WMA asked medical professionals to report cases of torture, as well as to report individual healthcare personnel involved or affiliated with torture to the proper authorities. Other protocols have been produced as a result of the wide-ranging collaboration of many actors. The *Istanbul Protocol* was initiated by the Human Rights Foundation of Turkey and the Physicians for Human Rights USA and involved more than 40 different organizations and institutions from 15 countries, becoming an official UN document in 1999. It provides a set of guidelines for the assessment of persons who allege torture and ill-treatment, for investigating cases of alleged torture, and for reporting such findings to the judiciary and any other investigative body.

The involvement of psychologists in torture is a phenomenon far less known and documented than that of physicians. In recent years, the issue has gained some popularity in the context of the US policy of torture. However, this phenomenon is not completely new: in the early 1980s in the so-called 'Libertad' prison in Uruguay, Dr Britos, a psychologist, master-minded a scientific policy of destabilization of prisoners over a ten year period (Amnesty International, 1991).

In the context of the 'war on terror', the CIA was allowed to use ten 'enhanced interrogation' methods designed by the Agency psychologists on detainees (Burton and Kagan, 2007; McCoy, 2006; Patel, 2007; Soldz, 2008). In the prison of Guantánamo Bay Naval Base, special teams of psychiatrists and psychologists and other health care personnel – known as BISCUITS, (Behavioural Science Consultation Teams) – were created and granted permission to assist in the use of such techniques for 'priority' detainees. These 'enhanced interrogation techniques', included stress positions, isolation for up to 30 days, light and sound deprivation, hooding, 20-hour interrogations and, in reference to waterboarding,[9] the use of a 'wet towel and dripping water to induce the misperception of suffocation' (McCoy, 2006: 127). Psychiatrists and psychologists were also employed to drag up information regarding areas of psychological vulnerability regarding the prisoner, for example phobias, or cultural, sexual and religious norms (Bloche and Marks, 2005a). The function of clinical personnel included consulting on interrogation plans and approaches, providing feedback on interrogation technique, assessing fitness for interrogation and reviewing interrogation plans (Lewis, 2005a, 2005b; Lifton, 2004; Miles, 2006; Patel, 2007; Rubenstein et al., 2005).

Stephen Soldz (2008) and Frank Summers (2008) make an important contribution to the understanding of the relationship between psychology and torture in the USA. Soldz (2008) provides a detailed report of how psychologists in the recent history of the United States helped develop, implement and standardize US torture techniques. His interesting investigation convincingly draws a historical line between the research programme into mind control techniques developed during the Cold War and similar techniques – or reversed techniques – utilized during the so-called 'War on Terror', via the CIA training manuals distributed throughout Latin America in the 1970s and 1980s. Rather than oppose this use of psychologists, the American Psychological Association (APA) closed ranks and provided cover for US interrogation abuses. As the rumours spread about the involvement of health professionals in torture, they formed the Psychological Ethics and National Security (PENS) task force. Following the PENS reports, the APA was convulsed with controversy. Its leadership deflected the issue by repeating its claim that psychologists have a critical role in keeping interrogations safe, legal, ethical and effective, and that interrogation abuses are the result of 'a few bad apples' rather than of systematically designed and conducted procedures. In the years since PENS, the anti-torture groups within the APA have tried to change the direction of its policies. In response, there have been several resolutions condemning torture, which have hardly changed the APA's pro-participation stance to any substantial degree (Altman, 2008; Reisner, 2007; Soldz and Olson, 2008; Woolf, 2007).

Summers (2008) offers an answer to the question why APA was so resolute to state that psychologists must have the right to participate in interrogations. He pinpoints how the dramatic growth of psychology after World War II is attributable to resources supplied by the Department of Defense and the CIA. He sets out in very great detail four critical historical periods, which consolidated the alliance between American psychology and governmental and defence agencies, all of which correspond to wartime periods: during World War II, the Cold War, the Vietnam War and the War on Terror. Psychology was employed in a variety of ways and made a substantial contributions to successful results through psychological warfare, consulting roles, clinical services, persuasion campaigns, development of interrogational and resistance techniques, etc. Summers substantiates with a rich mass of data and documents and a persuasive narrative his hypothesis that the historical and topical dependency of American psychology on the military for research funds, as well as clinical training and treatment has resulted in an enduring debt on the part of psychology to both of these organizations. This debt is repaid by an unquestioned endorsement of military policy. However, the debt is understood not only in historical but also in economic terms since American academic psychology and psychological research still depend to a great extent on military funding.[10] He defines the relationship between American psychology and the military as 'a symbiotic bond' (Summers, 2008: 632).

Passive opposition: between bystanders' and victims' states

In other contexts, bystanders adopt a role closer to that of victims. They remain silent despite the fact that they do not accept, or refuse to see, the deception in the prevailing definitions promoted and sustained by those in power. Their silence transforms them into victims.

Vaclav Havel analyzes the nature of the Marxian totalitarian system in the Soviet bloc countries during the Cold War and the role of the individual in it as both victim and supporter. He considers communist societies as constructed around what he called 'living within the lie' (1978: 148). According to Havel, by the late 1970s, true believers no longer existed in those countries, and socialism was a system of perpetuated power, privilege and corruption. Communism cloaked its claim to power in an all-embracing ideology, which demanded acceptance by everybody. The system was totally divorced from reality, but nothing could be permitted to cut through the veil of lies because, once truth penetrated the veil, even to the smallest degree, the foundation of the system would be threatened with collapse. The legitimacy of the system, therefore, required continual verbal and symbolic reaffirmation of its premises and rationale for existence. Everyone was required to play according to the system's rules of the game: repeating hollow slogans about class struggle, voting in sham elections, participating in well-organized 'spontaneous' demonstrations, etc. Through obedience to and participation in these legitimizing games, the people were forced to sanctify their oppression as victims and hide their fears, while the rulers justified their power and covered up their corruption. Public culture was centered not on fear of the 'sharp knives' of a violent police state, but on an all-encompassing dulled anxiety of what might happen if you did not at least pretend to go along with official definitions of reality. Everyone was so vulnerable because they had something to lose (work, status, children's education). Everyone was aware of the invisible web of controls, collaborators and informers, even if this could be neither seen nor touched. Official ideology encouraged a collective deception, which everyone knew to be a deception, which Havel calls 'evasive thinking'.

Another example of a population of bystanders, who were closer to being victims than perpetrators relates to the experience of Latin America (Argentina, Brazil, Chile, Uruguay, etc.) at different times between the 1950s and the 1980s, when a number of national populations were plunged into a culture of fear (Feitlowitz, 1998; Graziano, 1992; Hollander, 1992, 2007, 2008, 2010). Under different regimes, torture was directed against highly selected victims, and was supposed to be clandestine. Nonetheless, the public had to be given enough information to be persuaded that the repression was justified. For this reason, for example, the Argentinian military junta generated a richly verbal and sophisticated version of the 'double discourse' in a delicate balance between making state terror known, yet hiding or denying its details. The regime denied (by definition) the existence of the *desaparecidos*, while simultaneously proclaiming that victims got what they deserved. Everything was supposed to be normal, yet at the same time opponents were demonized, repression justified, and terror heightened by uncertainty. The regime used language to disguise its true intentions, saying the opposite of what was meant, inspiring trust, instilling guilt and instigating a paralyzing terror (Feitlowitz, 1998: 20). In between the constant noise of words, events were staged with an exaggerated theatrical quality. Abductions were 'public' spectacles, but also clandestine and later totally denied. Details of the torture, the killings, and the disposal of the bodies remained genuinely secret. State violence was enacted behind closed doors, but terror was continually projected onto the public. Life was in two parallel worlds, public and secret: bystanders recognized what they saw, yet avoided this recognition; knew the general facts, yet did not believe them. The political split between closed and open created a state of mind that was expressed afterwards in the common refrain 'We knew, but we didn't know'. And even if you did 'really' know, the price for openly expressing knowledge in public was too high (Hollander, 2008). Fear generated a state of self-censorship: you avoided talking in public or even with your friends, and you monitored internal thoughts. The Argentinian junta's media communiqué and news addressed the victims' family and friends, who were told to keep quiet about the disappeared person to avoid causing them dishonor. The disappearance was surely proof of guilt. Hence, the following refrains: *Por algo sera* ('It must be for something') and *Algo habra[n] hecho* ('He/she/they must have done something'). 'The[se] refrains were an informal rite of obeisance; they deferred to the military; they conceded in bad faith that the military knew the 'something' that the public did not know, the 'something' that made atrocity just and necessary' (Graziano, 1992: 77).

Rescuers

Usually in societies that move toward group violence, a vanguard initiates scapegoating and destructive ideological visions, others follow, and most others remain passive. However, there are usually some who will put themselves in danger in order to save lives (Staub, 1997). They will take action against the atrocity and even influence perpetrators, as shown in the case of Denmark during the Nazi regime. On that occasion, the climate of support for Jews apparently influenced some German officials to delay deportation orders, providing the Danish population with the time needed to complete a massive rescue effort towards Sweden (Staub, 2012).

Even in extremities, some people's moral instincts remain intact. Sometimes, in a very risky situation, a minority go beyond the requirements of ordinary morality. This has been observed in some cases of genocide (during the Holocaust in Countries of Nazi Europe [Oliner and Oliner, 1988; Tec, 1986] in Rwanda [Africa Rights, 2002], during the Armenian genocide and elsewhere).

Studies suggest that rescuers have experienced the kinds of socialization that have been found to develop caring and altruism (Eisenberg *et al.*, 2006; Oliner and

Oliner, 1988; Staub, 1978, 1997, 2003). Some of them are marginal to their group in some way, for example, belonging to a minority religion, having one foreign parent or being somewhat unconventional (Tec, 1986). This presumably makes it easier for them to take a different perspective and to dis-identify from the majority group. Their example shows that, even under circumstances that exert a powerful influence, there is a variation in how people respond to social pressure.

External bystanders

External bystanders are generally outside nations and groups, which usually remain passive in the face of atrocities. They are often complicit, simply ignoring facts and events and continuing with business as usual (Crelinsten, 2003: 310). Staub's analysis of external bystanders' motives presents a picture of mixed preoccupations about economic and other interests and the will of not interfering in 'domestic affairs' of another country, which could be a precedent for others interfering in their internal affairs (Staub, 2011, 2012). However, external bystanders' contribution is fundamental: for instance there is evidence that the practice of torture diminishes in response to negative publicity and reactions from external bystanders (Stover and Nightingale, 1985). The lack of punitive action or even condemnation from important bystanders, or support from some, may negate the efforts of others and encourage and affirm the perpetrators. Crelinsten (2003) takes a similar perspective: 'A torture regime can persist as long as other nations and multinational corporations take a 'business as usual' approach to affairs with the regime, such as focusing exclusively on issues of trade and development and turning a blind eye to more political and social concerns' (2003: 310). Conversely, international condemnation of the torture regime can also play a role in providing support to those within society who are attempting to deconstruct social denial. More specialized campaigns against professionals, such as doctors, psychologists, and lawyers, who aid in torture or repression, can help medical, psychological or bar associations within the torture regime to better resist the dominant reality and adhere to their respective codes of ethics (Crelinsten, 2003)

However, it seems that timing is critical for any action of the kind stated to be effective. Most groups, especially ideologically committed ones, have difficulty in seeing themselves and having a perspective on their own actions and evolution. They need others to act as mirrors. However, once commitment to the destruction of a group has developed and the destruction is in process, nonforceful reaction from bystanders will tend to be ineffective (Staub, 2012). Staub (2012: 318) recommends that individuals, groups and nations act when the danger to them is limited and the potential exists for inhibiting the evolution of increasing destructiveness.

Crelinsten (2003) recommends a more preventive approach to the problem: in order to impede the construction of a torture reality, early warning systems and monitoring projects should detect initial signs of reality construction, which are conducive to the installation of a torture regime.

Notes

1 Martha K. Huggins (2012) detected, within torturous societies, four types of actors: perpetrators, facilitators, bureaucratic organizations and bystanders. While facilitators span systemic boundaries, by lending legitimacy, procuring resources and managing protection, most torture perpetrators operate within the boundaries of their encapsulating micro systems. Torture facilitators traverse their own national State's government and non-government bureaucracies, while others cross national boundaries. Torture system actors operate from a legitimized position within normal bureaucratic organizations; they are not extra-systemic 'deviant' outsiders and their torturing does not result from an atypical organizational 'breakdown'. Some torture facilitators – such as 'private' military contract corporations – mediate between formal national and international bureaucracies and a privatized *terra incognita* – a 'nether world' simultaneously inside and outside government and state.
2 The experiment description is available online at: www.prisonexp.org (accessed 3 May 2012).
3 There is not well-established knowledge about female torturers. Nonetheless, we know that in the third Reich, for example, there were women actively involved in the camps as guards (Lower, 2014; Mailänder, 2015). According to Cesereanu's study (2006), although few in numbers, female torturers existed during the first stages of communism in Romania. Milgram's studies (1974) demonstrate that women are as obedient to authority as men. And women were also seen in pictures of torture in the prisons of Abu Ghraib and Guantánamo. However, the topic has not been widely and systematically explored.
4 In Greek Ελληνική Στρατιωτική Αστυνομία (ΕΣΑ) was the Greek Military Police, a branch of the Greek Army in the years 1951–1974. It developed into a powerful paramilitary organization, and became the main intelligence organization for internal security of the Greek military junta of 1967–1974. It was used by the ruling Colonels to interrogate, torture and execute political opponents.
5 Escuela de Mecánica de la Armada (ESMA) was the Navy School of Mechanics in Buenos Aires – a center where thousands of people, who were kidnapped during the 'Dirty War', were also tortured and disappeared.
6 Research on torture survivors has estimated prevalence rates from 14 per cent to 38 per cent for developing PTSD, 14 per cent to 67 per cent for depression, and 17 per cent to 60 per cent for anxiety (Hooberman, 2007: 118).
7 This pattern proves similar, in many respects, to that illustrated for the making of torturers.
8 The 'just world thinking' is the belief that in the world things always happen in a fair and just manner. If something good happens to someone, they must be a good person; if something bad happens to someone they must have done something bad or wrong and are a bad person. This belief helps people to feel safe, because in a 'just world' they themselves will not become the victims of random, unpredictable suffering.
9 A technique in which the detainee is tied to a board with the head lower than the feet so that they are unable to move. A piece of cloth is held tightly over the face, and water is poured onto the cloth. Breathing is extremely difficult and the detainee will fear imminent death by asphyxiation. Its use is expressly prohibited by the *US Army Field Manual 34–52 on Interrogation* but the CIA is exempt from this.
10 Summers estimates approximately $400 million annually.

References

African Rights (2002) *Rwanda: Tribute to Courage*. Kigali, Rwanda: African Rights Organization.
Allen, J.G. (1993) 'Traumatic bonding joins abused to abuser'. *The Menninger Letter*, 1(7): 4.
Allhoff, F. (Ed.) (2008) *Physicians at War: The Dual-Loyalties Challenge*. New York: Springer.

Allodi, F. (1991) 'Assessment and treatment of torture victims: a critical review'. *Journal of Nervous Mental Diseases*, 179(1): 4–11. doi:10.1097/00005053-199101000-00002

Allodi, F. (1993) 'Somoza's national guard: a study of human rights abuses, psychological health and moral development'. In Crelinsten, R.D. and Schmid, A.P. (Eds), *The Politics of Pain: Torturers and Their Masters*. Centrum voor Onderzoek van Maatschappelijke Tegenstellingen/Center for the Study of Social Conflicts, AK Leiden, Netherlands: Leiden University, pp. 125–40.

Altman, N. (2008) 'The psychodynamics of torture'. *Psychoanalytic Dialogues*, 18(5): 658–70. doi:10.1080/10481880802297681

American Psychiatric Association (2013) *Diagnostic and Statistical Manual of Mental Disorders, 5th Edition*. Arlington, VA: American Psychiatric Association.

Amnesty International (1977) *Torture in Greece: The First Torturers' Trial 1975*. London: Amnesty International Publications.

Amnesty International (1990) *Involvement of Medical Personnel in Abuses against Detainees and Prisoners*. AI Index: ACT 75/08/90, November 1990.

Amnesty International (1991) *Doctors and Torture: Collaboration or Resistance?* London: Bellew.

Amnesty International (2000) *Take a Step to Stamp out Torture*. London: Amnesty International Publications.

Amnesty International (2014) *Torture in 2014. 30 Years of Broken Promises*. London: Amnesty International Publications.

Amris, K. and Prip, K. (2000a) 'Physiotherapy for torture victims. (I) Chronic pain in torture victims: possible mechanisms for the pain'. *Torture*, 10(3): 73–6. Available at: http://doc.rct.dk/doc/TORT2000-3-3.pdf (accessed 3 January 2017)

Amris, K. and Prip, K. (2000b) 'Physiotherapy for torture victims. (II) Treatment of chronic pain'. *Torture*, 10(4): 112–16. Available at: http://doc.rct.dk/doc/TORT2000-4-5.pdf (accessed 3 January 2017)

Amris, K. (2005) 'Chronic pain in survivors of torture: psyche or soma?' In Berliner, P., Arenas, J. and Haagensen, J.O. (Eds.), *Torture and Organized Violence: Contributions To a Professional Human Rights Response*. Copenhagen: Danish Psychology Publishers, pp. 31–70.

Amris, K. and Prip, K. (2003) *Falanga Torture: Diagnostic Consideration, Assessment and Treatment*. Copenhagen: IRCT/RCT.

Amris, K. and Williams, A. (2007) 'Pain clinical update: chronic pain in survivors of torture'. *Pain Clinical Update*, 15(7): 1–6. Available at: http://iasp.files.cms-plus.com/Content/ContentFolders/Publications2/PainClinicalUpdates/Archives/PCU07-7_139026 2836391_10 pdf (accessed 3 January 2017)

Amris, K., Torp-Pedersen, S. and Rasmussen, O.V. (2009) 'Long-term consequences of falanga torture: what do we know and what do we need to know?' *Torture*, 19(1): 33–40.

Archdiocese of São Paulo (1998) *Brazil: Nunca Mais/Torture in Brazil: A Shocking Report on the Pervasive Use of Torture by Brazilian Military Governments, 1964–1979. Secretly prepared by the Archdiocese of São Paulo*. Austin: University of Texas Press (ILAS Special Publication).

Arendt, H. (1963) *Eichmann in Jerusalem: A Report on the Banality of Evil*. New York: Penguin Books, 1977.

Aronson, E. and Mills, J. (1959) 'Effect of severity of initiation on linking for a group'. *Journal of Abnormal Social Psychology*, 59(2): 177–81. doi:10.1037/h0047195

Auerhahn, N.C. and Laub, D. (1998) 'Intergenerational memory of the Holocaust'. In Danieli, Y. (Ed.), *International Handbook of Multigenerational Legacies of Trauma*. New York: Plenum, pp. 21–41.

Basoğlu, M. (Ed.) (1992) *Torture and Its Consequences: Current Treatment Approaches*. London: Cambridge University Press.

Basoğlu, M., Parker, M., Paker, Ö., Özmen, E., Marks, I., Incesu, C., Sahin, D. and Sarimurat, N. (1994) 'Psychological effects of torture: a comparison of tortured with matched non-tortured political activists in Turkey'. *American Journal of Psychiatry*, 151(1) (January): 76–81. doi:10.1176/ajp.151.1.76

Basoğlu, M., Jaranson, J.M., Mollica, R. and Kastrup, M. (2001) 'Torture and mental health: a research overview'. In Gerrity, E., Keane, T.M. and Tuma, F. (Eds.), The *Mental Health Consequences of Torture*. New York: Kluwer Academic/Plenum Publishers, pp. 35–62.

Bettelheim, B. (1943) 'Individual and mass behaviour in extreme situations'. In Bettelheim, B. (Ed.) *Surviving and Other Essays*. New York: Alfred A. Knopf, 1979, pp. 48–83.

Bettelheim, B. (1952) 'Remarks on the psychological appeal of totalitarianism'. In Bettelheim, B. (Ed.), *Surviving and Other Essays*, New York: Alfred A. Knopf, 1979, pp. 317–32.

Blass, T. (Ed.) (2000) *Obedience to Authority: Current Perspectives on the Milgram Paradigm*. Mahwah, NJ: Lawrence Erlbaum Associates.

Bloche, M.G. and Marks, J.H. (2005a) 'Doctors and interrogators at Guantanamo Bay'. *New England Journal of Medicine*, 353(1): 6–8. doi:10.1056/NEJMp058145

Bloche M.G. and Marks, J.H. (2005b) 'When doctors go to war'. *New England Journal of Medicine*, 352: 3–6. doi:10.1056/NEJMp048346

Bonanno, G.A. (2004) 'Loss, trauma, and human resilience: have we underestimated the human capacity to thrive after extremely adverse events?' *American Psychologist* 59: 20–8. doi:10.1037/0003-066X.59.1.20

Bonanno, G.A. and Mancini, A.D. (2008) 'The human capacity to thrive in the face of extreme adversity'. *Pediatrics*, 121(2): 369–75. doi:10.1542/peds.2007-1648

Bowlby, J. (1969) *Attachment and Loss. Vol. 1: Attachment*. London: Hogarth and the Institute of Psychoanalysis.

Bowlby, J. (1988) *A Secure Base: Parent-Child Attachment and Healthy Human Development*. NY: Basic Books.

Bracken, J. (1998) 'Hidden agendas: deconstructing posttraumatic stress'. In Bracken, J. and Petty, C. (Eds.), *Rethinking the Trauma of War*. London: Free Association Press, pp. 38–59.

Breuer J. and Freud, S. (1895) 'Studies in hysteria'. In Freud, S., *The Standard Edition of the Complete Psychological Works of Sigmund Freud*, Trans. and Ed. J. Strachey, vol. 2, London: The Hogarth Press.

Briere, J. and Spinazzola, J. (2005) 'Phenomenology and psychological assessment of complex posttraumatic states'. *Journal of Traumatic Stress*, 18(5): 401–12. doi:10.1002/jts.20048

British Medical Association (1992) *Medicine Betrayed: The Participation of Doctors in Human Rights Abuses*. London: Zed Books, 1998.

Browning, C.R. (1993) *Ordinary Men: Reserve Police Battalion 101 and the Final Solution in Poland*. New York: HarperPerennial.

Burton, M. and Kagan, C. (2007) 'Psychologists and torture: more than a question of interrogation'. *The Psychologist*, 20(8): 484–7.

Campbell-Sills, L., Cohan, S. and Stein, M. (2006) 'Relationship of resilience to personality, coping, and psychiatric symptoms in young adults'. *Behaviour Research and Therapy*, 44(4): 585–99. doi:10.1016/j.brat.2005.05.001

Carlsson, J. M., Olsen D. R., Mortensen E. L., Kastrup M. (2006) 'Mental health and health-related quality of life: A 10-year follow-up of tortured refugees.' *Journal of Nervous and Mental Disease*, 194: 725–31.

Cesereanu, R. (2006) 'An overview of political torture in the twentieth century'. *Journal for the Study of Religions and Ideologies*, 5(14): 120–43.

Christie, R. (1991) 'Authoritarianism and related constructs'. In Robinson, J.P., Shaver, P.R. and Wrightsman, L.S. (Eds.), *Measures of Personality* and *Social Psychology Attitudes*. San Diego, CA: Academic Press, pp. 501–71.

Cicchetti, D. and Luthar, S.S. (2003) *Resilience and Vulnerability: Adaptation in the Context of Childhood Adversities.* Cambridge: Cambridge University Press.

Clarke, A. and Clarke, A. (2003) *Human Resilience: A Fifty-Year Quest.* London: Jessica Kingsley.

Cohen, S. (2001) *States of Denial: Knowing about Atrocities and Suffering.* Cambridge: Polity Press.

Conner, K. and Davidson, R. (2003) 'Development of a new resilience scale: the Connor-Davidson Resilience Scale (CD-RISC)'. *Depression and Anxiety,* 18: 76–82. doi:10.1002/da.10113

Conroy, J. (2000) *Unspeakable Acts, Ordinary People: The Dynamics of Torture: An Examination of the Practice of Torture in Three Democracies.* New York: Knopf.

Courtois, C.A. (2004) 'Complex trauma, complex reactions: assessment and treatment'. *Psychotherapy: Theory, Research, Practice, and Training,* 41(4): 412–25. doi:10.1037/0033-3204.41.4.412

Crelinsten, R.D. (2003) 'The world of torture: a constructed reality'. *Theoretical Criminology,* 7(3): 293–318. doi:10.1177/13624806030073003

Crelinsten, R.D. and Schmid, A.P. (Eds.) (1993) *The Politics of Pain: Torturers and Their Masters.* Centrum voor Onderzoek van Maatschappelijke Tegenstellingen/Center for the Study of Social Conflicts, AK Leiden, Netherlands: Leiden University.

Cunningham, M. and Cunningham, J.D. (1997) 'Patterns of symptomatology and patterns of torture and trauma experiences in resettled refugees'. *Australian and New Zealand Journal of Psychiatry,* 31: 555–65. doi:10.3109/00048679709065078

Danieli, Y. (Ed.) (1998) *International Handbook of Multigenerational Legacies of Trauma.* New York: Plenum, 2013.

Darley, J.M. and Latané, B. (1968) 'Bystander intervention in emergencies: diffusion of responsibility.' *Journal of Personality and Social Psychology,* 8(4, Pt. 1): 377–83. doi:10.1037/h0025589

Daud, A., Skoglund, E. and Rydelius, P.A. (2005) 'Children in families of torture victims: transgenerational transmission of parent's traumatic experience to their children'. *International Journal of Social Welfare,* 14(1): 23–32. doi:10.1111/j.1468-2397.2005.00336.x

Dekel, R. and Goldblatt, M. (2008) 'Is there intergenerational transmission of trauma? The case of combat veterans' children'. *American Journal of Orthopsychiatry,* 78(3): 281–9. doi:10.1037/a0013955

De Jong, J.T.V.M. (2005) 'Analysing critique on PTSD in an attempt to bridge anthropology and psychiatry'. *Medische Antropologie,* 17(1): 91–106. Available at: https://pure.uva.nl/ws/files/2012335/149162_deJong2005MedAntropol17_1_p91t106.pdf

De Jong, J.T.V.M. (2004) 'Public mental health and culture: disasters as a challenge to Western mental health care models, the self and PTSD'. In Wilson, J.P. and Drožđek, B. (Eds.), *Broken Spirits: The Treatment of Traumatized Asylum Seekers, Refugees, War and Torture Victims.* New York: Brunner-Routledge, pp. 159–78.

De Jong, J.T.V.M. and van Ommeren, M. (2002) 'Toward a culture-informed epidemiology: combining qualitative and quantitative research in transcultural contexts'. *Transcultural Psychiatry,* 39(4): 422–33. doi:10.1177/136346150203900402

DeVoe, E.E., Klein, T., Bannon, W. and Miranda-Julian, C. (2011) 'Young children in the aftermath of the World Trade Center attacks'. *Psychological Trauma: Theory, Research, Practice and Policy,* 3(1): 1–7. doi: 10.1037/a0020567

de Zulueta, F. (2006a) *From Pain to Violence: The Traumatic Roots of Destructiveness.* Second edition, Chichester: John Wiley and Sons Ltd.

de Zulueta, F. (2006b) 'Inducing traumatic attachment in adults with a history of child abuse: forensic applications'. *The British Journal of Forensic Practice,* (September) 8(3): 4–15. doi:10.1108/14636646200600015

Dutton, D.G. and Painter, S. (1993) 'Emotional attachments in abusive relationships: a test of traumatic bonding theory'. *Violence and Victims*, 8(2) (January): 105–20.

Ehrenreich R. and Cole, T. (2005) 'The perpetrator-bystander-victim constellation: rethinking genocidal relationships'. *Human Organization*, 64(3) (Fall): 213–24.

Eisenberg, N., Fabes, R. and Spinrad, T. (2006) 'Prosocial development'. In Eisenberg, N., Damon, W. and Lerner, R. (Eds.), *Handbook of Child Psychology: Vol. 3. Social, Emotional and Personality Development*. 6th edition. Hoboken, NJ: John Wiley and Sons, pp. 646–718.

Elms, A.C. (1995) 'Obedience in retrospect'. *Journal of Social Issues*, 51: 121–31. Available at:www.ulmus.net/ace/library/obedience.html (accessed 14 December 2016)

Elms, A.C. and Milgram, S. (1966) 'Personality characteristics associated with obedience and defiance toward authoritative command'. *Journal of Experimental Research in Personality*, 1(4): 282–9. Available at: http://elms.faculty.ucdavis.edu/wp-content/uploads/sites/98/2014/07/2014_07_16_12_17_24.pdf

Fanon, F. (1963) *The Wretched of the Earth*. New York: Grove Press.

Fassin, D. and d'Halluin, E. (2005) 'The truth from the body: medical certificates as ultimate evidence for asylum seekers'. *American Anthropologist*,107: 597–608. doi:10.1525/aa.2005.107.4.597

Faulkner, W. (1951) *Requiem for a Nun*. New York: Random House.

Feitlowitz, M. (1998) *A Lexicon of Terror: Argentina and the Legacies of Torture*. New York: Oxford University Press.

Fenigstein, A. (1998) 'Were obedience pressures a factor in the Holocaust?' *Analyse and Kritik*, 20(1): 54–73. doi:10.1515/auk-1998-0104

Finkelhor, D. and Browne, A. (1985) 'The traumatic impact of child sexual abuse: a conceptualization'. *American Journal of Orthopsychiatry*, 55(4): 530–41. doi:10.1111/j.1939-0025.1985.tb02703.x

Finkelhor, D. (2007) 'Developmental victimology: the comprehensive study of childhood victimizations'. In Davis, R.C., Luirigio, A.J. and Herman, S. (Eds.), *Victims of Crime*. Thousand Oaks, CA: Sage Publications, pp. 9–34.

Freedom from Torture (2011) *Body of Evidence: Treatment of Medico-Legal Reports for Survivors of Torture in the UK Asylum Tribunal*. Available at: www.freedomfromtorture.org/document/publication/5317 (accessed 14 March 2014).

Friborg, O., Hjemdal, O., Rosenvinge, J., Martinussen, M., Aslaksen, P. and Flaten, M. (2006) 'Resilience as a moderator of pain and stress'. *Journal of Psychosomatic Research*, 6(3): 213–19. doi:10.1016/j.jpsychores.2005.12.007

Friedman, M. and Jaranson, J. (1994) 'The applicability of the posttraumatic stress disorder concept to refugees'. In Marsella, A.J., Bornemann, T., Ekblad, S. and Orley, J. (Eds.), *Amidst Peril and Pain: The Mental Health and Wellbeing of the World's Refugees*. American Psychological Association, pp. 101–15.

Galea, S., Resnick, H., Ahern, J. Gold, J. Bucuvalas, M., Kilpatrick, D. and Vlahov, D. (2002) 'Posttraumatic stress disorder in Manhattan, NYC, after the September 11th terrorist attacks'. *Journal of Urban Health Studies*, 79(3): 340–53. doi:10.1093/jurban/79.3.340

George, S.K. (2016) 'The familiar stranger: on the loss of self in intense bodily pain'. In George, S.K. and Jung, P.G. (Eds.), *Cultural Ontology of the Self in Pain*. India: Springer, pp. 51–74.

Geras, N. (1998) *The Contract of Mutual Indifference: Political Philosophy after the Holocaust*. London and New York: Verso.

Gerrity, E., Keane, T.M. and Tuma, F. (Eds.) (2001) *The Mental Health Consequences of Trauma*. New York: Plenum Publishers.

Gibson, J.T. (1990) 'Factors contributing to the creation of a torturer'. In Suedfeld, P. (Ed.), *Psychology and Torture*. New York: Hemisphere, pp. 77–88.

Gibson, J.T. and Haritos-Fatouros, M. (1986) 'Education of a torturer'. *Psychology Today*, 20: 50–8.
Glover, J. (2001) *Humanity: A Moral History of the Twentieth Century*. London: Pimlico.
Goldfeld, A.E., Mollica, R.F., Pesavento, B.H. and Faraone, S.V. (1988) 'The physical and psychological sequelae of torture: symptomatology and diagnosis'. *Journal of the American Medical Association*, 259(18): 2725–9. doi:10.1001/jama.1988.03720180051032
Gordon, N. and Marton, R. (1995) *Torture: Human Rights, Medical Ethics and the Case of Israel*. London and New Jersey: Zed Books.
Gorst-Unsworth C. (1992) 'Adaptation after torture: some thoughts on the long-term effects of surviving a repressive regime'. *Medicine and War* (Jul–Sep), 8(3):164–8.
Graziano, F. (1992) *Divine Violence: Spectacle, Psychosexuality, and Radical Christianity in the Argentine 'Dirty War'*. Boulder, San Francisco, Oxford: Westview Press.
Haney, C., Banks, C. and Zimbardo, P. (1973) 'A study of prisoners and guards in a simulated prison', *Naval Research Reviews*, 26(9): 1–17.
Harkness, L.L. (1993) 'Transgenerational transmission of war-related trauma'. In Wilson, J.P. and Raphael, B. (Eds), *International Handbook of Traumatic Stress Syndromes*. New York: Plenum Press, pp. 635–43.
Haritos-Fatouros, M. (1993) 'The official torturer: a learning model for obedience to the authority of violence'. In Crelinsten, R.D. and Schmid, A.P. (Eds.), *The Politics of Pain: Torturers and their Masters*. Centrum voor Onderzoek van Maatschappelijke Tegenstellingen/Center for the Study of Social Conflicts, AK Leiden, Netherlands: Leiden University, pp. 129–46.
Haritos-Fatouros, M. (2003) *The Psychological Origins of Institutionalized Torture*. London: Routledge.
Havel, V. (1978) 'The power of powerless'. In *Open Letters. Selected Writings, 1965–1990*, selected and edited by Paul Wilson. New York: Vintage Books, pp. 125–214.
Heinz, W.S. (1993) 'The military, torture and human rights: experiences from Argentina, Brazil, Chile and Uruguay'. In Crelinsten, R.D. and Schmid, A.P. (Eds.), *The Politics of Pain: Torturers and their Masters*. Centrum voor Onderzoek van Maatschappelijke Tegenstellingen/Center for the Study of Social Conflicts, AK Leiden, Netherlands: Leiden University, pp. 73–108.
Henry, J. (1997) 'Psychological and physiological responses to stress: the right hemisphere and the hypothalamic–pituitary–adrenal-axis, an inquiry into problems of human bonding'. *Acta Physiologica Scandinavica*, 161: 164–9.
Herman, J.L. (1992a) *Trauma and Recovery: The Aftermath of Violence – From Domestic Abuse to Political Terror*. New York: Basic Books.
Herman, J.L. (1992b) 'Complex PTSD: a syndrome in survivors of prolonged and repeated trauma'. *Journal of Traumatic Stress*, 5(3): 377–91. doi:10.1002/jts.2490050305
Hilberg, R. (1961) *The Destruction of the European Jews*. New York: Holmes and Maier, 1985.
Hilberg, R. (1992) *Perpetrators Victims Bystanders: The Jewish Catastrophe, 1933–1945*. New York: Aaron Asher Books.
Hinton, D. E. and Lewis-Fernandez, R. (2011). 'The cross-cultural validity of Posttraumatic Stress Disorder: implications for DSM-5'. *Depression and Anxiety*, 28(9): 783–801. doi:10.1002/da.20753
Hollander, N.C. (1992) 'Psychoanalysis and state terror in Argentina'. *American Journal of Psychoanalysis*, 52(3): 273–89.
Hollander, N.C. (2007) 'Scared stiff: trauma, ideology, and the bystander'. *International Journal of Applied Psychoanalytic Studies*, 4: 295–307. doi:10.1002/aps.102
Hollander, N.C. (2008) 'Living danger: on not knowing what we know'. *Psychoanalytic Dialogues*, 18(5): 690–709. doi:10.1080/10481880802297707

Hollander, N.C. (2010) *Uprooted Minds: Surviving the Politics of Terror in the Americas*. New York: Routledge.
Hooberman, J.B. (2007) *Resilience in Torture Survivors: The Moderating Effect of Coping Style on Social Support, Cognitive Appraisal and Social Comparisons*. Ann Arbor, MI: ProQuest LLC.
Horwitz, G.J. (1991) *In the Shadow of the Death: Living Outside the Gates of Mauthausen*. London: I.B. Tauris.
Huggins, M.K. (2000) 'Legacies of authoritarianism: Brazilian torturers' and murderers' reformulation of memory'. *Latin American Perspectives*, 27(2) (March): 57–78.
Huggins, M.K. (2002) 'State violence in Brazil: the professional morality of torturers'. In Rotker, S. (Ed.), *Citizens of Fear: Urban Violence in Latin America*. New Brunswick, NJ: Rutgers University Press, pp. 141–51.
Huggins M.K. (2012) 'State torture: interviewing perpetrators, discovering facilitators, theorizing cross-nationality – Proposing "Torture 101".' *State Crime Journal*, 1 (1) (Spring): 45–69.
Huggins, M.K. and Haritos-Fatouros, M. (1998) 'Bureaucratizing masculinities among Brazilian torturers and murderers'. In Bowker, L.H. (Ed.), *Masculinities and Violence*. Beverley Hills, CA: Sage Publications.
Huggins, M.K., Haritos-Fatouros, M. and Zimbardo, P.G. (2002) *Violence Workers: Police Torturers and Murderers Reconstruct Brazilian Atrocities*. Berkeley, CA: University of California Press.
Human Rights Foundation of Turkey (2004) *Torture and Impunity*. Ankara: HRFT Publications.
Imseis, A. (2001) '"Moderate" torture on trial: critical reflections on the Israeli Supreme Court judgment concerning the legality of General Security Service interrogation methods'. *Berkeley Journal of International Law*, 19(2): 328–49. doi:10.15779/Z381P9P
Jaranson M. and Popkin M.K. (1998) *Caring for Victims of Torture*. Washington, DC: America Psychiatric Press.
Johnson, H. and Thompson, A. (2008) 'The development and maintenance of post-traumatic stress disorder (PTSD) in civilian adult survivors of war trauma and torture: a review'. *Clinical Psychology Review*, 28(1): 36–47. doi:10.1016/j.cpr.2007.01.017
Keen, S. (1986) *Faces of the Enemy: Reflections of the Hostile Imagination*. San Francisco: Harper and Row.
Keiser, S. (2005) *Post-Memories of Terror. A New Generation Copes with the Legacy of the 'Dirty War'*. New York: Palgrave Macmillan.
Kelman, H.C. (1993) 'The social context of torture: policy process and authority structure'. In Crelinsten, R.D. and Schmid, A.P. (Eds.), *The Politics of Pain: Torturers and their Masters*. Centrum voor Onderzoek van Maatschappelijke Tegenstellingen/ Center for the Study of Social Conflicts, AK Leiden, Netherlands: Leiden University, pp. 21–38.
Kelman, H.C. (2005) 'The policy context of torture: a social-psychological analysis'. *International Review of the Red Cross*, 87(857): 123–34. doi:10.1017/S1816383100181214
Kelman, H.C. (2010) 'Violence without moral restraint: reflections on the dehumanization of victims and victimizers'. *Journal of Social Issues*, 29(4): 25–61. Available at: http://scholar.harvard.edu/files/hckelman/files/Violence_1973.pdf (accessed 4 January 2015)
Kelman, H.C. and Hamilton, V.L. (1989) *Crimes of Obedience: Toward a Social Psychology of Authority and Responsibility*. New Haven and London: Yale University Press.
Kilham, W. and Mann, L. (1974) 'Level of destructive obedience as a function of transmitter and executant roles in the Milgram obedience paradigm.' *Journal of Personality and Social Psychology*, 29(5): 696–702.

Kira, I.A. (2002) 'Torture assessment and treatment: the wraparound approach'. *Traumatology*, 8(2): 61–90.

Kira, I.A. Templin, T., Lewandowski, L., Clifford, D., Wiencek, E., Ham-mad, A., Al-Haidar, A. and Mohanesh, J. (2006) 'The effects of torture: two community studies'. *Peace and Conflict: Journal of Peace Psychology*, 12(3): 205–28. doi:10.1207/s15327949pac 1203_1

Kissane, M., Szymanski, L., Upthegrove, R. and Katona, C. (2014) 'Complex posttraumatic stress disorder in traumatised asylum seekers: a pilot study'. *The European Journal of Psychiatry*, 28(3) (Jul–Sept). doi:10.4321/S0213-61632014000300001. Available at: http://scielo.isciii.es/scielo.php?pid=S0213-61632014000300001&script=sci_arttext (accessed 1 July 2015).

Laqueur, W. (1980) *The Terrible Secret: Suppression of the Truth About Hitler's 'Final Solution'*. Boston: Little Brown, 1998.

Latané, B. and Darley, J. M. (1970) *The Unresponsive Bystander: Why Doesn't He Help?* New York: Appleton-Century-Crofts.

Levi, P. (1986) *The Drowned and The Saved*. Trans. R. Rosenthal, New York: Vintage Books, 1989.

Lewis, N.A. (2005a) 'Interrogators cite doctors' aid at Guantánamo: ethics questions raised'. *The New York Times*, 24 June.

Lewis, N.A. (2005b) 'Psychologists warned on role in detentions'. *The New York Times*, 6 July.

Lifton, R.J. (1986) *The Nazi Doctors: Medical Killing and the Psychology of Genocide*. New York: Basic Books, 1986.

Lifton, R.J. (1961) *Thought Reform and the Psychology of Totalism: A Study of 'Brainwashing' in China*. Chapel Hill, NC: University of North Carolina Press, 1989.

Lifton, R.J. (2004) 'Doctors and torture'. *New England Journal of Medicine*, 351: 415–16. doi:10.1056/NEJMp048065

Lower, W. (2014) *Hitler's Furies: German Women in the Nazi Killing Fields*. Boston, MA: Houghton Mifflin Harcourt.

Luci, M. (2016) 'Inner and outer travels: analytical psychology and the treatment of refugees.' *Quadrant*, XLVI(2): 35-55.

Mailänder, E. (2015) *The Violence of Female Guards in Nazi Concentration Camps: Reflections on the Dynamics and Logics of Power*. Online Encyclopedia of Mass Violence. Available at www.massviolence.org/IMG/article_PDF/The-Violence-of-Female-Guards-in.pdf (accessed 25 September 2015).

Maio, G. (2001) 'History of medical involvement in torture – then and now'. *Lancet*, 357: 1609–11.

Mancini, A.D. and Bonanno G.A. (2006) 'Resilience in the face of potential trauma: clinical practices and illustrations'. *Journal of Clinical Psychology*, 62(8): 971–85. doi:10.1002/jclp.20283

Mandel, D. (1998) 'The obedience alibi: Milgram's account of the Holocaust reconsidered'. *Analyse and Kritik*, 20(1): 74–94. doi:10.1515/auk-1998-0105

Marks, J.H. (2005) 'Doctors of interrogation'. *Hastings Center Report*, 35(4): 17–22. doi:10.1353/hcr.2005.0044

Marks, J.H. (2007b) 'Doctors as pawns? Law and medical ethics at Guantanamo Bay'. *Seton Hall Law Review*, 37(3): 711–31. Available at: http://scholarship.shu.edu/cgi/viewcontent.cgi?article=1143&context=shlr (accessed 13 October 2015)

Marsella, A., Friedman, M. J., Gerrity, E. T. and Scurfield, R. M. (Eds.) (1996) *Ethnocultural Aspects of Posttraumatic Stress Disorder: Issues, Research, and Clinical Applications*. Washington, DC: American Psychological Association.

Masmas, T.N., Møller, E., Buhmann C, Bunch, V., Jensen, J.H. and Hansen, T.N. (2008) 'Asylum seekers in Denmark: a study of health status and grade of traumatisation of newly arrived asylum seekers'. *Torture*, 18(2): 77–86.

Mastroianni, G.R. (2002) 'Milgram and the Holocaust: a re-examination'. *Journal of Theoretical and Philosophical Psychology*, 22(2): 158–73. doi:10.1037/h0091220

Mattar, S. (2012) 'Cultural diversity in trauma response'. In Figley, C.R. (Ed.), *Encyclopedia of Trauma: An Interdisciplinary Guide*. Thousand Oaks, CA: Sage, pp. 177–80.

McCoy, A. (2006) *A Question of Torture: CIA Interrogation, from the Cold War to the War on Terror (American Empire Project)*. New York: Metropolitan Books/Henry Holt.

McCoy, A.W. (2012) *Torture and Impunity: The U.S. Doctrine of Coercive Interrogation*. Madison, WI: University of Wisconsin Press.

Mc Culley, A. (2014) 'The physical and psychological sequelae in adult refugees or asylum seekers who have survived torture: literature review'. Available at: https://ethnomed.org/clinical/torture/torture-literature-review/the-physical-and-psychological-sequelae-in-adult-refugees-or-asylum-seekers-who-have-survived-torture-2 (accessed 20 September 2015).

Meeus, W.H.J. and Raaijmakers, Q.A.W. (1986) 'Administrative obedience: carrying out orders to use psychological – administrative violence'. *European Journal of Social Psychology*, 16: 311–25.

Meeus, W.H.J. and Raaijmakers, Q.A.W. (1995) 'Obedience in modern societies: the Utrecht studies'. *Journal of Social Issues*, 51(3): 155–75. doi:10.1111/j.1540-4560.1995.tb01339.x

Mikulincer, M. and Shaver, P.R. (2007) *Attachment in Adulthood: Structure, Dynamics, and Change*. New York: Guilford Press.

Miles, S. (2006) *Oath Betrayed: Torture, Medical Complicity and the War on Terror*. New York: Random House.

Milgram, S. (1963) 'Behavioral study of obedience'. *Journal of Abnormal and Social Psychology*, 67(4) (October): 371–8. doi:10.1037/h0040525.

Milgram, S. (1974) *Obedience to Authority: An Experimental View*. New York: Harper and Row.

Miller, A.G. (1986) *The Obedience Experiments: Case Study of a Controversy in Social Science*. Wesport, CT: Praeger.

Miller, A.G. (2004) 'What can the Milgram obedience experiments tell us about the Holocaust? Generalizing from the social psychology laboratory'. In Miller, A.G. (Ed.), *The Social Psychology of Good and Evil*. New York: Guilford Press, pp.193–239.

Miller, A.G. (Ed.) (2005) *The Social Psychology of Good and Evil*. New York: Guilford Press.

Millet, K. (1994) *The Politics of Cruelty: An Essay on the Literature of Political Imprisonment*. London: Penguin Books.

Mollica, R.F. (2004) 'Surviving torture'. *New England Journal of Medicine*, 351: 5–7. doi:10.1056/NEJMp048141

Montgomery, E., Krogh, Y., Jacobsen, A. and Lukman, B. (1992) 'Children of torture victims: Reactions and coping'. *Child Abuse and Neglect: The International Journal*, 16(6): 797–805.

Montgomery, E. (2011) 'Trauma, exile and mental health in young refugees'. *Acta Psychiatrica Scandinavica*, Suppl. 440 (124):1–46. doi:10.1111/j.1600-0447.2011.01740.x

Mostad, K. and Moati, E. (2008) 'Silent healers, on medical complicity in torture'. *Torture*, 18(3):150–60.

Oliner, S.B. and Oliner, P. (1988) *The Altruistic Personality: Rescuers of Jews in Nazi Europe*. New York: Free Press.

Olsen, D., Montgomery, E., Carlsson, J. and Foldspang, S. (2006) 'Prevalent pain and pain level among torture survivors'. *Danish Medical Bulletin*, 53(2): 210–14.

Ortiz, S.D. (2001) 'The survivors' perspective: voices from the center'. In Gerrity, E., Keane, T.M. and Tuma, F. (Eds.), *The Mental Health Consequences of Trauma*. New York: Plenum Publishers, pp. 13–34.

Orwell, G. (1949) *Nineteen Eighty-Four*. London: Penguin, 2008.

Palosaari, E., Punamäki, R.L., Qouta, S. and Diab, M. (2013) 'Intergenerational effects of war trauma among Palestinian families mediated via psychological maltreatment'. *Child Abuse and Neglect*, 37(11): 955–68. doi:10.1016/j.chiabu.2013.04.006

Papadopoulos, R.K. (2002) 'Refugees, home and trauma'. In Papadopoulos, R.K. (Ed.), *Therapeutic Care for Refugees. No Place Like Home*. London: Karnac, Tavistock Clinic Series, pp. 9–39.

Papadopoulos, R.K. (2004) 'Trauma in a systemic perspective: theoretical, organization and clinical dimensions'. Paper presented at the 14th Congress of the International Family Therapy Association, Istanbul.

Papadopoulos, R.K. (2005) 'Political violence, trauma and mental health interventions'. In Kalmanowitz, D. and Lloyd, B. (Eds.), *Art Therapy and Political Violence: With Art Without Illusion*, London: Brunner-Routledge, pp. 35–59.

Papadopoulos, R.K. (2007) 'Refugees, trauma and Adversity Activated Development'. *European Journal of Psychotherapy and Counselling*, September 2007, 9(3): 301–12. doi:10.1080/13642530701496930

Parry, J.T. (2010) *Understanding Torture: Law, Violence and Political Identity*. Ann Arbor, MI: University of Michigan Press.

Patel, N. (2007) 'Torture, psychology and the 'war on terror': a human rights framework'. In Roberts, R. (Ed.), *Just War: Psychology and Terrorism*. Ross-on-Wye: PCCS Books, pp. 74–108.

Pearlman, L.A. (2001) 'The treatment of persons with Complex-PTSD and other trauma-related disruptions of the self'. In Wilson, J.P., Friedman, M. and Lindy, J. (Eds.), *Treating Psychological Trauma and PTSD*, New York: Guilford Press, pp. 205–36.

Peters, E. (1996) *Torture*. Expanded edition. Philadelphia: University of Pennsylvania Press.

Physicians for Human Rights and School of Public Health and Primary HealthCare University of Cape Town, Health Sciences Faculty (2006) 'Dual loyalty and human rights in health professional practice: proposed guidelines and institutional mechanisms'. Available at: http://physiciansforhumanrights.org/library/report-dualloyalty-2006.html. (accessed 24 May 2011).

Pont, J., Stöver, H. and Wolff, H. (2012) 'Dual loyalty in prison care'. *American Journal of Public Health*, 102(3) (March): 475–80. doi:10.2105/AJPH.2011.300374

Prager, J. (2003) 'Lost childhood, lost generations: the intergenerational transmission of trauma'. *Journal of Human Rights*, 2(2): 173–81. doi:10.1080/1475483032000078161

Price, K. (Ed.) (1995) *Community Support for Survivors of Torture: A Manual*. Toronto, ON: Canadian Center for Victims of Torture.

Quiroga, J. and Jaranson, J. M. (2005) 'Politically-motivated torture and its survivors: a desk study review of the literature'. *Torture*, 16(2–3): 1–112.

Reisner, S. (2007) 'Ethical concerns about psychologists' participation in interrogation of detainees'. *Psychologist-Psychoanalyst*, 27: 23–9.

Reyes, H. (1995) 'The conflict between medical ethics and security measures'. In Gordon N. and Marton, R. (Eds.), *Torture: Human rights, Medical Ethics and The Case of Israel*. London and New Jersey: Zed Books, pp. 41–7.

Roche, P. (1992) 'Survivors of torture and trauma: a special group of patient with chronic pain'. *Australian Physiotherapy*, 38(1): 156–7.

Roncevic-Grzeta, I., Franciskovic, T., Moro, L. and Kastelan, A. (2001) 'Depression and torture'. *Military Medicine*, 166(6) (June): 530–3.

Rubenstein, L., Pross, C., Davidoff, F. and Iacopino, V. (2005) 'Coercive US interrogation policies: a challenge to medical ethics'. *Journal of American Medical Association*, 294: 1544–9. doi:10.1001/jama.294.12.1544

Schwab, G. (2010) *Haunting Legacies: Violent Histories and Transgenerational Trauma*. New York: Columbia University Press.

Saraceno, B., Saxena, S. and Maulik, P. (2002) 'Mental health problems in refugees'. In Sartorious, N., Gaebel, W., Lopez-Ibor, J.J., Maj, M. (Eds), *Psychiatry in Society*. New York: John Wiley, pp. 193–220.

Shalev, A.Y. (2002) 'Acute stress reactions in adults'. *Biological Psychiatry*, 51(7): 532–43.

Shalev, A.Y. (2004) 'Further lessons from 9/11: does stress equal trauma? *Psychiatry*, 67(2): 174–7. doi:10.1521/psyc.67.2.174.35958

Shannon, P.J., Wieling, E., McCleary, J.S. and Becher, E. (2015) 'Exploring the mental health effects of political trauma with newly arrived refugees'. *Qualitative Health Research*, 25(4) (April): 443–57. doi:10.1177/1049732314549475

Sherman, N. (2005) *Stoic Warriors: The Ancient Philosophy Behind the Military Mind*. New York, Oxford University Press.

Shoeb, M. Winstein, H. and Mollica, R. (2007) 'The Harvard Trauma Questionnaire: adapting a cross-cultural instrument for measuring torture, trauma and posttraumatic stress disorder in Iraqi refugees'. *International Journal of Social Psychiatry*, 53(5) (September): 447–63. doi:10.1177/0020764007078362

Sironi, F. (1999) *Borreaux et Victimes. Psychologie de la Torture*. Paris: Odile Jacob.

Sironi, F., Branche, R. (2002) 'Torture and the borders of humanity'. *International Social Science Journal*, 54: 539–48. doi:10.1111/1468-2451.00408

Smith, P.B. and Bond, M.H. (1993) *Social Psychology Across Cultures: Analysis and Perspectives*. Needham, MA: Allyn and Bacon.

Soldz, S. (2008) 'Healers or interrogators: psychology and the United States torture regime'. *Psychoanalytic Dialogues*, 18(5): 592–613. doi:10.1080/10481880802297624

Soldz, S. and Oloson, B. (2008) 'Psychologists rejects the dark side: American Psychological Association members reject participation in Bush detention centers'. Available at: www.zmag.org/znet/viewArticle/18906 (accessed 8 October 2009).

Somnier, F., Vesti, P., Kastrup, M. and Genefke, I.K. (1992) 'Psychosocial consequences of torture: current knowledge and evidence'. In Basoğlu, M. (Ed.), *Torture and Its Consequences: Current Treatment Approaches*. Cambridge: Cambridge University Press, pp. 56–71.

Sonntag, J. (2008) 'Doctors' involvement in torture'. *Torture*, 18(3): 161–75.

Spitz, S. (1989) *The Psychology of Torture*. Paper presented at the Center for the Study of Violence and Reconciliation, Seminar No. 3, 17 May.

Staub, E. (1978) *Positive Social Behaviour and Morality: Vol. 1. Social and Personal Influences*. New York: Academic.

Staub, E. (1989) *The Roots of Evil: The Origins of Genocide and Other Group Violence*. Cambridge: Cambridge University Press.

Staub, E. (1990) 'The psychology and culture of torture and tortures'. In Suefeld, P. (Ed.), *Psychology and Torture*. Washington, DC: Hemisphere, pp. 49–77.

Staub, E. (1993) 'Torture: psychological and cultural origins'. In Crelinsten, R.D. and Schmid, A.P. (Eds), *The Politics of Pain: Torturers and their Masters*. Centrum voor Onderzoek van Maatschappelijke Tegenstellingen/Center for the Study of Social Conflicts, AK Leiden, Netherlands: Leiden University, pp. 109–23.

Staub, E. (1997) 'The psychology of rescue: perpetrators, bystanders, and heroic helpers'. In Michalczyk, J. (Ed.), *Resisters, Rescuers and Refugees: Historical and Ethical Issues*. Kansas City: Sheed and Ward, pp. 137–47.

Staub, E. (1999) 'The roots of evil: social conditions, culture, personality and basic human needs'. *Personality and Social Psychology Review*, 3(3): 179–92. doi:10.1207/s15327957pspr0303_2

Staub, E. (2003) 'The psychology of bystanders, perpetrators and heroic helpers'. In Staub, E. (Ed.), *The Psychology of Good and Evil: Why Children, Adults and Groups Helps and Harms Others.* Cambridge: Cambridge University Press, pp. 291–324.

Staub, E. (2011) *Overcoming Evil: Genocide, Violent Conflict, and Terrorism.* Oxford, New York: Oxford University Press.

Staub, E. (2012) 'The roots and prevention of genocide and related mass violence'. In Anstey, M., Meerts, P. and Zartman, I.W. (Eds.), *The Slippery Slope To Genocide: Reducing Identity Conflicts and Preventing Mass Murder.* New York: Oxford University Press, pp. 35–54.

Steel, Z., Chey, T., Silove, D., Marnane, C., Bryant, R.A. and van Ommeren, M. (2009) 'Association of torture and other potentially traumatic events with mental health outcomes among populations exposed to mass conflict and displacement: a systematic review and meta-analysis'. *Journal of the American Medical Association*, 302(5): 537–49. doi:10.1001/jama.2009.1132.

Stover, E. and Nightingale, E.O. (1985) *The Breaking of Bodies and Minds: Torture, Psychiatric Abuse and the Health Profession.* New York: Freeman.

Suedfeld, P. (1990) 'Psychologists as victims, administrators, and designers of torture'. In Suedfeld, P. (Ed.), *Psychology and Torture.* New York: Hemisphere, pp. 101–14.

Suedfeld, P., Krell, R., Wiebe, R. and Steel, G.D. (1997) 'Coping strategies in the narratives of Holocaust survivors'. *Anxiety, Stress and Coping*, 10: 153–79.

Suedfeld, P. (2002) *Life After the Ashes: The Postwar Pain, and Resilience, of Young Holocaust Survivors.* Washington, DC: United States Holocaust Memorial Museum, Center for Advanced Studies, pp. 1–24.

Summerfield, D. (2001) 'The invention of post-traumatic stress disorder and the social usefulness of a psychiatric disorder'. *British Medical Journal*, 322: 95–8. doi:10.1136/bmj.322.7278.95

Summers, F. (2008) 'Making sense of the APA: a history of the relationship between psychology and the military'. *Psychoanalytic Dialogues*, 18: 614–37. doi:10.1080/10481880802297665

Sussman, D. (2005) 'What's wrong with torture'. *Philosophy and Public Affairs*, 33(1): 1–33. doi:10.1111/j.1088-4963.2005.00023.x

Taylor, S., Asmundson, G.J. and Carleton, R.N. (2006) 'Simple versus complex PTSD: a cluster analytic investigation'. *Journal of Anxiety Disorders*, 20(4): 459–72. doi:10.1016/j.janxdis.2005.04.003

Tec, N. (1986) *When Light Pierced the Darkness: Christian Rescue of Jews in Nazi-Occupied Poland.* New York: Oxford University Press.

Teegen, F. and Vogt, S. (2002) 'Survivors of torture: A study of complex posttraumatic stress disorders'. *Verhaltenstherapie and Verhaltensmedizin*, 23(1): 91–106.

Teegen, F. and Schriefer, J. (2002) 'Complex posttraumatic stress disorders: an investigation of the diagnostic construct in a sample of abused women'. *Zeitschrift für Klinische Psychologie, Psychiatrie und Psychotherapie,* 50(2): 219–33.

Teodorescu, D.S., Heir, T., Siqveland, J., Hauff, E., Wentzel-Larsen, T. and Lien, L. (2015) 'Chronic pain in multi-traumatized outpatients with a refugee background resettled in Norway: a cross-sectional study'. *BMC Psychology*, 3(1): 7. doi:10.1186/s40359-015-0064-5

Thomsen, A.M., Madsen, J.B., Smidt-Nielsen, K. and Eriksen, J. (1997) 'Chronic pain in torture survivors'. *Torture*, 7: 118–20.

Todorov, T. (1991) *Facing the Extreme: Moral Life in the Concentration Camps.* New York: Henry Holt, 1996.

Todorov, T. (2007) 'Torture in the Algerian war'. *South Central Review*, 24(1)(Spring): 18–26. Available at:www.jstor.org/stable/40039956 (accessed 4 January 2017)

Tower R. (2013) *Recognising Victims of Torture in National Asylum Procedures. A Comparative Overview of Early Identification of Victims and their Access to Medico-Legal Reports in Asylum-Receiving Countries*. Denmark: International Rehabilitation Council for Torture Victims.

Turner, S.W. (2000) 'Surviving sexual assault and sexual torture'. In Mezey, G.C. and King, M.B. (Eds.), *Male Victims of Sexual Assault*. Oxford, England: Oxford University Press, pp. 97–111.

United Nations High Commissioner for Human Rights, *Istanbul Protocol: Manual of the Effective Investigation and Documentation of Torture and Other Cruel, Inhuman and Degrading Treatment or Punishment*, Professional Training Series no. 8/Rev. 1, New York, Geneva, 2004.

Vaknin, S. (2005) *Malignant Self Love: Narcissism Revisited*. Prague and Skopje: A Narcissus Publications Imprint.

van der Kolk, B.A. (1989) 'The compulsion to repeat the trauma: re-enactment, revictimization, and masochism'. *Psychiatric Clinics of North America*, 12(2) (June): 389–411.

van der Kolk, B.A. (2001) 'The assessment and treatment of Complex PTSD'. In Yehuda, R. (Ed.) *Traumatic Stress*. Washington, DC: American Psychiatric Press, pp. 2–28.

van der Kolk, B.A. (2015) *The Body Keeps the Score: Brain, Mind, and Body in the Healing of Trauma*. New York: Penguin Books.

van der Kolk, B.A., Pelcovitz, D., Roth, S., Mandel, F.S., McFarlane, A.C. and Herman, J.L. (1996) 'Dissociation, affect dysregulation and somatization: the complex nature of adaptation to trauma'. *American Journal of Psychiatry*, 153(7): 83–93.

van der Kolk, B.A., Roth, S., Pelcovitz, D., Sunday, S. and Spinazzola, J. (2005) 'Disorders of extreme stress: the empirical foundation of a complex adaptation to trauma'. *Journal of Traumatic Stress*, 18(5): 389–99. doi:10.1002/jts.20047

van Ijzendoorn, M.H. and Bakerman-Kranenbers, M.J. (1997) 'Intergenerational transmission of attachment: a move to the contextual level'. In Atkinson, L. and Zucker, K.J. (Eds.), *Attachment and Psychopathology*. New York: Guilford Press, pp. 135–70.

Varvin, S. and Stajner-Popovic, T. (Eds.) (2002) *Upheaval: Psychoanalytical Perspectives on Trauma*. Belgrad: International Aid Network.

Verbitsky, H. (1996) *The Flight: Confessions of An Argentine Dirty Warrior*. New York: The New York Press.

Vesti, P. and Lavil, N.J. (1995) 'Torture and the medical profession: a review'. *International Journal of Humanities and Peace*, 11: 95–9.

Vorbrüggen, M. and Baer, H.U. (2007) 'Humiliation: the lasting effect of torture'. *Military Medicine*, 172: S29–S33. doi:10.7205/MILMED.173.Supplement_2.29

Weill, S. (2014) *The Role of National Courts in Applying International Humanitarian Law*. Oxford: Oxford University Press.

Wenzel, T., Greingl, H., Stompe, T., Mirzaei, S. and Kieffer, W. (2000) 'Psychological disorders in survivors of torture: exhaustion, impairment and depression'. *Psychopathology*, 33(6): 292–6. doi:29160

White, B., Driver, S. and Warren, A. (2008) 'Considering resilience in the rehabilitation of people with traumatic disabilities'. *Rehabilitation Psychology*, 53(1): 9–17. doi:10.1037/0090-5550.53.1.9

Williams, M. (2001) 'Survivors of torture: realities, responsible care, and rehabilitation'. *Journal of Applied Psychoanalytic Studies*, 3(3) (July): 259–71. doi:10.1023/A:1011531701210

Williams, A.C.D.C. (2003) 'Treating torture survivors: reduce pain and isolation'. *American Pain Society Bulletin*, (January–February): 3–6.

Williams, A.C.D.C. and Amris, K. (2007) 'Pain from torture'. *Pain*, 133(1–3): 5–8. doi: 10.1016/j.pain.2007.10.001

Wilson, J.P. and Drožđek, B. (2004) *Broken Spirits: The Treatment of Traumatized Asylum-Seekers, Refugees, and War and Torture Victims*. New York, Brunner-Routledge.

Wilson, J.P. and So-Kum Tang, C.C. (Eds.) (2007) *Cross-Cultural Assessment of Psychological Trauma and PTSD*. New York: Springer.

Witterholt, S. and Jaranson, J.M. (1998) 'Treating torture victims on site: Bosnian refugees in Croatia'. In Jaranson, J.M. and Popkin, M.K. (Eds.), *Caring for Victims of Torture*. Washington: American Psychiatric Association Press, pp. 243–52.

Wolfendale, J. (2006) 'Stoic warriors and stoic torturers: the moral psychology of military torture'. *South African Journal of Philosophy*, 25(1): 62–77. doi:10.4314/sajpem.v25i1.31434

Woolf, L.M. (2007, September 1) 'A sad day for psychologists: a major blow against human rights'. Available at: www.counterpunch.org/woolf09012007.htm (accessed 12 May 2012)

World Health Organization (1992) *The ICD-10 Classification of Mental and Behavioral Disorders: Clinical Descriptions and Diagnostic Guidelines*. Geneva, Switzerland: WHO.

World Medical Association, Declaration of Hamburg concerning Support for Medical Doctors Refusing to Participate in, or to Condone, the Use of Torture or Other Forms of Cruel, Inhuman or Degrading Treatment. Adopted by the 49th WMA Assembly, Hamburg, Germany, November 1997 and reaffirmed by the 176th WMA Council Session, Berlin, Germany, May 2007.

World Medical Association, Declaration of Tokyo – Guidelines for Physicians Concerning Torture and other Cruel, Inhuman or Degrading Treatment or Punishment in Relation to Detention and Imprisonment. Adopted by the 29th World Medical Assembly, Tokyo, Japan, October 1975, and editorially revised by the 170th WMA Council Session, Divonne-les-Bains, France, May 2005 and the 173rd WMA Council Session, Divonne-les-Bains, France, May 2006. Available at: www.wma.net/en/30publications/10policies/c18/ (accessed 15 December 2015).

Yawar, A. (2004) 'Healing in survivors of torture'. *Journal of The Royal Society of Medicine*, 97(8) (August): 366–70. doi:10.1258/jrsm.97.8.366

Yehuda, R., Halligan, S.L. and Grossman, R. (2001) 'Childhood trauma and risk for PTSD: relationship to intergenerational effects of trauma, parental PTSD, and cortisol excretion'. *Development and Psychopathology*, 13(3): 733–53. doi:10.1017/S0954579401003170

Yehuda, R., Halligan, S.L. and Bierer, L.M. (2002) 'Cortisol levels in adult offspring of Holocaust survivors: relation to PTSD symptom severity in the parent and the child'. *Psychoneuroendocrinology*, 27(1–2) (January–February): 171–80.

Yehuda, R., Engel, S.M., Brand, S.R., Seckl, J., Marcus, S.M. and Berkowitz, G.S. (2005) 'Transgenerational effect of post traumatic stress disorder in babies of mothers exposed to the World Trade Center attacks during pregnancy'. *Journal of Clinical Endocrinology and Metabolism*, 90(7): 4115–18. doi:10.1210/jc.2005-0550

Yordanova, K. (2015) 'Images of war: the place of the war past of the parents in the second generation's identity'. *Journal of Regional Security*, 10(1): 79–102. doi:10.11643/issn.2217-995X151SPY50

Young, A. (1997) *The Harmony of Illusions: Inventing Post-Traumatic Stress Disorder*. Princeton, NJ: Princeton University Press.

Zarowsky, C. and Pedersen, D. (2000) 'Rethinking trauma in a transnational world'. *Transcultural Psychiatry*, 37: 291–3. doi: 10.1177/136346150003700301

Zimbardo, P.G. (1972) 'The pathology of imprisonment', *Society*, 9(6): 4–8.

Zimbardo, P.G. (1975) 'On transforming experimental research into advocacy for social change'. In Deutsch, M. and Hornstein, H. (Eds.), *Applying Social Psychology: Implications for Research, Practice, and Training*. Hillsdale, NJ: Lawrence Erlbaum Associates, pp. 33–66.

Zimbardo, P.G. (2004) 'A situationist perspective on the psychology of evil: understanding how good people are transformed into perpetrators'. In Miller, A.G. (Ed.), *The Social Psychology of Good and Evil*. New York: Guilford, pp. 21–50.

Zimbardo, P.G. (2007) The *Lucifer Effect: Understanding How Good People Turn Evil*. New York: Random House.

Zimbardo, P.G., Haney, C., Banks, C. and Jaffe, D. (1999) *Stanford Prison Experiment*. Available at: www.prisonexp.org (accessed 2 February, 2009).

Zimbardo, P.G., Maslach, C. and Haney, C. (2000) 'Reflections on the Stanford Prison Experiment: genesis, transformations, consequences'. In Bass, T. (Ed.), *Obedience to Authority: Current Perspectives on the Milgram Paradigm*. Mahwah, NJ: Lawrence Erlbaum Associates, pp. 1–31.

PART 2
A psychoanalytic understanding of torture

4
PARADOXICAL MULTIPLE SELF STATES AND MONOLITHIC SELF STATES

Destinies of the Reflective Triangle

In this chapter, the theoretical foundations of a psychoanalytic understanding of torture are presented and discussed. The selected concepts proposed here are meant to lay the groundwork for a workable explanation of intrapsychic, interpersonal and group dynamics of social actors of torture, as described in Part 1.

Several authors from British object relations theories, American relational psychoanalysis and analytical psychology describe the development of the mind and its functioning in terms of a qualitative leap in mental and relational capacities in the passage from *states of twoness* to *states of thirdness*. In several theories, these mental states have been noticed and described under different terms. They are characterized by the use of different intrapsychic defence mechanisms, styles of feeling, thinking, and relating to internal objects and external subjects (i.e., from an interpersonal perspective).

These observations are well-suited to a conceptualization of self as a paradoxical multiplicity whose functioning is based on dissociation. In a number of psychoanalytic theories, be they Freudian or Jungian, the self is described as a paradox. The idea of a different quality of dissociation, corresponding to a different style of processing experience within the self, prompted here the hypothesis of a self, which is able to function in different modes. I am calling here *Monolithic Self State* (MSS) a self that is working predominantly in *states of twoness*, as well as *Paradoxical Multiple Self State (PMSS)*, a self in which *states of thirdness* are prevailing. In doing so, I suppose that in order to process experience in a flexible way, a self needs to keep open what I refer to as *in-between spaces* among different parts, i.e., splintered psyches, which is only possible under certain environmental conditions. Under such conditions, experience can be processed in a relatively creative way, since many elements and centers of experience of self are available for meaning-making activity. This is what I mean here as *states of thirdness*. The multiplicity and flexibility of a state of self not heavily dissociated, but dissociable in a flexible and adaptive way, enables self-reflection, relations to 'internal objects' and 'external subjects' and representation of the exchange between internal and external worlds through symbolization. This mode of functioning of self characterized by open *in-between spaces*, where thinking, symbolization, and reflectivity are possible, is the opposite of a self characterized by *foreclosed spaces*, in which the intrapsychic world is heavily shaped by sustained and rigid dissociation and splintered psyches orientate the functioning to a paranoid-schizoid mode. These states have interpersonal correlates, connecting people in a peculiar and strictly determined way. In such a mode, flexibility and plurality are not viable, while the perception of one's identity, the functioning of memory and the perception of time are also affected.

In the conclusion of the chapter, this dual functioning of self is illustrated through the idea of the *Reflective Triangle*, a modelling image to represent reflectivity. The image of the triangle is used to represent a state of mind, which differently connects three (real or phantasised) poles, i.e. Me, You and Other, to process emotions and thinking. The mode of using these three poles is critical to the way identity and difference are processed both intrapsychically and interpersonally, which, in turn, crucially affects the possibility of reflectivity and symbolization and relationships. I assume here that the *Reflective Triangle* is the underlying pattern of *states of thirdness*, in which the person is able to process simultaneously identity and difference in relation to others. Reflectivity arises out of the space of this triangle because it derives from the ability of keeping connections between these three ideal poles: Me, You and Other. The Me–You (and You–Me) segment of the triangle represents the processing of identity issues, while the Me–Other and You–Other segments represent the processing of issues of difference in relation to oneself and others. When this triangle splinters, we are in the grip of *twoness*: in different situations or in sequence, we are aware of either identity and not of differences (segment Me–You and You–Me), or of differences and not of identity (segment Me–Other and You–Other). As we will see, from a phenomenological point of view, this is linked to destructiveness as an attempt to look for difference when we are in the grip of identity, and to look for identity, when we are in the grip of difference (see Chapters 5 and 6).

A theoretical premise

The blend of theories used here, i.e., British object relations theory, American relational psychoanalysis and analytic psychology, is not very customary, although it has some legitimacy.

As is well known, these theories have different origins: relational psychoanalysis is a prolific development of the Freudian psychoanalytic tradition, partially including concepts from object relations theory, which expanded in the direction of a bi-personal conception of mind; analytical psychology is Carl Gustav Jung's theory, which explicates to some extent, although not exclusively, a monopersonal psychology. Nonetheless, I would make the point that there seems to be some cultural affinity between the two, which has not yet been sufficiently explored and recognized. As evidence for this common ground, a number of Jungian analysts are also members of the International Association of Relational Psychoanalysis and Psychotherapy or demonstrate in other ways their familiarity with relational thinking.[1]

This affinity between relational psychoanalysis and analytical psychology has been noticed previously (Fosshage and Davies, 2000; Giannoni, 2003, 2011; Kalsched, 2000; Lingiardi, 2000; Samuels, 2012; Young-Eisendrath and Dawson, 2008) and some conferences and review issues have been devoted to the subject in the last 15 years (see Beebe et al., 2001). For example, Young-Eisendrath and Dawson detect at least twelve vital psychoanalytic issues in which Jung can be seen as a precursor of recent development of 'post-Freudian' psychoanalysis, among them: 1) having moved the ego away from the center of the theoretical and the therapeutic projects of psychoanalysis; 2) an emphasis on a two-person psychology and intersubjective influences on unconscious relating; 3) the usefulness of the clinical use of counter-transference; and 4) the intertwining of the real relationship and therapeutic alliance in and out of the transference/counter-transference dynamics (Young-Eisendrath and Dawson, 2008: 4). Similarly, Giannoni (2011) points out that Jung's thinking created relational attitudes and meanings, in opposition to classical psychoanalysis, which are analogous to those developed in relational debates. He refers to: the idea that psychotherapy is interactive and the psychotherapist's involvement is the rule; the proposal that change occurs as a result of a psychic contagion in psychotherapy, where meaning-making activity results from an interaction of two unconscious minds, which are both transformed in the analytic encounter; and the suggestion of dissociation as a constant of the psychic functioning, rather than as a rare event. Recently, Jung was even regarded as a pioneering and prescient figure in the evolution of psychoanalysis in a relational direction (Samuels, 2012; Segdwick, 2013). Kalsched also expressly noted:

> I believe a Jungian approach has many modern elements that fit very well with contemporary psychoanalysis as practiced in the United States and Britain. I have alluded to several of these elements in the work of Bollas, Klein, Kohut, Khan, and others.
>
> (Kalsched, 2000: 483)

For space reasons and in order to avoid losing our main thread, we cannot go deeper into such an affinity. And, inevitably, similarities between these two different perspectives are here emphasized much more than differences, which are more evident and generally acknowledged.

This range of theories, different but similar, and to some respect complementary, allow for the mental correlates of the phenomenon of torture to be explored, bridging the gap between the internal and external realms, going from one area (the intrapsychic) to another (the interpersonal and even the social sphere) not feeling you are inappropriately crossing a disciplinary border between different fields of inquiry.

The paradox of the multiple self: multiplicity as unity and dissociation as continuity

The conception of self is crucial to understand many aspects of the phenomenon of torture, at different (intrapsychic, interpersonal, groupal) levels. For this reason, much space is devoted to theories exploring its functioning.

Beyond considerable differences, relational psychoanalysis and analytical psychology, each in its own terms, formulate an idea of self as a *paradoxical multiplicity* and dissociability as a crucial characterizing feature. In these theories, the self is at once represented as manifold and discontinuous, separate, integral and continuous (Mitchell, 1991; Bromberg, 1993, 1996; Jung, 1920, 1928), since it relies on dissociation as a crucial dynamic of its normal and pathological functioning (Mitchell, 1991, 1992; Bromberg, 1993, 1996, 1995a; Jung, 1920, 1934).

Stephen Mitchell

Stephen Mitchell offered an outstanding conceptualization of self, reworking the theoretical contributions of many authors in different theoretical traditions, i.e., object relations theory, self psychology, interpersonal theories, classical psychoanalysis and *infant research* (1991, 1993). In his theoretical review, he recognizes two main narratives of self: 1) a spatial representation derived from Freud's topographical and structural model, according to which the self is composed of parts and structures, and 2) a temporal metaphor, according to which the self is what people do and live in time, a subjective organization of meanings that a person creates in time, doing, feeling and reflecting on oneself and one's emotions.

For Mitchell, the unconscious is a constellation of meanings organized around relationships involving a way of being with others, a person in relation to other persons. The result is a plural and multiple organization of self around different images and representations of self and object. Thus, one of the paradoxes of self is that an individual experiences oneself in each moment as constituting a 'complete' self in the present with a sense of substantiality and integrity, despite the fact that this self is 'deeply embedded in relations with others' (Mitchell, 1991: 131). A common underlying idea of many object relations theories (Fairbairn, 1952; Winnicott, 1958) and interpersonal theories (Sullivan, 1950) is that we learn to become a person through interaction with different others and through different kinds of interactions with the same other, so that our experience of ourselves is discontinuous, composed of different self–other configurations, different selves with different others. Crucial is the ability to switch from one role and psychological state to another, as well as the flexibility with which this can be done (Mitchell, 1991: 128).

The arrangement of these relationships to different others is the source of both plurality and sense of continuity. The nature of self is interpersonal and dialectical, since it implies definitions of others; paradoxically, however, relations to others establish the inner possibility of a dialogue with ourselves, which ground the sense of privacy of the self. When we feel most 'private', most deeply 'into' ourselves, we are in some other sense most deeply connected with others through whom we learned to become a self (Winnicott, 1958).

Despite the importance of multiplicity and discontinuity of self, we can still recognize all our different versions of ourselves as versions of a more or less invariant 'myself'. There is an internal capability, operating as a self-reflective function, to perceive continuity of what is a passage from a state of self to another. Otherwise, we would have no way of prioritizing our goals, motives and impulses.

Mitchell derives from a complex of theories (Bollas, 1983; Grossman, 1982; Kohut, 1984; Stern, 1985) the idea that the self is nothing but a shift between multiple self-other representations, which characterizes the experience of selfhood in a particular moment.

Phillip M. Bromberg

In several seminal clinical papers, Phillip M. Bromberg (1993, 1994, 1996) recognizes 'the extraordinary capacity of human personality to negotiate continuity and change simultaneously' (1996: 509). According to his perspective, derived from the work of psychoanalysts such as Balint (1968), Fairbairn (1944, 1952), Searles (1977), Sullivan (1940, 1953), Winnicott (1960a, 1971) and Laing (1960), the self is a *decentred* unity and the mind is a 'configuration of shifting, non-linear, discontinuous states of consciousness in an on-going dialectic with the healthy illusion of unitary selfhood' (Bromberg, 1998: 270). Bromberg writes 'even in the most well functioning individual, normal personality structure is shaped by dissociation as well as by repression and intrapsychic conflict' (1996: 512). In this framework every person 'has a set of discrete, typically overlapping schemata of who he is, and . . . each is organized around a particular self-other configuration that is held together by a uniquely powerful affective state' (Bromberg, 1993: 161–2). The psyche is not unitary since its origin and it does not arise as a compact whole that becomes fragmented as a result of a pathological process. 'It is a structure that originates and continues as a multiplicity of self-other configurations . . . that maturationally develop a coherence and continuity that comes to be experienced as a cohesive sense of personal identity – 'an overarching feeling of "being a self"' (1998: 181). However, this experience of being a unitary self is a developmentally acquired adaptive illusion. In most people, this 'illusion' is taken for granted, while in other individuals the experience of continuity and integrity of the sense of self is not. In both cases, dissociation is at work. Paradoxically, dissociation functions in order to maintain personal continuity, coherence and integrity of the sense of self, *and* to avoid the traumatic dissolution of selfhood. It is not simply a defence mechanism, but a basic process that allows the individual self to function optimally when full immersion in a single reality, a single strong affect, and a suspension of one's own self-reflective capacity, is required by adaptation. This idea has a strong impact on the conceptualization of self, defence mechanisms, trauma, health and many other pivotal concepts of psychoanalysis (Bromberg 1993, 1995a, 1995b, 1996, 1998).

For example, the idea of trauma is reconceptualised as a disruption of this normal illusion of 'integration', which preserves most socially developed areas of the ego functioning, while the self state that is experienced as 'me' has little simultaneous access to other domains of personal experience or memory, and other self states holding incompatible experiences. In this way, dissociation preserves continuity by restricting the interpretation of experience, and in doing so, it masks the existence of this multiplicity (Bromberg, 1993, 1995a).

> Dissociation as an ego function is distinguished by the presence of a selectively amnesic mental state. As a global defence against on-going trauma or the fear of potential trauma, it represents an adaptive hypnotic capacity of the personality . . . to protect against . . . the real or perceived threat of being overwhelmingly incapacitated by aspects of reality that cannot be processed by existing cognitive schemata without doing violence to one's experience of selfhood.
>
> (Bromberg, 1998: 184)

In this way, it galvanizes the illusion of unitary selfhood by exploiting the incomplete autobiographical information available to the subject, furthering the human capacity for multiple engagements.

Carl Gustav Jung

Much earlier and within a different epistemological paradigm, Jung depicted the self as an irresolvable paradox. His conceptualization of self, his theory of complexes and the role played by dissociation in his theory partially overlap relational perspectives.

The early foundation of the paradox of self can be brought back to Jung's early empirical researches on associative processes (Jung, 1973), where he measured the physiological alterations that accompanied disturbances in associations to a list of stimulus words. Jung identifies these quantum units of unconscious activity by their psychosomatic, affect-laden, intrapsychic contents, which operate in discrete split-off bundles to become 'splinter psyches' with enough internal coherence and autonomy to invade conscious personality as *alien* states of mind (Jacobi, 1959). They are 'feeling-toned complexes' composed of core arousal states and emotional memories (in representational and non-representational forms), which may be either re-enacted or remembered (Jung, 1934: par. 201). Psychological complexes are both universal and personal, and both collective and individual in that they form around archetypes,[2] which are inherited but also express the psychic reality of an individual life. '[A] complex is capable of behaving for relatively short periods as if it were the dominant personality of the individual, who experiences this intrusion on the Ego's habitual standpoint with anxiety' (Beebe, *et al.*, 2001: 222). Only with considerable effort, complexes move into the field of awareness as elements of one's own personality and, even then, such complexes are only partially willing to be assimilated into consciousness (Jung, 1934).

For Jung, the ego is simply one complex among many, albeit the master complex with the capable image of the hero at its core, representing the archetypal tendency toward mastery. Jung saw the ego as the complex at the center of one's personal awareness, the unifying and integrating function, favouring a stable identity of perspective, i.e. a sense of 'I-ness'. However, given the multiplicity of selves other than the ego, even if they lack the latter's drive to achieve stability, each of these splinter selves has the potential to become a state of mind.

Some Jungian analysts have suggested that, rather than to speak of internal *objects*, we should speak of internal *subjects*, because complexes have their points of view, even their own ideologies (Knox, 2003b: 11, emphasis added). Often, they seem to possess a will, a life, and a personality of their own. Jung writes:

> The psyche is not an indivisible unity but a divisible and more or less divided whole. Although the separate parts are connected with one another, they are relatively independent, so much so that certain parts of the psyche never become associated with the ego at all or very rarely. I have called these psychic fragments 'autonomous complexes', and I base my theory of complexes on their existence. According to this theory, the ego-complex forms the centre characteristic of our psyche. But it is only one among several complexes. The others are more often than not associated with the ego-complex and in this way become conscious, but they can also exist for some time without being associated with it.
>
> (Jung, 1920: para. 582)

Jung's theory of complexes is a theory of healthy and pathological dissociation, according to the degree of autonomy, control and organizing power of the complex and its relation to the ego-complex. The complex has a healthy function to the extent that it has some reciprocal relationship to the ego-complex, processing some disconnected, unconscious part of personality, which performs a completing, restoring role. It is increasingly pathological to the extent that there is no recognition at all by the ego-complex and it acts as a completely *alien* part of personality, a case of divided self.

Besides this dissociative model of personality, expressed in the complex theory, Jung formulated a theory of integration and unity of self through its archetype (Young-Eisendrath, 2000).

Jung defined the self as an overarching personality structure encompassing the entirety of conscious and unconscious processes. Its nature is complicated, paradoxical, transcendent, and very potent. In Jung's works, the self is depicted at the same time as the center and the circumference of the psyche, and the ego as a 'content of that is in relation to it' (Jung. 1928: pars. 399–405). In *Psychology and Alchemy*, he writes:

I call this centre 'the self' which should be understood as the totality of the psyche. The Self is not only the centre, but also the whole circumference, which embraces both conscious and unconscious; it is the centre of this totality, just as the ego is the centre of consciousness.

(Jung, 1944: para. 41)

However, the nature of self, the essence of individuality, remains inherently out of reach and can be represented only through symbols of a numinous nature, producing a sense of wholeness that is self-validating: the king, the prophet, the hero, Christ (Jung, 1921: para. 790), and also 'the geometrical structures of the mandala containing elements of the circle and quaternity, namely circular and spherical forms . . . and quadratic figures divided into four or in the form of a cross' (Jung, 1951: para. 352). These symbols also have a quality of 'center' and convey the deeply satisfying sense of an ineffable and inviolable core of personality. This experience, more easily felt than conceptualized, is a mystical experience that results from a shift in the center from the ego, as the center of consciousness, to the self, as the center of consciousness and unconsciousness (Jung, 1928: para. 274).

Although much of Jung's writing on self emphasizes the results of a process of integration, his idea of self implies a model of mind as multiple. The concept of wholeness is not the same of unity, even if it does not exclude it. Speaking of a sense of 'center' implies that an organized multiplicity dwells within the self, as the symbol of mandala suggests.[3] The archetype of self provides Jung with a device toward ever-evolving consciousness and knowledge of ourselves, a developmental potential to become a 'psychological individual' who can be accountable for multiple centers of subjectivity and competing motivations, as well as a predisposition towards unity and integration (Young-Eisenrath and Hall, 1991; Young-Eisenrath, 1997), which is nonetheless, in Jung's words, a work against nature (*opus contra natura*).

The *in-between space*: an investigation into the phenomenology of *states of twoness* and *states of thirdness*

The aim here is to conceptualize the *in-between space* as something that psychoanalysis and analytical psychology have always revolved around. Several theorists from object relation theory, relational psychoanalysis and analytical psychology account for the development of mind by referring in some way to a shift from what it is here called a mental *state of twoness* towards a mental *state of thirdness*.

In infancy the mind develops as a result of interactions in a relational context, in the psychological intermediate space of a relational dyad, where an exchange of intentions and meanings occurs. From a developmental perspective, the aim of these exchanges is the arising of the baby's ability to connect its different self states and to symbolize from a third (among two) position, which is relatively unsaturated of pre-determined meanings. This prompts a range of intrapsychic and relational abilities, which includes the ability to understand one's own and others' mind, to think creatively, to recognize reality more appropriately, to take responsibility for one's own actions/decisions, and to develop a sense of subjectivity and agency. Different authors in psychoanalysis and analytical psychology stress different aspects and functions of this passage from *states of twoness* to *states of thirdness*.[4] I will clarify this point going through the following review.

Object Relations Theory

Melanie Klein

Melanie Klein's theory of the infant's passage from the paranoid-schizoid position to the depressive position can be considered one of the first developmental narratives of a transition from a mental *state of twoness* to a mental *state of thirdness*. Klein (1957, 1959) believed the infant was born with pre-programmed 'knowledge', the phantasy of the existence of the mother and basic body parts or functions, such as the breast. The paranoid-schizoid position (*a state of twoness*) predominates in the baby's first three months (Klein, 1946). She defines a 'part-object' as a part or aspect of the self or the other which may be all that the baby can perceive and relate to. The 'good-breast' and the 'bad-breast' are the prototypical part-objects, the initial focal points of the baby's mental life, which refer to the mother in her feeding role. Given the high intensity of living under the sway of absolute impulses ('death instinct' and 'life instinct'), with little life experience to modify their extremes, it would be impossible to relax into trust and love with the dread of imminent annihilation threat. So, by separating everything bad from everything good (splitting), the baby has the chance of experiencing total goodness and can introject this goodness (good object) as a base for his sense of self (Klein, 1946). The price of experiencing a kind of goodness that is uncontaminated by badness is that, at other times, the baby feels himself to be in the grip of pure evil, a 'persecutory anxiety', which is the hallmark of the paranoid-schizoid position. This dreadful experience partly arises out of an externally-derived bad experience, but also – Klein felt most powerfully – from the rebounding-back of the death instinct, which the infant has projected into the mother.

According to Klein, in the first months of the infant's life, mother and infant are involved in the interplay of projection and introjection of such mental contents on the basis of splitting (1946, 1963). In projection, impulses, which the baby cannot hold inside, are split off and propelled into the other, in order to get rid of one's own badness. Goodness is also projected. Introjection is another way of strengthening the division of experience into good and bad; it involves taking in goodness as a support, while taking in badness to make the outside world safer. Projection and introjection are rough-and-ready ways of coping with anxiety and making a link with another (Klein, 1957, 1959).

Projective identification is a more complex form of *twoness*, where the infant is busy in primitive non-verbal communication through projection into the caregiver's mind. In 1946, Klein introduced the phrase and defined it as 'the prototype of aggressive object-relationship' (1946: 101), by means of forcing parts of the ego into it the object in order to take over its contents or to control it (Hinshelwood, 1991). This defence may help to manage anxiety by appearing to get rid of a part of the self that feels painful or unmanageable, as well as offer the illusion of having some control over the other person. Under pressure, the other person starts acting according to this unwanted part, experiencing the feelings and impulses involved. The person projected into may have the urge to push the intruding forces straight back to the sender, without recognizing their projected origins (Hinshelwood, 1991: 179–208). Melanie Klein's theory suggests, in some way implicitly, that the mind develops from a mental *state of twoness* – the dynamic of projective identification – as the mother and the baby are two persons and, at the same time, they are one; they are already two persons, but, at the same time, they are yet to be.

During development, a qualitative leap in the skill to work through psychic contents occurs. It is the shift towards the depressive position (here understood as a *state of thirdness*) that comes into ascendancy in the second half of the first year, having begun to emerge more strongly at around three months (Klein, 1935). Klein does not fully qualify the exact nature of this change: when things go well enough, the baby is able to come to terms with the worst of the paranoid-schizoid anxieties. They have less need for the splitting, denial and projective defences, which have kept the persecutory anxiety at bay. With less need to distort their perceptions, the babies in the depressive position experience inner and outer reality more accurately, while recognize that the part-objects resulting from their splitting – the good and bad mother, father, self – are complex, whole people about whom they have mixed feelings. As internal and external objects become more integrated, the babies experience absence as the loss of the good, rather than simply as a result of a depraving attack by something bad. Instead of anger, their reaction is grief. Since the babies are now afraid of directing their anger outwards, they turns it inwards instead, criticizing themselves rather than the other person for being selfish and bad. The pain of guilt gives rise to a new capacity for reparation (Klein, 1940). This is the core of the depressive position. In the depressive position, a certain amount of conciliation among contradictory elements prevails, while the ego and its functions becomes more integrated, good and bad, me and other can be both contained, and the mind can keep playing with opposites. Consequently, the other can be recognized as a subject and so can the baby.

Wilfred R. Bion

Bion's narrative of psychic development advanced Klein's thinking by offering a more prominent description of how the mother potentiates such a progressive development. His focus is on the process of projective identification between mother and infant in order to highlight its communicative, empathetic role, promoting what is here conceptualized as a movement from a *state of twoness* to a *state of thirdness*. He understands that the concept of projective identification could bridge the intrapersonal and the interpersonal worlds.

According to Bion, thinking is a process that both requires and achieves emotional containment (1967, 1970). He uses the developmental image of the baby's experience of unverbalized and unverbalizable distress, which comes to be emotionally held by the parent's capacity to make some meaning out of the baby's experience and to have the baby and the baby's experience 'in mind' (Bion, 1962a, 1962b).

Bion (1962a) refers to *alpha function*, as the ability of the mother to create meaning out of raw, unprocessed sensory data from her infant, which he calls *beta elements*. Through her *rêverie* the mother can understand and modify the child's tensions and anxieties. She has a role as a container of her child's fear and apprehension, with mother and child forming a 'thinking couple', as container–contained, which is the prototype for the thinking process that continues developing throughout life. In Kleinian terms, satisfactory experiences with objects enhance the infant's feeling of attachment to, and love from, internal good objects and diminish the infant's fear of bad objects. The infant's split-off anxieties (projections) are contained, de-toxified and returned to the infant who introjects them, but now in a modified form. 'Unthinkable anxieties' and 'nameless dread' have (through the mother's *rêverie* or 'alpha function') become bearable. According to Bion's terms, the infant's *beta elements* (1962a), which are fit only for projection and splitting, are modified in *alpha elements* in a way similar to a chemical transformation: they become absorbable as food for thought. *Alpha elements* represent the *links* between our innate preconceptions and raw experiences of the external world. They form the building blocks of thought, upon which more complex systems can be built. The mother is thus responding to the infant by reflecting on the infant's own raw experience, about which he cannot think; over time, under such positive conditions, the infant gradually develops a capacity to think (and link) for himself as a result of the reintrojection of the modified bits of his primitive world. If the establishment of the *alpha function* with the mother's container function is impeded, thinking is seriously impaired. Bion (1959, 1962a) refers to the mothers' inability or unwillingness to accept the infant's projective identification as an 'attack on linkage' (1959, 1962a, 1962b). This behaviour is then internalized by the infant in the form of self-directed attacks on the efforts to link thoughts and generate emotional ties (linkages) to others.

However, the way this happens, is still problematic. Good experience of containment and maturation and the mother's ability to process the infant's raw material, do not fully account for the new acquired ability of the child; a modification of the quality of the infant's receptivity and meaning making system occurs in the interaction of projective identification. The child's mind becomes able to think their own *beta elements*. A third dimension is developed: the ability to create a distance from what is *happening* to oneself, thinking of it.

Donald W. Winnicott

In Winnicott's theory, the idea of mind as a *space in-between* resulting from a 'good enough' relationship with the mother becomes clearer (1965, 1971). Winnicott's infant develops a personal self through the protective care of a 'good-enough mother'. Through her initial close identification with her baby, which he terms 'primary maternal preoccupation' (Winnicott, 1956), she fosters an illusion of oneness with her baby, which makes them feel secure and even omnipotent. Gradually, the baby moves through bearable experiences of frustration and disillusionment to the point of realization that their own powers, while real, are limited. Winnicott suggests that with an 'average expectable environment' of loving care, the baby gathers a sense of continuity and coherence which coalesces into personal identity, with an emotional core of togetherness which he terms 'ego-relatedness' (Winnicott, 1958: 32–4).

The baby is, at first, only aware of their relative well-being or, conversely, the threat or actuality of falling into an unbearable state of 'annihilation', i.e. 'primitive agonies'. These latter are felt as 'going into pieces', 'falling forever', 'having no relation to the body', 'having no orientation in the world' and 'complete isolation' with no means of communication (1962, 1974). The 'good enough' mother protects the baby from these experiences through 'holding', 'handling' and 'object-presenting' (1945, 1956, 1960b, 1962, 1971). Her sensitive touch and responsive care of the baby's body will enable them to experience physical and emotional satisfaction in an integrated way. This will help the baby to bring together the worlds of sensation and emotion, thereby building a stable unity of mind and body (1945, 1962). The mother's protective holding is expressed through the way she carries, moves, feeds, speaks to and responds to her baby, and in her understanding of the baby's needs and experience (1953, 1960b: 47). The mother's holding enables the baby's 'true self', the spontaneous experience of being, to develop coherence and continuity. During periods of un-integration, the baby lays down his sense of existing over time and space as one being, existentially real and personally authentic. When the mother cannot give the baby the kind of holding and protection they need, they are jolted into shock and reaction. If these states of reactivity are frequent and prolonged, the baby will feel, to some extent, unreal, inauthentic, afraid of 'going to pieces'. They may cover their 'true self' with a 'false self', hiding their fraught inner state behind an outward appearance of coping and compliance (1960b). *Object-presenting* is the way in which the mother brings the outside world to the baby, giving the latter the possibility to find it and the illusion to create it. Through presenting objects and experiences in a way that is sensitive to her baby's state, the mother helps them to build a primitive conviction of omnipotence and 'dual unity', which is an essential prelude to disillusion. The baby develops a sense of oneness and trust in the world, which grows into an appreciation of both his connection with others and his separateness (1962).

Privation of attuned holding, handling or object-presenting will result in an overwhelming amount of unmanageable stimuli that will break the baby's peaceful state of simply being and the awareness of his separateness. Winnicott terms these traumatic experiences 'impingements', that is, fractures in the wholeness of being which the baby has no option but to accommodate (1962: 71). Failures in mother's adaptation to the infant's needs produce 'phases of reaction to impingement and these reactions interrupt the going on being of the infant. An excess of this reacting produces not frustration but a threat of annihilation' (1956: 303).

Winnicott's theory of transitional phenomena (Winnicott, 1971) is the closest developmental and relational idea of a *space in-between*. Transitional phenomena belong to the border between the child's early fusion with their mother and their dawning realization of their separateness. The transitional object is the blanket, rag or toy that the baby needs to be holding or sucking before they can go to sleep and which they may also carry around for most of the day. It is the emblem of the child's internal unity with a giving, accepting, nurturing mother. In this transitional zone, the baby finds they can use a particular object, sound, ritual or other happening as a way of managing their fears of being separate or alone. Its importance is that it both *stands for* and *is not* the mother. It is the beginning of the symbol-making, phantasy, play and thought process (1971), which moves beyond the single (transitional) object to words, play, culture, art and religion. It is a special area of psychological experience, personal to each of us, located between phantasy and reality and between one's inner and external worlds.

This is a creative space to express oneself, namely, 'potential space', a possibility for subjectivity to arise. It has a key role in the development and differentiation of the self and is the basis for play, creativity, empathy and all that lend richness to human experience. In this way, it facilitates psychological independence and the possibility to connect to other human beings (Winnicott, 1971).

Further developments

Thomas H. Ogden

For the purposes of our discussion, Thomas H. Ogden's theory (1986, 1989b, 1994a, 1994b) is particularly significant for its articulated reformulation of the Kleinian 'positions' as synchronic modes of organizing experience. His conceptualization of the passage from the *paranoid-schizoid mode* to the *historical mode* is a valuable and fitting elaboration of the shift from a mental *state of twoness* to a mental *state of thirdness*.

Ogden interprets Melanie Klein's view of psychological development as a biphasic development from the biological to the impersonal-psychological level, and from the impersonal-psychological to the subjective level. These are inherited modes of organizing experiences, constituted by characteristic forms of object relatedness, symbolization, mode of defence, type of anxiety, maturity of ego and superego functioning. They are not 'phases' that are passed through, but rather 'modes' that continue throughout life as co-existing and persisting ways of processing experience (Ogden, 1986). They do not exist in pure forms, and although emerging sequentially in early development, they also operate in dialectical tension with each other throughout the life cycle. The particular value of Ogden's contribution is its bridging between external and internal worlds, and between the intrapsychic object relations and interpersonal relationships.

Ogden's modes of organizing experience are referred to as: *autistic-contiguous*, *paranoid-schizoid* and *historical modes*.

The *autistic-contiguous mode* and bodily boundedness

The concept of the *autistic-contiguous mode* is an elaboration and extension of the work of Bick (1968, 1986), Meltzer (1975) and Tustin (1972, 1981, 1986). It is associated with an approach to experience that is of a sensation-dominated sort, characterized by protosymbolic impressions of sensory experience, which, taken together, help constitute an experience of bounded surfaces. The experience is at the level of sensation, particularly of the skin surface, in which raw sensory data are ordered by means of forming pre-symbolic connections between sensory impressions that come to constitute bounded surfaces, the rudiments of the experience of self (Ogden,1989a). To the infant, there is no dichotomy of body and mind, but a single, undifferentiated experience. In the early days, sensations and feelings are experienced as such, a primary whole of experience. Rhythmicity and experiences of sensory contiguity (especially at the skin surface) contribute, over time, to an elemental sense of continuity of being. In this position, the relationship to objects is one in which the organization of a rudimentary sense of 'I-ness', derives from the boundedness generated from relationships of contiguity, which give a sense of shape, created by the impression of the infant's skin surface when they are held by the mother, from the rhythmicity and regularity of the infant's sucking activity, and from the rhythm of the 'dialogue', in which mother and infant engage (Ogden, 1989a).

The *paranoid-schizoid mode*: a state of twoness devoid of an interpreting subject

The *paranoid-schizoid mode* (Ogden, 1986, 1994b) is a psychological organization characterized by a state of being relatively devoid of an interpreting subject, which mediates between the sense of 'I-ness' and one's lived sensory experience. It is a-historical, heavily reliant on splitting, idealization, denial, projective identification, and omnipotent thinking as modes of defence and part-object relations, as described by M. Klein (1946).

In paranoid-schizoid mode, the experience of loving and hating the same object generates intolerable anxiety, which constitutes the principal psychological dilemma to be managed. This problem is handled, in large part, by splitting in order to separate loving and hating facets of oneself, and loving and hating facets of the object. However, for Ogden, the assumption that the infant has a need to hate is not dependent upon the Kleinian assumption of the presence of powerful, constitutionally determined destructive wishes. The hate arises out of excessively frustrated needs. It is essential for a normal development that the infant, child or adult be able to experience this feeling without being too frightened by it. Splitting is not simply a defence, but a mode of organizing experience; it is about dividing experience into categories of pleasure and unpleasure, danger and safety, hunger and satiation, love and hate, me and not-me. 'Splitting is a boundary-creating mode of thought and therefore an order-generating (not yet a personal meaning-generating) process' (Odgen, 1986: 48). However, this mode prevents the existence of an interpreting subject with a continuous personal history through conscious and unconscious memory because of its discontinuities. In splitting, each event exists in itself, but not for a self: 'The early ego is devoid of subjectivity, a sense of "I-ness"' (1986: 48). In the paranoid-schizoid mode, the 'I', is an 'it'. Objects are valuable, but there is not yet an 'I' to love them or value them. According to Klein, the object is never split without a corresponding split in the ego (1946). Different facets of the object-related experience are isolated from one another. In splitting, one experience of relation between self and object has come apart from other similar or different experiences. The infant uses omnipotent thinking, projection, introjection, denial, idealization and projective identification to rearrange his internal object world in an effort to separate endangered aspects of self and object. The result is that early infantile experience is devoid of subjectivity: the infant is, at first, a prisoner of his own state of mind.

In this mode, there is no space between symbol and symbolized, which are emotionally equivalent: the symbol is what it represents (1988). It is a two-dimensional mode of experience, in which there is no interpreting subject mediating between the perception and one's thoughts and feelings. One does not interpret one's experience': one reacts to it with a high degree of automaticity, while omnipotent thinking magically 'resolves' the complexities of loving and hating. Thoughts and feelings are experienced as things in themselves: thinking has a concrete quality. The compartmentalization created by the massive use of splitting leads to a continual need of rewriting history (1986, 1988). The experience of time is that of an eternal present (1986: 61–4). However, the continual rewriting of history leads to a fragility and instability of the object, a rapidly shifting sense of self and object with each new affective experience of the object that 'unmasks' the other and discovers the 'truth' about whom the object is and always has been. In this realm of experience, anxiety takes the form of the fear of impending annihilation and fragmentation (1991: 595).

In this mode, the self is, to a large extent, a *self-as-object*, that is a self that does not perceive itself as the author of its own thoughts, feelings, sensations and perceptions, but as pounded by thoughts, feelings and sensations as if they were something that simply 'take place'. In the emotional vocabulary of this primitive mode of experience, guilt has no place. One's objects are not experienced as people with thoughts and feelings. They are experienced as things or forces that impinge on oneself, things to be loved, hated or feared, and not people valued as such. 'An object can be damaged or used up, but only a subject can be hurt or injured' (Ogden, 1988: 27).

A crucial question here arises as to how the infant ever breaks out of this state of mind. Ogden (1979, 1981, 1982, 1984, 1986), by reworking Klein's and Bion's contributions, notes that the concept of projective identification, implies an interpersonal component of the process. Klein emphasized that, in projective identification, unconscious contents are projected *into* (1946: 8), not *onto* the object. Bion (1962a) developed the idea of projective identification as a relationship of container and contained, which serves not only as a defence, but as a form of communication in which two personality systems modify each other (Bion, 1962a). Ogden takes a step further in this reasoning by learning from Winnicott: he states that the general significance of the concept of projective identification lies in its function as a bridge between the intrapsychic sphere of thoughts, feelings and phantasies and the interpersonal sphere of object relations with actual external subjects (Ogden, 1986: 46–7). The object is enlisted in playing a role in an externalized version of the projector's unconscious psychological state. *When a 'recipient' of a projective identification allows the induced state to reside within them without immediately attempting to rid themselves of these feelings, the projector-recipient pair can experience that which had been projected in a manner unavailable to the projector alone.* Ogden's understanding of projective identification emphasizes its being an interpersonal elaboration of the process of splitting, which creates a form of simultaneous oneness and twoness (unity and separateness of mother and infant), in turn, creating a potential for a kind of experience that is more generative than the previous one (Winnicott, 1956, 1971).

The *historical mode* and the rise of subjectivity

The *historical mode* of experience (partially overlapping Klein's depressive position) is characterized by a way of relating to other people and oneself as subjects (1988, 1991). It is a mode endowed with a sense of 'I-ness' mediating between oneself and one's lived experience. The other is experienced as a whole and separate subject with an internal life. The person has a historically-rooted sense of self, which is continuous, although shifting between different affective states, able to feel concern and guilt for the other, and wishing to make non-magical reparation for the possible damage done. In this mode, defence mechanisms are mature and allow the individual to tolerate psychological strain over time, instead of unthinkingly evacuating it into the other. Importantly, the interpreting subject develops the capacity for abstract symbolization and self-reflection through mediation between symbol and symbolized (Ogden, 1986, 1988, 1989b).

The psychological-interpersonal process of projective identification is one of the principal mechanisms by which the move from the paranoid-schizoid to the depressive position is carried out. Projective identification, here intended not simply as a defence mechanism, but also as a dynamic process enhancing psychic development, enables the infant to move from the initially closed system of a schizo-paranoid psyche to a more flexible integrating system, which is capable of creating subjective (and not predetermined) meaning out of experience.

According to Ogden, while the transition between these two modes has qualities of a quantum leap, it is misleading to talk about the 'achievement of the depressive position': it would be more accurate to say that one has begun to function to some extent in the mode of the depressive position, keeping in mind that this mode is undergoing continual development over the course of one's life, and that it always presupposes a simultaneous operation in the mode of the paranoid-schizoid position (1986: 69).

In this process of moving from part-object relatedness to whole-object relatedness, and from split-self experience to an experience of self as continuous, the range of transformations and advancements in the quality of experience are incredibly wide: an enhanced capacity to differentiate the self from the object, the development of the capacity for symbol formation, increased capacity to regulate affects, and more accurate reality testing and memory. As the infant becomes capable of experiencing themselves as interpreter of their perceptions, they were born as subject (1986: 72).

Once the infant has become an interpreting subject, for the first time they can project that state of mind into their sense of the other and consider that other people have feelings and thoughts in much the same way: empathy enters the scene of the mind. The awareness of the existence of others as subjects, as well as objects, lays the groundwork for the infant to feel concern for another person. As the infant or the adult becomes capable of feeling concern for another, as both a whole and separate person, i.e., a living human being, they then become capable of feeling guilt and wish to make reparation (1986: 80). It is possible for them to feel bad about the way they have hurt another person (in reality or in phantasy) and, to a certain extent, they become able to discriminate between real and imagined harm (1986: 74). Omnipotent solutions are no more a viable option.

This state of mind enables the person to develop a sense of history. The subject cannot pretend time does not exist, deleting the past and re-starting everything again and again indefinitely. The historical self comes into existence for the first time. History implies the capacity for self-reflection and symbolization. This is connected with a sense of responsibility towards one's actions. To the extent that there is not yet a subject in the paranoid-schizoid position, one cannot possibly take a responsibility for emotions that present themselves to a non-subjective self as forces and objects impinging upon. On the contrary, feelings of loss, guilt, sadness, remorse, compassion, empathy and loneliness are unavoidable burdens of a subject, as he becomes an historical human being. The advantage gained in this leap is a sense of humanity, empathy, and subjectivity, as well as the possibility of making relatively free choices (Odgen, 1986: 82–4).

Peter Fonagy

Although Peter Fonagy is not a relational analyst, but an attachment theorist, relationality is naturally at the core of his insights and creative theorizing. Fonagy and his collaborators coined the concepts of *mentalization* and *reflective function* (Fonagy, 2001; Fonagy and Target, 1996, 1997, 1998, 2002; Fonagy et al., 2002; Fonagy and Allison, 2012). *Mentalization* is defined as 'the capacity to understand and interpret human behaviour in terms of the putative mental states underpinning it as it arises through the experiences of having been so understood in the context of an attachment relationship' (Fonagy, 1999: 13). In turn, the *reflective function* is the capacity to reflect on the content of one's own mind, as well as others' minds, the ability 'to conceive of others' beliefs, feelings, attitudes, desires, hopes, knowledge, imagination, pretence, plans, and so on' (Fonagy, 2001: 165). Both arise in the form of end results of repeated early child-caregiver interactions, in which the parent provides links between reality and phantasy, while accurately reflecting the child's mental states.

According to Fonagy, the psychological self is a structure that evolves from infancy through childhood, with its development critically dependent upon interaction with more mature (benign and reflective) minds. It is not just a cognitive process, but developmentally commences with the 'discovery' of affects through primary object relationships. It involves both a self-reflective function and an interpersonal component, and is related to the development of both an agentive and a representational aspect of self (Fonagy and Allison, 2012).

Fonagy refers to the modern psychoanalytic theories of the development of self (Fairbairn, 1952; Kohut, 1977; Winnicott, 1960a) by assuming that the psychological self develops through the perception of oneself as someone with feelings and thoughts by another person's mind (Fonagy and Target, 1996). The internalization of this image performs the function of the 'containment of mental states'. Through the internalization of these perceptions, the infant begins to learn that his mind is not a direct replica of the real world, but a version of it (Target and Fonagy, 1996). The experience of containment involves the presence of another being, which not only reflects the infant's internal state, but represents it as a manageable image, as something that is bearable and can be understood. In this sense, although his theory is in continuity with the line of thinking of M. Klein, Bion, Winnicott, Ogden, Fonagy takes a step further, by grasping a crucial dynamic of this process: the *quality* of the caregiver's mirroring and containment. To favour the quality leap in the baby's mental functioning, the caregiver needs to communicate not only an accurate understanding of the baby's mental state, *but also* that she is able to manage it, which involves the symbolization of the baby's internal state and a finer affective regulation. For instance, in order to contain the baby's distress, maternal mirroring should involve a complex affect, combining anxiety with an affect unfitting with anxiety – e.g. irony. At some level, this combination communicates that there is nothing to be afraid of the caregiver's response is the same as the baby's, though not perfectly coincident with it. This paradox gives rise to the possibility of a second order representation of distress. This kind of communication of a widened cognitive-emotional response is at the origin of the symbolizing process (Fonagy, 2001).

In this way, mentalization offers to the child: 1) the opportunity to find meaning in people's actions; 2) a clear demarcation between inner and external reality, between 'me', and 'other'; 3) the capacity to handle mental representations; and 4) a good level of intersubjective contact with others; in other words, the possibility for the child to be more in touch with their own and others' feelings, beliefs, and desires (Target and Fonagy, 1996).

If the caregiver cannot reply with adequate mirroring, the baby's distress will be avoided or mirrored without being mentalized, with the baby tending to interiorize the caregiver's defences, thereby creating intolerable gaps in self-experience. In absence or in case of distortion of this mirroring function, what arises is a psychological functioning in which internal experiences are scarcely represented, with a desperate need for alternative ways to contain psychological tension (for example, some forms of self-harm behaviour or aggression towards other people) while the affect is used in an instrumental (manipulative) way, rather than in a signalling (communicative) way (Fonagy, 2001). If a child is mistreated and traumatized by their parent, in order to get rid of the thought of such a parent as malevolent and dangerous, the child may defend themselves by inhibiting the development of their ability to mentalize: the child stops thinking of others in terms of intentions, beliefs, and desires, as they involve the danger of becoming real. The child's incapacity to keep ideas in mind or to give meaning to actions will make them prone to action, increasing their impulsiveness and violence toward others and their own body, experienced as 'other'. The failure to find another's mind in which the child may see their own mind represented, will lead to continuous attempts to find alternate ways of containment with increasing use of projection, lower awareness of being separated from others, and more dependence (Fonagy, 1995; Fonagy and Target, 1997, 1998). An absent or insufficient reflective function leaves the individual in that state of disintegration that manifests itself through intrapsychic and interpersonal *states of twoness*, as described above, and documented in Fonagy's works on borderline personality and trauma (Bateman and Fonagy, 2004; Fonagy and Bateman, 2007; Fonagy and Target, 2008; Fonagy *et al.*, 2003).

American Relational Psychoanalysis

Philip M. Bromberg

As outlined before, Bromberg is interested in the introspectively and clinically observable coexistence of 'multiple versions of the self', that may represent crystallizations of different interactional schemes (1996, 1998). At the core of Bromberg's vision, is a complex view of mind as a nonlinear system of loosely-related self states and self-representations. What sets the degree of connection or foreclosure among the component self states is an ever-shifting balance between the individual's self-protective, conservative aims (the fear of trauma and its repetition, for example) and an intrinsic movement towards human relatedness, growth, and development (openness to eventuality and the future, trust in human relationships, etc.). Given this dialectic, Bromberg's proposal is that the self is a system in which dissociation is a normative developmental process central to both character formation (1996, 1998, 2006) and, when intensified by trauma, character pathology. In his theory, the self is portrayed as a field of continuity and discontinuity with dissociation as both a normal and a pathological mechanism, which also intervenes in regulating the self and intersubjective relations. His (clinical) ideas of 'enactment' and 'standing in the spaces' (1998) are here understood as intersubjective formulations of mental states *of twoness* and mental *states of thirdness*.

'Enactment' refers to both patient and analyst as 'an interpenetrating unit,' in which analyst and patient become enmeshed in a narrow and concrete 'tunnel of reality', whereby both become entrapped in a shared dynamic emanating from the patient's dissociation (Bromberg, 2001: 520). New relational experience emerges from working out these 'tunnels'.

One might suppose that what the patient is doing, when involving another in the enactment, is to look for a new object, trying to create the needed new experience, as well as tending to repeat the old unreflected one. In this sense, the dissociation implied in the enactment can be understood as a *foreclosed space*, where patient and analyst participate in this *state of twoness*, in which they 'enact' together something that has not reached reflection yet. The analyst needs to recognize each dissociated part of self, or each self state, in order not to invalidate any one, reinforcing dissociation. When therapists are willingly carried along into an enactment, they allow themselves to become therapeutic objects (1996, 1998).

I understand Bromberg's concept of enactment as an evolution, in interpersonal terms, of what object relations theorists thought in terms of projective identification. One can observe a line of development of this concept from the intrapsychic realm of object relational theorists to an emphasis on the co-construction of interpersonal dynamics of modern relational psychoanalysts (Bromberg, 1996: 527), who claim that the analyst is able to wake up the patient's dissociated aspects through the analyst's participation in the enactment with the patient. Bromberg (1993) argues that the narrative told by the patient 'cannot be edited simply by more accurate verbal input. Psychoanalysis must provide an experience that is perceivably (not just conceptually) different from the patient's narrative memory' (1993: 391). The central aspect of this process is that the patient–analyst relationship is inevitably drawn into the process. Enactment would be 'the primary perceptual medium that allows narrative change to take place' (1993: 391). This relational experience, in which the analyst is able to recognize and be personally responsive to the patient's dissociated negative affect, is generally a pivotal change moment.

'Standing in the spaces' (1993: 166; 1998) is Bromberg's shorthand way of describing a person's relative capacity to make room, at any given moment, for subjective reality that is not readily containable by the self but he experiences as 'me' at that moment. In other words, 'standing in the spaces' is a certain temporary capacity of linking different and possibly contradictory self states. It indicates the fragile texture of an empty *space in-between*. Bromberg effectively describes health as the ability of inhabiting what we have referred to as *state of thirdness*:

> Health is not integration. Health is the ability to stand in the spaces between realities without losing any of them. This is what . . . self-acceptance means and what creativity is really about – the capacity to feel like one self while being many.
>
> (Bromberg, 1993: 186)

Jessica Benjamin

Jessica Benjamin offers an outstanding investigation into mental *states of twoness* and *thirdness* from an intersubjective and feminist perspective, particularly in her works about domination (1988, 1990) and the 'shared third' (2004). Her point of view is focused on relationships as site of actualization of important psychic processes (1988, 1990, 1998, 2004). Benjamin proposes the intrapsychic and intersubjective realms as being complementary, even though they are sometimes presented as oppositional (1990). Her intersubjectivity is in contrast with the logic of subject and object, which is predominant in Western philosophy and science, and considers that the other is not merely the object of the Ego's need/drive or cognition/perception, but a separate and equivalent center of self. Intersubjectivity postulates as a crucial concept that the other must be recognized as another subject in order for the self to fully experience his or her subjectivity in the other's presence.

Benjamin's most remarkable contribution to the analysis of *states of twoness* is her work on the interplay between love and domination. In *The Bonds of Love* (1988), she conceives domination as a two-way process, a system involving the participation of those who submit to power, as well as those who exercise it. Benjamin's reasoning starts from Simone de Beauvoir's insight 'that woman functions as man's primary other, his opposite – playing nature to his reason, immanence to his transcendence, primordial oneness to his individuated separateness, and object to his subject.' (Benjamin, 1988: 7) This is the first fundamental premise of domination. Benjamin analyses the conflict between dependence and independence in infant life, and moves outward towards the opposites of power and surrender in adult sexual life. She describes how masculinity and femininity within their development, become associated with the posture of master and slave (1988).

In her view, in order to challenge the sexual split which permeates our psychic, cultural and social life, it is necessary to criticize not only the idealization of the masculine side, but also what she considers a reactive valorisation of femininity. In fact, to reduce domination to a simple relation of doer and done-to is an oversimplification that ends up reproducing the structure of gender polarity instead of dismantling it (Benjamin, 1988, 1990, 1998, 2002, 2004). Domination begins with the attempt to deny dependency. No one can truly extricate oneself from dependency on others, from the need of recognition. The child not only needs to achieve independence, but must be recognized as independent by the very people on whom he has been most dependent. He may be tempted to believe that he can become independent without recognizing the other, believing that the other is not separate. Alternatively, the child may continue to see the mother as all-powerful, and himself as helpless. Balance within the self depends upon mutual recognition between self and other. And 'mutual recognition is perhaps the most vulnerable point in the process of differentiation' (1988: 53).

In order to exist for oneself, one has to exist for an other. Benjamin conceptualises domination as the consequence of refusing this fundamental condition. 'Since the subject cannot accept his dependency on someone he cannot control, the solution is to subjugate and enslave the other – to make him give that recognition without recognizing him in return' (1988: 54). On the other hand, masochism is a search for recognition 'through an other' who is powerful enough to bestow this recognition. Submission becomes the 'pure' form of recognition, as much as violation becomes the 'pure' form of self-assertion. However, since a slave who is completely dominated loses the quality of being able to give recognition, the struggle to possess her must be prolonged. She must be enslaved piece by piece; new levels of resistance must be found, so that she can be vanquished anew (1988).

Thus, the basic tension of forces *within* the individual becomes a dynamic *between* individuals. Paradoxically, this erotic complementarity offers a way to simultaneously break through and preserve the boundaries: in the opposition between violator and violated, one person maintains his boundary and the other allows her boundary to be broken. One remains rational and in control, while the other loses her self. Thus, the desire to inflict or receive pain, even as it seeks to break through boundaries, is also an effort to find them. Master and slave, sadist and masochist become a complementary unit.

Interestingly, loss of tension represent both the beginning and inevitable end of this story. Benjamin points out that omnipotence and loss of tension actually refer to the same phenomenon: omnipotence, whether in the form of merging or aggression, means the complete assimilation of self to the other and, consequently, it corresponds to the zero point of tension between self and other (1988, 1990). But, this merging leaves the self encapsulated in the closed system of the omnipotent mind. This apparent first cause is itself the result of an earlier breakdown between self and other, deriving from a failure of differentiation: domination is an alienated form of differentiation, an effort to recreate tension through distance, idealization and objectification. It is destined to repeat the original failure unless and until the other makes a difference (1988, 1990). Winnicott's idea of the role of destruction becomes a pivotal concept in understanding the interpersonal dynamics of domination and submission (Winnicott, 1971). In Winnicott, the baby's aggression 'creates the quality of externality' (Winnicott, 1971: 110). Thus, destruction is a way to differentiate the self – an attempt to place the other outside one's phantasy in order to experience her as external reality. 'When destructiveness damages neither the parent nor the self, external reality comes into view as a sharp, distinct contrast to the inner phantasy world. The outcome of this process is not simply reparation or restoration of the good object but love, the sense of discovering the other' (Benjamin, 1999 [1990]: 192). Thus, in intersubjective terms, violation is the attempt to push the other outside the self, to attack the other's separate reality in order to finally discover it. The controlled practice of sadomasochism portrays a classic drama of destruction and survival. To halt this cycle of domination, the other must make a difference surviving the attack (Benjamin, 1988).

Benjamin is interested in the question of how we break out of retaliatory cycles and complementary (doer–done to) relations (1988, 2002, 2004). Elaborating on Ghent's idea of surrender (1990), Benjamin states that the third is that to which we surrender. In her thinking, the term surrender refers to a certain letting-go of the self, which, in turn, implies the ability to take in the other's point of view on reality. Surrender requires a third principle or process that mediates between self and other. In the complementary structure, dependency becomes coercive; and indeed, coercive dependence that draws each into the orbit of the other's escalating reactivity is a salient characteristic of the impasse. Conflict cannot be processed, observed, held, mediated or played with. 'The idea of complementary relations . . . aims to describe those push–me/pull–you, doer/done-to dynamics that we find in most impasses, which generally appear to be one-way.' (Benjamin, 2012 [2004]: 94). 'Symmetry is a crucial part of what unites the pair in complementarity . . . each feels unable to gain the other's recognition, and each feels in the other's power . . . each feels the other to be the abuser-seducer; each perceives the other as 'doing to me'.' (Benjamin, 2012 [2004]: 95) In complementary relations – the relation of states of twoness – there appear to be only two choices: either submission or resistance to the other's demands. Each partner feels their own perspective as the only right one. This is what Benjamin (2004) calls the *doer/done-to mode*.

Benjamin believes that the recovery of subjectivity requires the recognition of one's own participation. Once a person has deeply accepted one's own contribution to the co-created situation, that person will surrender to the principle of reciprocal influence in interaction, which fosters both responsible action and freely given recognition.

In her description of *thirdness* as a quality of mental space, Benjamin highlights the idea of the third as a reflective space based on mutual recognition. Benjamin's interest in the third is not in the reified 'thing', but in the *process of creating thirdness* – that is, in how we build relational systems and how we develop the intersubjective capacities for such co-creation. In close relation to Winnicott's idea of potential or transitional space, she thinks of thirdness as a quality or experience of intersubjective relatedness that has as its correlate a certain kind of internal mental space (1990, 2004). This opens up the potential to negotiate differences while connecting to others. The experience of surviving complementary breakdowns, or twoness, and the subsequent restoration of dialogue are crucial to this aim. From survival a more advanced form of *thirdness* can emerge, based on the symbolic or interpersonal third.

For the symbolic third to actually work as a true third, a person needs to have integrated the capacity for accommodation to a mutually created set of expectations. Benjamin retraces this ability back to the mother–infant dynamics of mutual regulation and resonance, referring to what the infant research calls rhythmicity (Sander, 2002). Rhythmic experiences help constitute the capacity for thirdness, while rhythmicity may be seen as a model principle underlying the creation of shared patterns (Benjamin, 2002). Benjamin thinks of the rising of thirdness as an intersubjective process already present in the early presymbolic experiences of accommodation and mutuality between mother and child, and in the intention to recognize and to be recognized by the other, which she terms *shared intersubjective third* (Benjamin, 2004, 2006, 2009). Benjamin goes back to the early experiences of this state of thirdness, finding them in rhythmic experience of *the one in the third* and *the third in the one* (Benjamin, 2004).

The rhythmic *one in the third* corresponds to the principle of *accommodation*, while *the third in the one* is more like the principle of *differentiation*. While it is crucial for the mother to identify with the baby's need – for instance, adjusting herself to the feeding rhythm – (*the one in the third*), there are also inevitable moments when *twoness* arises, for example, in the form of the mother's need for sleep, i.e., the claims of her own separate existence (*the third in the one*). Here, the function of the third is to help transcend twoness neither by self-abnegation, nor by fostering the illusion that mother and baby are one; instead, at this point, the principle of asymmetrical accommodation should arise from the sense of surrender to necessity, rather than from submission to another person's tyrannical demands or an overwhelming task. Thus, the synergy of the *attunement function* – the *one in the third* – with the *differentiating* and *containing function* – the *third in the one* – is the place where self-regulation and mutual regulation meet, combining differentiation with empathy, rather than creating projective confusion.

Nonetheless, recognition inevitably and repeatedly breaks down, and thirdness always collapses into twoness (Benjamin, 2004).

Analytical Psychology

Almost all Jungian theory might be expressed through the vicissitudes of mental *states of twoness* and *thirdness*. As a matter of fact, in Jungian terms the psyche is a self-regulating system based on principles of compensation and complementarity, and can be understood as inexhaustible play among polarities that join in tension, generating psychic dynamism. Consequently, a comprehensive analysis of Jungian concepts of twoness and thirdness is an arduous undertaking and beyond the goals of this work.

What follows is a limited investigation into *some* concepts of analytic psychology in order to indicate that Jung formulated a theory of mind firmly based on the crucial importance of such interplay between mental *states of twoness* and *thirdness*. Differently from other authors, Jung does not systematically address developmental issues. However, some of his ideas on intrapsychic or relational dynamics are coherent with a model of self as a paradoxical multiplicity regulated by dissociation, which works in terms of states of twoness and states of thirdness. The aim of this type of self is to develop a quality of 'midway' for psychic processes, i.e., to open potential *in-between spaces* among its splinter and oppositional psyches for meaning making activity, which is ultimately the realm of symbols.

States of twoness: 'participation mystique' and shadow

We have seen that in Jung's theory the paradoxical nature of self, as center and totality of personality, is conceptualized against the background of an idea of mind as a plurality of dissociable complexes and multiple centers of subjectivity, loosely organized around the ego-complex and with its core in the archetype of self.

Although everyone strives for a coherent and continuous sense of self, this state of being is not easily sustained or ever finally secured. 'Psychological complexes' are experienced as motivating forces with core affective and image components that are highly arousing (Jung, 1934). Young-Eisendrath (2000, 2004) notices that when unconscious complexes overtake ordinary consciousness, they seek an other person's participation by invitation, offer or demand. We can consider enactments of complexes as states of interpersonal twoness, in which one person communicates unconsciously inviting another to play out some aspect of the complex. The receiving person may be familiar with the projected material, because of the universal nature of archetypes and emotions. Identifying with the other's projection, we play a role in the other's inner theatre that fits closely enough with something of our own. With this idea, we are somewhere between 'projective identification' and 'enactment'.

Jung called this form of enmeshment – an apparent state of twoness – *participation mystique*, borrowing the term from the anthropologist Lévy-Bruhl, in order to conceptualize a state of unconscious identity between the individual and the environment (or others), without awareness of being in such a state. This expression also indicates all those cases in which the subject cannot be clearly distinguished from the object, but it is tied to it in a primitive relationship of partial identity. Jung writes,

> [*Participation mystique*] consists in the fact that the subject cannot clearly distinguish himself from the object but is bound to it by a direct relationship which amounts to partial identity ... Among civilized peoples, it usually occurs between persons, seldom between a person and a thing. In the first case, it is a transference relationship ... In the second case, there is a similar influence on the part of the thing, or else an identification with a thing or the idea of a thing.
>
> (Jung, 1921: para. 781)

The concept of *participation mystique* is also connected to that of *abaissement du niveau mental*, the effects of which are as follows: 1) a loss of entire sections of personality, which are normally in control; 2) the production of dissociated fragments of personality; 3) the obstruction of normal logic thinking; 4) a reduction in the sense of responsibility and adequate ego reactions; 5) incomplete representation of reality and triggers of inadequate emotional reactions; and 6) a lowering of consciousness, which causes an automatic penetration of unconscious contents into the field of consciousness. Negative aspects of this state, such as confusion, identity loss or panic often appear dominant; as Jung stressed, 'compulsion and impossible responsibility' (1957: para. 78) can accompany interactions dominated by *participation mystique*.

Thus, *l'abaissment* triggers a restriction of conscious personality and, at the same time, compensates this latter with characteristic unconscious phenomena, such as *rêveries*, which paradoxically may also have the effect of an enlargement of personality (Jung, 1934, para. 215). This is because *participation mystique* has the power to break down inner psychic boundaries, as well as those between a person and the object world. This breakdown of structures is essential to any qualitative personality change. In his *Commentary to the Secret of the Golden Flower*, Jung maintains that the goal in therapy is the dissolution of those fusion states between subject and object that can be considered *participation mystique* (1957: pars. 65–6). In analysis, a perspective gradually develops in the patient's personality that is 'midway' or between the ego-complex and other complexes, which encompass both. It is the work of the self, the depersonalized (not personified) 'character' which embodies the pure 'being between', the 'midway' of opposites. Once the self becomes the center of personality, *participation mystique* is done away with. Thus, Jung emphasized the role of the self in breaking the compulsive tie between subject and object.

Another Jungian concept that illustrates an intrapsychic state of twoness is that of *possession by the shadow*. The shadow is, in Jung's view, a well-defined 'figure' outside the firmly circumscribed ego boundary to which it bears a complementary relationship (Jung, 1917: para. 103). He writes: 'By shadow, I mean the 'negative' side of the personality, the sum of all those unpleasant qualities we like to hide, together with the insufficiently developed functions and contents of the personal unconscious' (Jung, 1917: 66, fn.5). Jung sees possession as a neurotic or even psychotic state, in which shadow contents override the ego and control the personality. The shadow is, in Jung's work, generally considered morally inferior and dark: integration of the shadow demands a 'dialogue' where the opposites are recognized, which has as its goal the overcoming of the conflict of opposites for the sake of totality (Jung, 1934: para. 85). There are two ways to experience shadow contents: they remain unconscious and are projected onto others; or the person identifies with them and assimilates them into a richer sense of personality. The confrontation with the shadow is conceived as a moral problem, since a 'moral differentiation is a necessary step on the way of individuation. Without knowledge of "good and evil", ego and shadow, there is no recognition of the self, but at most an involuntary and therefore dangerous identification with it' (Jung, 1973: 154). It is primitive identity, or possession. Identity with the shadow is a 'blinding' state of twoness: for example, we may consciously believe to be acting 'good', while unconsciously perpetrating 'evil'. Possession by the shadow is not, however, something that occurs only at an individual or personal level; it also includes the possibility of group possession by the collective shadow.

On the contrary, confrontation with the shadow should eventually result in a *coniunctio* (a term that Jung borrows from alchemy): in such a case, what was hidden behind the conventional mask of the shadow is raised to consciousness and integrated into the ego (Casement, 2006). It is a struggle that has to be lived through and cannot be abolished by rational means or repression. Shadow contents involve known and unknown aspects of the self, making the ego, the unconscious and the environment all play a role in its expression or repression.

States of thirdness: coniunctio oppositorum, transcendent function, symbol

We have seen that in Jung's theory states of twoness always tend towards thirdness, until they eventually breakdown into new states of twoness. *Coniunctio oppositorum* is the principle that opposites contain, generate and eventually join with each other in the psyche, thus enabling us to cope with duality, resolve divisive conflicts and resist one-sided ego. *Coincidentia oppositorum* and *unio oppositorum* transform conflicting opposites into a synthesis or homeostasis that preserves their essential tension and energy and generates new meaning. In alchemic terms, the opposites of the *prima materia* join with each other in a '*hieros gamos*', i.e. a ritual marriage (1955–1956: para. 207).

Accepting the principle of *coincidentia oppositorum* can encourage, for example, the integration of the shadow and discourage the corrupting hypocrisy, scapegoating and alienation, which occur when we repress and project the shadow (Jung, 1959: para. 814). *Coincidentia oppositorum* represents Jung's psychological and ethical ideas of: 1) a balanced wholeness that makes use of opposites, while maintaining their vital tensions; and 2) relational interdependence that ends alienation, while maintaining respect for the autonomy of others.

The process of individuation implies the resolution of a number of states of inner conflict and opposition. It results from the union of opposites (conscious and unconscious, spirit and matter, male and female, old and young, powerful and powerless, etc.) which brings about wholeness, psychic totality, integral personality, and the development of a mature self. However, it must be said that the self, as a goal or end product of the union of opposites, cannot be realized once and for all (Jung, 1955–1956: para. 759).

This work is carried out through the *transcendent function* (Jung, 1916, 1921, 1940), which opens the door to greater self-knowledge. In Jung's terminology, the *transcendent function* is the smallest unit of psychic movement. It is the symbolic function par excellence, thanks to which psychic elements, earlier differentiated and characterized as opposite or alien to each other, are rejoined in a non-synthetic unity. The term 'transcendent' emphasizes the fact that it 'facilitates a transition from one attitude to another' (Jung, 1921: para. 818). For Jung, 'transcendent' does not refer to a metaphysical nature, but the ability of mind (self in particular) to go beyond the border that separates and joins consciousness and unconscious or the elements of a couple in psychic dialogue, through the *symbol*. According to its Greek etymology, the term 'symbol' means 'put together', 'compose' (Jung, 1912). In it, a tendency towards the reunion of opposite psychic polarities can be observed. These opposites can be contents or structures of the psyche, being the main opposite consciousness and unconscious in the self (Jung, 1912).

However, this passage from *states of twoness* to *states of thirdness* is a process that produces suffering, particularly for the ego in a *state of twoness*. As far as consciousness cannot stay in contradiction, the unconscious can inhabit it. But, if the ego can recognize its being inhabited by the unconscious, psychic dynamism and significant psychic events are present because opposites have been kept in tension. It is the experience of

> an agonizing situation of conflict from which there seems to be no way out – at least for the conscious mind, since as far as this is concerned, *tertium non datur*. But, out of this collision of opposites, the unconscious psyche always creates a third thing of an irrational nature, which the conscious mind neither expects nor understands. It presents itself in a form that is neither a straight 'yes' nor a straight 'no' and is consequently rejected by both. For the conscious mind knows nothing beyond opposites and, as a result, has no knowledge of the thing that unites them. Since, however the solution of the conflict through the union of opposites is of vital importance, and is moreover the very thing that the conscious mind is longing for, some inkling of the creative act, and of the significance of it, nevertheless gets through. . . . For this reason all uniting symbols have a redemptive significance . . .
> (Jung, 1940: para. 285)

In other terms, in the disentanglement of opposites there is psychic calmness, while, in the tension between opposites, suffering is produced. Nonetheless, if the ego can face this painful condition by staying in it, a new psychic condition can emerge, bearing new knowledge about oneself and the world.

The suspension of opposites is a difficult condition to bear, with sacrificial features, but if the ego can seriously consider both positions to be similarly valid, without renouncing its own, this suspension can create the *in-between space* for a new meaning in the self. The unity of opposites is a paradox that resists representation; this is the reason why *tertium non datur*: such antinomy can simply be postulated. By allowing itself to be what it is, the *transcendent function* characterizes itself as a sign of a genuinely creative act.

However, this third element, that arises from an extreme tension between opposites, is not just a function of a self-regulated psyche as a monad. Some post-Jungians emphasize its relational aspect, which is not explicitly formulated by Jung (Samuels, 2006; Schwartz-Salant, 1988). Jung chooses alchemy as metaphor for the healing process of psychotherapy because alchemists projected their internal process into what they were doing, which was creating something valuable – gold – out of base elements of little value in themselves (Samuels, 2006). Samuels notices that the 'the alchemist . . . worked in relation to another person (sometimes real, sometimes an imaginary figure) called *soror mystica*, mystical sister . . . [because he] needed an 'other' with whom to relate to get his work done at all' (2006: 186). The image of the *coniunctio* in the *Rosarium Philosophorum* – representing an intercourse between a man and a woman – is at the same time the 'deep and pervasive intermingling of the two personalities involved in therapy', as well as a depiction of 'the movements between parts of the unconscious psyches of both therapist and client' (2006: 186). The images of Rosarium evidently illustrate the interpersonal medium of intrapsychic dynamics, and, in this way, according to

Samuels, alchemy managed to 'straddle the divide between intrapsychic and interpersonal dimensions' (2006: 186).

Schwartz-Salant (1988) had already noticed that the alchemical tradition only rarely involved two people working together, and it was Jung's great stroke of genius to use this image to represent the unconscious process, implying that there is an implicit relational principle in Jung's perspective. Schwartz-Salant interprets the couples imagery in the *Rosarium* as images of projective identification, which can initiate the process of gaining access to, and transforming, interactive fields of linking or relating. 'The alchemical process is devoted to overcoming the dangers of fusion states [the states of interpersonal and intrapsychic twoness], of the tendency to concretize processes in the third area into something belonging to the ego' (Schwartz-Salant, 1988: 44). By focusing upon processes in this third area, which is felt as an interactive field, rather than them to projections to be taken back into individuals, two people can thus interact with its processes and experience linking in a variety of forms (notably fusion, distance and union). If one conducts a projection-type analysis based upon taking back projections, one limits the creative potential of projective identification and of the alchemical process that reveal the transference-countertransference as situated in the third area (Jung, 1947: pars. 503–5). In the third area, phenomena can only be perceived with the eye of the imagination. The alchemists referred to both this area and the process occurring there as *Mercurius*; it is a third area, according to Schwartz-Salant, because two parties become involved in the transformation of the third (Jung, 1946: para. 399). Thus, opposites are distinguished and reunified in both intrapsychic polarities and interpersonal polarities of the therapeutic dyad. This third area is a potential for linking, and not something concrete, neither inside, outside, nor in-between persons. This area is also neither material nor psyche, 'neither flesh nor fleshless', but rather a subtle body, a realm of ethers' (Schwartz-Salant, 1988: 49).

Paradoxical multiple self-states and monolithic self-states: destinies of the Reflective Triangle

All the theories illustrated above point to the importance of the transition from a *state of twoness* to a *state of thirdness* as a developmental achievement and/or a temporary mental state characterized by the emergence of essential psychic abilities: symbolization, responsibility, sense of time, sense of reality, memory, capability to relate to whole objects and recognize the other as a separate human being, etc. This passage is almost invariably understood as the hallmark of developmental maturity and attainment of crucial mental skills.

This idea of a continuous shifting among different mental states fits with a conceptualization of self as a dynamic multiplicity that sometimes can bridge the gap between its multiple affective and cognitive centers and sometimes cannot (or does it differently). This activity of 'bridging' is a most creative act, generative of meaning, and involves empathic relationships with others perceived as subjects. We have seen that M. Klein's ideas of projective identification and the passage from a paranoid-schizoid to a depressive position (1946, 1935), Bion's description of the mother's 'containment' and 'alpha function' (1962a), Winnicott's concepts of the true and false self and the role of 'potential space' in the mother–baby relationship (1971), Ogden's shifting from paranoid-schizoid to historical mode (1986, 1988, 1994b), Fonagy's 'mentalization' and 'reflective function' (Fonagy, 1999, 2001; Fonagy and Target, 1996, 1997, 1998; Fonagy et al., 2002, 2003), Bromberg's idea of a paradoxical self and his understanding of dissociation and health as the ability of 'standing in the spaces' (1993, 1996, 1998), Benjamin's intersubjective concepts of 'recognition' and 'shared third' (1988, 1990, 1998, 2004), Jung's concepts of symbol as a result of *coniunctio oppositorum* and *transcendent function* (1912, 1916, 1921, 1939, among others), all of these ideas elaborate on different aspects of the ability of the mind to 'bridge' psychic opposites or splinter psyches, both in a cognitive and emotional sense, especially in the context of a relationship with another, which facilitates the emergence of symbolization and meaning–making activity.

The Reflective Triangle

My proposal is to understand the core psychic achievement of development as the capability to function in *states of thirdness*. Such states imply the ability to simultaneously work through elements of *identity* and elements of *difference* in the context of a relationship, be it actually present or internalized. This working-through of identity and difference is meant both in cognitive and emotional terms. Thus, *identity* means thoughts of 'sameness', but also the ability to feel empathy – 'we are feeling the same' – attunement, sharing and connecting; while *difference* means thoughts of 'otherness', but also feeling differently, a rupture in attunement, self-affirmation, disconnection.

The importance of the ability to process *identity* and *difference* at the same time emerges quite clearly from Fonagy's account (Fonagy, 2001; Fonagy et al., 2002) of the crucial interactions between mother and baby, which lead to 'mentalization'. In such interactions, the mother demonstrates her empathy towards the baby's negative emotions – 'I am understanding what you feel, we are feeling the same . . . but . . . ' – and through a 'marker', such as exaggerated mirroring, makes clear to the baby that her own fear or distress is not exactly the same the baby feels – 'I can take a distance from that feeling, I am different, I am an adult, and I can face it'. Fonagy et al. (2002) argue that mothers are driven to saliently mark their affect-mirroring displays in order to differentiate them from realistic emotional expressions. The baby is soothed by the fact that the mother is not herself distressed, but is reflecting and understanding their feeling. If the mother should simply communicate 'identity' in the meaning of 'likeness' (your anxiety is equal to my anxiety), this would produce psychosis in the baby. Symmetry, even in positive affective states, does not allow admittance to one's separateness and externality, and makes of mind an enclosed world. This might be the reason why the Winnicottian mother is 'good enough' and not 'totally good' (1965). Winnicott's notions of object relating and object usage illustrate (1968) this apparent paradox of the child's need to be in a relationship where identity and difference are viable. In fact, object relating is characterized by an experiencing of the other that is based on projective mechanisms, such that the other continues to be under the child's illusory control, thanks to the 'primary maternal preoccupation' (Winnicott, 1958: 300–5). Object usage represents a 'new awakening' based on perceptions of the others as real and existing outside the child's boundaries. The mechanism by which this shift occurs is one in which, paradoxically, the child destroys the mother, yet she survives. Mother then becomes 'totally other'; she can now be loved and the child can make use of her. Between these two extremes, there is a transitional area, that is, the child's transitional object, which is simultaneously recognized to be subjective and objective, inside and outside one's control (Winnicott, 1971: 44). If the tension between these two poles collapses in one direction or another, we have either madness or a failure of imagination and creativity (Winnicott, 1965: 140–53).

Benjamin (1988, 1990, 1998, 2004) builds her theory on this foundation and expands this issue. She develops a position that defines intersubjectivity in terms of a relationship of *mutual recognition:* a relation in which each person experiences the other as a 'like subject', another mind who can be 'felt with', yet has a distinct, separate center of feeling and perception. According to her, subjectivity is established through processes of both recognition and destruction (Benjamin, 1988, 1990, 1998). Benjamin highlights that recognition between persons is essentially mutual, while self-regulation is achieved through regulating the other. In trying to establish itself as an independent entity, the self must yet recognize the other as a subject like itself in order to be recognized by the self, immediately compromising the self's absoluteness. At the very moment we come to understand the meaning of I, myself, we are forced to see the limitations of that self. At the moment when we understand that separate minds can share similar feelings – what will be referred to as 'identity' – we begin to find out that these minds can also disagree – what will be referred to as 'difference'. From the standpoint of intersubjective theory, the ideal 'resolution' of the paradox of recognition is for it to continue as a *constant tension* between recognizing the other and asserting the self, the *one in the third* and *the third in the one* (Benjamin, 2004).

The importance attached by Jung to the tension of opposites and dynamics of transcendent function is a clear statement on the paradox of keeping together *identity* and *difference*. Transcendent function works to mobilize the self from an exclusive state of identity with the ego, in which consciousness cannot recognize being inhabited by the unconscious, to a contemporary and non-contradictory state of difference (Jung, 1916, 1921, 1940), in which the self can recognize its fundamental contradiction of being composed of consciousness and unconscious, and can live this state of crucible inconsistency. In Jungian thinking, all of psychic life is shaped according to oppositional dynamics between structures and contents of psyche and their interplay of fusion, distinction and re-unification. It is a continuous confrontation with the other.

The continual process of getting to know the counterposition in the unconscious I have called the 'transcendent function', because the confrontation of conscious (rational) data with those that are unconscious (irrational) necessarily results in a modification of standpoint. But an alteration is possible only if the existence of the 'other' is admitted, at least to the point of taking conscious cognizance of it.

(Jung, 1955–1956: para. 257)

However, this work is never-ending and the self, as irresolvable paradox (Jung 1921, 1928), is at once center and circumference which, in the end, means 'decentered' and 'indefinite'. Symbolization arises here as an ability of the mind in bridging deeply felt gaps (dissociation) both intrapsychically, through an internal object, and interpersonally, with an actual subject, processing sameness (states of identity and *partecipation mystique*) and difference (recognizing the unconscious without renouncing to consciousness, i.e. confronting the shadow) simultaneously, mirroring ourselves in others, while we are still able to distinguish us from them.

Here, I refer to the 'Reflective Triangle' as the pattern of interconnections that represent this mental ability. Ideally, it keeps together three poles: Me, You and Other, and represents the mental capability to process identity (the Me–You, You–Me segment) and difference (the Me–Other, You–Other segments) at the same time, creating 'space in-between' (the area of the triangle), that is an empty, not pre-determined, potential for meaning (see Figure 4.1).

With reference to the self, *states of thirdness* open up a reflective space among its different centers of experience, bridging the gaps opened by differences through some identity, while avoiding the collapse of identity through the recognition of some difference. I call this organization and functioning of self *Paradoxical Multiple Self States*, that is a dynamic conceptualization of self characterized by the ability to keep in tension different intrapsychic positions among different centers of experience and different relationships in the intersubjective realm by producing a potential space for symbolization. *PMSSs* are characterized by a sense of centre

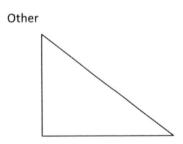

FIGURE 4.1 The Reflective Triangle

and wholeness (Jung, 1944), a sense of agency and shared power, responsibility (Ogden, 1986, 1988), in other words, a sense of being endowed with subjectivity (Benjamin, 1990, 1998; Ogden, 1986). This arises from a self which is a multiple and paradoxical whole, formed of differently connected parts, where dissociation is moderate and temporary (Bromberg, 1996; Jung, 1920, 1928, 1934). This structure of the self allows for unity and multiplicity (ego and self in Jungian terms) to be maintained in tension in order to keep open potential *in-between spaces*, which lead to workable temporary symbolization, mentalization, sense of time, memory, sense of continuity despite inconsistencies, recognition of the separateness of the other, and responsibility for one's own actions.

The Splintered Reflective Triangle

For states of thirdness to hold, some environmental condition needs to be in place (Bion, 1967, 1970; Fonagy, 2001; Target and Fonagy, 1996), for example, the mother's emotional containment in the Winnicottian developmental account (Winnicott, 1953, 1960b). Whereas the environment 'impinges' (Winnicott, 1956) on mind, the delicate working-through of the *Reflective Triangle* is interrupted and the latter 'splinters' flattening the *in-between space* available for the interplay of connections that are necessary to thinking and symbolization. The result of this 'splintering of the Reflective Triangle' is the foreclosing of the in-between spaces and the setting-out of consequent paired and linear connections between Me–You (and You–Me), Me–Other (and Other–Me) and You–Other (and Other–You).

These connections represent alternative horizontal and vertical relations with internalized objects and actual subjects. In such a state, we are in the grip of *twoness*: we are either aware of identity and not of differences (Me–You/You–Me segment) or we are aware of differences and not of identity (Me–Other/Other–Me and You–Other/Other–You segments).

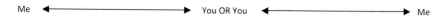

FIGURE 4.2 The Splintered Reflective Triangle: segment of identity

The first paired relation (with no-space-in-between) is the horizontal one (Figure 4.2), processing sameness and providing individuals with 'identity': what we are constituted of (as an individual or a group). This works at a paranoid-schizoid level, creating a delusional world that provides orientation for action and thinking and allowing to avoid, when convenient, the recognition of a too complex and/or frightening reality. As this mode prevails, the mental state is characterized by polarized oppositions, involving the defence mechanisms of a paranoid-schizoid position (splitting, denial, omnipotence, etc.) (Bion, 1962a, 1962b; M. Klein, 1946, 1957; Winnicott, 1956, 1962), with the self characterized by one-sidedness (Jung, 1921, 1957), and its functioning by sustained dissociation (Bromberg, 1996, 1998; Jung, 1934). We can feel totally dependent on and tied to, or absolutely

126 A psychoanalytic understanding of torture

independent and disconnected from the Other, according to what some authors refer to as states of mental 'omnipotence' (Benjamin, 1988, 1990, 1998; Winnicott, 1962) and schizo-paranoid mode of processing experience (Ogden, 1994).

Complementary and alternative to the first one, the second paired relations (with no-space-in-between) deal with a vertical processing of 'difference' (Figure 4.3), with a vertical distribution of power and value between someone powerful and/or valued and someone powerless and/or despised (Benjamin, 1988, 1990, 1998, 2004, 2007). This represents both interpersonal and intrapsychic dynamics of the relationship between self and other, as the triangle splinters.

We might even think of the internal object as an intrapsychic device appointed to maintain a dynamism between 'identity' and 'difference', since the object contains both elements of identification and recognition of oneself in the other, and rejected alien aspects which are unacceptable to the individual and, therefore, apt to be projected into the other. In this sense, the internal object might configure itself as an assembled system to activate this dynamic play between identity and difference in the relationship with the other.

Whenever fear and hatred impede play with these two aspects of the object, the self becomes *monolithic* because it cannot recognize any difference other than what is threatening and rejected, an absolute otherness. In this way, the self takes up a polarized 'I-dentification' with a narrow range of contents that can be accepted and recognized. Potential spaces between the ego and the object 'contract' and the 'other' is projected out onto someone who bears the rejected, disagreeable contents of this expulsive dynamic. This is to restore the boundaries of an endangered ego, whose survival is threatened by the merging with an unbearable 'otherness'. The object, in order to exist as a subjective element, needs a psychic space, in which an exchange between recognized and alien aspects of self may occur: the area of the Reflective Triangle. When the object becomes totally 'other', it is

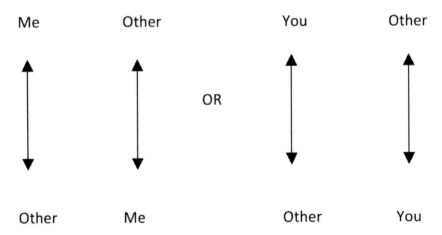

FIGURE 4.3 The Splintered Reflective Triangle: segments of difference

expelled as abject and the ego builds itself as 'whole' and pure (with that conflation of ego and self that Jung conceptualized as an inflation of ego). This dynamic in order to build up needs that in-between spaces collapse with a resulting splintering of the Reflective Triangle. As a consequence of this squeezing of *in-between spaces* in the self, different dissociated centers of experience (the splintered psyches) orientate emotions, thinking and actions according to the lines of the connections and dis-connections of the splintered triangles. This massive orientation of dissociated parts of self in the same direction is what constitutes a Monolithic Self State.

Ultimately, I use the term *Monolithic Self State* to characterize a certain functioning of self in its intrapsychic and relational dynamics, characterized by states of twoness in intrapsychic and/or interpersonal realms. The term '*monolithic*' points to a structural aspect of the self as a 'system' with dynamic implications, which are those of states of twoness. It is derived from ordinary language to convey the meaning of impenetrable lack of flexibility, that 'gives the impression that it will never change . . . and that people or parts in it are all very similar to each other' (Collins, 1987: 934). Here, the term is meant to refer to a mental state in which there is a prevalent need to take for granted a pretended 'homogenous identity', in which different parts of self work to compose a solid unity, silencing its multiplicity and contradictions. This shape would give the system the consistency of a rigid object with a lack of flexibility and adaptability to different situations, and an idea of intolerance of complexity and variations (only steady connections are possible like in solid states of matter – *lithos* is the Latin for stone). Monolithic Self States are more or less durable states, depending on the emotional atmosphere of the context in which the self is operating. They are characterized by no space and no tension among different positions, I-dentification with one-sided positions and 'black and white thinking' organized by splitting. At the same time, we can find a vertical distribution of power, a poor subjectivity, a sense of self-sufficiency and an adhesive relationality in terms of complementarity or similarity. The partiality of the psyche in Monolithic Self States is functional to the establishment of adhesive ties to other 'partial psyches' (or dissociated psyches), in order to form a whole with another or others, a dyad or a group and even a social organism, as will be illustrated in Chapter 5. In these relational contexts, there is often a sacrificial demand as a way to avoid tensions and to create adhesive relationality, which squeezes the empty potential space of *in-between states*. This provokes a severe impairment of reflective abilities. Difference can be processed only according to a vertical line of power.

Notes

1   Among contemporary Jungian authors who have come closer to relational psychoanalysis are: Margaret Wilkinson (2006), who, interested in the dialogue with neuroscience, explores the mind–brain relationship from a uniquely Jungian perspective; Jean Knox (2003a, 2003b), who elaborates on Fonagy's theory and his concept of reflective function, and redefines 'archetypes' in the light of cognitive neuroscience; George Hogenson (2004), who approaches the theory of complexity and emergent systems by proposing a new perspective on archetypes; Donald Kalsched (1996, 2000, 2013),

who explores the world of trauma through the dreams and fantasies of patients who have suffered unbearable experiences, finding connections between Jungian theory and Object Relations Theory; Vittorio Lingiardi, who writes about the similarities of relational models and analytical psychology (2000), while also investigating the 'relational turn' in Italian psychoanalysis (Lingiardi and Federici 2014); Andrew Samuels (1993, 2001, 2015), who relying on both Jungian thinking and relational psychoanalysis, approach the idea of a 'political psyche', suggesting that you cannot ignore the impact of social and political systems on individual psyche, and reflects on what ways is the personal political and the political personal; Massimo Giannoni, who has long been engaged in fostering a dialogue between analytical psychology and relational psychoanalysis in Italy (2003, 2004, 2011); Warren Colman (2013), who, having trained as a developmental Jungian analyst, recently explained how he became a 'relational analyst', showing the parallels between relational thinking and Jung's approach to clinical practice.

2 In Jungian psychology, archetypes are *a priori* structures, which organize and direct psychic activity. 'Archetypes are systems of readiness for action, and at the same time images and emotions. They are inherited with the brain structure–indeed they are its psychic aspect' (Jung, 1927: para. 53). It is not a question of inherited ideas but of inherited possibilities of ideas, instinctual images, i.e. the forms that the instincts assume. 'Psychologically . . . the archetype as an image of instinct is a spiritual goal toward which the whole nature of man strives; it is the sea to which all rivers wend their way, the prize which the hero wrests from the fight with the dragon' (Jung, 1947: para. 415).

3 In 1916, after his break with Freud and during a severe state of inner turmoil and conflict, Jung started painting mandalas and continued painting them during the 1920s. Later in his life, he recognized that they represented the goal of psychic development: the self (1963). About his dream of 1927, in which the city of 'Liver-pool' (which Jung referred to as the 'pool of life') was represented like a typical mandala, with a broad square in the center of the city and many streets converging, he writes: 'In the centre of the square was a round pool and in the middle of it a small island. On it stood a single tree, a magnolia. It was as though the tree stood in the sunlight and was at the same time the source of light' (1963: 224).

The mystical experiences lived by Jung in the period 1921–1928 become the source of his following inspiration about the self: '[This] centre of personality no longer coincides with the ego, but with a point midway between the conscious and the unconscious. This would be the point of a new equilibrium, a new centering of the total personality, a virtual centre' (Jung, 1928: para. 365). The total figure of the 'Pool of Life' is organized around a center, which exerts a numinous 'pull' and is both defining of the whole and defined by the whole. How not thinking of the double meaning of the word 'pool' as lake and as group? And how not thinking of the Jungian multicentered idea of psyche as formed by complexes, mini-centers, relatively autonomous clots, which are emotionally charged? Moreover, the urban structure of Liverpool is suggestive of the shape of the Panopticon, which is proposed in Chapter 5 as shape of self in Monolithic States.

4 It is noteworthy that, in the last three decades, a debate developed on the concept of 'third' and 'thirdness', with outstanding contributions (Benjamin, 2004, 2007, 2009, 2010; Britton, 1989; Cavell, 1998; Gerson, 2004, 2009; Green, 2004; Ogden, 1994a, 1994b). Although I did not rely on the debate for this formulation, there are relevant similarities, as well as differences, with these authors' ideas.

References

Balint, M. (1968) *The Basic Fault*. London: Tavistock.
Bateman, P. and Fonagy, P. (2004) *Psychotherapy for Borderline Personality Disorder: Mentalization-Based Treatment*. Oxford: Oxford University Press.
Beebe, J., Cambray, J. and Kirsch, T.B. (2001) 'What Freudians can learn from Jung'. *Psychoanalytic Psychology*, 18(2): . doi:10.1037/0736-9735.18.2.213

Benjamin, J. (1988) *The Bonds of Love: Psychoanalysis, Feminism & the Problem of Domination*. New York: Pantheon Books.

Benjamin, J. (1990) 'An outline of intersubjectivity: the development of recognition'. *Psychoanalytic Psychology*, 7: 33–46. Reprinted as 'Recognition and destruction: an outline of intersubjectivity', in Mitchell, S.A. and Aron, L. (Eds) (1999) *Relational Psychoanalysis: The Emergence of a Tradition*. Hillsdale, NJ and London: The Analytic Press, pp. 181–210.

Benjamin, J. (1998) *Shadow of the Other: Intersubjectivity and Gender in Psychoanalysis*. New York: Rutledge.

Benjamin, J. (2002) 'Terror and guilt: beyond them and us'. *Psychoanalytic Dialogues*, 12(3): 473–84. doi:10.1080/10481881209348681

Benjamin, J. (2004) 'Beyond doer and done to: An intersubjective view of thirdness'. *Psychoanalytic Quarterly*, 73(1): 5–46. Reprinted in Aron, L. and Harris, A. (Eds) (2012) *Relational Psychoanalysis, Vol. 4 Expansion of Theory*. New York and London: Routledge, pp. 91–130.

Benjamin, J. (2006) 'Crash: What we do when we cannot touch: commentary on paper by Meira Likierman'. *Psychoanalytic Dialogues*, 16(4): 377–85.

Benjamin, J. (2007) 'A review of *Awakening the Dreamer: clinical journeys* by Philip M. Bromberg. Mahwah, NJ: The Analytic Press, 2006'. *Contemporary Psychoanalysis*, 43: 666–80. doi:10.1080/00107530.2007.10745939

Benjamin, J. (2009) 'A relational psychoanalysis perspective on the necessity of acknowledging failure in order to restore the facilitating and containing features of the intersubjective relationship (the shared third)'. *The International Journal of Psychoanalysis*, 90(3): 441–50. doi:10.1111/j.1745-8315.2009.00163.x.

Benjamin, J. (2010) 'Can we recognize each other? Response to Donna Orange'. *The International Journal of Psychoanalysis and Self Psychology*, 5(3): 244–56. doi:10.1080/15551024.2010.485337

Bick, E. (1968) 'The experience of the skin in early object relations'. *The International Journal of Psychoanalysis*, 49: 484–6.

Bick, E. (1986) 'Further considerations on the function of the skin in early object relations'. *British Journal of Psychotherapy*, 2(4): 292–9. doi:10.1111/j.1752-0118.1986.tb01344.x

Bion, W.R. (1959) 'Attacks on linking'. In *Second Thoughts*. London: Heinemann, 1967.

Bion, W.R. (1962a) *Learning from Experience*. London: Heinemann.

Bion, W.R. (1962b) 'A theory of thinking'. *The International Journal of Psychoanalysis*, 43: 306–10.

Bion, W.R. (1967) *Second Thoughts: Selected Papers on Psychoanalysis*. London: Karnac Maresfield Library.

Bion, W.R. (1970) *Attention and interpretation*. London: Tavistock.

Bollas, C. (1983) 'Expressive uses of countertransference: notes to the patient from oneself'. *Contemporary Psychoanalysis*, 19(1): 1–33. doi:10.1080/00107530.1983.10746587

Britton, R. (1989) 'The missing link: parental sexuality in the Oedipus complex'. In Steiner, J. (Ed.), *The Oedipus Complex Today*. London: Karnac Books, pp. 83–101.

Bromberg, P.M. (1993) 'Shadow and substance: a relational perspective on clinical process'. *Psychoanalytic Psychology*, 10(2): 147–68. doi:10.1037/h0079464

Bromberg, P.M. (1994) 'Speak! That I may see you. Some reflections on dissociation, reality and psychoanalytic listening'. *Psychoanalytic Dialogues*, 4(4): 517–47. doi:10.1080/10481889409539037

Bromberg, P.M. (1995a) 'Psychoanalysis, dissociation, and personality organization: reflections on Peter Goldberg's essay'. *Psychoanalytic Dialogues*, 5(3): 511–28. doi:10.1080/10481889509539089

Bromberg, P.M. (1995b) 'Resistance, object-usage, and human relatedness'. *Contemporary Psychoanalysis*, 31(2): 173–91. doi:10.1080/00107530.1995.10746903

Bromberg P.M. (1996) 'Standing in the spaces: the multiplicity of self and the psychoanalytic relationship'. *Contemporary Psychoanalysis*, 32(4): 509–35. doi:10.1080/00107530.1996.10746334

Bromberg, P.M. (1998) *Standing in the spaces*. New York & London: Psychology Press, Taylor & Francis Group.

Bromberg, P.M. (2001) 'Hope when there is no hope: discussion of Jill Scharff's case presentation'. *Psychoanalytic Inquiry*, 21(4): 519–29. doi:10.1080/07351692109348955

Bromberg, P.M. (2006) *Awakening the Dreamer*. Mahwah, NJ: The Analytic Press.

Casement, A. (2006) 'The shadow'. In Papadopoulos, R.K. (Ed.), *The Handbook of Jungian Psychology*. Hove, East Sussex: Routledge, pp. 94–112.

Cavell, M. (1998) 'Triangulation, one's own mind and objectivity'. *The International Journal of Psychoanalysis*, 79: 449–67.

Fairbairn, W.R.D. (1944) 'Endopsychic structure considered in terms of object-relationships'. In *Psychoanalytic Studies of the Personality*. London: Routledge, 1952, pp. 82–132.

Fairbairn, W.R.D. (1952) *An Object Relations Theory of the Personality*. New York: Basic Books.

Fonagy, P. (1995) 'Psychoanalytic and empirical approaches to developmental psychopathology: an object-relations perspective'. In Shapiro, T. and Emde, R. N. (Eds.), *Research in Psychoanalysis: Process, Development, Outcome*. Madison, CT: International Universities Press, pp. 245–60.

Fonagy, P. (1999) 'Male perpetrators of violence against women: an attachment theory perspective'. *Journal of Applied Psychoanalytic Studies*, 1(1): 7–27. doi:10.1023/A:1023074023087

Fonagy, P. (2001) *Attachment Theory and Psychoanalysis*. New York: Other Press.

Fonagy, P. and Allison, E. (2012) 'What is mentalization? The concept and its foundations in developmental research'. In Midgley, N. and Vrouva, I. (Eds.), *Minding the Child: Mentalization-Based Interventions with Children, Young People and Their Families*. Hove, UK: Routledge, pp. 11–34.

Fonagy, P. and Bateman, A.W. (2007) 'Mentalizing and borderline personality disorder'. *Journal of Mental Health*, 16(1): 83–101. doi:10.1080/09638230601182045

Fonagy, P. and Target, M. (1996) 'Playing with reality: I. Theory of mind and the normal development of psychic reality'. *The International Journal of Psychoanalysis*, 77(2) (January): 217–33.

Fonagy, P. and Target, M. (1997) 'Attachment and reflective function: their role in self-organization'. *Development and Psychopathology*, 9(4)(Fall): 679–700.

Fonagy, P. and Target, M. (1998) 'Mentalization and the changing aims of child psychoanalysis'. *Psychoanalytic Dialogues*, 8(1): 87–114. doi:10.1080/10481889809539235

Fonagy, P. and Target, M. (2002) 'Psychodynamic approaches to child therapy'. In Kaslow, F.W. and Magnavita, J. (Eds.), *Comprehensive Handbook of Psychotherapy. Volume I: Psychodynamic/Object Relations*. New York, NY: John Wiley, pp. 105–29.

Fonagy P. and Target M. (2008) 'Attachment, trauma and psychoanalysis: where psychoanalysis meets neuroscience'. In Jurist, E.L., Slade, A. and Bergner, S. (Eds.), *Mind to Mind: Infant Research, Neurosciences and Psychoanalysis*. New York: Other Press, pp. 15–49.

Fonagy, P., Gergely, G., Jurist, E. and Target, M. (2002) *Affect Regulation, Mentalization, and the Development of the Self*. New York: Other Press.

Fonagy, P., Target, M. Gergely, G. Allen, J.G. and Bateman, A.W. (2003) 'The developmental roots of borderline personality disorder in early attachment relationships: a theory and some evidence'. *Psychoanalytic Inquiry*, 23(3): 412–59. doi:10.1080/07351692309349042

Fosshage, J. and Davies, J. (2000) 'Analytic psychology after Jung with clinical case material from Stephen Mitchell's *Influence and Autonomy in Psychoanalysis*'. *Psychoanalytic Dialogues*, 10(3): 377–88.

Gerson, S. (2004) 'The relational unconscious: a core element of intersubjectivity, thirdness, and clinical process'. *Psychoanalytic Quarterly*, 73:63–98.

Gerson, S. (2009) 'When the third is dead: memory, mourning, and witnessing in the aftermath of the Holocaust'. *The International Journal of Psychoanalysis*, 90(6): 1341–57. doi:10.1111/j.1745-8315.2009.00214.x

Ghent, E. (1990) 'Masochism, submission, surrender: masochism as a perversion of surrender'. *Contemporary Psychoanalysis*, 26(1), (January): 108–36. doi:10.1080/00107530.1990.10746643

Giannoni, M. (2003) 'Jung's theory of dream and the relational debate'. *Psychoanalytic Dialogues*, 13(4): 605–21. doi:10.1080/10481881309348759

Giannoni, M. (2004) 'Epistemological premise, developmental idea, main motivation in Jung's and Kohut's psychoanalysis: looking for some analogies'. *Journal of Analytical Psychology*, 49(2):161–75. doi:10.1111/j.1465-5922.2004.00451.x.

Giannoni, M. (2011) 'Psicoanalisi relazionale e psicologia junghiana'. In Lingiardi, V., Amadei, G., Caviglia, G. and De Bei, F. (Eds.), *La svolta relazionale. Itinerari italiani*. Milano: Raffaello Cortina, pp. 197–216.

Green, A. (2004) 'Thirdness and psychoanalytic concepts'. *Psychoanalytic Quarterly*, 73(1): 99–135. doi:10.1002/j.2167-4086.2004.tb00154.x

Grossman, W. (1982) 'The self as fantasy: fantasy as theory'. *Journal of American Psychoanalytic Association*, 30(4): 919–38.

Hinshelwood, R. (1991) *A Dictionary of Kleinian Thought*. London: Free Association Books.

Hogenson, G.B. (2004) 'What are symbols symbols of? Situated action, mythological bootstrapping and the emergence of the Self'. *Journal of Analytical Psychology*, 49(1): 67–81. doi:10.1111/j.0021-8774.2004.0441.x

Jacobi, J. (1959) *Complex/Archetype/Symbol*. Princeton, NJ: Princeton University Press.

Jung, C.G. (1912) 'Symbols of transformation'. In *Collected Works of C.G. Jung*, vol. 5, Read, H., Fordham, M. and Adler G. (Eds.), translated by R. Hull, Princeton, NJ: Princeton University Press/Bollingen Series XX (hereafter, *CW*).

Jung, C.G. (1916) 'The transcendent function'. In *CW*, vol. 8.

Jung, C.G. (1917) 'On the psychology of the unconscious'. In *CW*, vol. 7.

Jung, C.G. (1920/48) 'The psychological foundations of belief in spirits'. In *CW*, vol. 8.

Jung, C.G. (1921) 'Psychological types: Definitions'. In *CW*, vol. 6.

Jung, C.G. (1927) 'Mind and earth'. In *CW* vol. 10.

Jung, C.G. (1928) 'The relations between the ego and the unconscious'. In *CW*, vol. 7.

Jung, C.G. (1934) 'A review of the complex theory'. In *CW*, vol. 8.

Jung, C.G. (1939) 'Conscious, unconscious and individuation'. In *CW*, vol. 9.

Jung, C.G. (1940) 'The psychology of the child archetype'. In *CW*, vol. 9i.

Jung, C.G. (1944) 'Psychology and alchemy'. In *CW*, vol. 12.

Jung, C.G. (1946) 'The psychology of the transference'. In *CW*, vol. 16.

Jung, C.G. (1947) 'On the nature of the psyche'. In *CW*, vol. 8.

Jung, C.G. (1951) 'Aion'. In *CW*, vol. 9ii.

Jung, C.G. (1955–1956) 'Mysterium Coniunctionis'. In *CW*, vol. 14.

Jung, C.G. (1957) 'Commentary on the secret of the golden flower'. In *CW*, vol. 13.

Jung, C.G. (1959) 'Good and evil in analytical psychology.' In *CW*, vol. 17.

Jung, C.G. *Memories, Dreams, and Reflections* (1963) Edited by Aniela Jaffe, New York: Vintage Books.

Jung, C.G. (1973) *Letters, Vols. I and II*. Princeton: Princeton University Press.

Kalsched, D.E. (1996) *The Inner World of Trauma: Archetypal Defenses of the Personal Spirit*. New York: Routledge.
Kalsched, D.E. (2000) 'Jung's contribution to psychoanalytic thought'. *Psychoanalytic Dialogues*, 10(3): 473–88. doi:10.1080/10481881009348559
Kalsched, D.E. (2013) *Trauma and the Soul: A Psycho-Spiritual Approach to Human Development and its Interruption*. London and New York: Routledge.
Klein, M. (1935) 'A contribution to the psychogenesis of manic depressive states'. In *Love, Guilt and Reparation, and Other Works 1921–1945*. London: Vintage, 1998, pp. 262–89.
Klein, M. (1940) 'Mourning and its relation to manic-depressive states'. In Money-Kyrle, R. E. (Ed.), *The Writings of Melanie Klein, Volume 1*. London: Hogarth Press, 1981, pp. 344–69.
Klein, M. (1946) 'Notes on some schizoid mechanisms'. *The International Journal of Psychoanalysis*, 27: 99–110.
Klein, M. (1957) *Envy and Gratitude, and Other Works 1946–1963*. London: Vintage, 1997.
Klein, M. (1959) 'Our adult world and its roots in infancy'. In *The Writings of Melanie Klein, Volume 1*. London: Hogarth Press, 1975, pp. 247–63.
Kohut, H. (1977) *The Restoration of the Self*. New York: International Universities Press.
Kohut, H. (1984) *How Does Analysis Cure?* Chicago: University of Chicago Press.
Knox, J. (2003a) 'Trauma and defences: Their roots in relationship: An overview'. *Journal of Analytical Psychology*, 48(2): 207–33. doi:10.1111/1465-5922.t01-2-00007
Knox, J. (2003b) *Archetype, Attachment, Analysis: Jungian psychology and the Emergent Mind*. Hove: Brunner-Routledge.
Laing, R. D. (1960) *The Divided Self*. London: Tavistock.
Lingiardi, V. (2000) 'Modelli relazionali in psicoanalisi e in psicologia analitica'. *Studi Junghiani*, 6(1): 51–62.
Lingiardi V., Federici S. (2014) 'The relational turn in Italy: its history and evolution. Introduction to panel'. *Psychoanalytic Dialogues*, 24(5): 558–61. doi:10.1080/10481885.2014.949490
Meltzer, D. (1975) 'Adhesive identification'. *Contemporary Psychoanalysis*, 11(3): 289–310. doi:10.1080/00107530.1975.10745389
Mitchell, S.A. (1991) 'Contemporary perspectives on self: toward an integration'. *Psychoanalytic Dialogues*, 1(2): 121–47. doi:10.1080/10481889109538889.
Mitchell, S.A. (1992) 'True selves, false selves, and the ambiguity of authenticity'. In Skolnick, N.J. and Warshaw S.C. (Eds.), *Relational Perspectives in Psychoanalysis*. Hillsdale, NJ: Analytic Press, pp. 1–20.
Mitchell S.A. (1993) *Hope and Dread in Psychoanalysis*. New York: Basic Books.
Ogden, T.H. (1979) 'On projective identification'. *The International Journal of Psychoanalysis*, 60: 357–73.
Ogden, T.H. (1981) 'Projective identification in psychiatric hospital treatment'. *Bulletin of Menninger Clinic*, 45(4): 317–33.
Ogden, T.H. (1982) *Projective Identification and Psychotherapeutic Technique*. New York and London: Jason Aronson.
Ogden, T.H. (1984) 'Instinct, phantasy and psychological deep structure: a reinterpretation of aspects of the work of Melanie Klein'. *Contemporary Psychoanalysis*, 20(4): 500–25. doi:10.1080/00107530.1984.10745750
Ogden, T.H. (1986) *The Matrix of Mind: Object Relations and the Psychoanalytic Dialogue*. London: Maresfield Library, 1992.
Ogden, T.H. (1988) 'On the dialectical structure of experience: some clinical and theoretical implications'. *Contemporary Psychoanalysis*, 24(1): 17–45. doi:10.1080/00107530.1988.10746217

Ogden, T.H. (1989a) 'On the concept of an autistic-contiguous position'. *The International Journal of Psychoanalysis*, 70(Pt 1) (1) (February): 127–40.
Ogden, T.H. (1989b) *The Primitive Edge of Experience*. Northvale, NJ: Jason Aronson.
Ogden, T.H. (1991) 'Analysing the matrix of transference'. *The International Journal of Psychoanalysis*, 72: 593–605.
Ogden, T.H. (1994a) 'The analytic third: working with intersubjective clinical facts'. *The International Journal of Psychoanalysis*, 75: 3–20.
Ogden, T.H. (1994b) *Subjects of Analysis*. Northvale, NJ: Jason Aronson.
Samuels, A. (1993) *The Political Psyche*. London, New York: Routledge.
Samuels, A. (2001) *Politics on the Couch: Citizenship and Internal Life*. London: Profile Books; New York: The Other Press.
Samuels, A. (2006) 'Transference/countertransference'. In Papadopoulos, R.K. (Ed.), *Handbook of Jungian Psychology*. New York: Routledge, pp. 177–95.
Samuels, A. (2012) 'Jung and relational psychoanalysis'. Paper presented at the Panel '*The analyst is as much "in the analysis" as the patient' (1929): Jung as a pioneer of relational psychoanalysis*. International Association of Relational Psychoanalysis and Psychotherapy, Conference, 1–4 March 2012.
Samuels, A. (2015) *A New Therapy for Politics?* London: Karnac.
Sander, L. (2002) 'Thinking differently: principles of process in living systems and the specificity of being known'. *Psychoanalytic Dialogues*, 12(1): 11–42. doi:10.1080/10481881209348652
Schwartz-Salant, N. (1988) 'Archetypal foundations of projective identification'. *Journal of Analytical Psychology*, 33(1): 39–64. doi:10.1111/j.1465-5922.1988.00039.x
Searles, H.F. (1977) 'Dual- and multiple-identity processes in borderline ego functioning'. In *Borderline Personality Disorders*. New York: International Universities Press, pp. 441–55.
Sedgwick, D. (2013) 'Jung as pioneer of relational analysis'. Available at: www.cgjungpage.org/learn/articles/analytical-psychology/943-jung-as-a-pioneer-of-relational-analysis7 (accessed 12 March 2014).
Stern, D. (1985) *The Interpersonal World of the Infant*. New York: Basic Books.
Sullivan, H.S. (1940) *Conceptions of Modern Psychiatry*. New York: Norton.
Sullivan, H. (1950) 'The illusion of personal individuality'. In *The Fusion of Psychiatry and the Social Sciences*. New York: Norton, 1964, pp. 198–228.
Sullivan, H.S. (1953) *The Interpersonal Theory of Psychiatry*. New York: Norton.
Target, M. and Fonagy, P. (1996) 'Playing with reality: II. The development of psychic reality from a theoretical perspective'. *The International Journal of Psychoanalysis*, 77(3): 459–79.
Tustin, F. (1972) *Autism and Childhood Psychosis*. London: Hogarth Press.
Tustin, F. (1981) *Autistic States in Children*. Boston, MA: Routledge and Kegan Paul.
Tustin, F. (1986) *Autistic Barriers in Neurotic Patients*. New Haven, CT: Yale University Press, 1987.
Wilkinson, M. (2006) 'The dreaming mind-brain: a Jungian perspective'. *Journal of Analytical Psychology*, 51(1): 43–59. doi:10.1111/j.0021-8774.2006.00571.x
Winnicott, D.W. (1945) 'Primitive emotional development'. In *Through Paediatrics to Psycho-Analysis*. New York: Basic Books, 1975, pp. 145–56.
Winnicott, D.W. (1953) 'Transitional objects and transitional phenomena: a study of the first not-me possession'. *The International Journal of Psychoanalysis*, 34(2): 89–97.
Winnicott, D.W. (1956) 'Primary maternal preoccupation'. In *Collected Papers*. New York: Basic Books, 1958, pp. 300–5.
Winnicott, D.W. (1958) 'The capacity to be alone'. In *The Maturational Process and the Facilitating Environment*. London: Hogarth Press, 1965, pp. 29–36.

Winnicott, D.W. (1960a) 'Ego distortion in terms of true and false self'. In *The Maturational Processes and The Facilitating Environment*. New York: International Universities Press, 1965, pp. 140–52.

Winnicott, D.W. (1960b) 'The theory of the parent-infant relationship'. In *The Maturational Processes and the Facilitating Environment*. London: Hogarth Press, 1965, pp. 37–55.

Winnicott, D.W. (1962) 'Ego integration in child development'. In *The Maturational Processes and the Facilitating Environment*. New York: International Universities Press, 1965, pp. 56–63.

Winnicott, D.W. (1965) *The Maturational Processes and the Facilitating Environment*. New York: International Universities Press, 1965.

Winnicott, D.W. (1968) 'The use of an object and relating through identifications'. In *Playing and Reality*. London and New York: Tavistock Publications, 1971, pp. 86–94.

Winnicott, D.W. (1971) 'Playing: creative activity and the search for the self'. In *Playing and Reality*. London and New York: Tavistock Publications, 1971, pp. 53–64.

Young-Eisendrath, P. (1997) 'The self in analysis'. *Journal of Analytical Psychology*, 42(1): 157–66. doi:10.1111/j.1465-5922.1997.00157.x

Young-Eisendrath, P. (2000) 'Self and transcendence: a postmodern approach to analytical psychology in practice'. *Psychoanalytic Dialogues*, 10(3): 427–41. doi:10.1080/10481881-009348556

Young-Eisendrath, P. (2004) *Subject to Change: Jung, Gender and Subjectivity in Psychoanalysis*. London: Brunner-Routledge.

Young-Eisendrath, P. and Dawson, T. (2008) *The Cambridge Companion to Jung*. Cambridge: Cambridge University Press.

Young-Eisendrath, P. and Hall, J. (1991) *Jung's Self Psychology: A Constructivist Perspective*. New York: Guilford Press.

5
THE EMOTIONAL LIFE OF TORTUROUS SOCIETY

Monolithic societal states

The aim of this chapter is to reconsider the large group dynamics of torturous societies, as outlined in Chapter 2, in light of the psychoanalytic constructs built up in Chapter 4, in particular those of *states of twoness* and *Monolithic Self States* (MSSs).

It is here implied that, under favourable conditions, society, not very differently from self, is able to keep a compensatory balance between social multiplicity and social unity, between the representation of multiple interests and perspectives, and a sense of belonging to the same social body. This idea is rooted in a perspective according to which self and society are mutually constitutive and intertwined, and, to a certain extent, even isomorphic. Individuals are constituted by their social relations and human problems arise among people and are related to problems in the person's past or present relational contexts (Aron, 1996). Moreover, the social context may influence and even constitute the way a person perceives himself/herself and the other, and the way they interpersonally relate to others (Mitchell, 1988). Consequently, an indispensable premise here is that events occurring in the social domain have an impact, sometimes mediated by group and institutional life, sometimes directly impacting upon individual psyche.

As basic conditions of life, such as safety and nurture and a consequent feeling of trust, are guaranteed in society, this facilitates and implements social development and enables a finer processing of social issues and political conflicts. When this delicate balance cannot be kept, for several possible reasons, the social *in-between spaces* available for transactions, negotiations and meaning–making activities among different groups narrow, while the phenomena linked to *states of twoness* occur. Therefore, what we call here *Monolithic Societal State* (MSoS) is characterized, on the one hand, by an overemphasis of unity, in which *identity* becomes *identi-fication* among peers through a political and/or religious ideology that creates an overstated and artificial 'sameness'; and, on the other hand, by an overemphasis of *difference* that becomes social fragmentation, individual isolation and marginalization, thereby emphasizing and even creating 'difference' between social actors with a different power endowment. In both these conditions, social conflicts cannot be processed in the framework of a shared system of rules – the law, which is a 'social third' – and creative thinking is largely impeded.

The hypothesis developed in this chapter is that *Monolithic Societal States* arise as a result of Splintered Reflective Triangles in large group dynamics due to widespread, uncontained and overwhelming affects. Tremendous emotions, especially dread, triggered by a perceived threat to survival make the task of processing identity and difference in group relations impossible: as a consequence, identity is emphasized as a basis for togetherness among those who are perceived as the in-group (Me and You, You and Me are together on the basis of our similarity and our 'togetherness' cannot be disturbed by possible difference), usually found within majority groups. On the other hand, difference is overstated for out-group people: Me and the Other, You and the Other are separate on the basis of our/your difference, such that we/you are not disturbed and/or even contaminated by difference, usually the Other referring to members of a minority group. This dynamic results in a sense of fusion among peers (Me-You segment) through a unifying principle providing a sense of purity/identity/oneness within the majority group, merging this latter and its leader with a sense of triumphal superiority, and separateness from the powerless, the inferiors and those who, due to being different (or made different), are allocated to an inferior status (Me-Other, You-Other segments). This groupal defensive mechanism guarantees some degree of relief from dread and sense of vulnerability.

Monolithic Societal States can be detected in different historical and political phenomena throughout history. Totalitarianism, fascism, religious fundamentalism, communism, theocracy, and nationalism, which often used and are still using torture as a political instrument, are just a few examples of the forms that MSoSs may take in history. In Chapter 2, it was emphasized that, often, torturous societies are characterized by a rigid political and/or cultural context. Although different in their historical and political meaning, they show some recurring similarities: a common delusion of unity (of the nation, people, community of believers, comrades, etc.), while often hiding an extremely fragmented society, held together through a set of collectively assumed principles of identification. This pretended unity becomes the grounds for impeding a truly democratic processing of multiple opinions, economic interests, political positions, etc. The term 'monolithic' is to signal both this rigidity and the fact that, in such contexts, social and political life rely on fixed positions, ideological thinking, and a peculiar relational style, characterized by an 'adhesive' way to be together among peers (horizontal bonds) and between superiors and subordinates (vertical bonds), to form a distinct solid social body with no space between people, no mutuality, and very limited subjectivity. It is not only the case of totalitarian states but also of democracies that have entered into a monolithic mode of governance, where social processes of representation are in fact constrained, with the space for mutual recognition among different groups being very narrow.

It is worth emphasizing that the splintering of the Reflective Triangle that gives rise to MSoSs is not meant to be a 'pathology' of social functioning in itself, but a spontaneous organizing pattern that small or large groups take on in order to face powerful collective fears and threats. A flexible dynamic implying an alternation of social states of *twoness* and *thirdness* is normally part of the working through of important social issues. On the contrary, whereas groups rely massively on *states of twoness*, we may find a society that resorts to torture to make a distorted contact with the Other, plausibly in order to get out of the enclosed hallucinated social world based on sameness that spontaneously resulted from terror.

Freud: what kind of group psychology?

It is widely recognized that Freud considerably enriched the understanding of group psychology with the concept of the ego ideal (Chasseguet-Smirgel, 1985). I would make the point that, in *Group Psychology and the Analysis of the Ego* (1921), Freud's analysis deals not so much with groups in general but with groups in Monolithic Societal States.

Freud defines the 'primary group' as 'a number of individuals who have put one and the same object in the place of their ego ideal and have consequently identified themselves with one another in their ego' (1921: 116). He made the hypothesis that a group is formed out of two identifications: an idealizing identification with a leader, and an identification, based on similarity, with others who have adopted the same leader as their ego ideal.

The concept of the ego ideal appeared for the first time in his work 'On narcissism: an introduction' (1914), in reference to the part of the conscience concerned with aspirations and ideals. The conceptualization of the ego ideal and its differentiation from the superego is a debated topic because of Freud's frequently ambiguous use of the terms. Freud never reconciled his inconsistent usages of the ego ideal (1914) with his usage of the superego (1923). However, Freud's followers (Hartmann and Lowenstein, 1962; Rapaport, 1957) clarified the ego ideal, the heir of primary narcissism, as the organ of aspiration from which shame arises, while the proper superego, the heir to the Oedipus complex, as the organ of oedipal prohibition from which guilt derives. The ego ideal is formed when the child, through the crucial influence of parents, educators and others in the environment, is forced to abandon their infantile narcissism and to identify with the adults' superego, particularly with the paternal role (Freud, 1923). At this time, the child's ego ideal conflates with the superego – that includes the moral conscience – which compares the actual ego with the ego ideal. Thus, the ego ideal would become a superego's subset within the framework of a more mature moral conscience.

In *Group Psychology* (1921), Freud illustrates how members of the group are united by identifications based on their similarity, which in turn is the result of their common identification with a leader who functions as each individual's ego ideal. The consequences are well known. Similarly to what happens in the relationship between the hypnotizer and the hypnotist,

> The criticism exercised by that agency [the ego ideal] is silent; everything that the object does and asks for is right and blameless. Conscience has no application to anything that is done for the sake of the object; in the blindness of love remorselessness is carried to the pitch of crime. . . . The object has been put in the place of the ego ideal.
>
> (Freud, 1921: 113)

The group member no longer needs to discover or create purpose or meaning in their own life, but finds it in transcendent form in their dedication and service to the leader. Since the 'leader' of a group may be either a person, alive or dead, or a set of abstract principles, in Freud's theory, ideologies (see below) also qualify for the role of group leaders, according to Freud's theory.

For Freud, the group or the crowd has an almost magical power to create libidinal links between members, like in a chemical reaction. What Freud does not explain in his remarkable writing on group psychology is the reason why this happens: what is the motivating force behind these bonds? And what makes them so powerful? And why does he concentrate his attention on *Church* and *army*, among many other groups, to illustrate the group functioning?

He recognizes a similarity between Church and army on the basis that each institution has a leader (Christ and the commander in chief) who loves their subordinates with the same love. In addition, their members have libidinal links to their chief and between peers (brothers in Christianity and comrades in the army). Freud suggests that a mystical communion between members of the group does take place by replacing the ideal ego with the leader. But why does this happen? Why do people organize in such a group? Is it the only possible group organization?

I am proposing here that Freud gives implicit answers to these questions in the second part of his work, in which he addresses the effects of panic and collective fears on crowds and the potential rising-up of social destructiveness following the fantasized fall of some religious dogma (1921: 96–9). Freud seems to struggle with the idea that, in the face of collective fears, groups organize themselves in a way that enables their members to obtain guidance and protection by a leader, as well as the enjoyment of reciprocal social bonds between peers.

In the perspective here proposed, since dread is experienced as an intolerable otherness, which 'impinges' on people's minds and cannot be individually worked through, the Reflective Triangles of individual minds splinter impairing their ability to think of related social issues. This creates a potential to reshape groupal bonds. The group, in this regard, functions as a medium for the reorganization of itself. Indeed, the results of this splintering (at an interpersonal level) are isolated segments of this triangle, i.e., horizontal relationships based on a supposed identity with peers in comradery (horizontal bonds), and vertical relationships between superiors and subordinates, with the latter becoming the repository of non-conscious otherness and leaders representing the ego ideal and becoming the object of identification (vertical bonds). States of twoness predominate, while the large group starts functioning in a monolithic mode.

The role of the leader may also be played by an ideology, or a sacred or secular religion, no matter if collectivistic or individualistic, but embodied by an inflated power, which is often concerned with issues of purity, safety, identity, homogeneity of the large (national, religious, ethnic etc.) group, and the creation of a widely shared perspective on reality. However, what gets lost in this process is the connection with the Other, which is excluded by the conscious scenario, and comes back unconsciously in the vertical relationships with leaders. The Other ends up being embodied, not just by those deprived of citizenship, expunged from the community of decent people endowed with civil rights (the potential victims of torture), but also by those social actors who, on identifying with the monolithic power, are violently perpetrating evil in its name.

Application to torturous societies

In Chapter 2, we observed in torturous societies a pattern comprising the following:

1. An *emotional state* of collective terror.
2. A preformed pattern of knowledge that organizes thinking and orientates social action, which is made of: the *construction of a narrative* about a catastrophic threat and an omnipotent power protecting against a dangerous and often hidden enemy; a thinking shaped by clear-cut distinctions among opposites, to which a value in terms of good/bad is attributed; the promise of a better world; and the creation of categories of heroes and sub-humans.
3. A *peculiar style of social bonding* that goes along with this narrative.

In the following paragraphs each of these aspects will be discussed in the framework of the construct of *Monolithic Societal States*.

A nameless dread and the loss of group boundaries

We have seen in Chapter 2 that terror is a main ingredient of societies where torture appears. A non-recognized and widespread sense of dread and powerlessness, derived from having been victimized, exploited and traumatized, may be the trigger of a psychosocial process leading to torture. Fear and terror are different levels of intensity of the same emotion with a different sequel of psychic and somatic reactions. Terror is a powerful basic affect that is not easily described; it is by definition 'nameless', as Bion effectively conveys (1962b: 116). This feature describes the loss of any vestige of meaning because the incipient capacity to establish possible meaning has been reversed. From an individual perspective, Bion calls this process the 'reversal of alpha-function', which implies 'unthinkable anxieties' (1962a: 25). Whenever fear is powerful enough to become terror, complex systems collapse, with this collapse experienced as a loss of boundaries, a consequent threat of contamination, and the fear of a potential infectious mixture. Terror may be experienced as unbearable 'otherness' or indiscriminate contact with 'all', prompting a need to extrude what is 'alien' as a way to reinstate ego boundaries and identity.

When psychic pain is felt to be uncontained and therefore unbearable, there may be a fragmentation and withdrawal into closed-off states of petrified emotional isolation. In individual experience, Winnicott refers to a similar state as 'primitive agonies', which result from excessive impingement by the environment that interrupts the continuity of being for the infant in the very early stage of development (1960: 47). The sense of self can become annihilated. Can we suppose a similar emotional state for groups, even though not experienced by all group members in the same way?

The feeling of dread is a condition that Jungians theory calls archetypal. A primary and fundamental phylogenetic value can be recognized in the response to dread, in its being automatic, reflexive and immediate. Papadopoulos (2006: 92) notes that the etymological origin of the word terror is in the Greek *tromos*, which means trembling, quaking and quivering, especially out of fear. It is an onomatopoeic word coming from *trrr*, the sound of a shivering person: a very basic emotion with a direct somatic and universal basis. The experience of feeling terror is that of a sudden oneness with an unbearable otherness; an experience of invasion, violated borders and defilement. Formless dread is a threatening assault to one's integrity and generates an instinctive move towards distinguishing oneself from it, raising one's boundaries and delimiting one's own 'clear cut' identity. In the most physical experience of pain, we reflexively feel the urge to keep a distance from the source of pain; similarly, in terror, we unmindlessly feel the need to extrude something that is supposed to be the source of dread. Since the primary affect of terror is processed at the most primitive level of experience, the physical level, we suppose that the urge to contain this invading basic affect shapes, the psychic level, narratives of biological/physical contamination and lost boundaries.

Actually, in many social and historical contexts where torture is used, we can find a recurrence of racist accounts reflecting this preoccupation about distinctions, feeling of being threatened in bodily boundaries, skin contact, pollution, infections, etc. We can think of the Nazi discourse on the 'Arian race' and the need for a concrete purification from Jewish pollution that led to crematory ovens; or the need for segregation of races leading to that social system of institutionalized separations known as Apartheid. Millet (1994) notices that, under an Apartheid system, the internal sense of threat becomes the fear of corporal contamination, interracial marriage, sharing public spaces, contact and infection. Similarly, Sartre, in his 1958 introduction to Alleg's book, *The Question* (2006), understood that the French imperial reaction to Algerian independence was a fury that was not merely imperial, but racist, since the imperial/colonial nexus was built on racism and notions of race, ruling and subject races. Paxton (2004), in his analysis of the phenomenon of fascism, mentions different ways in which fascist movements promoted the growth of race and how a sense of corporal contamination drives the need for separation and the pursuit of the 'purity' of race. Furthermore, in those cases where no racist themes are exploited, the rhetoric of torturous powers often makes use of corporal metaphors of illness or physical contamination: the Argentine military described subversion as a disease infesting the nation and alluded to an epidemic similar to the plagues, which had scourged the world in previous centuries (Immerman, 1982: 113, in Hollander, 2010: 105). An Uruguayan psychologist, who was imprisoned for 13 months, recalls that she and hundreds of other female prisoners were kept in military prisons because they were considered a 'contagious infection' from which common criminals had to be protected (Hollander, 2010: 105).

While autistic-contiguous experience is not just the realm of dread, but the most fundamental and primitive mode of being – two skins or surfaces touching, one that is two, two surfaces whose contact creates one reality, shared skin (Ogden, 1989b: 35) – it may become transformed into dread in an instant. The experience of oneness with Otherness becomes an experience of loss of skin and consequently of self. Autistic-contiguous anxiety is experienced as a feeling of leaking or dissolving, disappearing or falling into shapeless unbounded space, pre-objectal life, the Other within.

Julia Kristeva (1982) develops a notion of *abjection* that contains both these corporeal and pre-objectal aspects, and provides an understanding of the dynamics of social oppression. She conceptualizes abjection as an operation of the psyche through which subjective and group identities are constituted by excluding anything that threatens one's own (or one's group's) borders, primarily, the materiality of death. Following Melanie Klein, Kristeva is interested in the earliest development of subjectivity, using the maternal body with its *two-in-one*, or *other within*, as a model for all subjective relations. Like the maternal body, each one of us is what she calls *a subject-in-process*. As *subjects-in-process*, we are always negotiating *the other within*, since we are never completely the subjects of our own experience. The abject marks the moment when we separated ourselves from our mother, when we began to recognize a boundary between 'me' and other, between 'me' and '(m)other'. The abject, then, at once represents the threat that meaning is breaking down and constitutes our reaction to such a breakdown, essentially a pre-lingual response, a conservative *manoeuvre of closure* (1982). 'The most archaic form of abjection is food loathing, nausea, a refusal to take it in, what others proffer. "I" want none of that element' (Kristeva, 1982: 3)

In this theoretical framework (1982), the abject refers to the human reaction to a threatened breakdown in meaning, caused by the loss of distinction between subject and object or between self and other. The primary example for what causes such a reaction is the corpse, which traumatically reminds us of our own materiality. The corpse especially exemplifies the breakdown of the distinction between subject and object, which is crucial for the establishment of identity and for our entrance into the symbolic order. The fear is caused by the breakdown of any distinction between subject and object, ourselves and the world of dead material objects (1982: 207). The reaction to the threat of such a breakdown is 'ab-jection' (from the Latin *abicere,* meaning 'to throw away, cast off; humble, degraded, lower' combining *ab-* 'away, off' + *iacere* 'to throw'), the casting-off of the object, the ejection of what is felt as totally 'other'.

In *Powers of Horror* (1982), which extends such a concept of the abject to the social realm, Kristeva persuasively writes:

It is thus not lack of cleanliness or health that causes abjection but what disturbs identity, system, order. What does not respect borders, positions, rules. The in-between[1], the ambiguous, the composite. The traitor, the liar, the criminal with a good conscience, the shameless rapist, the killer who claims he is a saviour . . . a terror that dissembles, a hatred that smiles, a passion that uses the body for barter instead of inflaming it, a debtor who sells you up, a friend who stabs you.

(Kristeva, 1982: 4)

In other less threatening encounters with the 'other', there is a negotiation of boundaries and an expansion of self, which tends toward the integration of the other (Winnicott, 1960). When the 'other within' (Kristeva, 1982) cannot be even partially recognized as belonging to me, it is extruded and evacuated into someone else who becomes the bearer of these 'alienated' contents. This evacuation makes a claim for borders, which means distinction, barrier, possibility to be separated from this otherness, and be safe.

Anzieu (1985, 1987) elaborates on this idea of groupal need for boundaries. He describes two early pre-structures of mind which he calls the 'psychic envelope' and 'ego-skin', viewed as membrane-like surfaces having some sort of proprioceptive or sensorimotor tonus, which protects the differentiation and individuation of the self by means of filtration and regulation of the permeability of the budding ego towards stimuli. Only stimuli that will be perceived as similar or compatible are allowed to draw upon images that give rise to a sense of pleasurable nonverbal communication. Similarly, groups have, or need to have, a common skin, a containing envelope that makes it possible for members to experience the existence of a groupal self and a groupal illusion, which corresponds to the founding moment when the group forms itself as such (1985: 95–7). This can then lead on to the formation of a group psychic apparatus, which might hold emotional states, thinking and effective group action (1985: 158). In Anzieu's work, this holding structure takes account of both individuals and group factors, a protective envelope in which thought and emotions can be registered and have some freedom to develop.

According to my hypothesis, in torturous societies the social organism has been somehow injured or terrified through a trauma, and its survival is in some other way threatened with dis-integration. In this condition, the reflective abilities of a group, what we have called the *Reflective Triangle* (i.e. its ability to process at the same time identity and difference in the social context), splinters, reorganizing social bonds in order to contain unbearable affects. Both terror and the urgent need for a containing border are processed at the most primitive bodily-level through fantasies of invasion and contamination, and consequent automatic psychic and social responses that create barriers and separations to resist this invasion of undifferentiated contents. This group reaction forces individual minds to conform to its functioning.

On the side of difference, unbearable dread is felt as 'abject' (Kristeva, 1982), an urge to expel some object from one's living body, in order to restore a sense of self and mastery. For this purpose, a minority group or a group with a minority status is exploited as the Other, someone in whom to evacuate formless dread via repetition of the initial trauma and intrusion into bodily boundaries, to give pre-symbolic form to the dread that is evacuated there. This guarantees some safety to the group from unbearable otherness.

On the side of identity, the collective need for a new border is satisfied through the identification with a narrow range of features, a reassuring merger with the group, the illusion of oneness with identical peers, but also the identification with a leader, whose body, symbolically representing their unity, offers containment of unbearable anxieties of dis-integration, its power protection, its leadership the reassuring or exciting phantasy of being capable of facing the threat. What is less apparent or difficult to recognize is the power imbalance (i.e. difference) and the internal unconscious otherness that one has become to that power. This awareness is sacrificed to the higher ideal of shaping a solid monolithic social body.

The shape of a Monolithic Societal State

In order to understand the preformed pattern of knowledge that seems to organize thinking, narratives and the style of social bonding in torturous societies, a reference to Michel Foucault's work is essential.

Foucault not only provides an outstanding analysis of how power works on body and subjectivity, but highlights with incredible clarity the geometry of power in emergency situations. Medicine had been a concern for Michel Foucault from the very beginning of his career. What is most relevant to our discourse is his description of the organization of community life by medical authorities in times of epidemic. According to his analysis, the Western world shaped two principal models to fight contagion during its history: the *model of leper* and *model of plague*. They were two distinctly different ways because, 'the leper gave rise to rituals of exclusion . . . the plague gave rise to disciplinary diagrams' (1975: 231). A society dealing with the leper is 'caught up in a practice of rejection, of exile-enclosure' (1975: 53), of partition and of separation because people with leprosy were removed and extruded from the rest of society. They were placed out of towns, in isolated places. On the contrary, a society dealing with plague requires the minute control and division of space: the town divided into districts, districts into quarters, quarters into isolated roads and individual houses, careful surveillance, detailed inspection, and order. These disciplinary diagrams require a strict spatial partitioning, careful surveillance, detailed inspection and order. This way of dealing with disease is not 'a massive, binary division between one set of people and another', rather, it is one that involves 'multiple separations, individualising distributions, an organisation in depth of surveillance and control, an intensification and a ramification of power' (1975: 231).

Foucault goes on to link these two models with their political/social counterparts: 'The first [the leper] is marked; the second [the plague] analyzed and distributed. The exile of leper and the arrest of the plague do not bring with them the same political dream. The first is that of a pure community, the second that of a disciplined society' (1975: 231–2). These are two ways of exercising power over men, of controlling their relations, of separating out their dangerous mixtures. They are different political projects, then, but not incompatible ones.

Foucault poignantly detects in the socio-political dream of control against the spreading of disease the psycho-social pattern at work in social reactions to terror. His brilliantly penetrating remarks on how a society stricken with the panic of contagion organizes itself against the epidemic illustrates, with outstanding clarity, the psychological pattern of the organization of societies in which the *Reflective Triangle* has splintered out of terror.

In torturous societies, we find both methods: on the one hand, exclusion and, on the other hand, systematic partitions. There are measures against mixture, contamination and contact with otherness (the model of exclusion used against leper) which are reserved for the out-group members, that is the minorities, the sub-human, whose otherness is perceived as external; and there are measures of systematic partitions (the model of control used against the plague), which are reserved for in-group members, the majority, the humans, whose otherness is perceived as internal to members of society.

In its conflation of political and psychological issues, Bentham's Panopticon, as discussed by Foucault, provides us with an interesting and poignant image, almost an ideal type, outlining the pure structure of power relations, organizational culture and ideology of a group in a monolithic mode of functioning.

The political geometry of ideology

Bentham's Panopticon is the architectural figure used by Foucault (1975: 200) to illustrate how discipline works: at the periphery, an annular building; at the centre, a tower which is pierced with wide windows that open onto the inner side of the ring; the periphery building is divided into cells, each of which extends the whole width of the building, and includes two windows, one on the inside, corresponding to the windows of the tower and the other, on the outside, allowing the light to cross the cell from one end to the other.

Foucault explains,

> All that is needed, then, is to place a supervisor in a central tower and to shut up in each cell a madman, a patient, a condemned man, a worker or a schoolboy. By the effect of backlighting, one can observe from the tower, standing out precisely against the light, the small captive shadows in the cells of the periphery. They are like so many cages, so many small theatres, in which each actor is alone, perfectly individualized and constantly visible. . . .
>
> Each individual, in his place, is securely confined to a cell from which he is seen from the front by the supervisor; but the side walls prevent him from coming into contact with his companions. He is seen, but he does not see; he is the object of information, never a subject in communication. The arrangement of his room, opposite to the central tower, imposes on him an axial visibility; but the divisions of the ring, those separated cells, imply a lateral invisibility. And this invisibility is a guarantee of order . . . The crowd, a compact mass, a locus of multiple exchanges, individualities

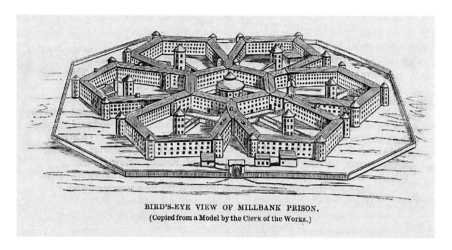

FIGURE 5.1 The Panopticon: the structure of a Monolithic Societal State. Bird's eye view of Millbank Prison (London), taken from *The Criminal Prisons of London, and Scenes of Prison Life*, by Henry Mayhew, published in 1862.

merging together, a collective effect, is abolished and replaced by a collection of separated individualities. From the point of view of the guardian, it is replaced by a multiplicity that can be numbered and supervised; from the point of view of the inmates, by a sequestered and observed solitude.

(Foucault, 1975: 200–1)

Foucault uses this model to explain the organization of the plague-stricken town, which is one where people's survival is menaced, a segmented, immobile, frozen space. Each individual is fixed in their place, and, if they move, they do so at the risk of their life, contagion or punishment. This enclosed, segmented space is observed at every point. In such a space, the individuals are inserted in a fixed place, the slightest movements are supervised, every event is recorded, the uninterrupted work of writing links the centre and periphery, power is exercised according to a continuous hierarchical figure and each individual is constantly located, examined and distributed (1975: 205–6). The plague is met by order; its function is to sort out every possible confusion. This means that, whenever the threat comes from mixture, society invents new mechanisms to shape according to partitioning, immobilization and hierarchy, thereby giving continuity to social action and allowing for central control. The Panopticon is the diagram of a mechanism of power reduced to its ideal form: it is in fact a figure of political technology.

It automatizes and de-individualizes power, which has its principle not so much in a person as in a certain concerted distribution of bodies, surfaces, lights and gazes, in an arrangement whose internal mechanisms produce the relations in which individuals are caught up. It is also polyvalent in its applications. It is a type of location of bodies in space, distribution of individuals in relation to one another, hierarchical organization, disposition of centres and channels of power, definition

146 A psychoanalytic understanding of torture

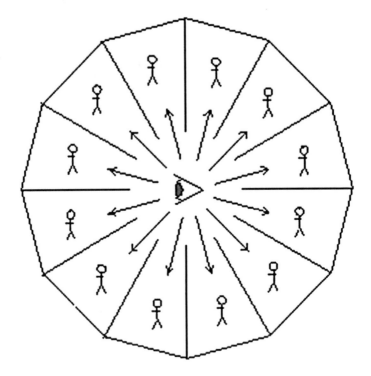

FIGURE 5.2 The political geometry of the Panopticon

of the instruments and modes of intervention of power, which can be implemented everywhere in society (Foucault, 1975). This is the reason why, in each of its applications, the Panopticon makes it possible to perfect the exercise of power because, without any physical instrument other than architecture and geometry, it acts directly on individuals; it gives 'power of mind over mind'.

The Panopticon geometry of relations and distributions perfectly fits with the geometry of the Splintered Reflective Triangle of MSSs, with its controlling social bonds set through a vision system: the web of towers controlling discrete individuals and, in turn, seen/controlled by a central tower. This illustrates how individuals can be controlled within groups or institutions, and how groups and institutions, in turn, can be controlled by a central power. It is precisely the architecture of torturous societies, where a system of social, institutional/groupal and intrapsychic partitions keeps individuals and groups disconnected through adhesive relationship between superiors and subordinates, established by means of being constantly seen, as well as keeps individuals aligned to the directives a central controlling power.

But the question still remains: what is the final device that keeps individuals in such positions? This question points to the issue of ideology. What is ideology from a psychological perspective?

That of ideology is a very complex theme. The notion of ideology emerges in the seventeenth and eighteenth centuries as a critical concept referring to representations that legitimate particular forms of authority, thereby securing the production and reproduction of particular socio-cultural formations (Barratt, 1985: 440). However, for the limited purpose of a possible psychosocial use, Baranger's definition of ideology refers to 'every system of abstract ideas (conscious or unconscious)', whether philosophical or religious and ethical, aesthetic and political, 'whose function it is to represent that which is real and man's action upon that which is real' (1958: 191).

In the psychological realm, psychoanalytic studies that describe mental *states of twoness* lend themselves to support a notion of ideology which is inherent not to the contents of the subject's psychic reality, but to the process of formation of representational contents. From a psychological point of view, we might suppose that ideologies imply two aspects of mental life, cognitive and emotional, in different proportions: a psychic architectural structure with its roots in human emotional needs and its branches in the realm of cognition, which, at their turn, shape the production of representations and material means of individual and social life. The more pressing and urgent are the emotional needs, the stronger and deeper their imprint on ideas that flow from them.[2]

Thus, ideology, as a system of ideas, may be conceived as the social reaction to powerful emotions that end up organizing people's thinking in closed systems of cognition (see Chapter 2), thereby creating acceptable perspectives and modes of interpreting reality, which sustain a certain mythology. They utilize and enforce selective attention and inattention on various aspects of interpersonal and social transactions, designing permissible thoughts and behaviours, which are congruent with the ethos of the ideological community. In so doing, they define the limits of knowing, structuring the future organization of experience and the nature of behaviour. Ideologies have a privileged relationship to truth and reality, and, for this reason, they have a remarkable capacity of making powerful transformations in the lives of individuals, uniting them into organized collectivities and converting ordinary fellow citizens and neighbours into brothers, sisters, comrades, and, especially, comrades in arms.

Ogden's paranoid-schizoid mode (1986, 1989b, 1994) can describe many features of ideologies, especially of those systems of ideas that are emotionally saturated. In such ideologies, thinking is constrained and organized by affective intolerance of ambivalence (love and hate, positive and negative emotions cannot be modulated); consequently, there is a massive use of splitting, denial, projection and, projective identification, which create a binary representation of the world that is divided into 'good' and 'bad', 'us' and 'them'. Moreover, it binds relational actors in fixed reciprocal positions through projective identifications. We have seen that the paranoid-schizoid mode is a state of mind that is relatively devoid of an interpreting subject; this is probably what favours the uncritical link to a prescriptive central power that can dictate even incoherent meanings, since it is founded on a compartmentalized system. Since mental *states of twoness* are the outcome of psychic fragmentation, individuals satisfy their need of coherence keeping themselves connected to a larger system (a group, an institution, society at large) in order to find meanings for their actions. These meanings can be conveyed from higher to lower spheres of society as incontestable 'truths'.

From a Jungian perspective, Papadopoulos illustrates in the concept of the *unipolar archetype*, the unconscious *twoness* of this collective mental state resulting in one-sided positions, and the interconnection between epistemology, positioning and action in them (2005a, 2005b, 2009). In Jungian theory, archetypes are inherited patterns of psychological functioning and, in this sense, they are impersonal and alike for everyone. Ordinarily, they are in a constant interaction and their coupled opposites can be modulated. However, during times of political upheaval, when powerful emotions flare up, unipolar archetypes tend to emerge with unprecedented power in everyone (Papadopoulos, 2005a), while archetypal polarization phenomena can be appreciated as manifestations of a state, where one pole of the archetype reigns supreme and almost totally suppresses any elements that belong to the other pole. Papadopoulos introduced the expressions 'archetypal dazzle', 'archetypal radiation' and 'archetypal whirlpool' to indicate the process for producing such unipolarity (Papadopoulos, 2005a, 2005b, 2006, 2009). My understanding of this 'archetypal radiation' is that, under certain conditions, people's minds perform an 'alignment' of archetypes (which are an inherited patterns of response) according to such unipolarity. Individuals find themselves in a groupal 'field of forces', operating a pressure to orientate their feelings and thinking according to the unipolarity of inherited patterns of response, which is susceptible to produce ideological thinking. Polarization implies simplistic perceptions, (i.e. black or white, good or bad, 'us *vs.* them') with the sacrifice of 'complexity' (Papadopoulos, 2009). This affects three distinct and yet inter-related areas: epistemology, position and action. As far as epistemology is concerned, under polarised conditions, there will be a selective perception within groups which interprets incidents in a way that strengthens the polarised beliefs and shapes everything around them according to its logic, with a certain degree of automaticity. Positioning refers to the active effect that discourses have in locating individuals and communities in certain positions: extreme images of pure good and pure evil tend to grip both sides of the conflict and polarised sharp divisions into 'us–good' *vs.* 'them–bad' organize social interactions and internal perceptions. Finally, action can only be the consequence of a certain positioning, given the specifics of the dominant epistemology that informs it. Thus, one encounters acts of unbelievable evil and depravity, or acts of generosity, self-sacrifice, and pure love, as we have seen in the bystander's phenomenology (Chapter 3). In this way, the epistemology, positioning and action keep strengthening and reproducing each other in mutually coherent ways.

The tower: identification with an inflated controlling power

The central tower of the Panopticon can be read as the actual controlling function of the power, as well as the unifying ideal principle, which makes a claim for identification through a shared ideal. It is the place where one pole – the good/powerful/valued – of the collective unipolar archetype is positioned (Papadopoulos, 2005a, 2006, 2009), or, put another way, where someone (the leader or their representative) has replaced the controlling ego ideal (Freud, 1921).

It works like a narcissistic core (a tall tower), i.e. an inflated power/leader/ideal invested with the qualities of goodness, perfection and purity, which protects individuals from contamination through control and partitioning. The central tower may also represent every kind of belief, both secular and sacred, providing a collective unifying set of principles, which produce knowledge and social organization.

Two aspects of ideological persuasion lend themselves particularly to narcissistic needs: the representation of one's magnificent identity and destiny, and a peculiar status of knowledge that gives the illusion of omniscience.

We have seen how a sense of cultural superiority characterizes torturous powers (Chapter 2). In these societies, the political and/or cultural context is fragmented, while there is the attempt to keep society united through a representation of one's destiny as great and superior than that of other groups. Their leader is often someone who best embodies and responds to the crowd's needs for narcissistic exaltation. There are plenty of examples of these narcissistic narratives. The early fascists were young and, in their rhetorical discourse, there was a celebration of youth, strength, future and destiny (Paxton, 2004). In their analysis of Israel, Gordon and Marton (1995) notice that the Jewish *Weltanschauung* was nourished by myths about the moral superiority of one's own people, the idea of equality, the 'purity of weapons', the narrative of the empty desert that the Zionists redeemed and turned into a blooming garden, all of which became agents of socialization. Graziano (1992: 124) shows how the Junta nourished Argentina's sense of grandiosity, emphasizing its pretended role in redeeming the 'Western and Christian civilization worldwide from the protracted international hostilities associated with world war'. As Ariel Dorfman states,

> Every regime that tortures does so in the name of salvation, some superior goal, some promise of paradise. Call it communism, call it the free market, call it the free world, call it the national interest, call it fascism, call it the leader, call it civilisation, call it the service of God . . . torturers everywhere do not think of themselves as evil, but rather as guardian of the common good, dedicated patriots who get their hands dirty and endure perhaps some sleepless nights in order to deliver the blind ignorant majority from violence and anxiety.
>
> (Dorfman, 2004: 36)

'Social narcissism' assumes the shape of an over-evaluation of one's own identity. Michael Ignatieff, writing about ethnic war in his book, *The Warrior's Honour* (1998), devotes a chapter to the 'narcissism of minor difference'. The narcissism of minor differences inscribes itself within a primitive and concrete mode of experiencing reality, which makes of the essentialist discourse on body and genetics its own language: we are the best, the fittest, the strongest, and this is inscribed in our genes. He explains that, 'by overvalue, I mean we insist that we have nothing in common, nothing to share. At the heart of this insistence lurks the phantasy of purity, of boundaries that can never be crossed' (Ignatieff, 1998: 62).

Ignatieff (1998) refers to a pathological form of groupal narcissism as a difficulty to process similarities with others, in which grandiosity – the overvaluing of our own identities – serves a defensive purpose. Boundaries must be clearly, and rigidly, delineated and imposed (because of a sense of internal threat). The narcissistic psyche will also more often than not be governed by a severe superego, which has had to develop in a Gestapo-like manner. Safety is then achieved through a kind of political correctness, which transforms minor differences into major ones.

Freud first used the phrase, 'narcissism of minor differences', in the course of his essay, 'The taboo of virginity', which he wrote in 1917. This was towards the end of the First World War, when mankind's aggression towards one another was powerfully evident and foremost in people's minds. Freud observed that, 'it is precisely the minor differences in people who are otherwise alike that form the basis of feelings of strangeness and hostility between them . . . ' (1917: 48, I).

Freud elaborated on this idea in terms of his clinical experience and his observation of the anxiety caused by the perception of the difference between the sexes. In his patients' material, Freud found that the sheer difference or otherness presented by the opposite sex was threatening and produced hostility.

Extending his views to groups, five years later, Freud wrote in, *Group Psychology and the Analysis of the Ego* that the closer the relation between groups, the greater is the potential hostility (1921: 49).

By 1921, he began to live through his own painful experience of witnessing how differences would turn into hostilities in Hitler's Germany and the widespread transformation of minor racial differences to major differences. In this same monograph on group psychology, Freud links the phenomenon directly to narcissism. He writes:

> In the undisguised antipathies and aversion which people feel towards strangers with whom they have to do we may recognize the expression of self-love of narcissism. This self-love works for the preservation of the individual, and behaves as though the occurrence of any divergence from his own particular lines of development involved a criticism of them and a demand for their alteration.
>
> (Freud, 1921: 50)

Freud recognizes within the aversion to strangers a merging into sameness, self-love and purity, which grants security and the constitution of an ego, a group or a national self. The ego ideal is thus the original mental agency that performs this defence of an early narcissistic identity based on a mirrored sameness. Thus, we gain potency and a new narcissistic integrity, in all its meaning of honesty, goodness, wholeness and unity. This satisfies the demand for the narcissistic ideal of purity. This ideal implies elevation, but also a movement *away from reality*.

This idea of purity, narcissistic identity, merging into sameness is maintained through the controlling system of the Panopticon. One major effect of the Panopticon is to induce in the inmate a state of conscious and permanent visibility, which assures the automatic functioning of power. In order to achieve this condition, Bentham laid down the principle that power should be visible and unverifiable: visible, so that the inmate will constantly have before their eyes the tall outline of the central tower from which they are spied upon; unverifiable, so that the inmate must never know whether they are being looked at at any one moment, while being certain that they could always be looked at (Foucault, 1975: 201).

This mechanism of the Panopticon dissociates the see/being seen dyad to induce a sustained and prolonged paranoid-schizoid state, which locks controllers and controlled in the same grip: in the peripheric ring, one is totally seen, without ever seeing; in the central tower, one sees everything without ever being seen. The same principle of unidirectional control can be seen in action in Orwell's *Nineteen Eighty-Four*, where a screen in every house has the function of a window to be seen, while the Thought Police represents the internalization of that surveillance (1949: 4–5; 219–20).

The dissociation of the see/being seen dyad is a very powerful device for control, which squeezes the relational in-between space and, in so doing, undermines mutuality in its fundamentals. From an intersubjective perspective, Benjamin (1988, 1990, 2002, 2004) illuminates the importance of 'mutual recognition' between mother and baby, which, in the beginning of this earliest human relationship, relies on mutual gazes. Research on mother–infant face-to-face play shows how the adult and the infant align with a third, establishing a co-created rhythm that is not reducible to a model of action–reaction, with one active and the other passive, or one leading and the other following. Action–reaction characterizes our experience of complementary twoness, the one-way direction. This is how the Panopticon works: through the internalization of the controlling function, with the state of twoness resulting from being continuously seen and under siege. Once the self is monolithic, there is no need for an external tower, the control function is performed by the ego ideal (Freud, 1921).

Adopting a similar technology of power, political systems often resort to the rhetoric of a religious monotheistic discourse: the idea of God serves the inflated power with a unifying principle, which prescribes the right behaviour and controls through the unidirectionality of sight and an impossible system of mutual checks. As Stein writes, 'monotheism is about the One, who is *invisible* [the controlling tower]. It is usually patriarchal, that is, it has at its core the belief in a masculine and paternal deity' (2006: 202, emphasis added). God, like some secular ideologies, seems to work here to bind individual experience to social action. The maximum expression of monolithic power is the merging of power, state and divine law, by a theocratic state. Millet (1994) exemplifies this conflation of religious and political aims leading to the sacred One that structures a monolithic social reality, in her analysis of the Islamic Republic of Iran. She comments that Iran is unusual in having legalized certain tortures in its criminal code, while other tortures, which are technically illegal, have come to be viewed as punishments of the same religious order, namely, expressions of the will of God.

The appeal to the unifying principle of a monotheistic God is so effective and fascinating that, in certain circumstances, even secular democratic states turn to it (Bacevich and Prodromou, 2004). This conflation of religion and power works as a penetrating device for social control, binding the private individual behaviour to the aims of a central power and, thereby, obtaining a *monolithic* unity of the social body.

The cells: the status of knowledge, partitions and omniscience

Barnett (1973) points out that ideology, being a closed system, lends itself to the illusion of omniscience. Doubts and uncertainties are replaced by the conviction (and by group support and validation) that it alone possesses and guards absolute truth. This absolute status of knowledge is the result of a fragmentation of consciousness, supported by multiple partitions in society, which enable those in power to keep control of reality. A shared language, premises and rules of discourse reinforce this illusion. Multiplicity is sacrificed to a false idea of unity based on the sharing of this state of twoness, which is at the foundation of the binary thinking ('good/bad', 'us/them') that also marks the exclusion of the Other. What is sought-after through these *states of twoness* is the grandiosity of certainty, which secures the self in an enclosed *i-dentity*. This *identi-fication* with the good leader/party/nation/ethnicity implies an *adhesive* fidelity to the power that claims to the need for unwearyingly moment-to-moment flexibility in the treatment of facts, conferring a special status on knowledge. For this purpose, a memory of real events is not required, only 'official truths', which can change on a moment-to-moment basis. This fidelity to power is based on the partitions that results from the contraction of reflective in-between social spaces. Such a contraction of the potential space for connections, means that pieces of information, perceptions, memories cannot make contact with each other with a consequent *freezing* of individual's reflective abilities. Because of this dissociating device, knowing is impeded. Similarly, the isolation of individuals (the cells of the Panopticon) through different levels of separations (divisions of roles, limitation of competence, professionalism) in society (see Todorov, 1991), produces a state of knowledge characterized by closure and massive use of splitting and denial. The result is what Orwell calls *blackwhite* and *doublethink*, which have a deep impact on the functioning of memory, the sense of history and the sense of time, a continuous unmasking of 'truth' and rewriting of history.[3] It is the reign of the paranoid-schizoid mode (Ogden, 1986, 1988, 1994) which sustains Monolithic Societal States.

As described in Chapters 3 and 6, disavowal is the mechanism by which we disregard acknowledging the reality of our perceptions (Cohen, 2001; Feitlowitz, 1998; Hollander 2008, 2010; Kaatz, 2006). Disavowal involves a *doublethinking*, a splitting of the ego, which knows but ignores at the same time. This produces the mental ability to believe what the power says it is true, while disbelieving one's own perceptions.

The vertical segment of difference: the process of 'othering', hierarchical relationships and the narrative of sacrifice

In torturous societies, the extrusion of the Other creates an artificial two-dimensional reality where individuals are alienated from genuine political life. The splintering of the Reflective Triangle, on the one hand, has the effect of creating a merging of individuals in the large group identity through the adoption of a shared ideology, while on the other hand, it processes difference by producing a power gradient, which shapes society in vertical hierarchical systems that perpetuate some level of violence on their own group members. In this way, the Other which was extruded as a safety measure – according to Foucault's leper model – re-enters the social scene.

As such, the closed world of the ideological mental state, if it guarantees the illusion of safety, also produces the suffering of being subjected to an emptying process of de-subjectification. Through a process of atomization of society into isolated and ineffectual individuals, along with the imposition of a set of values and the systematic use of terror, individual self is more and more 'othered' and objectified (Ogden, 1986, 1988, 1994).

As Abed describes,

> the disappearance of any semblance of legal protection for the individual results in a state of constant vulnerability and near-complete powerlessness that leads to depoliticization, infantilization and a state of passivity of the individual. Citizens are systematically deprived of autonomous decision-making and action in whole areas of their life.
>
> (Abed, 2005: 3)

In MSoSs, trust between individuals is systematically destroyed by rendering every citizen a potential informer for the state. The destruction of trust leads to a wider suppression of cooperative and collaborative behaviour and potentially to the suppression of altruistic behaviour towards others (even in totalitarian regimes that profess an egalitarian ideology) (Abed, 2005; Hollander, 2008, 2010). As shown in Chapter 3, terror may be used as a routine instrument of governance and not simply as a deterrent or punishment for opponents of the regime. If we cannot control the object of terror, we align ourselves with it. For the social context, this takes the form of believing that reality can be defended against by aligning with measures that support state terror, or with authoritarian figures who are imagined terminators of terror. For the citizen in Oceania,

> it is necessary that he should have the mentality appropriate to a state of war. It does not matter whether the war is actually happening, and, since no decisive victory is possible, it does not matter whether the war is going well or badly. All that is needed is that a state of war should exist. The splitting of the intelligence which the Party requires of its members, and which is

more easily achieved in an atmosphere of war, is now almost universal, but the higher up the ranks one goes the more marked it becomes.

(Orwell, 1949: 200)

Since a mental state of terror produces a range of partitions in individuals' psyche and in social relationships, the mind relies on a preformed pattern of knowledge to interpret reality, which becomes a principle of organization of society. People's thinking aligns with a common paranoid-schizoid mode, which is functional to a reshaping of society in a hierarchical way such that it provides continuity by filling the gaps of social fragmentation. The Panopticon seems to be a perfect alienating device, transforming individuals into an object of control, in the role of both controller and controlled.

This empties individuals of personal dimensions and 'sacrifices' individual subjectivity to the collective dimension. Worries and enthusiasms are focused on society as a whole and the individual dimension is sacrificed to the collective one. Paxton (2004) lists an entire repertory of collective themes within fascism that perfectly fits into this pattern. He writes: 'At its fullest development, fascism redrew the frontiers between private and public, sharply diminishing what had once been untouchably private' (2004: 11), affirming 'the primacy of the "race" or the "community" or "the people" (the *Volk*, for Germans) over any individual rights' (2004: 38); 'the virtue and beauty of violent action on behalf of the nation'(2004: 38); 'the excitement of participating in a vast collective enterprise' (2004: 17); 'the gratification of submerging oneself in a wave of shared feelings, and of sacrificing one's petty concerns for the group's good; and the thrill of domination' (2004: 17).

On December 24, 1976, at the close of the first year of the 'Dirty War' and on the eve of the Son-God's rebirth into Christendom, President Jorge Rafael Videla addressed the people of Argentina with the following message:

> Sacrifice has been, without a doubt, the sign of the year that is ending. A shared and indispensable sacrifice that constitutes the beginning of the arduous journey toward the true reencounter of all Argentines; sacrifices ... that permit us to assume the essential theme of the great Argentine family: that of national union.
>
> (Graziano, 1992: 191)

Having narrativized the 'Dirty War' around the 'sign' of *sacrifice*, the Junta discourse reinforced the propriety of exacting a 'personal quota' from each Argentine by positing the military and, above all, the Junta itself, as paradigms of self-sacrifice for the *patria*. The sacrifice was qualified by Videla as 'shared', an act of service that, with faith in God he offered to the Fatherland, to the army and to all the Argentine people, as he put it. Graziano (1992: 192) comments that, outside this mythology, it was difficult to justify the distribution of the heaviest sacrificial burden among the military because the 'Dirty War's' primary strategy – abduction,

Monolithic Societal States 155

torture, execution – situated the Junta more readily in the role of sacrificial executioner than in the role of victim.

This paradigm of self-sacrifice for perpetrators of torture becomes more understandable if we reverse the terms and think of it as the *sacrifice* of *self*, dedicating oneself to the required partiality that favours adhesive links, especially among military and civil superiors, to a paternal dominating figure.

Lazar (2006) writes that the English word *sacrifice* is derived from 'sacred'. It refers to a ritual in which the sacrificial victim is destroyed in order to achieve a desired relation between the individual who makes the sacrifice and the god to whom the offering is made and on whose good will the individual depends. The sacrifice nourishes the deity and, at the same time, atones for any destructiveness against it. The objective is to make an offering that would please the deity or to institutionalize a value or an order of things, which are important to the individual who makes the sacrifice or to their close environment. Lazar (2006) stresses the feature of sacrifice as that of acting out an idealization of the other for whom the sacrificial offering is made, typically a paternal deity. In the founding myths, the maker of sacrifice is portrayed as a victim of their own vows or their master's command, and not as a suffering independent actor, free of remorse. The act of sacrifice comprises fusion, a blurring out of identity, whereas relinquishment comprises surrender, a response to an-other as a value.

In Jungian terms, this psychic position of sacrifice may be understood as possession by a tyrannical father. On the theme of the tyranny of power, Colman (2000) recognizes the mythological figure of Chronos/Saturn, who, persuaded by his mother Gaia to overthrow his father, attempts to prevent the same fate eating all his children as soon as they are born. Chronos, according to Jung (1955–1956: para. 298), is the archetype of the *senex* and subsequent writers have elaborated on the devouring aspect of the Saturnine *senex* as 'the sick father', an archetypal metaphor for a situation of stagnation and decay in the psyche, and its need for rejuvenation and rebirth by its archetypal opposites, the *puer* (notice two opposite expressions of narcissism). Colman (2000) suggests that this is the archetypal situation operating under a totalitarian power: *a state of total projective identification between father and son*, similar to living inside the stomach of Chronos with no access to the maternal feminine and no possibility to escape. The omnipotent dictator, whether internal or external, seeks to crush all forms of opposition, especially any possibility of creativity. The children are consumed by the father, kept under his control by remaining a part of himself, inside him, denied any life of their own. This myth applies to tortured and torturers. Neumann distinguishes between those sons who are *captives* of the father (those in the cells of the Panopticon), and those who are *possessed* by him (those in the tower), the torturers (1954: 187), two different ways of oppression produced by the same social device. In both, there is an element of sacrifice and adhesive relationality to the father.

Apparently, torture might be understood as a continuation of this line of sacrifices, part of the same social process of 'othering' its members. Graziano (1992) notices that, in torture, the opposite logic of self-sacrifice seems to be at work –

that of the scapegoat. This logic is one in which the projection of one's otherness/badness onto someone else serves the purpose of one's own rescue.

Torture

In conclusion, what is the role of torture in such a framework? In a MSoS, the difference (represented by the Other) has been extruded, but the resulting state of mind is an enclosed delusional world, which ultimately threatens all members of society with objectification, depletion and plundering. If this process does not encounter resistance, the end point will be unthinkable horrors of objecthood: what has been expelled and put into a distanced other becomes an Other, and finally a thing, a body, a corpse. However, if torture may end with death, it is not aimed at the material sacrifice of the victim. On the contrary, it seems to be a way to reintroduce dynamism where the tension between self and other collapsed.

At an early stage, a Monolithic Societal State seems an appropriate and most successful way to approach existential and social tasks: it provides mastery over difficulty, a sense of agency and control, a defence against threats, the avoidance of reality, the possibility to rewrite the past, thereby avoiding painful memories and awareness, and facing powerful emotions. However, this is a mental state in which the mind loses the ability to symbolize, to manage those signs which enable a correct perception, to hierarchically classify dangers from the outside world and discriminate between imagination and reality (Ogden, 1986, 1988, 1994).

Torture seems to be introduced here in the attempt to find a bulwark to this slippery slope and stop this disastrous process. The collective seems to intrude into the victim's tortured body/mind in search for borders, seeking for resistance to this relentless paralysing process.

We have seen that Benjamin (1988) conceives domination as a two-way process, a system involving the participation of those who submit to power, as well as those who exercise it (1990, 2004). In her theory, domination is an attempt to deny mutual dependence and, in the dynamic of master and slave, there is a kind of unconscious symmetry (a *state of twoness*) that guides the enactment – an inverse mirror in which each feels done to (Benjamin, 1990, 2004). Benjamin is interested in the question of how we break out of retaliatory cycles and complementary (doer–done to) relations (1988, 1990, 2002, 2004). However, her understanding of the interpersonal sadomasochistic dynamics, i.e. the masochist's recognition of one's own participation in the dynamics of submission, might sound inappropriate if applied individually to victims of torture, and risks resulting in a 'blaming of the victim'.

As an alternative, if we look at 'recognition' and 'domination' as two opposite modes of relating connected to the Reflective Triangle at individual, groupal and social level, we reintroduce in our understanding the difficulties of reflectivity in the interactions between different levels of experience.

From this perspective, torture would be that practice of segregation and violence through which a political power wants to conquer the subjectivity of the tortured converting them to its monolithic functioning (in this sense, the individual *is* a victim, see Chapter 6). However, at the same time, it is also an attempt to regain what has been primarily lost in society, that is the reflective abilities which have been destroyed through the violent intrusion of otherness. In other words, I am proposing torture as a distorted way to make contact with the Other in an attempt to make reality reappear.

We have seen that groupal defences tend to create the conditions in which an illusionary – ideological – knowledge can develop, with a depletion of symbolizing abilities: that same knowledge which has been lost (together with subjectivity) is now looked for. Torture might be understood as repetition of the (group felt) attack, a concrete attempt to stage what happened as primary move, a gruesome attempt to reconnect with that initial point of disconnection, where the reflective abilities dis-integrated. This need there might be beyond the fictionality of torture. Scarry notes that, in the Philippines, in the torturers' idiom, the room in which the brutality occurred was known as the 'production room', in South Vietnam the 'cinema room', and in Chile the 'blue lit stage'. Scarry interprets this fictional vocation of torture simply as a means of converting the physical pain of the victim into a 'fantastic illusion of power', 'a compensatory drama' (Scarry, 1985: 28). However, in this account an aspect of the phenomenon may have been missed: the possible unconscious claim for restoring reflective abilities, a failed attempt of symbolization and re-presentation. Paradoxically, the chance of regaining such an ability may only lie in the possibility that the victim, the most powerless, makes a difference by surviving (Benjamin, 1988, 2004), reassuring the attacker that a world is still in there.

What is really sacrificed in torture are *social reflective in-between spaces*, individual and communal subjectivities that are transformed into power subjects. The social transactions, interactions, conflicts, negotiations and meaning making activities are constrained in coercive dynamics. The *in-between space* becomes a *no man's land* where neither law nor sovereignty of any subject can be claimed. The protector and the protected, the powerful and the powerless, the subjector and the subjected, the slave and the master, the torturer and the tortured: they are each one half of the entire social body, in a deep *state of twoness* (Benjamin, 1988), enacting what cannot be thought.

Notes

1 Here the term 'in-between' is used in the sense of 'mixed' by Kristeva.
2 This is probably the reason why Paxton states that, although fascism did not rest on an elaborated philosophical system, it was nonetheless considered an ideology (Paxton, 2004: 15). Fascist leaders made no secret of having no programme. Mussolini exulted in that absence. Paxton alerts us to the risk of identifying fascism with its leader and details its historical analysis with the role of people's emotional needs (2004: 40–1). Even scholars who are specialized in the quest for fascism's intellectual and cultural origins, such as George Mosse (1982), declare that the establishment of a 'mood' is more important than 'the search for some individual precursors' (1982: 16).

3   Like so many Newspeak [the project of a new language in Oceania] words, this word [blackwhite] has two mutually contradictory meanings. Applied to an opponent, it means the habit of impudently claiming that black is white, in contradiction of the plain facts. Applied to a Party member, it means a loyal willingness to say that black is white when Party discipline demands this. But it means also the ability to *believe* that black is white, and more, to *know* that black is white, and to forget that one has ever believed the contrary. This demands a continuous alteration of the past, made possible by the system of thought which really embraces all the rest, and which is known in Newspeak as *doublethink*. . . . Thus history is continuously rewritten. This day-to-day falsification of the past, carried out by the Ministry of Truth, is as necessary to the stability of the regime as the work of repression and espionage carried out by the Ministry of Love.

(Orwell, 1949: 221–2, emphasis in original)

References

Abed R.T. (2005) 'Tyranny and mental health'. *British Medical Bulletin*, 72(1): 1–13. doi: 10.1093/bmb/ldh037

Alleg, H. (1958) *The Question*. Preface by Jean-Paul Sartre, with a new afterword by the author. Lincoln and London: University of Nebraska Press, 2006.

Anzieu, D. (1985) *The Ego-Skin*. New Haven, CT: Yale University Press.

Anzieu, D. (1987) *Psychic Envelopes*. London: Karnac Books.

Aron, L. (1996) *A Meeting of Minds: Mutuality in Psychoanalysis*. Hillsdale, NJ: The Analytic Press.

Bacevich, A.J. and Prodromou, E.H. (2004) 'God is not neutral: religion and U.S. foreign policy after 9/11'. *Orbis*, 48(1) (Winter: 43–54.) doi:10.1016/j.orbis.2003.10.012

Baranger, W. (1958) 'The ego and the function of ideology'. *The International Journal of Psychoanalysis*, 39: 191–5.

Barnett, J. (1973) 'On ideology and the psychodynamics of the ideologue'. *Journal of American Academy of Psychoanalysis*, 1(4): 381–5.

Barratt, B.B. (1985) 'Psychoanalysis as critique of ideology'. *Psychoanalytic Inquiry*, 5(3): 437–70. doi:10.1080/07351698509533598

Benjamin, J. (1988) *The Bonds of Love*. New York: Pantheon Books.

Benjamin, J. (1990) 'An outline of intersubjectivity: the development of recognition'. *Psychoanalytic Psychology*, 7(Suppl): 33–46. Reprinted as 'Recognition and destruction: an outline of intersubjectivity', in Mitchell, S. A. and Aron, L. (Eds) (1999) *Relational Psychoanalysis: The Emergence of a Tradition*. Hillsdale, NJ and London: The Analytic Press, pp. 181–210.

Benjamin, J. (2002) 'Terror and guilt: beyond them and us'. *Psychoanalytic Dialogues*, 12(3): 473–84. doi:10.1080/10481881209348681

Benjamin, J. (2004) 'Beyond doer and done to: an intersubjective view of thirdness'. *Psychoanalytic Quarterly*, 73(1): 5–46. Reprinted in Aron, L. and Harris, A. (Eds) (2012) *Relational Psychoanalysis, Vol. 4 Expansion of Theory*. New York and London: Routledge, pp. 91–130.

Bion, W.R. (1962a) *Learning from Experience*. London: Heinemann.

Bion, W.R. (1962b) 'A theory of thinking'. *The International Journal of Psychoanalysis*, 43: 306–10.

Chasseguet-Smirgel, J. (1975) *The Ego Ideal: A Psychoanalytic Essay on the Malady of the Ideal*. London: Free Association Books, 1985.

Cohen, S. (2001) *States of Denial: Knowing about Atrocities and Suffering*. Cambridge: Polity Press.
Colman, W. (2000) 'Tyrannical omnipotence in the archetypal father'. *Journal of Analytical Psychology*, 45(4): 521–39. doi:10.1111/1465-5922.00189
Dorfman, A. (2004) *Other Septembers, Many Americas: Selected Provocations 1980–2004*. New York: Seven Stories Press.
Feitlowitz, M. (1998) *A Lexicon of Terror: Argentina and the Legacies of Torture*. New York: Oxford University Press.
Foucault, M. (1975) *Discipline and Punish: The Birth of the Prison*. New York: Random House, 1979.
Freud, S. (1914) 'On narcissism: an introduction'. In *The Standard Edition of the Complete Psychological Works of Sigmund Freud*, Trans. and Ed. J. Strachey, vol. 14. London: The Hogarth Press (hereafter, *SE*).
Freud, S. (1917) 'The taboo of virginity'. In *SE*, vol. 11.
Freud, S. (1921) 'Group psychology and the analysis of the ego'. In *SE*, vol. 18.
Freud, S. (1923) 'The Ego and the Id'. In *SE*, vol. 19.
Gordon, N. and Marton, R. (1995) *Torture: Human Rights, Medical Ethics and the Case of Israel*. London and New Jersey: Zed Books.
Graziano, F. (1992) *Divine Violence. Spectacle, Psychosexuality, and Radical Christianity in the Argentine 'Dirty War'*. Boulder, San Francisco, Oxford: Westview Press.
Hartmann, H. and Lowenstein, R. (1962) 'Notes on the superego'. *Psychoanalytic Studies of the Child*, 17: 42–81.
Hollander, N.C. (2008) 'Living danger: on not knowing what we know'. *Psychoanalytic Dialogues*, 18(5): 690–709. doi:10.1080/10481880802297707
Hollander, N.C. (2010) *Uprooted Minds: Surviving the Politics of Terror in the Americas*. New York: Routledge.
Ignatieff, M. (1998) *The Warrior's Honour: Ethnic War and the Modern Conscience*. New York: Holt Paperbacks.
Jung, C. G. (1955–1956) 'Mysterium Coniunctionis'. In *Collected Works of C.G. Jung*, vol. 14, Read, H. Fordham M. and Adler G. (Eds.), translated by R. Hull, Princeton, NJ: Princeton University Press/Bollingen Series XX.
Kaatz, M. (2006) 'The beheading of America: reclaiming our minds'. In Layton, L., Hollander, N.C. and Gutwill, S. (Eds.), *Psychoanalysis, Class and Politics: Encounters in the Clinical Setting*. London, New York: Routledge, pp. 141–53.
Kristeva, J. (1982) *Powers of Horror: An Essay on Abjection*. New York: Columbia University Press.
Lazar, R. (2006) 'In the beginning was love?' *The Psychoanalytic Review*, 93(3): 391–410. doi:10.1521/prev.2006.93.3.391
Millet, K. (1994) *The Politics of Cruelty: An Essay on the Literature of Political Imprisonment*. London: Penguin Books.
Mitchell, S.A. (1988) *Relational Concepts in Psychoanalysis*. Cambridge, MA: Harvard University Press.
Mosse, G. (1964) *The Crisis of German Ideology: Intellectual Origins of the Third Reich*. New York: Grosset and Dunlap.
Neumann, E. (1954) *The Origins and History of Consciousness*. Princeton, NJ: Princeton University Press, 1970.
Ogden, T.H. (1986) *The Matrix of Mind: Object Relations and the Psychoanalytic Dialogue*. London: Maresfield Library, 1992.
Ogden, T.H. (1988) 'On the dialectical structure of experience – some clinical and theoretical implications'. *Contemporary Psychoanalysis*, 24(1): 17–45. doi:10.1080/00107530.1988.10746217

Ogden, T.H. (1989a) 'On the concept of an autistic-contiguous position'. *The International Journal of Psychoanalysis*, 70(Pt 1) (1) (February): 127–40.

Ogden, T.H. (1989b) *The Primitive Edge of Experience*. Northvale, NJ: Jason Aronson.

Ogden, T.H. (1994) *Subjects of Analysis*. Northvale, NJ: Jason Aronson.

Orwell, G. (1949) *Nineteen Eighty-Four*. London: Penguin, 2008.

Papadopoulos, R.K. (2005a) 'Mythical dimensions of storied communities in political conflict and war'. In Dulic, T., Kostic, R., Macek, I. and Trtak, J. (Eds.), *Balkan Currents: Essays in Honour of Kjell Magnusson*. Uppsala: Uppsala Multiethnic Papers, 49.

Papadopoulos, R.K. (2005b) 'Political violence, trauma and mental health interventions'. In Kalmanowitz, D. and Lloyd, B. (Eds.), *Art Therapy and Political Violence. With Art, Without Illusion*. London: Brunner-Routledge, pp. 35–59.

Papadopoulos, R.K. (2006) 'Terrorism and panic'. *Psychotherapy and Politics International*, 4(2): 90–100. doi:10.1002/ppi.105

Papadopoulos, R.K. (2009) 'Extending Jungian psychology: working with survivors of political upheavals'. In Heuer, G. (Ed.), *Sacral Revolutions*. London: Routledge, pp. 192–200.

Paxton, R.O. (2004) *The Anatomy of Fascism*. London: Penguin Books.

Rapaport, D. (1957) 'A theoretical analysis of the Superego concept'. In Gill, M. (Ed.) (1967), *Collected Papers of David Rapaport*. New York: Basic Books, pp. 685–709.

Scarry, E. (1985) *The Body in Pain: The Making and Unmaking of the World*. New York, Oxford: Oxford University Press.

Stein, M. (2006) 'Fundamentalism, father and son, and vertical desire'. *The Psychoanalytic Review*, 96(2): 201–29. doi:10.1521/prev.2006.93.2.201.

Todorov, T. (1991) *Facing the Extreme: Moral Life in the Concentration Camps*. New York: Henry Holt, 1996.

Winnicott, D.W. (1960) 'Ego distortion in terms of true and false self'. In *The Maturational Processes and The Facilitating Environment*. New York: International Universities Press, 1965, pp. 140–52.

6
THE SPLINTERED REFLECTIVE TRIANGLE IN BYSTANDERS, PERPETRATORS AND VICTIMS OF TORTURE

In this chapter, the phenomena related to bystanders, perpetrators and victims of torture, as described in Chapter 3, will be illustrated with the use of concepts elaborated in Chapters 4 and 5, particularly the idea of the *Splintered Reflective Triangle*.

Relying on psychoanalytic literature, I have proposed that reflective ability is the capacity to simultaneously hold in the mind three poles, Me, You and Other, which enables a paradoxical mental activity that at once processes difference and identity in relationships. This concept can also be expressed through the idea of keeping open *in-between spaces* among multiple positions in mind and society: potential spaces among multiple centers of experience that can be 'bridged' through symbolization, which is strictly connected to abilities like mutual recognition, appropriate mirroring and affective containment (see Chapter 4).

In this chapter, I am defending the hypothesis that the phenomena described in Chapter 3, those related to bystanders, perpetrators and victims of torture, can be understood as consequences of a massive use of *states of twoness*, which results from the splintering of the *Reflective Triangle*. Such a break is supposed to disconnect the three poles, but tends to leave the horizontal segment Me–You (or You–Me) and the vertical Me–Other (or Other–Me) and, You–Other (or Other–You) segments intact (see Figures 4.2 and 4.3). The horizontal segment points to the dynamics of social construction of a collective identity through a massive use of the paranoid-schizoid modes of processing experience. This offers some explanation for the phenomena observed predominantly among bystanders and perpetrators. The second segments illustrate the establishment of a power gradient among members of society, most clearly between victims and perpetrators, but also between leaders and the general population of bystanders. This unconscious vertical alignment serves multiple purposes, such as re-enacting the violence endured on a weaker other to unburden unbearable emotions and find some relief, while having a feeling of control and a sensation of being protected.

Me–You and You–Me: bystanders and the phenomenon of the 'missing witness'

We have seen that, in a society shaped according to the Panopticon pattern, individuals are subjected to a range of partitions and in a submissive relation with a controlling 'central' power. They can neither see each other nor the controller, but they are seen by him. In this state of being continuously seen, relationships are shaped in blinding states of twoness, binding those who perceive themselves as peers in horizontal 'psychotic' states of identity, and those in condition of inequality and/or hierarchical contexts in vertical 'perverse' phenomena of difference, such as blind obedience to authority.

Literature shows that the characterizing features of the bystander state are: 1) a relentless and continuous dissociation of the individual self sustained through an emotional climate of terror that prompts a peculiar status of knowledge called 'disavowal', 'denial' or 'knowing and not knowing'; and 2) compliance with a Monolithic Societal State, which offers some fake 'protection' from terror: this implies to be bound to the large group's massive use of defence mechanisms, such as splitting and projective identification, that guarantees alignment with a terrific object.

The 'bystander' is a pivotal figure in torture, epitomizing a state of *absence* of an internal witness in society. Whereas a society is transformed into a mass of bystanders, what is lacking are borders, groupal skin (Anzieu, 1985, 1987), boundaries, community links, articulation in groups, spaces where experience can be shared and reflected upon, also thanks to the emotional 'containment' (Bion, 1967; Winnicott, 1965), which enables thinking. Being constantly observed, as the Panopticon suggests, means being under siege, compelled by an adhesive and controlling state of *twoness* with no access to a third position, and with no links of empathy and mutual recognition, only controlling hierarchical relations between superiors/subordinates. From the central tower, the power 'impinges' on individuals' psyche through vision (Foucault, 1975): it is a society of control and security. The social environment of fear and control alters the self, making it dissociate and requiring it to work in paranoid-schizoid mode. This determines a condition in which the 'internal witness' is missing because the *in-between* spaces of self are contracted. The 'internal witness' is a third part which is present at and recognizes something happening. It is a function of the ego that, being 'decentred' and mobile within the self, allows multiplicity promoting links between different parts of self. It is not concerned with 'control' but with 'listening' partial truths and rights, 'bridging' multiple perspectives through symbolization (Bromberg, 1993, 1994, 1996; Jung, 1916, 1920, 1921, 1928, 1934, 1940; Mitchell, 1991). As seen in Chapter 5, this is linked to the ability of creating meaning out of experience, recognizing partial and even contradictory realities, something which seems lost under threat, with a loss of reflectivity.

The continuum between bystanders and perpetrators

We have seen that some bystanders are more similar to perpetrators than others for their active participation in social violence (Cohen, 2001; Hilberg, 1961, 1992; Laqueur, 1980; Staub, 1989 among others).

Straker (2000) shows that the immersion in contexts of exposure to continuous/repetitive traumas or intense stress, such as a climate of political repression and/or violence, makes individuals' cognition change. He researched mental health professionals who were immersed in the context of continuing traumatic stress generated by South Africa's political repression, civil conflict and the struggle for liberation during the 1980s. All the interviewees indicated that, during immersion in the continuous traumatic stress, they thought more about good and evil, life and death, meaning and meaninglessness, than they did previously. These preoccupations were often linked to the need to resolve pressing ethical dilemmas in the present, which required fairly immediate action. The professionals also reported differences in their manner of thinking: they spoke of how acts of violence committed by their allies became more acceptable and were justified by them in ways that were not conceivable before the civil conflict. Straker (2000) understands this in relation to Lifton's (1973) and Bar-On's proposition (1992) that, in contexts of continuing traumatic stress such as war, one develops a split morality: one pertaining to peace and one pertaining to war. Their epistemological position was, we might say, somewhere in the continuum between bystanders and perpetrators.

Papadopoulos illustrates how unipolar archetypes work on individuals in pushing them towards action (1998: 464–5). He points out that violence can have an exhilarating, even 'liberating' effect on the individual, for at least four reasons: 1) the individual is relieved by the burden of thinking. This idea of thinking refers to the ability to create a space in which when one is not overwhelmed by pressing impulses (Bion, 1962b, 1967, 1970). Thus, not having such space provides a tragic kind of 'relief' from the pain caused by contradictions and conflicts. 2) Violence provides people a false sense of 'wholeness', since, in acting out, there is no division between thoughts, feelings and actions: all become one and action flows with exceptional consistency. 3) Destructiveness can have a certain kind of chilling purity, which is extremely seductive. 4) Individual identity is subsumed by a wider collective identity, which is polarized under the effect of unipolar archetypes.

I understand this to be an affirmation of a MSS where individuals are required by group pressure to function in states of twoness, while the intrapsychic fragmentation produced is compensated by a sense of unity derived from the merging within the group, which provides a satisfying and reassuring sense of identity and deservingness.

As seen in Chapter 3, institutions of doctors and psychologists are no exception to this dynamic and may act in collusion with monolithic states within their institutions (especially if the professional group has some material convenience for espousing the hegemonic ideology) (Allhoff, 2006; Altman, 2010; Bloche, 1987; Bloche and Marks, 2005a, 2005b, 2005c; Lifton, 1986, 2004; Miles, 2006, 2007;

Patel, 2007; Physicians for Human Rights, 2007; Rasmussen *et al.*, 1988; Soldz, 2008; Summers, 2008; Vesti, 1990; Vesti and Lavik, 1991). Even in their case, morality may become one of a 'state of war' (Schwager, 2004). If the professional community does not offer any containment, any protected *in-between space* where reflectivity is viable, and sticks to a polarized wider societal discourse, professionals have only a binary choice: to adhere to the morality of war (to join) or disassociate (to leave) (for the active involvement of the American Psychological Association in the US 'war on terror', see: Altman, 2010; Patel, 2007; Soldz, 2008; Summers, 2008).

The continuum between bystanders and victims

If involvement and 'action' represent one aspect of the 'bystander' position, as seen in the previous paragraph, the other characterizing feature is 'silence' (see Chapter 3). The silence of those bystanders who do not accept the prevailing definitions of the situation, makes of them victims of power.

Nancy Caro Hollander (1992, 2006a, 2007, 2008, 2010) illustrates how, in the context of the authoritarian regimes of Latin American Countries during the 1960s, 1970s and 1980s, political and economic institutions impacted on people's unconscious and conscious mental functioning. She examines the powerful and dialectical interaction between the unconscious mind and hegemonic ideology, arguing that, in such a context, individuals internalize notions and values of mass culture, which become aspects of the unconscious world of inner representation and object relationships (Hollander, 2006a, 2007, 2008). She extends the concepts of denial and splitting to capture the defensive mechanisms employed by individuals who are forced to deal with a threatening political environment (2008). In Argentina, torture generated an emotional atmosphere of widespread fear, silence and inhibition, while self-censorship resulted in depoliticization and the destruction of a sense of community. She remembers that, in the attempt to deal with persecutory anxiety, people disavowed significant aspects of the self. The traumatogenic political environment drove citizens to disavow not only their identities, but often their capacities to believe and act on their perceptions of reality (Hollander, 2006a, 2006b, 2007, 2008) (see Chapter 5).

Hollander makes the important observation that the symbols of state terror are 'subject-seeking' (Hollander and Gutwill, 2006), in the sense that they are designed to penetrate private life and phantasy. They are created to be in active pursuit of their subjects in order to ensure the dominance of the social interests they represent.

This observation is crucial because, just as there can be no baby without a mother, according to Winnicott's thinking (1952: 99), there can be no individual who does not reside within the context of a community or culture. Embedded in the self is the knowledge that it is impossible to live outside the culture or community in which one is born. This makes both the baby and individual extremely vulnerable to the expectations and requirements of both the maternal and societal environment. Schwager (2004) points out that many theorists of early infancy (Beebe, 1985, 1988;

Bick, 1986; Bion, 1959, 1962a; Mitrani, 1996; Ogden, 1989, 1994b; Winnicott, 1971) have shown that the early lack of a containing, holding and empathic environment results in an inability to separate from the maternal object. This results in a fused self/object sense of self and catastrophic anxieties, which can derail the evolution of the symbolic process.

I proposed the Panopticon as a social counterpart of this kind of bond to a powerful other. This social state, often called ideology, works in people's mind producing control through the simple device of being constantly visible (Foucault, 1975). Being constantly seen means being under the scrutiny of some superior and never being alone; Winnicott (1971) referred to the developmental relevance of the capability of being alone to explain the arising of a true self, which is only possible through experiences that promote also reflectivity. If a true self (or its correlate, the *Reflective Triangle*) is not in place, a false self (or a *Splintered Reflective Triangle*) cannot be anything but compliant to official truths. This happens because, at some level, consistency is needed. In this regard, Schwager (2004) remarks on the similarity between the use of terror by parents and leaders: both are coupled with ideology and utopian visions that justify and even encourage them to feel good about using violent means in order to bring about so called 'good results', 'virtuous ends' or a better or ideal society, generally diminishing an other.

If the self cannot rely on the other's recognizing and mentalizing mirroring gaze (Benjamin, 1988, 1990, 1998; Bion, 1962a, 1962b; Fonagy, 2001; Winnicott, 1953, 1956, 1965) – and here I extend this function to communities within society – *Paradoxical Multiple Self States* leading to symbolization, responsibility, sense of self and other as whole subjects, are not viable. Instead, we find monolithic selves based on inflexible *states of twoness* that cement them with others selves in the same state. If the gaze is one-way, the Winnicottian false self 'adheres' to authority, and cannot separate from this kind of Other: the perception of oneself as an independent but relational agent fades away.

Once the self is deprived of its ability to find meanings, and must cohere with the meanings provided by the authority, reality may suffer that unwearyingly moment-to-moment flexibility in the treatment of facts by the powerful other described above (Chapters 3 and 5). Reality becomes something that can be manipulated at will through the massive use of denial and splitting (Hollander, 2008), which have a deep impact on the functioning of memory and the sense of time (Ogden, 1986). *Doublethinking*, as Orwell calls splitting and denial, means the ability to believe that black is white; better still, to know that black is white and to forget that one has ever believed the contrary (Orwell, 1949: 37). This demands a continuous alteration of the past which is based on fragmentation. History is continuously rewritten, through day-to-day falsification of the past, carried out by authority that makes mutability of the past a central tenet of changing society. Orwell seems to suggest the importance of a sense of threat to sustain the status of knowledge of bystanders: sustained terror is represented through the shocks produced by continuous explosions of bombs and the silent disappearance of people, deleted from the collective memory (1949). This is used to maintain consent on the legitimacy of the rule of Big Brother. The mental state of an endless war[1] works to sustain this state of mind where you know and you do not know and, at the same time, you are ready to accept the 'official' definition of reality, as provided by leaders.

This defensive process to keep knowledge apart requires a continuous effort because, in order to keep something out of mind, the individual needs to constantly keep it in mind, so that it does not pass through the boundary or frame of the sequestrated area. Thus, paradoxically, the individual is constantly mindful of that which is repressed.

In psychoanalysis, denial is understood as an individual unconscious defence mechanism for coping with guilt, anxiety and other disturbing emotions. The psyche blocks off information that is literally unthinkable or unbearable. Freud first referred to *Verleugnung* ('disavowal'), in the specific sense of 'a mode of defence which consists in the subject's refusing to recognize the reality of a traumatic perception' (Laplanche and Pontalis, 1985: 118) – in his theory, the perception of the absence of the woman's penis (Freud, 1923: 143–4; 1925: 248–58). Freud distinguished between neurotic and psychotic denial of reality, but created some confusion by seeing them both as forms of repression. In neurosis, the ego, following a reality principle, suppresses a 'piece of the id', that is of instinctual life, for the sake of adaptation. In psychosis, the ego, being in the service of the id, withdraws from reality and recreates it anew. (Freud, 1924: 183–7): 'neurosis does not disavow the reality, it only ignores it; psychosis disavows it and tries to replace it' (Freud, 1924: 185). Some awkward facts of life are too threatening to confront, but impossible to ignore. The compromise solution is to deny and acknowledge them at the same time. Freud insisted that what is denied is the 'unwelcome idea' associated with the perceived reality, rather than the objective existence of the phenomenon itself (at least at the neurotic level). Unless there is a wholly psychotic interference, the subject is perfectly able to describe things accurately. Disavowal and denial, as originally described by Freud, do not imply an absence or distortion of an actual perception, but rather a failure to appreciate fully the significance or implications of what is perceived (Trunnel and Holt, 1974: 771). This is crucial, because it suggests that there is a failure in symbolization, the meaning is missed because of sustained mental discontinuities.

However, the original Freudian theory makes the assumption that there is a unified integrated self. By contrast, the late-modern and post-modern self has, in essence, no essence. To this fragmented, fluid and compartmentalized self, disavowal and denial, far from being aberrations, are only to be expected, and those contents of self that are not symbolized at an individual level may be processed in wider relational systems, at interpersonal, groupal and social levels.

According to the relational perspective, the primary psychic basis is interactive and, by nature, undifferentiated (Mitchell, 2000). Out of it, the individual gradually grows to become a distinct entity, while always keeping explicit or implicit contact with an other. From this perspective, there can be no subject without an other. Therefore, subjectivity and intersubjectivity go hand in hand (for example, Benjamin, 1988, 1990, 1998, 2002a, 2002b, 2004; Mitchell, 1988, 1993, 2000; Ogden, 1986, 1992a, 1992b, 1994a, 1994b; but also differently Aron, 1996,

Atwood and Stolorow, 1984; Stolorow and Atwood, 1992; Stolorow et al., 1994). Fonagy comments poetically: 'At the core of the mature child's self is the other at the moment of reflection' (2001: 173). But this other at the core of the self is not really other because, by definition, it is part of the self. And, since it is part of the self, one recognizes the other in the self and the self in the other.

In this perspective, the affect is not just an isolated intrapsychic event, but context-dependent. It is a co-structuring, albeit unconscious, which is directed towards and with the other. In addition, we need the other not only to recognize but also to formulate and consolidate our experience. For this reason, a system of external and internalized relations supporting discontinuities installs an epistemological fracture in which people 'know and not know' because of the absence of a properly reflecting other (Cohen, 2001; Laub and Auerhan, 1993). Knowing depends on the ability to keep multiple perspectives in oneself, or to keep the *self multiple*. Actively supported discontinuities in the mind and society work against this ability to link the pieces of one's experience.

While society becomes more and more fragmented, reflective social contexts and relations vanish. This process increasingly 'sequesters' in-between social spaces. Since there is no such a thing as an isolated individual, the continuity with institutions (and groups) and survival within them demands compliance and acceptance of the reality they establish. As Schwager (2004) observes, at this stage, the development of one's creative, transcendent capacities (locating power and authority within oneself through the integration and transcendence of dualities and autonomous and creative thinking) is often neglected out of fear that this state of mind may challenge the existing power and the continuity of the group as it is presently organized. Thus, whole societies may slip into collective modes of denial and induce more and more individuals to comply with this state, without telling them what to think about or what not to think about. This happens in a silent and crawling way: it is sufficient for the monolithic power to just keep control of a piece of everybody (Todorov, 1991): a piecemeal involvement, often starting with the professional self and then encroaching on more and more space within personal self (as seen in Chapter 3). Then, ideology provides an appearance of unity and control that covers the emotional situation of fear, fragmentation and powerlessness. Recognizing its multiple and chameleon-like forms is not an easy task. However, the knowledge so produced lacks the complexity of multiple perspectives of experience and reality.

'Bystander' is a term for an absence. It is the 'missing witness' of individual and social experience. This absence, if sustained, is what allows other citizens to move just along the line of perpetrators and victims.

Other–Me and Me–Other: the objectification of perpetrators

Bureaucratic perpetrators

In Chapter 3, we have seen that actual torturers and bureaucratic officials may be very ordinary people (Arendt, 1963; Browning, 1993; Christie, 1991; Conroy, 2000;

Milgram, 1963, 1974; Todorov, 1991; Zimbardo, 1972, 1975, 2004; Zimbardo *et al.*, 1999, 2000). Their psychological and relational dynamics partially look like those of bystanders who are positioned somewhere in the continuum between bystanders and perpetrators. In the previous paragraph, I argued that, in a general sense, the emotional flooding from the social context creates the 'impingement' (Winnicott, 1958) that makes the individual mind ready for a reshaping of thought and the ideological interpretation of reality. This is actualized through an unconscious structuring of *Monolithic Self States* ready to link to others' *Monolithic Self States* within institutions and groups. Zimbardo (1972, 1975, 2004), Milgram (1963, 1974) and Conroy (2000), in their studies on obedience, show one important feature of these phenomena: the slippery slope of obedience towards authority can escalate to unthinkable violence when it is multiplied through groupal or institutional organization and may easily be perceived as morally acceptable. The monolithic functioning of institutions may reverberate among its members' selves.

Schwager (2004) accurately describes the state of mind we called *monolithic* with the following features:

1 it is dualistic,
2 it establishes a defensive, self-righteous, judgemental position,
3 it projects the shadow side on the other,
4 it lacks integration of self and is characterized by inner fragmentation,
5 the authority is located outside of self,
6 it operates in respect of the dominance of or the compliance with others, and makes others compliant with you, rather than operating from a creative, spontaneous core,
7 it has selective empathy: only for those who are like oneself; while empathy and love are conditional,
8 ideology is taken for reality, replacing reflective, on-going doubt and openness,
9 love in part depends on coercion, thereby becoming a form of violence and manipulation,
10 it has symbiotic issues,
11 it is vulnerable to taking on ideas of and seeking approval from others in order to be part of a relationship or group,
12 it shows impairment in symbolic capacity and capacity for creativity, reflection and thinking.

The training of torturers and reorganization of self

There is considerable evidence in the literature that torturers, during their training, undergo a downright process of 'institutional colonization' of their self. In their case, the wider social process of identification with a rigid set of values is taken to extremes, through an institutionalized method consisting of isolating individuals, breaking their previous social bonds and sense of community, and replacing those relations with institutional ones. The personal transformation produced is extremely powerful and carried out by attacking the trainee's body and psyche. The treatment they undergo disorganizes their self, enabling them to reorganize it according to the institutional tasks of specialized monolithic institutions, usually deputed to the administration of violence (army, police, special operational forces, etc.). These institutions demand trainees to re-enact the violent treatment they underwent during their training with designated others (Conroy, 2000; Crelinsten, 2003; Crelinsten and Schmid, 1993; Haritos-Fatouros, 2003; Huggins, 2002; Huggins et al., 2002).

Joan C. Golston (1993) suggested that the process for the creation of torturers relies heavily on the creation and exploitation of dissociative responses. The process is promoted through: 1) an abusive introduction or initiation, 2) the ensnarement in the 'torturer's bind', 3) programming which ratifies their growing identification with their abuser.

As seen in *Chapter 3*, the training of torturers begins with physical and psychological abuse, even torture, and continues with rituals that mark the passage to a new identity, namely, that of a torturer. According to Golston (1993), from then on, the trainee is operating from a post-traumatic personality, which lays the foundation for their accommodation to abusive authority and their susceptibility towards further personality change. The trainee will struggle to manage recurrent intrusive imagery or physical sensations; they will go through both the voluntary and unconscious numbing of their normal responses; their attachment to themselves and others will be damaged, while they will experience emotional irritability and hyper-responsivity. The trainee's psychological needs and defences are likely to become more primitive and predisposed to action. If the abuse is repeated, their suffering denied and their chances for restoration of self blocked, then their initial dissociative responses may become lasting mechanisms, their memory may become selective, their susceptibility to trance will increase, their perceptions will be distorted and the meaning they attach to their life may dramatically alter. According to Golston, the trainee's trainers will exploit the features of this adjustment, so that, regardless of the trainee's psychological state as they enter training they will evolve from being an externally vigilant trauma victim, to simply accommodating to their abuser/trainer, with an increasing identification with their trainers' world view.

Stanley Rosenman (2003) calls this process 'assaultive projective identification and the plundering of the victim's identity'. The predator group establishes a bridge hold in the psyche of their members who are taken over by an 'alien' force. To badge the victim from within, the predators hold out many lures. These start with the cessation of initial violence, torture, menacing or imprisonment. In return for fidelity, the group can offer advancements in terms of career prospects, security, income, esteem, and companionship. Sacrificial services for an elite slaughterous organization will find ample reward and invitation to identify with the totalistic power that has guaranteed it will exist forever. This promise of an everlasting state is an important source of an anticipated extended period of symbolic existence for the raptor. The intimidating or even beloved abuser may forbid speaking of this exchange or persuade the victim that they were to blame. The victim's shame and dread add to the reluctance to talk about the violence. This ensures that the trauma endures, with the metamorphosed victim separated from their true affects, and destined to have a character stamped with sado-masochism and compelled to revisit the abuse.

Ruth Stein (2010) explores the processes at work in mind control methods, which rely on brain functioning, as well as on relational–transferential factors. Using Margaret Singer's words, she defines mind control as 'a behavioural change technology' which is 'applied to cause the learning and adoption of an ideology or set of behaviours' (Singer and Lalich, 2003, in Stein, 2010: 252). During military training, emotional overload, as well as physical techniques such as prolonged rhythmical pounding and drumming, music and dance, chanting and praying, fasting and sleeplessness, are vehicles for changing waves and brain functioning. Trance states can be evoked by rhythmic and acoustical activities, and by deregulating body functioning, such as sleep and food deprivation. Powerful emotions, too, can cause brain functioning that disconnects from reality and runs 'by itself'. The 'snapping' chaotic–change moment can be followed by a far-reaching transformation, amounting to a religious conversion or ideological 'illumination'. This process can be understood in physiological terms as a condition whereby the experience becomes more intense than the ability of the brain to encompass and contain it, followed by a feeling of being powerfully swept away, of losing control over actions and speech, combined with a sense of loss of self, and being pulled by some exterior power. Such moments can be short and abrupt, or they can be slow and drawn out. In the wake of such a rupture, the information-processing centers of the brain become disorganized and leave the mind open and receptive to new ideas, and even to a radical reorganization, similarly to what happens in religious enlightenment.

Stein (2010) suggests that the literature on varieties of mind control calls for distinguishing two main processes of coercive and indirect influence: 1) love is proffered, which later turns into abuse, coercion and humiliation; in this type of engineered abuse, the redemption seeker is lured by the grace, warmth and gentleness of their new acquaintances, with the coercive demands revealed only gradually; 2) the prisoner/indoctrinator relates to the prisoner with cruelty, after which they change their face to become kind, friendly and warm: what comes first is not love, but hate, the harsh practices of attack and imprisonment, and the mental or physical kidnapping, all of which impose discipline and utter obeisance. Following the 'softening' by these attacks, they are granted a reprieve and acceptance by the group to which they now feel a belonging once they begin to comply. Hence, they are rewarded in direct proportion to their self-denunciation and immersion in what is dictated to them. None of the coercive–persuasive environments and procedures is a pure type, but hate turning into 'loving kindness', seems to be more perverse and chilling. This is consistent with some different narratives that torturers have given about their introduction to torture, as reported in Chapter 3.

Jay Lifton's work on thought reform (1961) is a well-documented psychological study of the experience of individuals who underwent the thought reform programmes during China's Cultural Revolution in the 1950s and 1960s. These programmes exploited the effects of systematically administered guilt/anxiety/shame in the context of strong emotional arousal and inescapably enclosed settings (prisons for Westerners, 'revolutionary universities' for Chinese intellectuals) where people were both forcibly confined and exposed to massive social and psychological pressures. Thought reform programmes worked through the systematic instillation and amplification of the feeling of being evil. Initially, the individual would struggle with themselves and with others against the assault on their self-respect and sense of self. However, any attempt on their part to reassert their own identity was considered arrogant and dishonest, as well as a symptom of their error, which led to renewed pressures on them to capitulate. The external attacks, accompanied by sleep deprivation and harsh conditions, led many people to inner submission. They began to exist in a twilight state between no sleep and no wakefulness, in which they were increasingly susceptible to the influence from an ostensibly just and flawless outside, while being more vulnerable to destructive and self-destructive impulses from within themselves. The relief from this experience was offered by conversion into ideological fanaticism. Confession played a most crucial role in the indoctrination process, in particular, the confession of having committed terrible, albeit vague crimes. Confession was a means to call into existence a hateful, regretful self-condemnation. It was self-betrayal beyond the betrayal of friends and family that the prisoner was pressured to denounce. The more of one's self one was led to betray, the more deeply one became involved with one's captors. Dissociation was used to resolve the horrific contradiction between one's own history and beliefs, and the 'truths' the prisoner was coerced to believe in. When dissociation did not help, annihilation anxieties, suicidal thoughts and psychotic hallucinations emerged.

From Lifton's description, it is clear that the 'thought reform' techniques were torture, i.e. methods to destroy the prisoner' old internal objects, loyalties, and internalized relationships in order to re-build them anew in relation to the attackers.

Coercion and mind control are not just negative processes of oppression and domination, but positive ones of enhancing one's self-negating parts. In this way, the sense of inner evil can be transcended in the ecstatic experience of being purified and pronounced good. The message of the thought reform was that self-abhorrence could be corrected by applying oneself to the doctrine. Having achieved this, the prisoner now felt in harmony with surroundings that were not experienced as strange anymore. At this point, they experience many of their responses as personal discoveries. As O'Brien says in *Nineteen Eighty-Four*: 'We are not content with negative obedience, nor even with the most abject submission. When finally you surrender to us, it must be of your own free will' (Orwell, 1949: 267). What is described here is the process of the installation of an internal Panopticon, a restoration of self according to the lines of power and control of the new social and/or institutional bonding diagram.

Physical and psychological pain can have a primary role in this reorganization. When sufficient pain is inflicted on a person, the victim ends by feeling sympathy and affection toward the perpetrator (i.e., Stockholm syndrome). Certain aspects of childrearing are analogous to these processes. Ferenczi (1933), in his classic 'Confusion of tongues between adults and the child' describes how, when a child attains a certain level of anxiety, they become submissive to the will of the attacking adult, and will, from then on, try to guess each of the adult's desires and strive to gratify them. Ferenczi also points out the introjection of the feeling of guilt towards the aggressor: 'When recovering from the attack he feels enormously confused, in fact split – innocent and guilty at the same time – and his trust in his own perception is broken' (Ferenczi, 1933: 162).

Ferenczi sensed a principle that applies beyond the specific issue of sexual seduction. The 'confusion of tongues' is the conflict between the adult's construction of reality and that of the child, their different desires and needs. Ferenczi simply described one such typical reaction to trauma: children compliantly identify with the adult construction of reality, which results in a loss of trust in their own judgement of reality. In this situation, the child forgets himself/herself and identifies with the aggressor, while maintaining the fiction of being loved. Through this fiction they internalize their seducer's worldview. It is a huge transferential fusion with the attacker's self.

Winnicott's theory of the transitional object (1971) describes the opposite process indicating how the constructions of reality of mother and child can interact with each other in a creative and healthy way. It is here that Winnicott positioned the formation of a third area of reality, which he called 'potential space'. This latter is an illusory world that belongs neither to the subject nor to the object; it is neither inner reality nor external fact. It represents the subject's creative transformation of the external world. This interplay of separateness and union with the other permits one to learn from others, while maintaining the autonomy of the self.

We have seen that Bion, Winnicott, Fonagy and Benjamin (among others) have differently elaborated on the idea that it is crucial that the parent connects with infant anxieties and 'digests' them by creating a mirroring analogue, albeit different from the infant's self state. This prevents the child (the self) having to adapt to the parent (the object), that is to an alienated presence in their own psyche, as if it were an integral part of themselves. On the contrary, if this paradoxical process is impeded, the infant is forced to internalize the other not as an internal object, but as a core part of the self.

Ronald Fairbairn (1952) believed that every internalization is a measure of coercion that occurs only when the object is tantalizing or withholding, not when it is good and gratifying. We paradoxically internalize bad objects, writes Fairbairn, because we cannot resign ourselves to their badness and accept it, thereby differentiating ourselves from them. Thus, we withdraw (sometimes schizoidically) from people in the external world, but we strive to overcome our helplessness in relation to them by struggling to become their masters, to possess them and to force them to change into good objects in our inner world.

We have seen that several psychoanalysts emphasized the importance of an interaction with another that enables the self to be differentiated but not isolated (Benjamin, 1988, 1990, 1998; Fonagy, 2001; Fonagy and Target, 1995, 1996, 1997, 1998; Winnicott, 1953, 1958, 1960). For this to happen, one also needs to experience the other's hatred, but in a benign way. Winnicott finds that it is not aggressiveness as a primary instinctual element, but motility, i.e. the force of life, that gives the individual their sense of reality. The baby's 'ruthless love', a primitive, cruel and demanding love, which is aimed at the object available to them, certainly will arouse the mother's hatred – 'objective hatred', in Winnicott's terms. A growing child can only believe in being loved after reaching being hated. The mother's hate is inevitable, but she must carry it for her child, not deny it but also not act upon it. She must carry it for them so that they can meet it and, in due time, hate too, and thus create the world as a real world for themselves (Winnicott, 1947). This is Winnicott's account for the importance of becoming able to tolerate the flooding of positive and negative affects, and the discovery of the object–mother as someone with her own independent existence from one's own destructive feelings. These two developmental achievements favour the establishment of permeable boundaries between self and non-self, along with the ability to make contact with the other, and to process, at the same time, difference and identity in the *Reflective Triangle*.

At a low or moderate level of affectivity, the boundaries of self are always negotiated in the relationship between Me and Other. At a level of affectivity beyond one's tolerance, when environmental 'impingements' disturb the isolation of the core of personality (Winnicott, 1960b), the experience of self is always an experience of fusion with the other. In this fusion, a splitting occurs: a split object is no more an object, a split ego is no more an ego, but something whose bad and good aspects are arranged in a way that they are in control.

Rina Lazar (2003) makes sharp distinctions between hostility, rage, hatred and evil, which represent affective experiences on a continuum. Hostility is the most immediate response to exaggerated pain; it is an organismic ridding reaction *vis-à-vis* a noxious life-threatening element. Rage is a physiological-based affective reaction to high levels of excessive unpleasure. Hatred is an affective experience of hostility, which has two additional components: 1) it is an enduring and stable or stabilizing affective experience, which persists as affect, once it is activated, and seems to be less dependent than hostility upon the continuation of the event that triggered it; and 2) it is more related to internalized representations of self-object experiential events than to current and concrete events. Lazar (2003) suggests that hatred is a sort of defence, a detaching, flattening and simplifying modality of relation, facing an uncontainable emotional complexity. This defence is not only intrapsychic, but exists between the subject and an other who is perceived as threatening due to its very existence, and, for this reason, it is objectified and reduced to a part-object. Akhtar (1995) makes acute distinctions between rage and hatred, marking the latter as defensive. Rage is acute, whereas hatred is chronic. Rage releases the ego from the object because its aim is to remove a source of pain or irritation, whereas hatred binds the subject to a threatening idealized object. Rage is focused on the present, whereas hatred focuses on the past and on the future. Rage has an impeding effect on the intellect, whereas hatred may sharpen the individual's reasoning, although it may also narrow its focal range. Hatred provides a sense of continuity as the basis for a link and a core of identity. Hatred may protect against fear, guilt, dependent longing, repressed mourning, abandonment anxiety and the fear of psychotic disintegration, as well as from passivity, helplessness and the need to be loved.

In other words, differentiation between self and object is possible in low-level affect situations. Hence, it is clearer how the rage triggered by mistreatments during the training of torturers is put at the service of a fusion of self with its environment, the institution, with a consequent reshaping of self accordingly. The assaultive projective identification with its burden of physical pain, psychological suffering and induced rage compels the trainee to internalize the 'alien' persecutor or to become bound to them in a symbiotic bond. The ego becomes the territory of this alien presence, which identifies with good and aligns with vertical bonds to superiors and/or leaders, while projecting badness into the pretended inferior others. Torturers' learning sessions are not actual 'learning' sessions, but attacks on the self's boundaries to induce a mind-narrowing trance, often interspersed with demonstrations of the leader's knowing, healing and predictive powers (see Chapter 3). The enormous relief of having their uncertain, fragile, individual ego ideal taken over by the leader fuels a sense of renewal, happiness, even bliss, and rebirth fantasies within the trainee. Ties to family and former friends are generally cut, while autonomous thinking and planning for the future are relinquished. Human ties are sacrificed for the joy of refinding the powerful parent, who dispenses unconditional love and promises of salvation. The participants become increasingly bonded to such a figure, while working harder and harder not to disappoint them nor to be disillusioned themselves.

This relates to the installing of what Novick and Novick refer to as a 'closed system superego' within individuals. Novick and Novick (2003) postulate two systems of superego self-regulation. One system, the 'closed-system superego', avoids and denies reality, is unchanging, circular, and repetitive and is characterized by a static omnipotent sadomasochistic mode of functioning. The other system is the 'open-system superego'; this is attuned to inner and outer reality, constantly expands and changes, and is characterized by joy, competence and creativity in self-regulation, problem-solving and conflict resolution. The open-system superego contains a range of ego-ideals, values and standards, all of which are related to realistic aspirations and experiences, as well as to practical possibilities and consequences. Another difference touches on the style or quality of superego functioning. A closed-system superego is global and total, with black-and-white standards. Here belong issues of perfectionism, ideas of tyrannical, unending punishment, omnipotent beliefs and so forth. Differentiation, complexity, balance and an increasing capacity to encompass benefits and consequences are typical in the open-system superego.

The closed system super-ego and the confinement of self in a limited part of itself may be what links, in a vertical way, members of society in a close, intimate and adhesive power relationship between a superior and a sub-ordinate, a shared pattern of mental functioning through which the power replicates itself.

Stein, in her analysis of religious fundamentalism (2002, 2003, 2006), observes that monotheism, sanctifying a single, integrative entity, may be the source of a violent, homoerotic, self-abnegating father–son relationship. Stein's picture of the 'vertical mystical homoeros' is significant for the understanding of *torturous societies* because of her inquiry into this vertical structure of desire, which transforms hate and self-hatred into idealized love. This kind of love (often expressed as 'love for Truth') is far from being simply a love of God; rather it has the character of reverence and fear, and a desire for a God who manifests Himself through absoluteness and unconditionality. Stein (2003) calls this 'regression to the Father'. When the Father, as legislator and protector, assumes the traits of a primitive, inexorable figure, He becomes the object of a certain kind of vertical desire, marked by a dissociated tone and a secret, alienated intimacy.

Thus, groups and societies may take a vertical shape in relation to a hyper-idealized and split paternal object (Jones, 2006; Stein 2002, 2003, 2006; Colman, 2000). The nature of such relationships becomes based on the principle of authority, adhesive bonds, dissociation of action from decision, external control and blind obedience (the unifying vertical paternal principle symbolized by the tower of the Panopticon). So are the bonds tying torturers within a hierarchy: they provide not only protection, but also a special relationship with superiors. Verticalization of difference engenders vertical desire. Vertical desire is a mystical longing for the merger with an idealized fa(o)ther who requires one's inferior sub-jection (Billow, 1980; Stein, 2003).

Understanding the future of a torturer

At this point, the reason why former torturers experience themselves and their memories as ambivalently shifting among different 'truths' should be clearer. Lifton, informed by his twenty years of research on Nazi doctors and their psychological adjustment to their life stories of cruelties perpetrated on Jews during the Third Reich (1986), puts forward the principle of *doubling* as a psychological mechanism for handling conflicts of identity. *Doubling* is the division of the self into two separate functioning wholes, so that each part of the self can act as an entire self. He believes this allowed the Germans to more easily tap into the underlying potential for evil. Doubling provided two separate selves for two separate tasks.[2] Some authors, who interviewed former torturers, registered their strange inconsistent need to 'talk' (Lifton, 1986; Schwager, 2004; Verbitsky, 1996). This ambivalence may be considered as the trace of a struggle to liberate oneself from the internalized abuser and/or the shifting between the two selves and the consequent burden of guilt and helplessness. For example, in his interview with Horacio Verbitsky (1996), Scilingo, the former 'dirty warrior' mentioned in Chapter 3, reveals this dramatic internal struggle between a part of himself who wants to talk and one who does not want to. Finally, he makes the decision to talk and break the 'shell' of the torturer and executioner, feeling entitled to use the 'correct' words to say what he was demanded to do: 'kidnapping', 'torturing', 'murdering', in place of 'arresting', 'interrogating' and 'eliminating the enemy' (Verbitsky, 1996). However, during the interview, his internal struggle persisted, such that, in the end, he retracted his version of the facts for his own trial. Nonetheless, something in his behaviour, as narrated by Verbitsky, leaves the reader with the feeling that he wanted to be tried and condemned. Still, his main concern was not the crimes he committed but the fact of having been cheated by his military superiors and political leaders: the lost state of vertical fusion with the Father.

Schwager (2004) calls this 'speaking with double heart': a heart that has been terrified into 'loving and hating', that is loyal to a master it fears and that has learned to label this loyalty 'love'. Out of this loyalty, the torturer hates whom their master hates and has learned to call this 'justice', and so pretends to survive. This 'heart' is one in bondage, the heart of the symbiotic mentality that fears differentiating for fear of breaking up the symbiosis and losing its master.

Other–You and You–Other: de-subjectification of the victim

The horizontal segment of identity: a shattered self

Torture distinctly appears as a *technology* of unmaking of the self. Physical and mental boundaries of individuals and groups are attacked, therefore, victims' identity and sense of belonging are destroyed. In the CIA's 1963 manual *KURBAK – Counterintelligence Interrogation*, we can find a clear formulation of torture as a destructive 'technology' to impair the affective abilities of the prisoner and, in this way, win their subjectivity[3].

Indeed, many after-effects of torture on victims can be described as bodily, intrapsychic and interpersonal states resulting from a 'shattered self' (Ulman and Brothers, 1993), a 'broken spirit' (Wilson and Drožđek, 2004), a condition of 'world dissolution' (Scarry, 1985: 38–45) and lost 'trust in the world' (Améry, 1980). Scarry writes that 'Intense pain is world-destroying' (1985: 29) and refers both to the obliteration of contents of consciousness through the clearing action of pain ('seeing the stars') and to its ability to destroy language (1985: 4, 54). Améry (1980) masterly describes the way that the concreteness of physical pain and its intentionally malignant use in torture work on the mind to produce an explosion of mental contents: 'Whoever is overcome by pain through torture experiences his body as never before. In self-negation, his flesh becomes a total reality . . . Whoever was tortured, stays tortured. Torture is ineradicably burned into him' (Améry, 1980, in Schulz, 2007: 83).

In torture, the assaultive projective identification is made concrete through an invasive attack on borders, a violent intrusion into the body: the zones of interchange between the inside and the outside of the body are often attacked (through electric shocks, beatings, cigarette burns, injuries, etc.), substances that are normally outside the body are forced into or back into it (vomit, urine, faeces, such as in the various 'bathtub' variations), rape and every other kind of sexual assault, often committed with objects forcibly introduced inside through the anus, vagina, mouth, etc. Sironi and Branche (2002) maintain that making every boundary one that can be transgressed is part of the torturers' repertoire.

However, this attack on boundaries is also carried out by other more subtle psychological means: 1) the systematic destruction of the privacy and intimacy in the life of the prisoner; 2) techniques disrupting biological rhythms and the ability to discriminate perceptively or psychologically (such as sleep deprivation, sensory deprivation or overload, head-covering, the alternation between 'bad cop and good cop',[4] etc.); 3) various techniques of material or psychological assault/annihilation; 4) techniques aimed at increasing the sense of helplessness and isolation of the victim; 5) techniques to break the cultural ties between the individual and their group (Sironi, 1999, 2001; Sironi and Branche, 2002).

The concept of trauma, widely used in medical and psychological literature, deals with the transgression of (bodily and psychic) boundaries of self. In medicine, the term 'trauma' was previously presumed to mean a blow to 'the tissues of the body' (Erichsen 1866) and its meaning was expanded to also signify, in a telling way, 'the tissue of the mind' (Breuer and Freud, 1895). Later, psychoanalysis referred the concept to the crucial function of associations and connections of feelings and ideas; the metaphor of 'the tissue of the mind' may be referred to the fabric of connections implied in the symbolic process (Bion, 1967, Jung, 1912, 1916, 1947). If the concept of trauma grasps a central feature of torture, i.e. the blow to the connections that keep together the bodily and psychic self, the psychiatric discourse about PTSD often risks contributing to the further 'objectification' of survivors of torture. Indeed, disconnecting the consequences of torture from personal meaning and social and political issues risks generating a detached language of symptoms and syndromes that produce 'dry narratives'. In other words, the discourse about trauma easily disconnects itself from its subjects, thus contributing to the process of de-subjectification of survivors initiated by torture.

Even though it is often the corporeality of the body that is most obviously attacked during torture, it is not the material body but the psychic body – the body in the mind that is the host to agency, the interpreter of volition, the container of affect – that fragments when the psychic skin no longer offers protection against assaults from the world. Massive psychic trauma collapses the distinction between the external world and internal experience; as Tarantelli writes, 'there is no longer an outside from which a perception came or an inside which can register it' (2003: 919).

The 'post-traumatic condition' is a state lacking middle ground processing, where in-between spaces of self have come apart and are not available to meaning making activity.

Van der Kolk and Fisler (1995) argue that, while ordinary sensory input is immediately synthesized and translated into a personal story, traumatic experiences remain 'imprinted' as sensations or emotional states without narratives. The failure to symbolize traumatic experiences is at the core of PTSD and other common after-effects of torture, as described in the *Instanbul Protocol*. Neuropsychological studies reviewed by van der Kolk, McFarlane and Weisaeth (1996) and van der Kolk (2002) and other works (van der Kolk et al., 2005) provide evidence of the brain's failure to formulate thoughts efficiently under extreme stress: traumatic memories are quite literally short-circuited and stored as somatic sensations and visual images in the amygdala, as linguistic memory is frequently inactivated during trauma. After the traumatic event, these unprocessed somatic, visual and affective sensations may persecute the survivors, who may be unable to find the thoughts that might be attached to them, inducing more hyper-reactivity to stimuli and withdrawal. This somatic, perceptual and affective sensation may correspond to Bion's (1959) 'beta elements', raw sense impressions that cannot be linked to one another, making them unavailable for reflection. Thinking requires that words be used symbolically, as signifiers, implying that there is a distance between the experience of the words and what they signify. Thinking and meaning are disrupted by the transgressive nature of trauma.

Varvin (2002, 2003) agrees on this point and delves deeper into this question. In post-traumatic state, there is a lack of integration between perceptions, feelings and thoughts in symbol formation. The perceptions may be judged according to symmetry, condensation and contiguity: any sign that bears some likeness to the characteristic of the earlier perceived danger is evaluated as a signal of danger (the characteristic hyper-reactivity to stimuli under post-traumatic conditions). Trauma turns the experience of time into a fragmented experience, totally disconnected from the framework of biographical time. Under these conditions, the perceptions and sensations of the body and environment are not even linked by means of imaginary modes of thinking. Instead, they may be said to be of an indexical nature, i.e. immediate, perceptual, non-symbolic intrusions on the mind.

Boulanger investigated into these states, seeing in the survivor's process of healing a crucial passage from the state of a 'voyeur' to the state of a 'witness' (2002a, 2002b, 2005, 2007, 2008). In the state of a 'voyeur', the traumatic experiences are 'wild', in the sense that the person has no capacity to process and organize them: they are traces from alienated worlds. The clinging of the traumatized mind to specific moments may undermine a correct sense of chronology in the subjectively felt flow of time. The distinctions between present, past and future become blurred and the existential experience of time is heavily conditioned by dream states and fantasies.

Boulanger (2002b, 2005, 2007) and Grand (2000), among others, have drawn parallels between the paranoid-schizoid position and the survivor's psychic state. When the psyche is in survival mode, the lens through which the world is perceived reverts to the concrete logic of the paranoid-schizoid position, where the self that acts as a mediator between words and what they stand for, between symbols and symbolized, between immediate and mediated experience, is no longer accessible. Perception and interpretation are one and the same, while thought cannot be relied up on to provide a different perspective. The distinction between signifier and signified has collapsed. The loss of the self as interpreter of experience also implies that the self as maker and conveyer of meaning has been lost.

Laub and Auerhahn refer to 'knowing and not knowing' (1993) when talking about the state of mind resulting from massive trauma. Their account is a very detailed description of different levels of this failure to connect perceptions, thoughts and memories with a sense of subjective narrative, rooted in time and space. According to them, we all hover at different distances between knowing and not knowing about trauma, caught between the compulsion to complete the process of knowing and the inability or fear of doing so. Trauma is *per se* something eluding our knowledge because of both defence and deficit. The knowledge of what is going on in trauma is fiercely defended against, involving an appraisal of events and our own injuries, failures, conflicts and losses, which affects us so violently that it exceeds the ego's capacity for regulation. Much of knowing is dependent on language. Victims often cannot find categories of thought or words for their experience. Knowing, in the sense of articulation, analysis, elaboration and reformulation, requires the preservation of a relatively detached sensibility, which is destroyed in situations of dread.

Not only trauma-related events, but also experiences not related to the original traumatic experience, can be affected, creating a generalized instability in the network of mental representations. A continuous defect of symbolization may arise from the ability to deal with emotional experience. The plethora of symptoms, signs and personality features associated with post-traumatic conditions, as described in different diagnostic systems and phenomenological descriptions, may be an expression of attempts to rescue oneself from this mental confusion.

Even somatic symptoms, as Varvin (2003) suggests, can be a way to use the body as an arena for built-up tensions caused by non-metabolized affects. Acting may provide a means of dealing with aggression, either through acts of violence or self-harm behaviour or by mere hyperactivity. Re-experiencing may be seen partly as a deficit-avoiding strategy and partly as the ego's attempt to revert to the original helplessness by returning to 'the scene of the crime'.

The vertical segment of difference: the traumatic bonding

The psychological and physical suffering of torture survivors becomes the concrete mark of taking possession of the self by a tormentor. According to Miguel Benasayag (1981), who went through the experience of torture in Argentinian prisons, the torturer's aim is always to bring the prisoner to the point where the personality shatters, the point in which there is no other person, only a sort of fusion, when the victim is glued to the torturer. As in a nightmare, deprived of one's landmarks and previous identity, the body is broken at the torturer's mercy, with the victim likely seeing no exit other than submitting to the only other person available, namely, the torturer. The subject, endowed with self-awareness and autonomous will, is 'no longer there'.

Here, we can see at work the same relational dynamic of the traumatic bondage which the torturer underwent but with roles reversed. In an outstanding description of this nightmare from Orwell's novel *Nineteen Eighty-Four*, O'Brien foretells

Winston his capitulation under torture: 'You will be hollow. We shall squeeze you empty, and then we shall fill you with ourselves' (1949: 269).

After the attack, often the victim's body becomes the theatre where the malignant relationship with the torturers is perpetuated and made long-lasting. The physiological changes occurring during the episodes of torture are registered at an implicit level in the body and in after-effects they re-present the abusive relationship between the victim and the torturers.

A survivor of torturous imprisonment vividly recounted to sister Dianna Ortiz:

'Once I was safe, I thought I was free of my torturers. I actually believed that I would never see them again, that I would never have to smell them or hear their voices. But what I soon realized was they were within me: they literally had made their home in my soul. So often I felt as if they were dancing within me, reminding me they were a part of my life.'
(Ortiz, 2001: 18–19)

From an object relations perspective (Rosenman, 2003), this condition corresponds to a failure of protection by the internal object with a decline in related feelings of basic trust and mastery. This may be experienced as a sense of betrayal or damage to internalized object relations, with a consequent difficulty in finding meaning in thoughts and actions (Bion, 1962a, 1962b; Fonagy, 1999, 2001; Fonagy and Target, 1996, 1997, 1998; Fonagy et al., 1998, 2002; Winnicott, 1956, 1965, 1971). When this internal ability is damaged or destroyed, attachment to others may be perceived as dangerous, so that a withdrawal pattern will emerge. In brief, the attack of torture is an attack on that internal object, which once allowed self-differentiation and access to the process of symbolization through the modulation of affects and creation of meaning within a benign relationship of mutual recognition (Benjamin, 1988, 1990, 1998, 2004).

This interpretation of the meaning of the post-traumatic condition after torture is full of relational implications. Rosenman (2003) understands the post-traumatic suffering following torture as a consequence of the impact of torture on the victim's internalized relational world. According to him, the identity of the victim is impoverished through the cognitive dedifferentiation, the variety of dissociative experiences and the memory impairment that follow abuse. Good internal figures are crushed, with the void contrived to be filled by the evil-doer. The symptoms of PTSD reveal the decimated, newly possessed psyche of the victim, and their feeling of having been swooped down upon and appropriated by an alien, besmirching consciousness. Recurrent fantasies, flashbacks and nightmares suggest the tenacious grasp of the tormentor. Avoidant responses, such as emotional numbing, lack of responsiveness and amnesia, are also strained efforts to avoid thinking about the calamity and its perpetrators. In these ways, the victim divulges their preoccupation with the tormentor, signalling the hold by the latter on the victim's psyche. The trauma victim often suffers a 'derealization' that jumbles the aspects and markers of the surrounding world, so that it no longer looks familiar; while 'depersonalization' make them feel dead, not real, lost, utterly alone, debased, detached from the situation or taken over by an alien consciousness. By remaining ailing or dysfunctional, some injured parts of the body feel foreign. In the subject's unravelled state, they may view these parts as belonging to the enemy who has cleaved the body ego and now racks them from within (Goldfeld *et al.*, 1988; Scarry, 1985). Their suffering may turn against the organ that drew the abuse. It is as though the victim can no longer discern what they are supposed to guard or to protect, or what an appropriate defence looks like. The trauma may also result in states of intense absorption or trance, which in addition to an effort towards a defence, may end up as a takeover of consciousness by the assaulter.

For these reasons, meeting with others becomes potentially frightening to a survivor. Relationships may be felt as complicated, confusing or as an immersion in an internal power struggle. In meeting with other people, there may be more or less space for the interplay between the negative and the positive, a variable transitional space for the creation of symbols and protosymbols referring to opposing forces (Varvin, 2003). The relationships are exposed to the repetition of the logic of the 'traumatic bonding' (van der Kolk, 1989; see Chapter 3).

Transgenerational transmission of trauma

The working-through of this kind of trauma tends to occur spontaneously through the repetition of the same relational pattern that produced the original traumatic bonding, involving people in asymmetric relationships. In this way, trauma is easily transmitted up through the generations from parents to children (Daud *et al.*, 2005).

Schwager (2004) observes that the parent-survivor typically creates a sense of emotional inaccessibility because of their own neediness, requiring the child to parent them through symbiotic attachment, especially when the parent tends to maintain defences against trauma. This makes the child's sacrifice of their own subjectivity necessary, with consequent loss of their self. What often happens is that the child takes on the horrific pain that the parent attempts to deny. Accepting the parent's projective assault may be the only way that the child feels they have meaning in relation to their parent, the only way not to be abandoned. Auerhahn and Prelinger (1983) find that survivors' children, with their empathic capacity and relative distance from the actual experience of torture, may serve as an easier medium for knowledge to evolve and memories to emerge, with association and imagery. Unfortunately, theirs is a displaced knowledge, an event that defies representation and, instead, is experienced as an absence. An ironic outcome emphasized by Rosenman (2003) is that the abusive situation creates a child who is forced to play parental host to the internal representation of the predator. Cajoled into being a repository for their parents' terrible experience, the child's pervasive assignments can fill them to bursting: in this situation there is no room for the child to discover and find themselves. Guilt, shame and abashment may become salient features of the next generation's character, which is designated to be a mute container of the parents' imperative needs (Bar-On, 1989; Bergman and

Jucovy, 1982; Brown, 2007; Heck, 1988; Heimannsberg and Schmidt, 1993). However, victims, when chronically abused, often seek out increased contact with their attackers and with others in an attempt to placate and prevent further assaults (Ainsworth and Eichberg, 1991; Main and Hesse, 1990). Abused children cling to the abusing parent often in direct proportion to the perversity and extremity of the abuse. This creates a form of perverse or 'negative intimacy', not unlike a love-sick relationship (Twemlow, 1995), narrowing the visual world on the attacker. At the same time, most other thoughts are absent from the conscious mind, except for intrusive thoughts about the attacker. These states seem to install the paranoid-schizoid position as a permanent feature (Bion, 1970; Ogden, 1986) with its correlates of diminished self-awareness, self-as-object and a world experienced as containing only omnipotent, powerful, persecuting bad objects, which are capable of annihilating the victim.

As Alice Miller writes,

> The child's dependence on his or her parent's love also makes it impossible in later years to recognize these traumatizations, which often remain hidden behind the early idealization of the parents for the rest of the child's life.
> (Miller, 1983: 4)

The concrete projective assault of torture, which actualizes the traumatic bondage between the torturer and the victim, is often passed to children who become entrapped in a massive projective identification with the parent, in which they are unconsciously coerced to engage in a sustained *state of twoness* in relation to the survivor-parent in the attempt to de-freeze the parent's monolithic self. The vertical segment of difference (Other–Me) actualized in torture victims' children, once again becomes a concrete subjection of a weaker other to a process of 'othering', which risks transforming the other's self into a rigid monolithic system, as both a repetition of and an attempt to work through the experience of torture through generations.

Positive responses to torture

In Chapter 3, we have seen that positive responses to torture are possible and, conceptualized as resilience, post-traumatic growth, and Adversity Activated Development. Most studies on this topic focused on internal and external factors contributing to positive responses.

A long-standing result is that internal factors of resilience include strong individual religious or political beliefs. For example, Basoğlu et al. (2001) contend that the inmates of a prison in Turkey, who were jailed for political reasons and, therefore, politically committed, prepared for and expecting torture, did better than a control group with no record of political activity. Holtz (1998) similarly found that a group of tortured Tibetan nuns were found to be almost as non-pathological as their sister nuns who were not tortured.

Among external factors, Rosenman (2003) reports that it is commonly believed by clinicians that, when impunity is given to the torturer, resilience for the victim is more difficult to attain. It would seem that impunity makes the abuser more present, less under the survivor's control, not subject to justice. This is confirmed by other studies (Amnesty International, 2001; Herman, 2003).

Combining these data with the idea of the *Reflective Triangle* at both individual and social levels, we can make the inference that the possibility of maintaining trust in the world and a framework of meanings to understand (adverse) life events is a crucial key point for positive responses to torture. The most striking example is probably that of Nelson Mandela, who found in his political commitment the meaning to withstand his experience of torture and 27 years of prison, with a final extraordinary accomplishment of his political ideas, i.e. the end of Apartheid in South Africa, when he became the President (Mandela, 1994).

In terms of resilience, we may speculate that a strong belief system is helpful because it provides individuals with emotional containment, *vis-à-vis* the dramatic experience of torture, through the intelligibility of events in one's (political, religious, etc.) framework of beliefs, and the sense of an emotional connection to an ideal (political or religious) community.

On the other hand, if a society can restate a principle of justice by trying persecutors, we can similarly expect that the victims' recovery process will be faster and more likely to succeed, because the social processing of torture will help a parallel individual working-through, making sense of the traumatic experience.

However, the concept of AAD (Papadopoulos, 2004, 2007) is much more challenging than that of resilience, because it establishes a causal connection between adversities, in this case torture, and development. I speculate that this kind

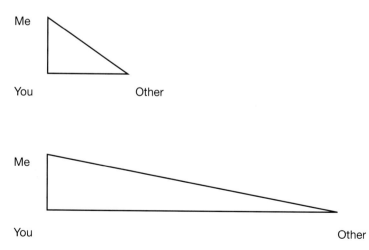

FIGURE 6.1 The expansion of the Reflective Triangle in Adversity Activated Development

of development might be connected to the process of exploration and pursuit of meaning of the terrible experience, which powerfully entered into the survivor's life. One way out from the enormous suffering produced by torture, is the possibility for the self to widen the range of its possible meanings, including the experience of torture itself. Instead of expelling it from the consciousness and alienating it as 'other', the containment and integration of this extreme experience in the self, may be tremendously developmental for the self. In the *Reflective Triangle*, if the pole of the Other is very far from Me and You, i.e. the experience is truly 'alien', in order to connect Me, You and Other, the area of the *Reflective Triangle* will necessarily be expanded, indicating an enlargement of the reflective capacity. Images can help to grasp this phenomenon (see Figure 6.1).

Nevertheless, the factors that influence this dynamic process, and contribute to such a paradoxical and significant result, still need to be satisfactorily explored and clarified.

Notes

1 The war, therefore, if we judge it by the standards of previous wars, is merely an imposture. . . . But though it is unreal it is not meaningless. . . . it helps to preserve the special mental atmosphere that a hierarchical society needs. . . . The war is waged by each ruling group against its own subjects, and the object of the war is not to make or prevent conquests of territory, but to keep the structure of society intact. The very word 'war', therefore, has become misleading. It would probably be accurate to say that by becoming continuous war has ceased to exist.

(Orwell, 1949: 207)

2 Lifton (1986) attributes five essential characteristics to the process of *doubling* in the Nazi physicians: 1) there is a dialectic between two selves: an Auschwitz self that functioned in the concentration camp, and a prior self that needed to see oneself as part of the human family and in the medical role of the past; 2) doubling is different from splitting or dissociation, since the personality successfully sustains its functioning over a long period of time, in conjunction with the other self, but often taking over and seeming to speak for the whole personality; 3) the Auschwitz self was a killing self, paradoxically needed for survival; 4) doubling seems to appease guilt, in that only 'one' self is doing the horrific work of killing; 5) doubling involves an unconscious dimension, which can significantly change moral consciousness.

3 'All coercive techniques are designed to induce regression . . . the result of external pressures of sufficient intensity is the loss of those defences most recently acquired by civilized man . . . the circumstances of detention are arranged to enhance within the subject his feelings of being cut off from the known and the reassuring and of being plunged into the strange . . . once this disruption is achieved, the subject's resistance is seriously impaired. He experiences a kind of psychological shock, which may only last briefly, but during which he is far . . . likelier to comply . . . Frequently the subject will experience a feeling of guilt. If the 'questioner' can intensify these guilt feelings, it will increase the subject's anxiety and his urge to cooperate as a means to escape'

(quoted in Danner 2004: 30–1)

4 The alternation is so contiguous and the phase change so frequently, that the discrimination of logical distances breaks down, producing confusion, perplexity and 'sideration'.

References

Ainsworth, M.D.S. and Eichberg, C. (1991) 'Effects on infant-mother attachment of mother's unresolved loss of an attachment figure, or other traumatic experiences'. In Parkes, C.M., Stevenson-Hinde, J. and Marris, P. (Eds.), *Attachment Across the Life Cycle.* London: Routledge, pp. 160–85.

Akhtar S. (1995) 'Some reflections on the nature of hatred and its emergence in the treatment process: Discussion of Kernberg's chapter "Hatred as a core affect of aggression"'. In Akhtar, S., Kramer, S. and Parens, H. (Eds.), *The Birth of Hatred: Developmental, Clinical, and Technical Aspects of Intense Aggression.* New Jersey: Jason Aronson, pp. 83–103.

Allhoff, F. (2006) 'Physician involvement in hostile interrogations'. *Cambridge Quarterly of Healthcare Ethics,* 15(4): 392–402. doi:10.1017/S0963180106060506.

Altman, N. (2010) 'Torture and the American Psychological Association: a one-person play'. In Harris, A. and Botticelli, S. (Eds.), *First Do No Harm: The Paradoxical Encounters of Psychoanalysis, Warmaking, and Resistance.* New York: Routledge, pp. 143–52.

Améry, J. (1980) 'Trust in the world'. In W.F. Schulz (Ed.), *The Phenomenon of Torture: Readings and Commentary.* Philadelphia, PA: University of Pennsylvania Press, 2007, pp. 80–7.

Amnesty International (2001) *End Impunity: Justice for Victims of Torture.* London: AI.

Anzieu, D. (1985) *The Ego-Skin.* New Haven, CT: Yale University Press.

Anzieu, D. (1987) *Psychic Envelopes.* London: Karnac Books.

Arendt, H. (1963) *Eichmann in Jerusalem: A Report on the Banality of Evil.* New York: Penguin Books, 1977.

Aron, L. (1996) *A Meeting of Minds: Mutuality in Psychoanalysis.* Hillsdale, NJ: The Analytic Press.

Atwood, G.E. and Stolorow, R.D. (1984) *Structures of Subjectivity: Explorations in Psychoanalytic Phenomenology.* Hillsdale, NJ: The Analytic Press.

Auerhahn, N.C. and Prelinger, E. (1983) 'Repetition in the concentration camp survivor and her child'. *International Review of Psycho-Analysis,* 10(1): 31–46.

Bar-On, D. (1992) 'A testimony on the moment before the (possible) occurrence of a massacre: on a possible contradiction between the ability to adjust which means mental health and the maintaining of human moral values'. *Journal of Traumatic Stress,* 5(2): 289–301. doi:10.1002/jts.2490050213.

Basoğlu, M., Jaranson, J.M., Mollica, R. and Kastrup, M. (2001) 'Torture and mental health: a research overview'. In Gerrity, E., Keane, T.M. and Tuma, F. (Eds.), *The Mental Health Consequences of Torture.* New York: Kluwer Academic/Plenum Publishers, pp. 35–62.

Beebe, B. (1985) 'Mother-infant mutual influence and precursors of self and object representations'. In Masling, J. (Ed.), *Empirical Studies of Psychoanalytic Theories,* Vol. 2. Hillsdale, NJ: Analytic Press, pp. 27–48.

Beebe, B. (1988) 'The contribution of mother-infant mutual influence to the origins of self and object representations'. *Psychoanalytic Psychology,* 5(4): 305–37. doi:10.1037/0736-9735.5.4.305.

Benasayag, M. (1981) *Malgrado tutto: racconti a bassa voce dalle prigioni argentine.* Napoli: Filema.

Benjamin, J. (1988) *The Bonds of Love.* New York: Pantheon Books.

Benjamin, J. (1990) 'An outline of intersubjectivity: the development of recognition', *Psychoanalytic Psychology,* 7: 33–46. Reprinted as 'Recognition and destruction: an outline of intersubjectivity', in Mitchell, S. A. and Aron, L. (Eds) (1999) *Relational Psychoanalysis: The Emergence of a Tradition.* Hillsdale, NJ and London: The Analytic Press, pp. 181–210.

Benjamin, J. (1998) *Shadow of the Other: Intersubjectivity and Gender in Psychoanalysis.* New York: Routledge.

Benjamin, J. (2002a) 'Terror and guilt: beyond them and us'. *Psychoanalytic Dialogues*, 12(3): 473–84. doi:10.1080/10481881209348681.
Benjamin, J. (2002b) 'The rhythm of recognition: comments on the work of Louis Sander'. *Psychoanalytic Dialogues*, 12(1): 43–53. doi:10.1080/10481881209348653.
Benjamin, J. (2004) 'Beyond doer and done to: an intersubjective view of thirdness'. *Psychoanalytic Quarterly*, 73(1): 5–46. Reprinted in Aron, L. and Harris, A. (Eds) (2012) *Relational Psychoanalysis, Vol. 4 Expansion of Theory*. New York and London: Routledge, pp. 91–130.
Bergmann, M.S. and Jucovy, M.E. (Eds.) (1982) *Generations of the Holocaust*. New York: Basic Books.
Bick, E. (1986) 'Further considerations on the function of the skin in early object relations'. *British Journal of Psychotherapy*, 2(4): 292–9. doi:10.1111/j.1752-0118.1986.tb01344.x.
Billow, R.M. (1980) 'On reunion'. *Psychoanalytic Review*, 67: 253–70.
Bion, W.R. (1959) 'Attacks on linking'. In *Second Thoughts: Selected Papers on Psychoanalysis*. London: Heinemann, 1967, pp. 93–109.
Bion, W.R. (1962a) *Learning from Experience*. London: Heinemann.
Bion, W.R. (1962b) 'A theory of thinking'. In *Second Thoughts: Selected Papers on Psychoanalysis*. London: Karnac Maresfield Library, 1967, pp. 110–19.
Bion, W.R. (1967) *Second Thoughts: Selected Papers on Psychoanalysis*. London: Karnac Maresfield Library.
Bion, W.R. (1970) *Attention and Interpretation*. London: Tavistock.
Bloche, M.G. (1987) *Uruguay's Military Physicians: Cogs in a System of State Terror*. Washington: AAAS.
Bloche, M.G., Marks, J.H. (2005a) 'Doctors and interrogations'. *New England Journal of Medicine*, 352: 1633–4. doi:10.1056/NEJMc051947.
Bloche, M.G. and Marks, J.H. (2005b) 'Doctors and interrogators at Guantanamo Bay'. *New England Journal of Medicine*, 353(1): 6–8. doi:10.1056/NEJMp058145.
Bloche M.G. and Marks, J.H. (2005c) 'When doctors go to war'. *New England Journal of Medicine*, 352(1): 3–6. doi:10.1056/NEJMp048346.
Boulanger, G. (2002a) 'The cost of survival: psychoanalysis and adult onset trauma'. *Contemporary Psychoanalysis*, 38(1): 17–44. doi:10.1080/00107530.2002.10745805.
Boulanger, G. (2002b) 'Wounded by reality: the collapse of the self in adult onset trauma'. *Contemporary Psychoanalysis*, 38(1): 45–76. doi:10.1080/00107530.2002.10745806.
Boulanger, G. (2005) 'From voyeur to witness: recapturing symbolic function after massive psychic trauma'. *Psychoanalytic Psychology*, 22(1): 21–31. doi:10.1037/0736-9735.22.1.21.
Boulanger, G. (2007) *Wounded By Reality: Understanding and Treating Adult Onset Trauma*. Mahwah, NJ: The Analytic Press.
Boulanger, G. (2008) 'Witnesses to reality: working psychodynamically with survivors of terror'. *Psychoanalytic Dialogues*, 18(5): 638–57. doi:10.1080/10481880802297673.
Breuer, J. and Freud, S. (1895) 'Studies in hysteria'. In *The Standard Edition of the Complete Psychological Works of Sigmund Freud*. Trans. and Ed. J. Strachey, vol.2. London: The Hogarth Press.
Bromberg, P.M. (1993) 'Shadow and substance: a relational perspective on clinical process'. *Psychoanalytic Psychology*, 10(2): 147–68. doi:10.1037/h0079464.
Bromberg, P.M. (1994) 'Speak! That I may see you: some reflections on dissociation, reality and psychoanalytic listening'. *Psychoanalytic Dialogues*, 4(4): 517–47. doi:10.1080/10481889409539037.
Bromberg P.M. (1996) 'Standing in the spaces: the multiplicity of self and the psychoanalytic relationship'. *Contemporary Psychoanalysis*, 32(4): 509–35. doi:10.1080/00107530.1996.10746334.

Brown, E.M. (2007) 'A child survivor of the Holocaust comes out of hiding: two stories of trauma'. *Psychoanalytic Perspectives*, 4(2): 51–75. doi:10.1080/1551806X.2007.10472995.
Browning, C.R. (1993) *Ordinary Men: Reserve Police Battalion 101 and the Final Solution in Poland*. New York: HarperPerennial.
Christie, R. (1991) 'Authoritarianism and related constructs'. In Robinson, J.P., Shaver, P.R. and Wrightsman, L.S. (Eds.), *Measures of Personality and Social Psychology Attitudes*. San Diego, CA: Academic Press, pp. 501–71.
Cohen, S. (2001) *States of Denial: Knowing about Atrocities and Suffering*. Cambridge: Polity Press.
Colman, W. (2000) 'Tyrannical omnipotence in the archetypal father'. *Journal of Analytical Psychology*, 45(4): 521–39. doi:10.1111/1465-5922.00189.
Conroy, J. (2000) *Unspeakable Acts, Ordinary People: The Dynamics of Torture: An Examination of the Practice of Torture in Three Democracies*. New York: Knopf.
Crelinsten, D. (2003) 'The world of torture: a constructed reality'. *Theoretical Criminology*, 7(3): 293–318. doi:10.1177/13624806030073003.
Crelinsten, R.D. and Schmid, A.P. (Eds.) (1993) *The Politics of Pain: Torturers and Their Masters*. Centrum voor Onderzoek van Maatschappelijke Tegenstellingen/Center for the Study of Social Conflicts, AK Leiden, Netherlands: Leiden University.
Danner, M. (2004) 'The logic of torture'. In Danner, M., Ehrenreich, B. and Levi Strauss, D. (Eds.), *Abu Ghraib: The Politics of Torture*. Berkley, CA: North Atlantic Books, pp. 17–46.
Daud, A., Skoglund, E. and Rydelius, P.A. (2005) 'Children in families of torture victims: transgenerational transmission of parent's traumatic experience to their children'. *International Journal of Social Welfare*, 14(1): 23–32. doi:10.1111/j.1468-2397.2005.00336.x.
Erichsen, J. (1866) *On Railway and Other Injuries of the Nervous System*. London: Walton and Maberly.
Fairbairn, W.R.D. (1952) *An Object Relations Theory of the Personality*. New York: Basic Books.
Ferenczi, S. (1933) 'Confusion of tongues between adults and the child'. In Balint, M. (Ed.), *Final Contributions to the Problems and Methods of Psychoanalysis*. New York: Brunner/Mazel, vol. 3, 1955, pp. 156–67.
Fonagy, P. (1999) 'Male perpetrators of violence against women: an attachment theory perspective'. *Journal of Applied Psychoanalytic Studies*, 1(1): 7–27. doi:10.1023/A:1023074023087.
Fonagy, P. (2001) *Attachment Theory and Psychoanalysis*. New York: Other Press.
Fonagy, P. and Target, M. (1995) 'Understanding the violent patient: the use of the body and the role of the father'. *The International Journal of Psychoanalysis*, 76(3): 487–501.
Fonagy, P. and Target, M. (1996) 'Playing with reality: I. Theory of mind and the normal development of psychic reality'. *The International Journal of Psychoanalysis*, 77(2) (January): 217–33.
Fonagy, P. and Target, M. (1997) 'Attachment and reflective function: their role in self-organization'. *Development and Psychopathology*, 9(4) (Fall): 679–700.
Fonagy, P. and Target, M. (1998) 'Mentalization and the changing aims of child psycho-analysis'. *Psychoanalytic Dialogues*, 8(1): 87:114. doi:10.1080/10481889809539235.
Fonagy, P., Target, M., Steele, H. and Steele, M. (1998), *Reflective-Functioning Manual*, Version 5. London: University College.
Fonagy, P., Gergely, G., Jurist, E. and Target, M. (2002), *Affect Regulation, Mentalization, and the Development of the Self*. New York: Other Press.
Foucault, M. (1975) *Discipline and Punish: The Birth of the Prison*. New York: Random House, 1979.
Freud, S. (1923) 'The infantile genital organization'. In *SE*, vol. 19.

Freud, S. (1924) 'The loss of reality in neurosis and psychosis'. In *SE*, vol. 19.
Freud, S. (1925) 'Some psychical consequences of the anatomical distinction between the sexes'. In *SE*, vol. 19.
Goldfeld, A.E., Mollica, R.F., Pesavento, B.H. and Faraone, S.V. (1988) 'The physical and psychological sequelae of torture: symptomatology and diagnosis'. *Journal of the American Medical Association*, 259(18): 2725–9. doi:10.1001/jama.1988.03720180051032.
Golston, J.C. (1993) 'Ritual abuse: Raising hell in psychotherapy. Creation of cruelty: the political military and multigenerational training of torturers: violent initiation and the role of traumatic dissociation'. *Treating Abuse Today*, 3(6): 12–19.
Grand, S. (2000) *The Reproduction of Evil: A Clinical and Cultural Perspective*. Hillsdale, NJ: The Analytic Press.
Haritos-Fatouros, M. (2003) *The Psychological Origins of Institutionalized Torture*. London: Routledge.
Heck, A. (1988) *The Burden of Hitler's Legacy*. Meridian, New York.
Heimannsberg, B. and Schmidt, C.J. (Eds.) (1993) *The Collective Silence*. San Francisco: Jossey-Bass.
Herman, J.L. (2003) 'The mental health of crime victims: impact of legal intervention'. *Journal of Traumatic Stress*, 16(2) (April): 159–66. doi:10.1023/A:1022847223135.
Hilberg, R. (1961) *The Destruction of the European Jews*. New York: Holmes and Maier, 1985.
Hilberg, R. (1992) *Perpetrators Victims Bystanders: The Jewish Catastrophe, 1933–1945*. New York: Aaron Asher Books.
Hollander, N.C. (1992) 'Psychoanalysis and state terror in Argentina'. *American Journal of Psychoanalysis*, 52(3): 273–89.
Hollander, N.C. (2006a) 'Trauma, ideology, and the future of democracy'. *International Journal of Applied Psychoanalytic Studies*, 3: 156–67. doi:10.1002/aps.97.
Hollander, N.C. (2006b) 'Negotiating trauma and loss in the migration experience: roundtable on Global Woman'. *Studies in Gender and Sexuality*, 7: 61–70.
Hollander, N.C. (2007) 'Scared stiff: trauma, ideology, and the bystander'. *International Journal of Applied Psychoanalytic Studies*, 4(3): 295–307. doi:10.1002/aps.102.
Hollander, N.C. (2008) 'Living danger: on not knowing what we know'. *Psychoanalytic Dialogues*, 18: 690–709. doi:10.1080/10481880802297707.
Hollander, N.C. (2010) *Uprooted Minds: Surviving the Politics of Terror in the Americas*. New York: Routledge.
Hollander, N.C. and Gutwill, S. (2006) 'Despair and hope in a culture of denial'. In Layton, L., Hollander, N.C. and Gutwill, S. (Eds.), *Psychoanalysis, Class and Politics: Encounters in the Clinical Setting*. New York: Routledge, pp. 81–91.
Holtz, T.H. (1998) 'Refugee trauma versus torture trauma: a retrospective controlled cohort study of Tibetan refugees'. *Journal of Nervous and Mental Diseases*, 186(1): 24–34. doi:10.1097/00005053-199801000-00005
Huggins, M.K. (2002) 'State violence in Brazil: the professional morality of torturers'. In Rotker, S. (Ed.), *Citizens of Fear: Urban Violence in Latin America*. New Brunswick, NJ: Rutgers University Press, pp. 141–51.
Huggins, M.K., Haritos-Fatouros, M. and Zimbardo, P.G. (2002) *Violence Workers: Police Torturers and Murderers Reconstruct Brazilian Atrocities*. Berkeley, CA: University of California Press.
Jones, J.W. (2006) 'Why does religion turn violent? A psychoanalytic exploration of religious terrorism'. *Psychoanalytic Review*, 93(2): 167–90. doi:10.7282/T38K77FT.
Jung, C.G. (1912) 'Symbols of transformation'. In *Collected Works of C.G. Jung*, vol.5, Read, H., Fordham, M. and Adler, G. (Eds.), translated by R. Hull, Princeton, NJ: Princeton University Press/Bollingen Series XX. (hereafter *CW*)

Jung, C.G. (1916) 'The transcendent function'. In *CW*, vol. 8.
Jung, C.G. (1920) 'The psychological foundations of belief in spirits'.In *CW*, vol. 5..
Jung, C.G. (1921) 'Psychological types: Definitions'. In *CW*, vol. 6.
Jung, C.G. (1928) 'The relations between the ego and the unconscious'. In *CW*, vol. 7.
Jung, C.G. (1934) 'A review of the complex theory'. In *CW*, vol. 8.
Jung, C.G. (1940) 'The psychology of the child archetype'. In *CW*, vol. 9i.
Jung, C.G. (1947) 'On the nature of the psyche'. In *CW*, vol. 8i.
Laplanche, J. and Pontalis, J.B. (1985) *The Language of Psycho-Analysis*. Trans. Donald Nicholson-Smith. London: Hogarth Press and Institute of Psycho-Analysis.
Laqueur, W. (1980) *The Terrible Secret: Suppression of the Truth About Hitler's 'Final Solution'*. Boston: Little Brown, 1998.
Laub, D. and Auerhahn, N.C. (1993) 'Knowing and not knowing massive psychic trauma: Forms of traumatic memory'. *The International Journal of Psychoanalysis*, 74(2): 287–302.
Lazar, R. (2003) 'Knowing hatred'. *The International Journal of Psychoanalysis*, 84: 405–25. doi:10.1516/Y9P5-7M1N-PP5H-X3YQ.
Lifton, R.J. (1961) *Thought Reform and the Psychology of Totalism: A Study of 'Brainwashing' in China*. Chapel Hill, NC: University of North Carolina Press, 1989.
Lifton, R.J. (1973) *Home From the War: Vietnam Veterans Neither Victims Nor Executioners*. New York: Touchstone, Simon and Schuster.
Lifton R.J. (1986) *The Nazi Doctors: Medical Killing and the Psychology of Genocide*. New York: Basic Books, 1986.
Lifton, R.J. (2004) 'Doctors and torture'. *New England Journal of Medicine*, 351(5): 415–16. doi:10.1056/NEJMp048065.
Main, M. and Hesse, E. (1990) 'Parents' unresolved traumatic experiences are related to infant disorganized status: Is frightened/frightening parental behavior the linking mechanism?' In Greenberg, M.T., Cicchetti, D. and Cummings, E.M. (Eds.), *Attachment in the Preschool Years*. Chicago: University of Chicago Press, pp. 161–82.
Mandela, N. (1994) *Long Walk to Freedom: the Autobiography of Nelson Mandela*. Randburg, South Africa : Macdonald Purnell.
Miles, S. (2006) *Oath Betrayed: Torture, Medical Complicity and the War on Terror*. New York: Random House.
Miles, S. (2007) 'Medical ethics and the interrogation of Guantanamo 063'. *The American Journal of Bioethics*, 7(4): 5–11. doi:10.1080/15265160701263535.
Milgram, S. (1963) 'Behavioral study of obedience'. *The Journal of Abnormal and Social Psychology*, 67(4): 371–8. doi:10.1037/h0040525.
Milgram, S. (1974) *Obedience to Authority: An Experimental View*. New York: Harper and Row.
Miller, A. (1983) *For Your Own Good*. New York: Meridian.
Mitchell, S.A. (1988) *Relational Concepts in Psychoanalysis*. Cambridge, MA: Harvard University Press.
Mitchell, S.A. (1991) 'Contemporary perspectives on self: toward an integration'. *Psychoanalytic Dialogues*, 1(2): 121–47. doi:10.1080/10481889109538889.
Mitchell S.A. (1993) *Hope and Dread in Psychoanalysis*. New York: Basic Books.
Mitchell, S.A. (2000) *Relationality: From Attachment to Intersubjectivity*. New Jersey: The Analytic Press.
Mitrani, J. (1996) *A Framework for the Imaginary*. Northvale, NJ: Aronson.
Novick, K.K. and Novick, J. (2003) 'Two systems of self-regulation and the differential application of psychoanalytic technique'. *The American Journal of Psychoanalysis*, 63: 1–20. doi:10.1023/A:1022323003802.
Ogden, T.H. (1986) *The Matrix of Mind: Object Relations and the Psychoanalytic Dialogue*. London: Maresfield Library, 1992.

Ogden, T.H. (1989) *The Primitive Edge of Experience*. Northvale, NJ: Jason Aronson.
Ogden, T.H. (1992a) 'The dialectically constituted/decentered subject of psychoanalysis. I: The Freudian subject'. *The International Journal of Psychoanalysis*, 73(3): 517–26.
Ogden, T.H. (1992b) 'The dialectically constituted/decentered subject of psychoanalysis. II: The contribution of Klein and Winnicott'. *The International Journal of Psychoanalysis*, 73: 613–26.
Ogden, T.H. (1994a) 'The analytic third: working with intersubjective clinical facts'. *The International Journal of Psychoanalysis*, 75: 3–19.
Ogden, T.H. (1994b) *Subjects of Analysis*. Northvale, NJ: Jason Aronson Inc.
Ortiz, S.D. (2001) 'The survivors' perspective: voices from the center'. In Gerrity, E., Keane, T.M. and Tuma, F. (Eds.), *The Mental Health Consequences of Trauma*. New York: Plenum Publishers, pp. 13–34.
Orwell, G. (1949) *Nineteen Eighty-Four*. London: Penguin, 2008.
Papadopoulos, R.K. (1998) 'Destructiveness, atrocities and healing: epistemological and clinical reflections'. *Journal of Analytical Psychology*, 43(4): 455–77. doi:10.1111/1465-5922.00047.
Papadopoulos, R.K. (2004) 'Trauma in a systemic perspective: theoretical, organization and clinical dimensions'. Paper presented at the 14th Congress of the *International Family Therapy Association*, Istanbul.
Papadopoulos, R.K. (2007) 'Refugees, trauma and Adversity-Activated Development'. *European Journal of Psychotherapy, Counselling and Health*, 9(3): 301–12. doi:10.1080/13642530701496930.
Patel, N. (2007) 'Torture, psychology and the "war on terror": a human rights framework'. In Roberts, R. (Ed.), *Just War: Psychology and Terrorism*. Ross-on-Wye: PCCS Books, pp. 74–108.
Physicians for Human Rights (2007) *Leave No Marks: Enhanced Interrogation Techniques and the Risk of Criminality*. Washington, DC. Available at: http://physiciansforhumanrights.org/library/report-2007-08-02.html (accessed 24 March 2013).
Rasmussen, O.V., Lopez J., Udsen P. and Espersen O. (1988) 'Doctors involved with torture'. *Lancet*, 14(1) (May)(8594):1112–12.
Rosenman, S. (2003) 'Assaultive projective identification and the plundering of the victim's identity'. *Journal of American Academy of Psychoanalysis*, 31(3): 521–40. doi:10.1521/jaap.31.3.521.22131.
Scarry, E. (1985) *The Body in Pain. The Making and Unmaking of the World*. New York, Oxford: Oxford University Press.
Schwager, E. (2004) 'Transforming dualism and the metaphor of terror. Part II: From genocidal to dialogic mentality: an intergenerational struggle'. *The Psychoanalytic Review*, 91(4): 543–89. doi:10.1521/prev.91.4.
Schwan, G. (2001) *Politics and Guilt: The Destructive Power of Silence*. Lincoln, NE: University of Nebraska Press.
Singer, M.T. and Lalich, J. (2003) *Cults in Our Midst: The Continuing Fight with the Hidden Menace*. San Francisco: Jossey-Bass (Wiley).
Sironi, F. (1999) *Bourreaux et victimes: Psychologie de la torture*. Paris: Odile Jacob.
Sironi, F. (2001) 'Les stratégies de déculturation dans les conflits contemporains. Nature et traitement des attaques contre les objets culturels'. *Sud Nord*, 12: 29–47.
Sironi, F. and Branche, R. (2002) 'Torture and the borders of humanity'. *International Social Science Journal*, 54: 539–48. doi:10.1111/1468-2451.00408.
Soldz, S. (2008) 'Healers or interrogators: psychology and the United States torture regime'. *Psychoanalytic Dialogues*, 18(5): 592–613. doi:10.1080/10481880802297624.
Staub, E. (1989) *The Roots of Evil: The Origins of Genocide and Other Group Violence*. Cambridge: Cambridge University Press.

Stein, R. (2002) 'Evil as love and as liberation'. *Psychoanalytic Dialogues*, 12(3): 393–420. doi:10.1080/10481881209348675.

Stein, R. (2003) 'Vertical mystical homoeros: an altered form of desire in fundamentalism'. *Studies in Gender and Sexuality*, 4(1): 38–58. doi:10.1080/15240650409349214.

Stein, R. (2006) 'Fundamentalism, father and son, and vertical desire'. *The Psychoanalytic Review*, 93: 201–29. doi:10.1521/prev.2006.93.2.201.

Stein, R. (2010) 'Notes on mind control: the malevolent uses of emotion as a dark mirror of the therapeutic process'. In Harris, A. and Botticelli, S. (Eds.), *First Do No Harm. The Paradoxical Encounters of Psychoanalysis, Warmaking, and Resistance.* New York, London: Routledge, pp. 251–77.

Stolorow, R.D. and Atwood, G.E. (1992) *Contexts of Being*. Hillsdale, NJ: The Analytic Press.

Stolorow, R.D., Atwood, G.E. and Brandchaft, B. (1994) *The Intersubjective Perspective*. Northvale, NJ: Jason Aronson Inc.

Straker, G. (2000) 'Thinking under fire: psychoanalytic reflections on cognition in the war zone'. *Free Associations*, 7(4): 1–12.

Summers, F. (2008) 'Making sense of the APA: a history of the relationship between psychology and the military'. *Psychoanalytic Dialogues*, 18(5): 614–37. doi:10.1080/10481880802297665.

Tarantelli, C.B. (2003) 'Life within death: towards a metapsychology of catastrophic psychic trauma'. *The International Journal of Psychoanalysis*, 84(4): 915–28. doi:10.1516/NPEL-X40F-3QH3-MXAX.

Todorov, T. (1991) *Facing the Extreme: Moral Life in the Concentration Camps*. New York: Henry Holt and Company, 1996.

Trunnel, E.E. and Holt W.E. (1974) 'The concept of denial or disavowal'. *Journal of the American Psychoanalytic Association*, 22(4): 769–84. doi:10.1177/000306517402200403.

Ulman, R.B. and Brothers, D. (1993) *The Shattered Self: A Psychoanalytic Study of Trauma*. New York, London: Routledge.

van der Kolk, B.A. (1989) 'The compulsion to repeat the trauma: re-enactment, revictimization, and masochism'. *Psychiatric Clinics of North America*, 12(2): 389–411.

van der Kolk, B.A. (2002) 'Posttraumatic therapy in the age of neuroscience'. *Psychoanalytic Dialogues*, 12(3): 381–92. doi:10.1080/10481881209348674.

van der Kolk, B.A. and Fisler, R. (1995) 'Dissociation and the fragmentary nature of traumatic memories: overview and exploratory study'. *Journal of Traumatic Stress*, 8(4): 505–25. doi:10.1007/BF02102887.

van der Kolk, B.A., McFarlane, A.C. and Weisaeth L. (Eds.) (1996) *Traumatic Stress: The Effects of Overwhelming Experience on Mind, Body and Society*. New York: Guilford.

van der Kolk, B.A., Roth, S., Pelcovitz, D., Sunday, S. and Spinazzola, J. (2005) 'Disorders of extreme stress: the empirical foundation of a complex adaptation to trauma'. *Journal of Traumatic Stress*, 18(5): 389–99. doi:10.1002/jts.20047.

Varvin, S. (2002) 'Body, mind and the other. Symbolisation and mentalisation of extreme trauma'. In Varvin, S. and Stajner-Popovic, T. (Eds), *Upheaval: Psychoanalytic Perspective on Trauma*. Belgrade: IAN.

Varvin, S. and Rosenbaum, B. (2003) 'Extreme traumatisation: strategies for mental survival'. *International Forum of Psychoanalysis*, 12(1): 5–16. doi:10.1080/08037060310005223.

Verbitsky, H. (1996) *The Flight: Confessions of An Argentine Dirty Warrior*. New York: The New York Press.

Vesti, P. (1990) 'Extreme man-made stress and anti-therapy: doctors as collaborators in torture'. *Danish Medical Bulletin*, 37(5): 466–8.

Vesti, P. and Lavik, J. (1991) 'Torture and the medical profession: a review'. *Journal of Medical Ethics*, 17 (Suppl.) (December): 4–8. doi:10.1136/jme.17.Suppl.4.

Twemlow, S.W. (1995) 'Traumatic object relations configurations seen in victim/victimizer relationships'. *Journal of American Academy of Psychoanalysis*, 23: 563–80.

Wilson, J.P. and Drożdek, B. (2004) *Broken Spirits: The Treatment of Traumatized Asylum-Seekers, Refugees, and War and Torture Victims*. New York: Brunner-Routledge.

Winnicott, D.W. (1947) 'Hate in the countertransference'. In *Through Paediatrics to Psycho-Analysis*. New York: Basic Books, 1975, pp. 194–203.

Winnicott, D.W. (1952) 'Anxiety associated with insecurity'. In *Collected Papers*. London: Tavistock, 1958, pp. 97–100.

Winnicott, D.W. (1953) 'Transitional objects and transitional phenomena: a study of the first not-me possession'. *The International Journal of Psychoanalysis*, 34(2): 89–97.

Winnicott, D.W. (1956) 'Primary maternal preoccupation'. In *Collected Papers*. New York: Basic Books, 1958, pp. 300–5.

Winnicott, D.W. (1958) 'The capacity to be alone'. In *The Maturational Process and the Facilitating Environment*. London: Hogarth Press, 1965, pp. 29–36.

Winnicott, D.W. (1960a) 'Ego distortion in terms of true and false self'. In *The Maturational Processes and the Facilitating Environment*. New York: International Universities Press, 1965, pp. 140–52.

Winnicott, D.W. (1960b) 'The theory of the parent-infant relationship'. *The International Journal of Psychoanalysis*, 41: 585–95.

Winnicott, D.W. (1965) *The Maturational Processes and the Facilitating Environment*. New York: International Universities Press, 1965.

Winnicott, D.W. (1971) 'Playing: creative activity and the search for the self'. In *Playing and Reality*. London and New York: Tavistock Publications, 1971 pp. 53–64.

Zimbardo, P.G. (1972) 'The pathology of imprisonment', *Society*, 9(6): 4–8.

Zimbardo, P.G. (1975) 'On transforming experimental research into advocacy for social change'. In Deutsch, M. and Hornstein, H. (Eds.), *Applying Social Psychology: Implications for Research, Practice, and Training*. Hillsdale, NJ: Lawrence Erlbaum Associates, pp. 33–66.

Zimbardo, P.G. (2004) 'A situationist perspective on the psychology of evil: understanding how good people are transformed into perpetrators'. In Miller, A. G. (Ed.), *The Social Psychology of Good and Evil*. New York: Guilford, pp, 21–50.

Zimbardo, P.G., Haney, C., Banks, C. and Jaffe, D. (1999) *Stanford Prison Experiment*. Available at: www.prisonexp.org (accessed 2 February, 2009).

Zimbardo, P.G., Maslach, C. and Haney, C. (2000) 'Reflections on the Stanford Prison Experiment: genesis, transformations, consequences'. In Bass, T. (Ed.), *Obedience to Authority: Current Perspectives on the Milgram Paradigm*. Mahwah, NJ: Lawrence Erlbaum Associates, pp. 1–31.

PART 3
Implications for human rights

7
THE PERMISSIBILITY OF TORTURE

This chapter intends to critically review the main arguments of the debate on the permissibility of torture within the context of human rights, as well as in light of previous understandings of the phenomenon. A central concern is to reveal the configuration of phantasies, emotions, defences, assumptions and values underlying such a debate, and the psychologically implicit meanings of arguments both for and against torture.

What can particularly be seen from this review is that most pro-torture arguments are shaped according to an ideological pattern of thinking based on polarizations, terrifying phantasies of annihilation, and omnipotent phantasies of defence and protection, combined with a logic of self-sacrifice. Overall, the debate on the permissibility of torture seems to confirm that torture is the result of an emotional climate of terror and the consequent social defence response, as described in Chapters 4, 5 and 6.

Arguments for torture

Many authors who support the legitimacy of torture do so on the basis of the argument of utilitarianism (Allhoff, 2005, 2012; Bagaric and Clarke, 2005; Dershowitz, 2002, 2003, 2004a, 2004b, 2006; Posner, 2004; among others). The basic value of utilitarianism is sentience as the capacity to experience pain and pleasure: pleasure is good and pain is bad. According to an utilitarian moral practice, we seek to maximize pleasure and/or to minimize pain. As a result, whenever we act or construct laws, we should always act with a view towards maximizing good and/or minimizing harm. Although utilitarians share a commitment to sentience and happiness maximization, different utilitarian theories can diverge considerably over how best to maximize good consequences.

The most popular utilitarian arguments that appeal to the necessity of torture are articulated around the themes of: 1) the 'supreme emergency' state and 'necessity reasons', 2) the 'ticking-time bomb scenario', 3) the 'dirty hands' problem and 4) the 'self-defence' issue.

'Supreme emergency' and 'necessity reasons'

The canonical statement of the argument of 'supreme emergency', as used in many pro-torture reasonings, can be found in the modern literature on the 'just war'. In *Just and Unjust Wars*, Michael Walzer (1977) suggests that the idea of a 'supreme emergency' is, in fact, a compound of two conditions, both of which must be present if the idea of supreme emergency is to be justifiably invoked: *danger* and *imminence*. Evidently, the corollary of this is that, when these two conditions run out, the idea of 'supreme emergency' loses its hold (Walzer, 1977: 252). Walzer illustrates this thesis with two detailed examples: 1) the case of the strategic bombing of the German cities by the British between 1940 and 1943, which, he argues, was a situation in which 'supreme emergency' was legitimately deployed; and 2) the decision to drop the atomic bomb on Japan, which, he argues, cannot be seen as a case of 'supreme emergency' and was therefore doubly a crime. In the British case, Walzer's argument depends on the claim, disputable of course, but nonetheless very widely believed at the time, that the possibility of German victory in 1940–1941 seemed real and that a German victory, given the character of the Nazi regime, was an appalling prospect. Walzer makes the case that, while the bombing offensive was justified when Britain stood alone, by 1942, when other military options had become available, it no longer was. According to these criteria, Truman's decision to drop the atomic bomb cannot be seen as a case of 'supreme emergency', although it is often portrayed as such, since the determining condition (that of possibly suffering unimaginably large casualties on both sides) was not a fixed and appalling possibility (Walzer, 1977: 259).

The 'necessity doctrine' has been expressed in numerous ways, which cannot be exhaustively addressed here. However, it 'represents a concession to human weakness in cases of extreme pressure, where the accused breaks the law rather than submitting to the probability of greater harm if he does not break the law' (Ashworth, 1975: 106). The idea, in its simplest form, is that it is unjust to penalize someone for violating the law when the action produces a greater good or averts a greater evil. Today, many states have enacted varying forms of a statutory necessity defense. English and American courts have long recognized the defence of necessity reasons as a common law principle, even in the absence of statutory law on the subject. For instance, in the aftermath of 9/11, similar arguments were adopted by former US Vice President, Dick Cheney.[1] From this perspective, torture has been portrayed as the only way to deal with particularly dangerous 'evil doers'. The argument here is not only that 'we are under threat', but that the current enemy is unlike any other, of exceptional dangerousness, and hence only torture will allow us the defeat of this particular threat. This logic led to the creation of internment camps at Abu Ghraib and Guantanamo Bay, the latter a deliberately 'extra-legal' area outside formal US jurisdiction, yet wholly controlled by the US government, where torture was practiced. This situation has led some in the USA – most notoriously, Alan Dershowitz – to argue for the incorporation of torture into US law under specific circumstances through the creation of what Dershowitz called 'torture warrants' (Dershowitz, 2002, 2003, 2004b). This argument has also been adopted by other authors in the legal field (although from different positions: Elshtain, 2004; Ignatieff, 2004; Posner, 2004 and others) who have proposed an understanding of the supreme emergency situation as being faced with a choice between two evils – torture or terrorism. In this binary choice, all we can do is to choose the lesser evil – i.e. torture.

The 'ticking-time bomb scenario'

The 'ticking-time bomb scenario' is a sophisticated phantasy that contains the ingredients of the 'supreme emergency' argument – *threat* and *imminence* – disguised under the cover of a rational argument. It is a thought experiment that invokes some catastrophic threat, such as the detonation of an atomic bomb, or perhaps the release of a similar weapon of mass destruction, and asks us to consider whether we could justify refusing to torture a terrorist, given that the consequences arising from the detonation of the likely device are so severe (Allhoff, 2005, 2012; Bagaric and Clarke, 2005; Curzer, 2006; Dershowitz, 2002; Elshtain, 2004; Levin, 1982; Shue, 1978).

The philosopher Michael Levin anticipated by almost twenty years this debate about whether the conditions for torture were morally and legally permissible by illustrating the ticking-time bomb case:

> There are situations in which torture is not merely permissible but morally mandatory . . . Suppose a terrorist has hidden an atomic bomb on Manhattan Island which will detonate at noon on July 4 unless . . . (here follow the usual demands of money and release of his friends from jail). Suppose, further, that he is caught at 10 am of the fateful day, but – preferring death to failure – won't disclose where the bomb is. What do we do? If we follow due process . . . millions of people will die. If the only way to save those lives is to subject the terrorist to the most excruciating possible pain, what grounds can there be for not doing so? . . . Torturing the terrorist is unconstitutional? Probably. But millions of lives surely outweigh constitutionality. Torture is barbaric? Mass murder is far more barbaric. . . . Once you concede that torture is justified in extreme cases, you have admitted that the decision to use torture is a matter of balancing innocent lives against the means needed to save them.
>
> (Levin, 1982, in Schulz, 2007: 227)

This argument prevails from book to book (Allhoff, 2005, 2012; Bagaric and Clarke, 2005; Dershowitz, 2002, 2004; Elshtain, 2004; Shue, 1978, 2006).

The ticking-time bomb argument provides a substantial reason for implementing an actual policy of torture (Dershowitz, 2002, 2004). Derived intellectually from Jeremy Bentham (Twining and Twining, 1973), it consists of two parts. First, there are some extraordinary cases where interrogational torture is, or is regarded as, the least bad option, namely, variants of the ticking-time bomb scenario. Second, since torture is *de facto* used in these cases, it is better to drop the hypocritical pretence that it is something 'we don't do' and legalize its use. Dershowitz argues that it would be better to issue 'non-lethal torture warrants in extraordinary cases' (Dershowitz, 2004b: 20) than to go along with the hypocrisy of torture's 'selective use beneath the radar screen' (Dershowitz, 2002: 163).

Dershowitz thinks that, although torture is morally wrong, it should nevertheless be legalized, to control and regulate the practice (Dershowitz, 2004b, 2006). He argues that we are sometimes faced with an unavoidable moral dilemma, which demands that we choose the lesser of two evils: however you decide, someone is going to suffer the consequences. Since such circumstances are inevitably going to arise, it is better that torture be legally regulated, so as to avoid abuse and to ensure that it is used as sparingly as possible.

A different perspective on this dilemma reverses the question: torture should be banned as a legal matter *and* nevertheless may also be morally permissible. Parry claims:

> We cannot completely reject the evil of torture as a method of combating terrorism, regardless of what international law provides. If torture provides the last remaining chance to save lives in imminent peril, the necessity defence should be available to justify the interrogators' conduct. [. . .]
>
> Technical legal terms cannot mask or limit torture's evil . . . Yet torture may be the legitimate option — the lesser of two evils — in rare circumstances. In theory, we can admit an exception to an otherwise universal prohibition without undermining the values that gave rise to that prohibition.
>
> (Parry, 2004: 158–60)

Not all uses of the ticking-time bomb argument advocate torture policy. Other authors state that torture ought to be prohibited in all cases, but concede that the ticking-time bomb argument shows that the universal illegality of acts of torture can, in some cases, be overlooked (Gross, 2004; Gur-Arye, 2004; Elshtain, 2004). This is not the same as allowing a policy of torture. It is rather a way of acknowledging that certain violations of the law admit to ex-post ratification (Gur-Arye, 2004).

Even some clear and robust critics of interrogational torture have taken a softer and more complex position regarding the ticking-time bomb scenario. Jonathan Allen, for example, states that, for the 'ticking-time bomb' scenario to constitute a truly compelling case for torture, we would have to know: a) that we are holding the right person; b) that the person being tortured really does possess the information we need; c) that acquiring the information the captured terrorist possesses would be very likely to put us in a position to avert a disaster, and that their accomplices have not already adopted a contingency plan of which the person in question is ignorant; and d) that the information we obtain through torture is reliable (Allen, 2005). Allen reminds us that real cases, even those that approximate the ticking-time bomb scenario, involve much more uncertainty, and, therefore, require complex judgements.

The problem of 'dirty hands'

Another argument framing the moral question of torture is that of 'dirty hands'. The moral responsibility to save lives goes beyond the ticking-time bomb scenario: the greater the number of lives involved, the greater the sense of obligation one might feel to engage in whatever is required to save those lives. To refuse to torture, the argument runs, is to place one's own moral purity over the lives of the people who would otherwise be saved. In this respect, the decision to *immorally* torture is a decision to sacrifice one's own moral standing for a greater good (Walzer, 1973; Elshtain, 2004; Curzer, 2006). Morality here demands the sacrifice of self-interest or, better still, of one's own *innocence*, if there is something much more important on the line. Here, a philosophical paradox in moral philosophy can be identified: is it possible that an immoral action in ordinary circumstances can be morally required in exceptional circumstances?

A variation on the above argument can be found in the idea that politicians have a responsibility to engage in ostensibly immoral actions based on their political positions. In literature, this is referred to as the problem of 'dirty hands', based on Sartre's play of the same name (1955), and largely due to Michael Walzer's seminal discussion in 'Political action: the problem of dirty hands' (1973):

> I do not think I could govern innocently, nor do most of us believe that those who govern are innocent ... even the best of them. ... It means that a particular act of government (in a political party or in the state) may be exactly the right thing to do in utilitarian terms and yet leave the man who does it guilty of a moral wrong.
> (Walzer, 1973 in Levinson, 2004: 61–2)

Despite the immorality of torture, one might argue that our leaders have the political obligation to engage in it in order to protect the lives of citizens. The argument here goes that accepting office entails accepting a set of duties that one would otherwise not have. By accepting a public office, one vows to protect the public that one represents.

A number of jurists, philosophers and political scientists defend the idea that torture should be permitted (morally speaking), even while it remains illegal. For example, Allen (2005) and Shue (1978, 2006) think that, while interrogational torture might be morally justified 'in principle and at the extreme', its remaining illegal is also morally justified on the grounds that the likely consequences of its legalization are morally undesirable. They differ from Dershowitz in their assessment of the likely consequences of legalization.

In this respect, many resolve the problem of torture by concluding that, as lamentable as it is, we want leaders willing to get their hands dirty, that is, to compromise their moral conscience by ordering immoral courses of action.

'Necessity defence' and 'self-defence' arguments

A standard necessity argument may be used as a defence for engaging in illegal actions, which are reputed necessary to save people's life. We can find an example of such a formulation of the problem in a judgement of the Supreme Court of Israel[2]. Indeed, the judges noted that an explicit authorization permitting the General Security Service (GSS) to employ physical means can be found in specific cases by virtue of the criminal law invoking the 'necessity defence', as prescribed in the Penal Law, Article 34 (1)/5737-1977:

> A person will not bear criminal liability for committing any act immediately necessary for the purpose of saving the life, liberty, body or property, of either himself or his fellow person, from substantial danger of serious harm, imminent from the particular state of things [circumstances], at the requisite timing, and absent alternative means for avoiding the harm.

From this flowed the legality of the directives with respect to the use of physical means – i.e. torture – in GSS interrogations (Kassim, 2002: 278).

Miriam Gur-Aye argues that, in rare situations, the use of interrogational force may be justified under the limited boundaries of 'self-defence' rather than 'necessity' (2004: 183). Indeed,

> self-defence is not limited to defending one's own self; it applies also when third parties are being attacked. Like necessity, the use of force seeks to prevent an imminent danger to legitimate interests. Unlike necessity, preventing the danger in cases of self-defence does not involve the sacrifice of innocent people's interests. The self-defender repels the attack by using force . . . against the attacker who has unlawfully created the danger. The moral basis of self-defence is, therefore, stronger than that of mere 'necessity'.
>
> (Gur-Aye, 2004: 194)

Arguments against torture

Against the 'necessity reasons' and 'supreme emergency' arguments

As shown in Chapter 2, whereas a policy of torture is invoked to defend national security, it is also possible to trace some notion of 'necessity reason'. Larry May makes the important point of distinguishing between 'necessity' *simpliciter* and 'military necessity':

> The principle of military necessity is different from the defence of necessity . . . the defence of necessity is indeed a post-hoc or post-factum defence . . . many believe that there is a principle of military necessity that establishes

pre-emptory authorization, that is, where a State is permitted to use otherwise impermissible tactics in certain cases of extreme emergency.

(May, 2005: 203)

On the contrary, May clarifies that the International Law Commission maintains that 'necessity' can be legitimately invoked by nations to ensure the protection of certain vital interests, provided that the threat is imminent, that there are no available alternatives, and that the action to be carried out 'does not seriously impair an essential interest of the State or the States towards which the obligation exists, or of the international community as a whole' (2005: 204). Therefore, international law does not allow *carte blanche* when it comes to claims of necessity. Several circumstances must occur for the military necessity being positively met, namely: a) the imminence of threat, b) the absence of alternative means by which to prevent the harm, and c) the balance between the harm prevented and the harm caused. 'If cases of torture are ever justified by reference to military necessity, they are far fewer, and much harder to justify fully, than people like to think' (May, 2005: 205).

Wisnewski (2010) focuses on the implications of the necessity arguments to establish a policy of torture. He makes the point that the effects of such a policy have seriously been underestimated. In order to have persons capable of using torture effectively, one needs to organize significant amounts of training. In many cases, the training is achieved by inducing persons to torture, or even subjecting themselves to torture, in order to bring about and then exploit a post-traumatic personality. To this, one must add, the substantial overall damage to the reputation of that society, both internally and internationally.

Against the 'ticking-time bomb' argument

Many authors have criticized the ticking-time bomb argument as a logically incoherent justification for torture. According to Vittorio Bufacchi and Jean Maria Arrigo (2006), this reasoning reveals two kinds of fallacy:

1 *A deductive fallacy.* The ticking-time bomb argument follows a deductive line concerning the efficacy of torture interrogation: a) the terrorist is captured; b) if the terrorist is tortured, they will reveal information regarding the location of the primed bomb before the bomb detonates; c) the terrorist ought to be tortured; d) the information regarding the location of the primed bomb is retrieved; e) the bomb is found and disconnected before it explodes, saving the lives of many innocent people. However, c, d, e do not follow on from premises a and b.
2 *A consequentialist fallacy.* In order to deduce c, d, e, other invisible premises are required: f) it is almost certain that this is the terrorist holding information regarding a primed bomb; g) if the terrorist is tortured, they will reveal the information regarding the location of the primed bomb before the bomb detonates.

The deductive argument is indeed problematic for a number of reasons: intelligence is always fallible, torture is not always effective, torture is less likely to work in short time spans, torture elicits false information, etc. (Bufacchi and Arrigo, 2006: 362).

Many other authors point out that the ticking-time bomb case is unrealistic (Brecher, 2007; Luban, 2005; Matthews, 2008; Wisnewski, 2010 among others).

David Luban (2005) considers the ticking-time bomb story an intellectual fraud, a rhetorical move designed to convince liberals that there are cases in which torture is morally required. This story may paint an unrealistic picture, which tricks us into thinking that torture is justifiable and that the torturer is not a sadistic brute, but a heroic public servant trying to save innocent lives. Luban claims the story cheats by assuming too much: that officials know there is a bomb, that they have captured the one who planted it, that torture will make them talk, and so on. None of this is certain in the real world. Furthermore, the story assumes it is rational to choose between the certainties of torture *vs.* the uncertainty of saving lives and that a decision can be made by calculating costs and benefits. The liberal ideology of torture presupposes a torturer impelled by the desire to stop a looming catastrophe, not by cruelty. Implicitly, this image presumes that the interrogator and the decision maker are the same person. On the contrary, the defining fact about real organizations is the division of labour. The basic rule in every bureaucratic organization is that operational details and the guilty knowledge that goes with them get pushed down the chain of command as far as possible, while credit is pulled up. Luban cautions that the conditions of the ticking-time bomb case are so remote from the real world that the wiser course is to deny the possibility. Besides, back in the real world, once it is granted that torture is permitted in the imaginary tick-bombing case, we end up with a torture culture, and torture practices, training and institutions.

Matthews (2008) also argues that the ticking-time bomb hypothesis works through a logical illusion deliberately constructed to justify torture. Its ingredients are:

1   *Imminence*. Every ticking-time bomb hypothesis presupposes an imminent threat. The reason is clear: the greater the time available, the more likely it is that intelligence methods alternative to torture will be available to resolve the dilemma.
2   *Threat*. The ticking-time bomb hypothesis presupposes that there is a risk of evil, injury, loss or destruction. The point is to establish that conditions exist where we are morally obligated to torture.
3   *Necessity*. The necessity has to do with a hypothetical imperative to minimize harm and the absence of alternatives. Yet, in real interrogation situations, there is always a variety of alternative interrogation strategies.[3]
4   *Epistemic state of interrogator*. What is at stake here is the distinction between the infallibility of knowledge and the fallibility of belief. In the strict case of the ticking-time bomb, interrogators know that: there is a bomb and the clock is ticking, that the threat is real and imminent and that the 'terrorist' knows where the bomb is and how to defuse it. However, if the interrogators had

the knowledge they required, they would not need to resort to torture. The strict case has the advantage that it avoids a host of morally controversial consequences like the torture of the innocent, while limiting cases of torture only to those that are absolutely necessary. If we eliminate knowledge from the ticking-time bomb hypothesis and replace it with belief, we inevitably factor in a range of ills that the stricter model manages to avoid.

5   *Suspect/source*. Since the category of 'suspect' is irredeemably vague, and plausibly includes not just the suicide bomber, but also a whole range of individuals, the interrogators must be tempted to extend the class of suspects with no limits. At the point when interrogators lack detailed information, the pool of possible suspects is the entire target population.

Moreover, Matthews (2008) remarks that the ticking-time bomb hypothesis claims to model the behaviour of a single interrogator reacting to a catastrophic threat. Yet, in all cases involving governments or non-state groups, we are talking about individuals who act in a public capacity as representatives. Soldiers do not act independently of their institutions, but in terms of established training practices and defined policies, often secret, which determine the frame of possible actions they may employ. A secretary of defence does not usually order a single torture event. If a torture policy is constructed, it will have to be interpreted by a wide range of people. The interpretation will lead to a variation of practices, which the policy-maker will not anticipate and hence will not be able to control.

Matthews' point is that, not only are the scenarios of the ticking-time bomb unlikely, but that they are empirically impossible. The hypothesis systematically and deliberately ignores the empirical circumstances under which torture takes place; it ignores the institutional nature of torture and its problems; it fails to understand the difference between the behaviour of individuals and the policies of institutions; it fails to account for the social nature of either the victims or torturers; it creates a demonizing myth about the 'terrorist'; it refuses to introduce any real consequence of torture at all; it provides no analysis of the nature of torture; and it pays no attention to problems of conceptual or fog-of-war vagueness (Matthews, 2008).

Wisnewski (2010) advances a similar criticism. He notices that the ticking-time bomb case is *unrealistic*, epistemologically, psychologically and pragmatically. From the epistemological point of view, Wisnewski emphasizes that the most obvious instance of unrealism concerns the multiple levels of certainty that we must assume to make the thought experiment work. Three particular issues make the certainty unlikely: the probability that the person is a terrorist, the probability that they have the required intelligence, and the probability that the intelligence, once acquired, will still allow us to stop the bomb. In the *psychological* domain, the logical error is in the assumption that torture will work on *anyone* in terms of efficacy and timing. Three kinds of problem arise at this point: 1) pain responses are not predictable; 2) the appeal to intuitions is problematic because our intuitions may be informed by latent racism and sexism; and 3) the amount of time a successful interrogation may require cannot be predicted in advance. Finally, Wisnewski makes a *pragmatic* argument. He points out that the idea of torture 'working' is ill-defined. If 'working' consists merely of someone talking, then this does not seem enough to confirm that torture works. Torture 'working' involves actionable, current and true information that could not be acquired in an equally effective way.

Jean Maria Arrigo, along with several other psychologists and former trained interrogators, came to the conclusion that prisoner/detainee abuse and torture are counterproductive to an intelligence gathering mission (Arrigo and Wagner, 2007: 393). In addition, a policy of torture is likely to spread social violence by producing more terrorists, and promoting competent torturers who will substantially increase the likelihood of acts of gross immorality carried out on command.

In his book, *Torture and the Ticking Bomb*, Brecher (2007) also shows concern about how to limit the applicability of torture to a weapon of mass destruction and a captured bomber, rather than to all situations in which the authorities need information. After a strict analysis of many authoritative opinions on the ticking-time bomb scenario, he concludes that government apologists want to keep this scenario alive because it keeps the level of fear high within the population, making it possible to implement all sorts of controls. It works because it is easy to imagine the weapon, the perpetrator and the consequences.

Against the 'dirty hands' argument

The 'dirty hands' argument considers taking decisions against moral sense as a moral duty of higher-ups. Some authors expose the 'fairy tale' nature of this narrative, emphasizing the 'real' consequences of this supposed moral self-sacrifice of superiors.

The assumption of opinions advocating legalized torture (such as Dershowitz, 2002) is that torture can be controlled, regulated and effectively administered by superiors. Rejali claims that, 'legalizing torture makes rogue operations inevitable, . . . [while] civil servants cannot exercise selective control once they have licensed armed men to exercise unlimited power over individuals' (Rejali, 2007: 529). Richard Matthews puts it this way:

> When states torture, they attack not individuals but groups and communities . . . state torture is one tactic in a coercive assault on some community . . . [the harm of torture] spreads out across these entire groups in complicated ways. This spreading is intrinsic to torture and cannot be avoided.
> (Matthews, 2008: 202)

Winsnewski (2010) observes that torture requires institutions; there cannot be a solitary act of torture. If excess emerges at the hands of torturers, it also does, with certainty, at the level of the institutions that support the use of torture. As a matter of fact, the nature of torture is to escalate.

Moreover, the use of torture can actually undermine other investigative techniques for two significant reasons. First, the ability to detain and arrest criminals deteriorates as investigators increasingly rely on torture. Conviction rates rise in tandem with false arrests and coerced confessions. Second, the reliance on torture by police investigators undermines the classical skills of solid detective work. De-skilling, as a consequence of the systematic use of torture, thus leads with some regularity to more torture.

Furthermore, Rejali emphasizes that torture leads to organizational decay, because torturers tend to disobey orders and regulations (2007: 456–500). The tendency of torture to gravitate towards excess, as well as to stray across boundaries, along with a decreased ability to gather information effectively, ultimately aids in the destruction of a public trust, which has already been eroded by the ability to suspend the rule of law. Carlos Castresana confirms that, 'torture affects the basic pillars of the legal structure of democratic States, its very essence . . . [accepting torture] compromises the safety and threatens the collapse of our whole legal system' (2008: 136). Claudia Card (2002) observes that engaging in torture could damage our ability to find the citizens of our nation trustworthy. This, in turn, could significantly minimize the value of our society, as well as the life we might live within it. Our contentedness with politics in whatever nation we call home is affected by our ability to trust our leaders. Living under a torturous regime has devastating psychological effects on both the ruled and rulers.

Against the 'self-defence' argument

Wisnewski (2010) considers the argument of self-defence to be begging the question: is self-defence only viable if there are no other alternatives? In the case of torture, the standards of a 'just war' do not seem to apply. One's right to kill the enemy, for example, is only warranted because the enemy has an identical opportunity. Once one is captured, no reciprocal threat exists. As Henry Shue notices,

> part of the peculiar disgust which torture evokes may be derived from its apparent failure to satisfy even this weak constraint of being a 'fair fight'. The supreme reason, of course, is that torture begins only after the fight is – for the victim – finished. Only losers are tortured. . . . now that the torture victim has exhausted all means of defence and is powerless before the victors, a fresh assault begins. . . . [torture] is a cruel assault upon the defenceless.
>
> (Shue, 1978: 130)

Gur-Aye (2004) recognizes that self-defence does not justify every response to one's attacker. It justifies only those actions that are absolutely necessary to thwart one's attacker. If one is entitled to engage in violent actions in self-defence, provided that such violence is reasonably thought to be necessary to defend oneself, it would follow that no action directly against a perpetrator is justified when an alternative to such direct action is available. Moreover, self-defence is permissible only insofar as it follows the basic principle of proportionality.

Emotional undercurrents of rational arguments

Looking at the main themes of philosophical debate on the permissibility of torture in light of the psychoanalytic understanding illustrated in Chapters 4, 5 and 6, it becomes clearer that the subject of rational philosophical or moral arguments, on the basis of which free-will political or legal decisions are taken, has its internal emotional rationale.

We can find in the arguments of this debate, particularly in pro-torture arguments, the main ingredients of the ideological thinking that results from monolithic societal states:

1 The emotional climate of *terror* linked to a perceived threat to survival: the cipher of the threat is conveyed by the variety of themes about the exceptional circumstances of *imminent danger*: the state of 'necessity', the 'supreme emergency' that demands exceptional measures, the self-defence argument, the imminence of a catastrophic event such as the explosion of a nuclear bomb. The discourse of necessity implies an argument of threat, feeling emotionally overwhelmed, and urgency to act in self-defence. We have seen how fear is crucial to the emotional life of large groups (Chapters 2 and 5). Brecher's remark (2007) that the thought experiment of a ticking bomb is a way in which to exploit an emotional state of fear within the public is relevant here.

2 *Ideological thinking*: in Chapter 5, ideology is portrayed as a structure of thinking which, to some extent, is rooted on the emotional need to keep mental contents divided through splitting, denial, idealization, etc. In many arguments of the debate for and against torture, we can find a representation of self and other as split into 'us and them', 'good and bad', 'superior and inferior'. In this state of mind, what is overlooked is that, while we think to be the 'good guys', we act the evil, as in Jung's idea of being possessed by the shadow (Jung, 1945). The simple criterion of utilitarianism (to maximize good and minimize pain) is an obvious bipolar structure of thinking, which lends itself to the logic of splitting and denial that is typical of the paranoid-schizoid mode of thinking.

3 The phantasy of an *omnipotent* response to such a threat: this element is particularly clear in the ticking-time bomb scenario, where the mission to save innocent lives requires us to take the exceptional measure of torture. Some authors emphasize the logic lapses of this reasoning, but, emotionally, this logic has its own consistency: it feeds the illusion of being able to face the threat, denying one's own vulnerability and guaranteeing an epistemic position of *certainty* (the status of knowledge of paranoid-schizoid mode). In Chapters 2 and 5, we saw how ideology offers society a sense of unity, while it is menaced by fragmentation. Thus, an ideological stance provides an epistemic position of knowledge, shared by the members of the group, on the condition that members align with the prevailing *Monolithic Societal State*. Perhaps on the wave

of such a need, so many thinkers and citizens find the ticking-time bomb thought experiment logically persuasive. The exceptionality of torture is also functional to a display of agency by the torturer. Omnipotence is at the service of a certain status of knowledge: clear-cut individuation of evil, the certainty of what is fair and reasonable to do in order to face the situation, perceiving oneself as on the right side, possessed with a feeling of being invested in a 'sacred' mission, and consequently a sense of restored self-esteem. Altman (2008) emphasizes that, after a defeat has produced the humiliation of having been unable to control events, torture produces the illusion of restored control and omnipotence. He observes that this movement is compensatory towards the initial helplessness of authorities, possibly agents of a great nation, in relation to this single individual who is supposed to possess crucial knowledge (the location of the bomb).

4   Within the 'dirty hands' argument, an emotional need of protection by a powerful superior entity is revealed. This deals with that verticality, which shapes society within the context of a social climate of widespread terror (Chapter 6), as well as with the issue of self-sacrifice. The problem of 'dirty hands' reveals the need to be in a protector–protected relationship with regard to leaders, who must sacrifice their morality and themselves by disregarding ethical and reality considerations. They are required to automatically take the guilt of immoral and illegal decisions upon themselves in the name of a supposedly 'salvific' mission on behalf of society. Here, we find ourselves in that social space, which demands that the individual self is 'sacrificed' in the name of the societal monolithic functioning.

Utilitarianism is particularly akin to the ideological turn of thinking, given its emphasis on a simple end: maximizing overall 'happiness' and reducing pain and unpleasure. However, in this regard, it is important to make the distinction, as introduced by Matthews (2008), between *act utilitarianism* and *rule utilitarianism*.

Act utilitarians argue that we need to focus on specific happiness-maximizing 'actions', rather than specifically on 'policies' or 'laws'. Morality is concerned with individual choice making. As a consequence, obeying the law will generally be good, but there are occasions in which to disobey the law will cause less harm. Act utilitarian defenders believe there are times when we have to choose between greater and lesser harms. The number of these cases is always believed to be small. The conditions under which torture is justified are those outlined in the ticking-time bomb hypothesis. *Rule utilitarians* argue that happiness is best maximized through the establishment of effective rules and laws. The general practice of upholding and following laws will provide greater benefits than any tendency to break the law, whenever the good consequences are believed to maximize happiness. Violating laws will produce more harm than one might think. So the apparent plausibility of encouraging the violation of a rule for the sake of some good masks much greater difficulties. William Casebeer (2005: 262), although allowing torture in principle, suggests that utilitarians should never justify torture in practice, because the problem is that effective torture requires harmful policies, institutions and practices, which entail far more than the infliction of violence on a torture victim on a discrete occasion. The problem with institutionalization is crucial. Jean Maria Arrigo (2004) makes of this question one of her main points: 'the establishment of an official torture interrogation programme produces long-term dysfunctions in key institutions – notably health care, biomedical research, the police, the judiciary, and the military – due to institutional dynamics that are independent of the original moral rationale for torture' (2004: 544).

At this point of reasoning, it seems appropriate to suggest that the passage between *act utilitarian* and *rule utilitarian* arguments significantly reminds the shift from the simplifying binary thinking of ideological positions inspired by fear, based on the paranoid-schizoid pattern of defence (splitting/denial/omnipotence), compelled to action, to a more complex, articulated, and reality-based thinking characteristic of states of thirdness, which can consider the multiple contextual factors in which torture can emerge and the dramatic consequences of its use.

Notes

1. Typical of Cheney's confident declarations is that 'enhanced interrogation techniques were absolutely essential in saving thousands of American lives and preventing further attacks against the United States' (Dick Cheney, interviewed by Chris Wallace, Fox News Sunday, Fox News Channel, 30 August 2009). Also see, Dick Cheney, 'Cheney Warns of New Attacks', interview by John F. Harris, Mike Allen and Jim Vandehei, Politico.com, 4 February 2009. Available at: www.politico.com/news/stories/0209/18390.html (accessed 8 May 2012).
2. *Public Comm. Against Torture in Israel v The State of Israel* 53(4)PD 817 (1999)
3. Some professional interrogators, like those employed by the FBI, the US army and other bodies, are sceptical about the value of torture as an interrogation tool (Borum, 2006: 8; Coulam, 2006: 18–19; Wahlquist, 2006: xxi).

References

Allen, J. (2005) 'Warrant to torture? A critique of Dershowitz and Levinson', ACDIS Occasional Paper, Program in Arms Control, Disarmament, and International Security, University of Illinois at Urbana-Champaign, 13. Available at: www.acdis.uiuc.edu (accessed: 10 January 2016).

Allhoff, F. (2005) 'A defence of torture: separation of cases, ticking-time bombs, and moral justification'. *International Journal of Applied Philosophy*, 19(2): 243–64. doi:10.5840/ijap 200519213.

Allhoff, F. (2012) *Terrorism, Ticking Time-Bombs, and Torture*. Chicago, IL: University of Chicago Press.

Altman, N. (2008) 'The psychodynamics of torture'. *Psychoanalytic Dialogues*, 18: 658–70. doi:10.1080/10481880802297681.

Arrigo, J.M. (2004) 'A utilitarian argument against torture, interrogation and terrorists'. *Science and Engineering Ethics*, 10(3) (July): 543–72. doi:10.1007/s11948-004-0011-y.

Arrigo, J.M. and Wagner, R.V. (2007) 'Psychologists and military interrogators rethink the psychology of torture'. *Peace and Conflict: Journal of Peace Psychology*, 13(4) (November): 393–8. doi:10.1080/10781910701665550.

Ashworth, A.J. (1975) 'Reason, logic and criminal liability'. *Law Quarterly Review*, 91: 102–44.
Bagaric, M. and Clarke, J. (2005) 'Not enough official torture in the world? The circumstances in which torture is morally justifiable'. *University of San Francisco Law Review*, 39(3) (Spring): 581–616.
Borum, R. (2006) 'Approaching truth: behavioral science lessons on educing information from human sources'. In Fein, R.A. (Ed.), *Intelligence Science Board Study Phase I Report: Educing Information*. Washington, DC: NDIC Press, pp. 17–44.
Brecher, B. (2007) *Torture and the Ticking Bomb*. Malden, MA, Oxford, UK, Victoria, Australia: Blackwell Publishing.
Bufacchi, V. and Arrigo, J.M. (2006) 'Torture, terrorism and the state: a refutation of the ticking-bomb argument'. *Journal of Applied Philosophy*, 23(3): 355–73. doi:10.1111/j.1468-5930.2006.00355.x.
Card, C. (2002) *The Atrocity Paradigm: A Theory of Evil*. Oxford: Oxford University Press.
Casebeer, W. (2005) 'Torture interrogation of terrorists: a theory of exceptions (with notes, cautions, and warnings)'. In Shanahan, T. (Ed.), *Philosophy 9/11: Thinking about the War on Terrorism*. Peru, IL, Open Court, pp. 261–72.
Castresana, C. (2008) 'Torture as a greater evil'. In Hilde, T.C. (Ed.), *On Torture*. Baltimore, MD: Johns Hopkins University, pp. 133–44.
Coulam, R. (2006) 'Approaches to interrogation in the struggle against terrorism: considerations of cost and benefit'. In Fein, R.A. (Ed.), *Intelligence Science Board Study Phase I Report: Educing Information*. Washington, DC: NDIC Press, pp. 7–16.
Curzer, H.J. (2006) 'Admirable immorality, dirty hands, ticking bombs and torturing innocents'. *The Southern Journal of Philosophy*, 44(1): 31–56. doi:10.1111/j.2041-6962.2006.tb00002.x.
Dershowitz, A. (2002) *Why Terrorism Works: Understanding the Threat, Responding to the Challenge*. New Haven, CT: Yale University Press.
Dershowitz, A. (2003) 'The torture warrant: a response to Professor Strauss'. *New York School of Law Review*, 48: 275–94.
Dershowitz, A. (2004a) 'Tortured Reasoning'. In Levinson, S. (Ed.), *Torture: A Collection*. New York: Oxford University Press, pp. 257–80.
Dershowitz, A. (2004b) 'When torture is the least evil of terrible options'. *Times Higher Education Supplement*, 11 (June): 20–1.
Dershowitz, A. (2006) 'Should we fight terror with torture?' *Independent* 3 July (unpaginated). Available at: www.independent.co.uk (accessed 18 April, 2012).
Elshtain, J.B. (2004) 'Reflection on the problem of 'dirty hands''. In Levinson, S. (Ed.), *Torture: A Collection*. Oxford: Oxford University Press, pp. 77–92.
Gross, O. (2004) 'Are torture warrants warranted? Pragmatic absolutism and official disobedience'. *Minnesota Law Review*, 88 (June): 1481–555.
Gur-Arye, M. (2004) 'Can the war against terror justify the use of force in interrogations? Reflections in light of the Israeli experience'. In Levinson, S. (Ed.), *Torture: A Collection*. Oxford: Oxford University Press, pp. 183–98.
Ignatieff, M. (2004) *The Lesser Evil: Political Ethics in an Age of Terror*. Toronto: Penguin.
Jung, C.G. (1945) 'Psychology and religion. The definition of demonism'. In *Collected Works of C. G. Jung*, vol. 18, Read, H. Fordham M. and Adler G. (Eds.), translated by R. Hull, Princeton, NJ: Princeton University Press/Bollingen Series XX.
Kassim, A.F. (Ed.) (2002) *The Palestine Yearbook of International Law 2000–2001*. Vol. 11, 2000/2001, The Hague: Kluwer Law International.
Levin, M. (1982) 'The modern case for torture'. In Schulz, W.F. (Ed.), *The Phenomenon of Torture. Readings and Commentary*. Philadelphia, PA: University of Pennsylvania Press, 2007, pp. 227–9.

Luban, D. (2005) 'Liberalism, torture and the ticking bomb'. *Virginia Law Review*, 91(6) (October): 1425–61.

Matthews, R. (2008) *The Absolute Violation. Why Torture Must Be Prohibited*. Montreal and Kingston, London, Ithaca: McGill-Queen's University Press.

May, L. (2005) 'Torturing detainees during interrogation'. *International Journal of Applied Philosophy*, 19(2): 193–208. doi:10.5840/ijap200519214.

Parry, J.T. (2004) 'Escalation and necessity: defining torture at home and abroad'. In Levinson, S. (Ed.), *Torture: A Collection*. Oxford: Oxford University Press, pp. 145–64.

Posner, R. (2004) 'Torture, terrorism, and interrogation'. In Levinson, S. (Ed.), *Torture: A Collection*. Oxford: Oxford University Press, pp. 291–8.

Rejali, D. (2007) *Torture and Democracy*. Princeton, NJ: Princeton University Press.

Sartre, J.P. (1955) 'Dirty hands'. In *No Exit and Three Other Plays*. New York: Vintage.

Shue, H. (1978) 'Torture'. *Philosophy and Public Affairs*, 7(2) (Winter): 124–43. Reprinted in Levinson, S. (2004) (Ed.), *Torture: A Collection*. Oxford: Oxford University Press, pp. 47–60.

Shue, H. (2006) 'Torture in dreamland: Disposing of the ticking bomb'. *Case Western Reserve Journal of International Law*, 37(2–3): 231–9. Available at: http://scholarlycommons.law.case.edu/jil/vol37/iss2/4 (accessed 5 January 2016)

Twining, W.L. and Twining, P.E. (1973) 'Bentham on torture'. *Northern Ireland Legal Quarterly*, 23(3): 305–57.

Wahlquist, J. (2006) 'Educing information: interrogation – science and art'. In Fein, R.A. (Ed.), *Intelligence Science Board Study Phase I Report: Educing Information*. Washington, DC: NDIC Press, pp. xv–xxvi.

Walzer, M. (1973) 'Political action: the problem of dirty hands'. *Philosophy and Public Affairs*, 2(2) (Winter): 160–80. Reprinted in S. Levinson (Ed.), *Torture: A Collection*. New York: Oxford University Press, 2004, pp. 61–76.

Walzer, M. (1977) *Just and Unjust Wars*. New York: Basic Books, 1978.

Wisnewski, J.J. (2010) *Understanding Torture*. Edinburgh: Edinburgh University Press.

8

THREE FIELDS OF APPLICATION IN HUMAN RIGHTS

Responsibility of perpetrators, reparation for victims and the problem of truth

The idea for this study was to elaborate a comprehensive understanding of torture, which might also function as a workable conceptual tool to initiate a meaningful dialogue between psychoanalysis and human rights. In Chapter 7, the model was used to grasp substantial emotional undercurrents of the debate on the permissibility of torture. However, its potential, it is argued, might be deployed in relation to more applicative issues within the human rights field.

My proposal for future research concerns its application to the topic of torture in three fields of inquiry: 1) the responsibility of perpetrators of torture; 2) the issue of reparation for survivors; 3) the problem of 'truth'. Understandably, these would form three considerable chapters within the human rights discourse on torture, which cannot be run out here. The following paragraphs have the limited aim of framing a few questions in these areas of investigation.

Responsibility of perpetrators of torture

Torture poses a delicate question about the allocation of criminal liability. The problem in the legal field is often posed in terms of whether the abuse perpetrated by ordinary soldiers can be imputed, and to what extent, to the higher military echelons, to the top-level policy makers and legal officers, or even to political leaders (Allen, 2004; Human Rights Watch, 2006; Pokempner, 2005).

Pursuant to general principles of criminal law, not only the direct perpetration of acts of torture, but also any form of participation or complicity thereto, is criminally relevant. This principle is guaranteed by Article 4(1) of the UN Convention against Torture. Under this article, high-ranking officials who have instigated, ordered, authorized or approved the commission of illegal techniques amounting to torture by their soldiers, are criminally liable of torture for their participation or complicity in the crimes committed by subordinates. The group that drafted the UN Convention against Torture, concluded that 'complicity or participation' also embraced acts relating to 'cover-up' or concealment of incidents of torture, or leaving them unpunished.

However, in practice, the prosecution of higher-rank officers and, above all, political leaders is difficult and controversial (Bantekas, 1999, 2000; Bonafé, 2007; Martinez, 2007; Meloni, 2010; Mettraux, 2009; Sengheiser, 2008) nor is it clear what kind of link there may be between political and military fields. Orders become mini-policies or grand-policies as one moves up a chain of command, while policy is logically much more general in nature than a specific order or the actions carried out in response to it. However, as Sengheiser writes, 'Instead of flowing up the chain of command, command responsibility is relegated to the lower ranking troops' (2008: 694).

The 'culpable state of mind' (mens rea) in a superior–subordinate relationship

The doctrine of command responsibility was developed over the course of the twentieth and twenty-first centuries, mainly via the sentences of war crimes tribunals for wartime malpractices. The doctrine has become part of customary international law and been incorporated into the statutes of *ad hoc* international criminal tribunals – for example, the International Criminal Tribunal for the former Yugoslavia (ICTY) and the International Criminal Tribunal for Rwanda (ICTR) – and into the Rome Statute of the International Criminal Court (ICC). For space reasons, this interesting history cannot be reviewed here (for an introductory history, see Markham, 2011; for analyzes of the doctrine and the emerging case law, see Cassese and Gaeta, 2013; Cryer *et al.*, 2010; van Sliedregt, 2012; Werle, 2009). From this history, it emerges clearly that the law of *superior responsibility* has been the object of both great expectations and much criticism. Its doctrine is perceived as an indispensable tool to ascribe criminal responsibility to military and political leaders for international crimes committed at the collective and state level. However, it has also raised much concern, being perceived as a fall-back position for prosecutors to improperly expand the scope of individual criminal responsibility (Lael, 1982; Mettraux, 2009). On the other hand, its application seems to fail in prosecuting high-level military and civil authorities, which were responsible for introducing and organizing the policy for torture (Bantekas, 1999, 2000; Martinez, 2007; Pokempner, 2005).

This doctrine comprises three constituent elements, reflecting, respectively, power and agency ('effective command and control'), *mens rea* ('they knew or should have known'), and the omission that actually triggers criminal responsibility ('failure to take the reasonable and necessary steps'). The superior incurs criminal responsibility for failing to have prevented (or repressed) criminal acts committed by their subordinates on the basis that command responsibility implies a crime of *omission*. As the superior may be held *criminally* responsible, the doctrine has to observe the basic principles of criminal law, in particular, the principle of individual guilt. Criminal law is predicated on the idea of free human agency, implying that the accused has the capacity to act in conformity with the legally and morally desirable norm and that they know that they will be held responsible whenever they flout that norm.

One of the main controversial aspects surrounding the developments of the doctrine has been the level of knowledge that commanders must possess before they become criminally responsible. While it is accepted that actual knowledge of subordinates' crimes is sufficient, debates have centered on the appropriate level of 'constructive' knowledge required to warrant individual criminal responsibility (Ambos, 2002; Bantekas, 1999, 2000; Bonafé, 2007, Martinez, 2007; Mettraux, 2009; Mitchell, 2000; Pokempner, 2005; Stryszak, 2002). Two different formulations of 'constructive knowledge' have emerged. The stricter standard assesses whether, under the circumstances, a commander should have known of their subordinates' unlawful actions, thereby placing the commander under a proactive duty to keep informed of troops' activities. Under a more lenient standard of 'constructive knowledge', the commander is only held responsible when they fail to discover their subordinates' actions based on information already available to the commander. Both tests have received support in jurisprudence on command responsibility following the Second World War (see Levine, 2005).

In *The Law of Command Responsibility*, Mettraux (2009) conceptualizes command responsibility as a *sui generis* form of liability for culpable omission. He analyzes each element of such a doctrine: the underlying offence, the issue of causation, the superior–subordinate relation, effective control and *mens rea*. From his perspective, the core of the commander's *culpa*, and the basis of their liability, stands not in the contribution that they made to the crime of the subordinate, but in a culpable dereliction of duty. Ultimately, the question at the heart of this issue concerns the point at which the superior has such effective control over their troops' actions that it amounts to control over the crime itself. If a critical threshold is crossed (e.g., by an omission that amounts to facilitation), the superior may become an indirect (co-) perpetrator of the crime.

Mettraux stresses that customary law does not consider superior responsibility to be a form of objective or strict liability, such that liability may not be entailed by a superior in the absence of proof that the superior knew or had reason to know of crimes committed or about to be committed by their subordinates. For this reason, his argument claims that, a failure or a neglect to acquire such knowledge does not constitute a sufficient basis for liability. In his perspective, while customary law stepped away from an objective sort of liability for superiors, the Rome Statute of the ICC has gone back to such a standard, insofar as it concerns military(-like) commanders, by providing that such a commander could be held criminally responsible, not only where they knew or had reason to know that crimes had been or were about to be committed by subordinates, but also where they 'should have known' that to be the case.

Sengheiser (2008) agrees that part of the challenge in applying the doctrine of command responsibility is determining what constitutes a 'culpable mental state'.

This author identifies two difficulties in this field. The first one is a reluctance to punish upper-level commanders for omissions in the command responsibility framework. Applying the doctrine of command responsibility to enemy forces helps to de-legitimize them. When applied to one's own forces, it would be detrimental to these interests for senior military leaders. Therefore, when command responsibility is applied to one's own forces, there is an interest in limiting the scope of liability. The second difficulty is about the standard for punishing criminal omissions. Specifically, a balance must be found within the doctrine of command responsibility so that it can hold commanders criminally liable for certain, but not all omissions. According to Sengheiser, such a balance is only achieved when it is possible to transform a commander's omission into an act by proving it had the effect of encouraging the commission of war crimes by subordinates. He finds in *accomplice liability* the well-developed principle of criminal law upon which command responsibility for acts is based. However, in so doing, the specificity of the *superior responsibility* principle becomes lost.

Martinez (2007) analyses the reasons why the concept of *mens rea* for command responsibility is still the most controversial aspect of the doctrine in both theory and application. The effort is to situate 'wilful blindness' somewhere between knowledge and negligence. According to Martinez, there is substantial, if not incontrovertible, support in the case law of international tribunals, as well as in state practice, for finding in international customary law a military commander's 'duty of knowledge' that goes beyond a simple prohibition on the most egregious forms of wilful blindness, that is, the duty to take reasonable steps to acquire information about whether their subordinates have committed or are about to commit crimes. The demonization of such a standard as 'simple negligence' or strict liability fails to acknowledge how the 'duty of knowledge' fits within the superior's broader duty to prevent crimes by subordinates. Moreover, it fails to take into account the unique context in which the command responsibility doctrine emerged, a context that distinguishes it from ordinary complicity liability in municipal criminal law.

Bantekas (2000) appropriately clarifies a major problem of superior responsibility, which accounts for the limited application of its doctrine: this issue is at the crossroads of legal and political interests. He highlights the opposing interests of criminal justice and the states in cases involving the criminal liability of military officers and political leaders. The doctrine of superior responsibility determines the criminal liability of those persons who, by being in positions of command, whether military officers or civilians placed in positions of command, have failed to either prevent or punish the crimes of their subordinates. While there can be little doubt about the necessity of this rule of international law for ensuring command diligence at all levels, and thus deterring future violations of humanitarian law, some states have voiced their concern about the possible abuse of the doctrine for political purposes.

Until very recently, the vast majority of states abstained from prosecuting nationals accused of fostering criminal acts by their subordinates. The sanctioning of such behaviour was achieved either through the application of domestic standards for the ascertainment of superior liability, or in terms of clouding responsibility by assigning it to a supposedly national disciplinary context. Bantekas (2000) notes that the decline in the use of the doctrine of superior responsibility at the national level is closely connected to the political climate and warzone conflicts. States will be much more inclined to shield their officials in times of armed conflict than to give priority to upholding criminal justice. In a climate of conflict, it is feared that if military personnel were prosecuted in strict accordance with the doctrine of command responsibility, enemy states would find ample grounds for accusing the former of violating international law in general. While the doctrine of superior responsibility seems to be gradually acquiring a clearly defined field of application, the fact nonetheless remains that a number of states conceive it to be a threat to their military and civilian forces.

In conclusion, the doctrine of command responsibility seems to have the following weaknesses:

1 at the level of interpretation of the doctrine: on the one hand, the *mens rea* requirement, interpreted as 'vicarious liability', arises out the fears of an excessive enlargement of boundaries of culpability; on the other hand, arguments against its application make the intentionality and possible criminal plans of political leaders and military officials invisible.
2 At the level of its actual application: the conflicting interests of states and international criminal justice make the prosecution of political leaders and high ranking military officials less likely on the basis of the defence of state reason, except in the situations where an armed conflict creates a weaker party (such as in the case of Japan in the tribunals following the Second World War).

Responsibility for crimes of obedience

At the low levels of the military echelon, the classical line of defence of those accused of crimes of obedience is that they were 'only following orders'. Indeed, many torturers have adopted this line of defence (Verbitsky, 1996; Senese, 2006). The legal thinking about superior orders allows for the detection of three main approaches:

1 *The idea of the 'absolute defence' (or* respondeat superior *principle).* According to the notion of the *respondeat superior*, a soldier who commits an offence while following an order should be entirely exempted from responsibility, such that it is the superior who has to take all the blame for issuing an illegal order. The rationale behind this approach is the utmost upholding of military discipline (Dinstein, 2012; Insco, 2003).
2 *The notion of 'absolute liability'.* According to the doctrine of 'absolute liability', soldiers are not required to obey illegal orders. Its rationale is the safeguard of the supremacy of law. However, this principle ignores the claim that a successful military is built on a foundation of discipline that demands total and unqualified obedience to orders without any hesitation or doubt (Dinstein, 2012).

3. *The concept of 'limited liability' for following manifestly illegal orders.* According to the 'manifest illegality principle', for the defence to succeed, the accused must demonstrate the absence of the subjective knowledge of the illegality of the order and that the order was not 'manifestly illegal' in the objective (Hendin, 2003).

It is generally recognized that it is difficult for subordinates to evaluate whether an order is legal or illegal, as well as to choose between obedience and disobedience on that basis, particularly in military settings with their strong presumption that subordinates will follow orders. Thus, there is often a tendency to accept the defence of superior orders, as long as the defendants have a reasonable basis for claiming that they did not know the orders were illegal. Such a defence has influenced amnesty laws. In Argentina, for instance, the defence of superior orders had actually been legally established by the 1987 'Due Obedience Law' and applied to all but the highest military officers. This law established an irrefutable presumption that a subordinate who committed a violation acted under orders without any ability to resist or to assess the order's lawfulness.

Even if superior orders are not accepted as full exoneration, they may at least serve as mitigating factors. Thus, those accused of crimes have potentially much to gain from the claim that they were only following orders, since it may help them escape punishment or reduce its severity.

The simplest cases, from the point of view of defining crimes of obedience, are those in which the actors show reluctance to carry out the actions ordered, but nevertheless do so because they feel obligated to follow orders. These are clear cases of obedience, in which the actors experience a conflict between obligation and preference, but act in accordance with their perceived obligation.

In many cases that we would describe as crimes of obedience, however, the picture that emerges is much more complicated. One major category of cases consists of those in which the evidence clearly suggests that the actors had motives for their criminal acts beyond the duty to obey. They may act out of ideological zeal, they may derive personal gratification from their activities, they may reap material gains from their activities (for example, Nazi storm troopers and Argentinian kidnap squads confiscated victims' property), or they may regard their activities or indeed their dutiful acts of obedience themselves as ways of advancing their careers (as Adolf Eichmann and perhaps Kurt Waldheim did in the context of Nazi Germany, and William Calley may have done in the context of the Vietnam war).

In these cases, the motives and nature of the actions make it difficult to conceive of the defendants as reluctant participants in crime, who were merely following orders because they saw themselves as having no other choice. One can reasonably ask in these cases whether one is really dealing with crimes of obedience, or with cynical use of the defence of superior orders to avoid or reduce criminal responsibility. From a legal point of view, evidence that the criminal actions satisfied any personal motive or represented a high level of personal involvement clearly undermines the credibility of a defence of superior orders, as well as greatly reduces whatever exonerating or mitigating role it may have played. Moreover, the psychic or material gains that were accrued by the actors, and their active identification with the actions taken, increase their personal culpability, even if the actions took place in the context of superior orders.

Both the legal standard of command responsibility and the 'manifestly illegal order' developed within international law should be incorporated in national military manuals and codes of military justice. While the actual effect of these kinds of military manuals and codes on training, institutional structures and commanders' behaviour is an empirical question that has yet to be answered, neither can their impact be discounted without some empirical evidence that they are insignificant or are completely ignored. If the requirement that military commanders take reasonable steps to acquire knowledge about whether their troops are committing crimes were firmly endorsed by international courts as a principle of customary international law, it is quite likely that this standard would be incorporated into a significant number of national military manuals and domestic codes of military justice, where it might have some salutary effect on military training and institutional structures. A similar assumption may be made for the manifestly illegal order principle.

Responsibility and knowledge: a state of thirdness in psychoanalysis and law

We have seen how Monolithic Societal States promote the denial of knowledge and the group enactment of unconscious emotional states, which enables personal responsibility for actions to be overlooked. At an individual level, responsibility and knowledge that result from psychic reflective abilities tend to disappear, while other interpersonal, groupal and social phenomena that foreclose *in-between spaces* tend to emerge. The results are emotional and cognitive splitting, the prominence of denial, the state of knowledge that some authors have referred to as 'knowing and not knowing' (Laub and Auerhan, 1993) or *doubling of self* (Lifton, 1986), the shaping of the intersubjective fields in vertical power relations of subjection and control, an asymmetrical distribution of subjectivity in terms of subject/object, polarizations in the social domain, etc. Groups deputed to the administration of violence (military corps, police, etc.) become the section of society in charge of enacting violently unconscious emotional states, restructuring themselves in monolithic mode.

In the superior responsibility doctrine, some interpretations of the concept of *mens rea* refer to conscious knowledge and information ('knew'), but the 'should have known' principle seems to extend responsibility, more or less, to unconscious knowing and disregard leading to complicity. In other words, there is the assumption that somewhere the information was available and not picked up, or it was more or less consciously ignored in compliance with group violence. Role responsibility implies the contribution of both collective phenomena of delegation to political and executive officers of collective intentions, and the individual responsibility and liberty in decision-making. The unconscious knowing, understood not so much as dynamic unconscious, but as non-conscious interpersonal or groupal enactment, appears in the social and subsequently the legal fields, which is why this doctrine is so debatable. The superior responsibility doctrine seeks to establish how to 'allocate' this knowledge in a social or groupal context, which seems to be designed to make it disappear. Whereas *states of twoness* predominate, there is a social enactment of uncontained powerful emotional contents that are delegated to particular social institutions. In this framework, torture emerges as a policy of large group violence, rather than as an incidental event that has run out of control, the premises of which can be traced back to a systemic collapse of the large group.

This aim of allocating knowledge is pursuable if we understand the unconscious knowledge as something inhabiting social action. In this perspective, 'truth' (i.e., knowledge) and responsibility established through trials may be seen as a 'correction' to the perception of reality and may mark the exit from the delusional *states of twoness* of a heavily fragmented social context. From this perspective, international law on *superior responsibility* can be understood as a border along the slippery slope of a fading reality and of withdrawal into the intrapsychic world of illusions supported by the group. In this sense, these social states do not need pathological personalities, because dissociation is lived at group or institutional and social levels. This does not mean that the social context is not a source of suffering for individuals. This phenomenon is dramatically witnessed in the literature on torturers, which describes their internal torment, the paradoxical relief they experience in being judged, and the contradictions of their statements in trials, or their internal struggle between talking and not talking about their misdeeds (Arendt, 1963; Verbitsky, 1996). A captive individual self is in there, engaged in the struggle to exit from the enclosed world of the schizo-paranoid state to make reality reappear.

The 'manifest illegality principle' is the other border (besides 'superior responsibility') the legal doctrine poses to an illegitimate, this time down-top, relieving of the burden of responsibility. From this perspective, a *culpable state of mind* is the standard for prosecuting both superiors and subordinates and can be established in consideration of the person's knowing and its use of the other and group dynamics. Judgement about personal responsibility means in both cases re-establishing a state of thirdness, i.e., that *in-between space* that enables the working-through of the meaning of one's own actions and possible misdeeds. This is not so paradoxical if we remember that, according to the theories of Winnicott and Benjamin, destruction can be read as a pursuit for the boundaries needed to become newly in touch with one's own otherness (and difference), which has been abruptly extruded in those *Monolithic Self* and *Societal States* that emphasize pure identity. Winnicott's account of the constitution of externality, in which the object maintains itself outside the subject's destructive orbit (1963), culminates in a liberating feeling about the subject/object difference which allows for the use of the object. Benjamin (1990) draws heavily on Winnicott's notions of object relating and object usage, alongside Hegel's master–slave analogy, in order to demonstrate the need for both recognition and negation in the establishment of human subjectivity. Intersubjective theory postulates that the other must be recognized as another subject in order for the self to fully experience their subjectivity in the other's presence (Benjamin, 1990, 2004, 2007).

Torture tremendously reveals the initial failure of this task and the desperate collective search for a renovated ability to perceive one's own limits and borders, to make contact with otherness, to make reality reappear and to restore one's own ability to 'reflect' (the search for 'truth' in Chapter 1). In other words, the need is to find an *in-between space*, a third position from which we become witness to our conflicts and can hold them at a distance, through a process of dis-identification, i.e., exiting from a state of identity, namely, Me–You. To become responsible means to recognize one's own unconscious 'otherness' – literally, our own unconscious assumption of an-other (interpersonal, groupal/institutional or collective) subjectivity – and be present to oneself. This is the core of subjectivity, which is restored only if we are able to open up space between our different states of being (Bromberg, 1993, 1998; Jung, 1920, 1928, 1934). This third position is transformative because, from its perspective, our subjectivity enlarges to comprehend multiple different self states that allow a process of multiple identifications, empathy and understanding for others, and a critical internal debate; while remembering that this cannot be anything but a transient state, ever at risk of disappearing in threatening situations.

Reparation for survivors of torture

Victims' right to reparation for a wrongful act is a well-established principle of international law. Reparation is an umbrella term to designate a set of measures that provide redress for victims of gross violations of international human rights law, serious violations of international humanitarian law and violations of international criminal law (Gillard, 2003; Rebout and Vandeginste, 2003; REDRESS, 2003, 2006a, 2006b; Echeverria, 2006).

The right to reparation for having been victim of the crime of torture is, for example, grounded in many treaties, such as in Articles 2, 3 and 7 of the International Covenant on Civil and Political Rights, Article 39 of the Convention on the Rights of the Child, and in Article 14 of the Convention Against Torture (CAT). The latter guarantees torture victims the right to obtain reparation, such as redress, adequate compensation and the means for as full rehabilitation as possible. However, the Convention Against Torture does not define 'redress', 'compensation' or 'rehabilitation'; neither does it contain a strict definition of whom is considered to be a 'victim'. Two other UN documents have attempted to address the issues: the Declaration of Basic Principles of Justice for Victims of Crimes and Abuse of Power and the UN Basic Principles and Guidelines on the Right to a Remedy and Reparation for Victims of Gross Violations of International Human Rights Law and Serious Violations of International Humanitarian Law. These two documents move away from the treatment of violations as abstract phenomena towards an increasing emphasis on the subjects of the violations: on the one hand, the victim, whose rights have been violated, who continues to suffer the consequences of the wrongful act, and whose right to obtain full reparation should be facilitated by the state; on the other hand, the perpetrator, who must be brought to justice, in part to afford reparation to the victim, but also to satisfy States Parties' obligations under the CAT to investigate, prosecute and punish.

In particular, the Basic Principles and Guidelines is one of the most significant achievements in developing the right to reparation. They identify mechanisms and procedures, as well as clarify the scope of the states' obligations to prevent, investigate, punish and remedy violations of human rights. Furthermore, they emphasize that victims are entitled to 'adequate, effective and prompt reparation' which should be 'proportional to the gravity of the violations and the harm suffered'.[1] However, they do not create new legal obligations for states and are not legally binding *per se*. The term 'remedy' is here used to include the right to access national and international procedures for the protection of human rights, as well as effective disciplinary, administrative, civil and criminal procedures. Meanwhile, 'reparation' is used to encompass the content aspects (e.g., monetary compensation) and the procedural aspects (e.g., civil and/or administrative remedies to obtain such compensation), including individual and collective measures. 'Redress' is the action taken to repair or restore.

Damages of torture

It is axiomatic that torture victims suffer from a variety of pecuniary and non-pecuniary damages. Pecuniary damages include the victim's loss or reduction in income (lost earnings), as well as expenses incurred by the victim or their family as a result of the human rights violation(s) (Rodriguez-Pinzon and Martin, 2006: 146).

According to Sandoval and Duttwiler (2010), the Inter-American Court of Human Rights identified various forms of non-pecuniary harm resulting from torture:

1 *Harm to physical or mental integrity*: as torture, by definition, inflicts severe physical and/or mental pain, it cannot be disputed that the anguish resulting from torture is a non-pecuniary form of harm for which reparations should be granted. This equally applies to the next of kin of a torture victim, who also experiences mental harm as a result of the suffering of their loved one.
2 *Damage to reputation*: reputation, being defined by how people see a person, is an example of a protected interest, which is separate from mental integrity in that it encompasses an interpersonal dimension.
3 *Harm to the integrity of the family*: in most torture cases, the victims are in some form of detention while being tortured, thus separated from their families. Consequently, an obvious non-pecuniary damage arises out of the disruption of family life.
4 *Damage to the 'life plan'*: the Inter-American Court explained that: 'the concept of "life plan" is akin to the concept of personal fulfilment, which, in turn, is

based on the options that an individual may have for leading his life and achieving the goal that he sets for himself.[2] Those options, in themselves, have an important existential value. It is clear that the persons eligible for reparations are those who have been subjected to torture, but also persons who have suffered non-pecuniary damage *as a result* of the original violation, namely the next of kin of the victims of torture, given that they have shared the victim's suffering.

This list offers an effective summary of the range of damages caused by torture that are generally eligible for reparation.

Forms of reparation

The core idea beyond reparation is that 'reparation must, as far as possible, wipe out all the consequences of the illegal act and re-establish the situation which would, in all probability, have existed if that act had not been committed'.[3] However, it is obvious that the extent of what can be repaired and the rationale behind reparation may differ among such cases. For this reason, inherent to the concept of reparation is the recognition that different types of remedies need to exist in order to fulfil the principle of reparation.

The term 'reparation' encompasses *restitution, compensation, rehabilitation*, measures of *satisfaction* (such as public apologies, public memorials), *guarantees of non-repetition* and changes in relevant laws and practices, as well as bringing to justice the perpetrators of human rights violations (Antkowiak, 2008; REDRESS, 2006a, 2006b; van Boven, 2010).

The guiding principles of a proper reparation program are meant to acknowledge the wrongdoing done to victims to re-impose quality on their lives, to afford recognition through affirmation and acknowledgment of the harm suffered, and to build civic trust and solidarity.

Restitution: the idea of going back to a previous state

Restitution most closely conforms to the general principles that the responsible state is bound to wipe out the legal and material consequences of its wrongful act by re-establishing the situation that would have existed if that act had not been committed.[4] For this reason, it comes first among the forms of reparation, and the terms 'restitution' and '*restitutio in integrum*' are copiously used as a synonym for 'full reparation'.

Restitution takes two main forms: material and legal. Material restitution is the most common within state practice and may involve the liberation of individuals who are illegally seized or detained, the restoration of property or of territory illegally taken or occupied, and the return of property. Legal restitution denotes the alteration or revocation of a legal measure taken in violation of international law, whether a judicial decision or an act of legislation or even a constitutional provision. In some cases, both material and juridical restitution may be sought, such as the return of exiled persons to their country and the restoration of their rights, including property rights and, if possible, the return of their property or the compensation of its value at the time of the indemnification. What will be required in terms of restitution will often depend on the content of the primary obligation that has been breached' (Crawford et al., 2010).

Restitution, as the main form of reparation, is of particular importance when the obligation breached is of a continuing character. Van Boven (1993), discussing his encounters with relatives of the 'disappeared' in Chile and Argentina, stressed that this form of reparation was particularly important to survivors. Apart from establishing an independent record of what had happened, he found that many relatives also expressed a desire for some 'normalization' of their legal position, such that inheritance rights could come into play, marital positions could be clarified, etc.

Although certain aspects of restitution might be possible (such as restoring an individual's liberty, legal rights, social status, family life and citizenship, return to one's place of residence, restoration of employment and return of property), it is generally not possible to restore torture survivors to their original situation before the violations occurred, since it is not possible to 'undo' the pain and suffering caused by the violations. This form of restitution could be supplemented by compensation where appropriate to provide full reparation.

Compensation: the idea of filling gaps created by damage

Compensation is a secondary form of reparation, in the sense that a state has an obligation of compensation for damage 'not made good by restitution', covering any financially assessable damage including loss of profits insofar as it is established (REDRESS, 2003). The idea of compensation is to fill the gaps created by the damage caused by the act, whether material or moral, suffered by the injured party as a result of the breach. Compensation for immaterial damage is a form of monetary reparation for physical or mental suffering, distress, harm to reputation or dignity, or other moral damage.

The right to compensation for individuals because of human rights violations is explicitly recognized in a wide range of treaties, as well as the jurisprudence of courts and human rights bodies.[5]

The amount of compensation is equivalent to what restitution in kind would have offered, i.e., based on the value lost as compared to the situation if the illegal act had not occurred.

If monetary compensation is meant to act as a replacement for losses, the main issues with regard to torture, say Arcel et al. (2000), involve determining the particular losses suffered and deciding what constitutes 'just' compensation. The problem, they suggest, is that torture survivors may have experienced many 'losses' that are invisible to the observer. Some authors (Sveaass and Lavik, 2000) suggest that the specific character of torture, as a particularly egregious violation and man-made infliction of pain, has a moral dimension that is difficult to evaluate. This difficulty to establish the severity of trauma and to measure subjective distress and psychological problems results in the struggle surrounding compensation decisions (Reisman, 1999). The consequence is that, when compensation is paid, it often seems unsatisfactory and, 'ironically inconsistent with the fundamental notion of the humanity of the victim' (Reisman, 1999: 67).

In the aftermath of atrocities as grievous as torture, financial measures may be particularly inadequate, and perceived as forms of buying silence (Mignone, 1992). They may lead survivors and their representatives to seek other forms of reparation. Wise (1993) describes the emotional turmoil and demonstrations in Israel against what was perceived as 'blood money' in response to the Claims Conference.[6] On the other hand, this organization persists in seeking benefits for the thousands who have not received reparation, insisting that memory and commemoration are insufficient.

Thus, survivors' pleas for recognition may often be made in the form of monetary requests. It is worth investigating whether this is (even partly) because other forms of redress are not available or are less obvious.

Satisfaction and guarantees of non-repetition: the idea of establishing truth, responsibilities and preventive measures

Satisfaction and guarantees of non-repetition refer to the range of measures that may contribute to the broader and longer-term restorative aims of reparation. A central component is the role of public acknowledgment of the violation, and the victims' right to know the truth and have the perpetrators held accountable. The Commission on Human Rights, in its resolution of April 25, 2001, recognized that,

> for the victims of human right violations, public knowledge of their suffering and the truth about perpetrators, including the accomplices, of these violations are essential steps towards rehabilitation and reconciliation, and urges States to intensify their efforts to provide victims of human rights violations with a fair and equitable process through which these violations can be investigated and made public to encourage victims to participate in such a process.[7]

One of the most common forms of satisfaction is a declaration of the wrongfulness of the act by a competent court or tribunal. Given that any court or tribunal which has jurisdiction over a dispute has the authority to make a declaration of its findings as a necessary part of the judicial process, such a declaration may sometimes act as a precondition to other forms of reparation, or may be the only remedy sought. In some instances, the European Court of Human Rights has held that a finding of a violation is a sufficient 'just satisfaction', even when the petitioner has specifically sought compensation; though in others, the Court awarded the full amount of compensation sought for pecuniary and non-pecuniary damages 'in view of the extremely serious violations of the Convention . . . and the anxiety and distress that these undoubtedly caused'.[8]

Implementing guarantees of non-repetition to prevent future violations and/or general safeguards to prevent violations also represents a common obligation included in human rights instruments. The vital role of prevention, as one means of reparation, has been enshrined by the European Convention on the Prevention of Torture, as well as the Optional Protocol to the Convention Against Torture and the Robben Island Guidelines.[9] Significantly, Article 14 of the latter notes that: 'States should prohibit and prevent the use, production and trade of equipment or substances designed to inflict torture or ill-treatment and the abuse of any other equipment or substance to these ends'. Prevention is also cited in paragraph 10(a) of the Istanbul Protocol: Manual on the Effective Investigation and Documentation of Torture and other Cruel, Inhuman or Degrading Treatment: 'Taking effective legislative, administrative, judicial or other measures to prevent acts of torture. No exceptions, including war, may be invoked as justification for torture'.

Satisfaction and guarantees of non-repetition may include establishment of the truth, acknowledgment, apology and guarantee of non-repetition, etc. Other possible forms may include active involvement of the survivor of torture in the reparative process and/or an opportunity to speak about their experiences in a public forum. The meaning for the individual survivor of these measures may be difficult to ascertain. Nevertheless, it is clear that many survivors attach immense significance to them.

Rehabilitation: the idea to restore functionality

Rehabilitation is an important component of reparation and a right specifically recognized in some international human rights instruments.[10] Artical 14 of the UN Declaration of Basic Principles of Justice for Victims of Crime and Abuse of Power stipulates that: 'victims should receive the necessary material, medical, psychological and social assistance through governmental, voluntary, community-based and indigenous means'. Principle 21 of the Basic Principles and Guidelines equally establishes that 'rehabilitation should include medical and psychological care as well as legal and social services'. Rehabilitation may be provided 'in kind' or the costs may form part of a monetary award. It is important to distinguish between indemnity paid in the form of compensation (for material and/or moral damage) and money provided for rehabilitation purposes.

The Inter-American Court has been the most active of the regional courts in referring to the importance of rehabilitation in the overall framework of reparations. A series of judgements has awarded rehabilitation as part of broader awards.[11] In other cases, the Court provided for the future medical treatment of victims where there was a direct link between the condition and the violation. The Committee Against Torture and to an apparently lesser extent the Human Rights Committee have also addressed rehabilitation.

The differences in the way rehabilitation is addressed highlight the question of whether the right to rehabilitation exists independently, or within the right to restitution, compensation and satisfaction. Rehabilitation has been described as one component of 'restitution' (Shelton, 2005), although the extent to which rehabilitation can ever 'fully repair' or restore a victim's health or well-being to a pre-violation state is questionable, rendering the inclusion of rehabilitation within restitution at best theoretical. Where compensation includes monetary awards for non-pecuniary damage, and for treatment costs already incurred or anticipated, rehabilitation can be said to partly exist within compensation measures. Satisfaction measures, including the building of health facilities, free healthcare or the provision of health programs for a community, can legitimately be seen as encompassing rehabilitation, albeit partially and not necessarily for each individual victim.

Rehabilitation is commonly described in terms of services or activities, including psychological therapies, medical and physical examination and treatment, and social, welfare and legal support. Nonetheless, entrenched controversies exist amidst and between centers as to the most appropriate service model and health interventions, with broad agreement only on the need for rehabilitation to be multidisciplinary, both short and long term, and addressing the well-being of survivors and their families. Medical activities vary according to the emphasis of a center, country context and available resources, typically including medical assessment, documentation, and referral to appropriate healthcare services available within the center, or in mainstream health services. Psychosocial activities for torture survivors are, by far, the most diverse and controversial in their emphasis placed on a continuum of being exclusively 'trauma-focused' or, more broadly, 'human-rights focused'. Trauma approaches are most similar to traditional rehabilitation approaches in mental health, which focus on traumatic reactions and are aimed at symptom-elimination, reduction or management. Rehabilitation is not a term that is used or familiar in such approaches; more typical terms used are 'treatment' of 'clinical problems' or 'disorders'. Some centers emphasize diagnostic, 'trauma approaches', while others reject traditional diagnosis of Post-Traumatic Stress Disorder and other psychological or medical labels, instead addressing distress within the wider context of human rights violations and injustice. These distinctions have profound implications for the conceptualization and practice of rehabilitation. Centers also vary in their emphasis on torture, organized violence and violations by state or non-state actors.

However, the process of rehabilitation for a tortured person must deal with more than mere psychotherapy and medical treatment; it must include consideration towards survivors' existential situation: the relationship with their family, their social and occupational environment, and the political realm in which they reside. For this reason, it is also worth investigating whether or not a combination of measures has a different meaning for, or effect on, survivors. Shelton (2005) contends that establishing the truth of their experiences is more important for some survivors than the receipt of monetary compensation. Indeed, if the 'best' form of reparation (from the point of view of the recipient) often involves some mixture of financial and non-financial measures, the question is raised regarding its nature, weight and proportions: or what Zedner has called the 'elusive "recipe" for reparation' (Zedner, 1994: 238).

The other way round: reparation as 'therapy'

A number of authors have commented that the search for reparation has a therapeutic benefit for the victim, in addition to more targeted forms of medical or psychosocial treatment and support. Carmichael *et al.* (1996: 7) take the view that seeking reparation is an important part of the rehabilitation process, both for the individual and for the society in which the torture occurred. The pursuit of reparation can be empowering for a victim, allowing them to overcome feelings of isolation and pain in a public process closely linked to the disclosure of unacknowledged events and the naming of the guilty (Sveaass, 1994).

A debated issue concerns whether some forms of reparation may be more therapeutically beneficial than others. Some commentators have discussed the relative merits of civil and criminal proceedings. For example, Gordon (1995) discusses the advantage of civil suits over criminal proceedings for victims of torture in terms of control over the proceedings, as well as the opportunity to compromise and raise matters of principle, which cannot be addressed in criminal cases, thereby raising the prospect of a speedier resolution.

On the other hand, McFarlane (1996) warns of potential problems in both civil and criminal justice systems. Many victims perceive legal processes to lack empathy, a problem that is perhaps more prevalent in civil litigation, where court officials and advocates are unused to dealing with victims of torture or other violent crime.

The best reparation for survivors of torture is probably a combination of measures tailored to the single case, and to reflect each survivors' needs. A participatory reparations process is important for several reasons. First, as underlined in the Basic Principles and Guidelines, reparations should be *effective* and *adequate*. This can only be achieved if reparations meet the needs of victims, which have materialized as a result of the harm suffered. Therefore, in deciding on reparation awards, it is crucial to consult victims because only they can provide the court with in-depth information as to their real needs, the extent of the harm suffered as a result of the crime, and the priorities of individual persons and communities with regard to reparations. Taking these factors into account maximize the possibility that the reparations ordered have a positive impact on victims' lives (Magarell, 2007). Second, a participatory process creates a sense of local ownership of a reparations policy. Involving victims in designing and implementing reparations from the very beginning of the process may assist in managing their expectations of what the court can and cannot do for them (Suchkova, 2011).

Obviously, a participatory reparative process does not end when the court issues a decision on reparations. It is important to receive victims' feedback about the effectiveness of the distribution and quality of services provided within the reparation framework. Having victims' feedback made available could provide the court with the possibility to make certain, albeit limited, adjustments to the implementation of the reparations it has ordered, either directly or through the on-going work of another body. Furthermore, the constant monitoring of implementation of reparation measures should shed light on the best way forward.

A well-organized participatory process has a potential healing effect on victims and communities. Being consulted and treated as rights holders, whose dignity is respected (OHCHR, 2008: 15–16), helps victims to move forward and be better integrated into society. In this respect a participatory process is particularly important for marginalized and discriminated groups (Muddel, 2009). Victims' participation in defining and implementing reparations contributes to rebuild social links within communities and safety nets, which might have been destroyed as a result of internal violence.

This can be understood as 'simultaneous therapy' for individuals and society. While the victims' damages are repaired, society has the opportunity to rebuild social relationships among its members in a new and more flexible way. The foreclosed spaces of social transactions become available again to reflective activity, in which action and thinking may be reconnected in a meaningful social action. Recognizing the harm inflicted on victims and establishing responsibility for such harm are therapeutic actions for individual victims and for society. Torture victims may find in this recognition a principle of justice reaffirmed, the opportunity to restore trust in humanity, and recreate social bonds. On the other hand, society that underwent that social process of fragmentation and reorganization, which we have referred to as a Monolithic Societal States, is presented with the opportunity to re-open its foreclosed spaces. In this sense, '*restitutio in integrum*', instead of a misleading ideal, may be understood in the sense of 'restitution [of self and society] to the former wholeness'.

In this way, reparation becomes a political process that seeks to re-establish a community based on meaningful bonds and restore a new equilibrium to society, in which victims have their status as such recognized and can potentially take on a new role in the political and social arena (Gómez Isa, 2013). Indeed, such a recognition is what allows for them to leave their victimhood, even assuming beneficially a leading role in social transformation. This latter is more than an eventuality for social change. We have seen in Chapter 1 that the 'truth' in torture is searched in the victim. This suggests that society itself senses it has located the 'truth', i.e. some knowledge, into the persecuted victims as part of a massive projective identification, and as a result, it demands it back. In this sense, victims of torture, as bearers of social 'truths', may potentially be powerful catalysts of social change, in the event they decide to use such knowledge for this aim.

The question of 'truth'

In *If This Is a Man*, Primo Levi (1947) describes a recurring dream that he and his fellow-prisoners used to have: the prisoner would be reunited with their family and talking about what had happened to them, but nobody would listen. 'Why', he wondered, 'was the pain of every passing day translated so consistently in our dreams into the scene of the story being told over and over again, and nobody listening?' Being tortured is not only being reduced to an object of violence, but being disconnected from other human beings, exiled from the human community through experiences that are not communicable: voices that cannot be heard, messages that cannot be received.

Torture has a peculiar potential to distort the 'truth', while pretending to discover it. For this reason, restoring the reality of facts which have been denied for a long time is the first necessary task: to establish exactly what did happen, remove the silence surrounding often still painful and controversial events, and make the relevant information publicly accessible, so that it cannot be further denied.

At a social level, Truth Commissions can play a critical role in a country struggling to come to terms with a history of massive disruption of human rights. To date, there have been more than 30 Truth Commissions around the world, including in Argentina, Chile, Timor-Leste, El Salvador, Guatemala, Sierra Leone, the Democratic Republic of Congo and South Africa. A number of these Truth Commissions has had notable successes. Their investigations have been welcomed by survivors of violence and by human rights advocates alike, while their reports have been widely read, and their summary of facts considered to be conclusive and fair. Such commissions are often referred to as having a 'cathartic' effect on society, fulfilling the important step of formally acknowledging a long-silenced past (see Hayner, 2011).

However, not all Truth Commissions have been so successful. Some have been significantly limited in achieving a full and fair account of the past (for example limited by mandate, political constraints or restricted access to information, or a basic lack of resources), and have reported only a narrow slice of the 'truth'. Some commission reports have even been kept confidential after being submitted to the respective government.

In cases of systematic use of torture, Truth Commissions have always shied away from a full consideration of the crime itself, instead preferring to include it in a wider list of crimes committed in the context of situations of social upheaval. Only in recent past has a debate emerged in the USA on the possible use of a specific Truth Commission to investigate the Bush Administration's political use of systematic torture in Guantánamo Bay and in other sites (Kristof, 2008; Chanbonpin, 2011; Streichler, 2010, among others). However, even in this case, such a Commission has not been established.

Although the question of truth and knowing is crucial in torture, Truth Commissions are problematic ways in which to heal society following torture. They have a complex relation to criminal trials and tools of redress. Revealing what happened is just a first step, and the price paid for its emergence needs to be well balanced with other measures. The revelation of truth itself, with no consistent effects, is not enough for a society to 'get out' of torture.

Truth Commissions: definitions and aims

Truth Commissions are truth-seeking bodies (Gonzalez and Varney, 2013), which became common in the 1990s as 'commissions established to research and report on human rights abuses which have occurred over a certain period of time in a particular country under a particular regime or in relation to a particular conflict' (Knoops, 2006: 1). They are created, vested with authority, sponsored and/or funded by governments and international organizations such as the UN and non-governmental organizations. Most Truth Commissions are established during a political transition phase, after a period of civil war or military rule/dictatorship. Their general aim is to officially investigate and provide an accurate record/analysis of the broader pattern of abuses committed during repression and civil war. Inherent to this investigation is the hearing of victims and perpetrators. Although known as 'Truth Commissions' or 'Truth and Reconciliation Commissions', they are not all formally referred to as such.[12] Nevertheless, these bodies all share certain common elements and are created for similar purposes: 1) they are focused on the past; 2) they investigate a record of abuses over a period of time; 3) they are temporary, and generally conclude with the submission of a report; 4) they are somehow officially sanctioned by the government to investigate the past and 5) they make recommendations to the government. There are differences among commissions, as each country must shape a process out of its own historical, political and cultural context. Furthermore, commissions' mandates differ according the types of abuses to be investigated, perhaps including acts by the armed opposition as well as government forces, for example, or perhaps limited to certain specific practices, such as disappearances. Such variations are a natural reflection of the differences in countries' politics, political culture, history and needs (Hayner, 1997).

Truth Commissions, however, are not engaged in prosecution, although their mandates are related to investigating into human rights violations and abuses. In most instances, Truth Commissions are also required by their mandate to provide recommendations in order to prevent a recurrence of such abuses, as well as to facilitate reconciliation by means of exchanging information, promoting dialogue, and providing mediation by third parties (arbitrage) or even via court procedures. This reconciliation process might also require to facilitate the reintegration of minor criminal offenders who submit their confessions. Additionally, they can, by means of their report, directly or indirectly contribute to the reparations for victims.

Not many Truth Commissions have held public hearings, due to serious concerns for security and a fear of witness intimidation. For this reason, public hearings in Latin America have been considered virtually unthinkable. On the contrary, in Africa, a number of commissions has held public hearings, allowing victims a public stage to receive recognition for the pains suffered, and allowing the process of the Truth Commission to be shared nationally.

The truth of perpetrators and the truth on perpetrators: the relationship between Truth Commissions and International or National Courts

In periods following a conflict/war or dictatorship, two methods are typically adopted in order to establish a record of grave human rights crimes: prosecutions at a national or international level (see Chapter 8) and Truth Commissions that, under various names, investigate situations and submit reports (Aukerman, 2002; Kilpatrick and Ross, 2001; Yav Katshung, 2005). Some authors (Chapman and Ball, 2001; Humphrey, 2003) consider the model of the Truth Commission, based on the official acknowledgment of severe abuses by a government-sanctioned body, to be less traumatic to the nation than an adversarial tribunal approach, and more effective in deterring future abuses.[13]

Surely, these are two different approaches to the truth of past events in a transitional society. A Truth Commission can do many things that courts cannot or generally do not attend to. Trials focus on the actions of specific individuals, while Truth Commissions focus on the large pattern of overall events, which happened during a period of socio-political turmoil. It is true that some trials help shed light on overall patterns of human rights violations, but this is generally not their focus or intent. Furthermore, courts do not typically investigate the various social or political factors which led to the violence, or the internal structure of abusive forces, such as death squads or the intelligence branch of the armed forces, all of which might be the focus of a Truth Commission. Courts do not submit policy recommendations or suggestions for political, military or judicial reforms. Finally, while courts' records may be public, court opinions are generally not widely distributed nor widely read, unlike typical of Truth Commission reports. In other words, a Truth Commission's strengths are in those very areas that fall outside the parameters or capabilities of a court. For example, the South Africa Truth and Reconciliation Commission had the overall task of developing a comprehensive picture of the nature, causes and extent of human rights violations and, for this purpose, had three committees. The first one interviewed witnesses and took testimony from survivors and perpetrators; the second committee made recommendations regarding reparations for survivors; and the third committee reviewed petitions from perpetrators asking for amnesty. Its tasks were wide and targeted victims, perpetrators and other witnesses of past abuses, who were involved to different extents in the investigated events.

This kind of structure is to enforce restorative justice principles, but may be in conflict with retributive justice (prosecutions, trials). In fact, although these commissions offer space for perpetrators to reveal the 'truth' about past abuses, they cannot prosecute and try alleged human rights abusers, and so justice is not actually done. They can only offer alternative forms of justice. On the contrary, as to the main purpose of international tribunals, one can say that they are primarily focused on retribution and deterrence through the prosecution of international crimes. Moreover, international tribunals may form a response to amnesty, which is often granted to perpetrators by national authorities.

As to what is relevant to our understanding, Truth Commissions and national and international courts may be considered as two different ways of dealing with the relationship between perpetrators and truth. Truth Commissions are the site in which the 'truth *of* perpetrators' can be revealed, while courts are the site in which the 'truth *on* perpetrators' is presented and where its consequences in terms of justice are drawn.

Truth Commissions offer spaces to everyone (those who are here called victims, perpetrators and bystanders) to reveal what they know, and, for this reason, space is given to those who, to a different extent responsible for past abuses, are willing to reveal what they did, what they know about facts, and their personal understanding. Offering their accounts of the past and their experience, they disclose not only precious testimony about people and truth but also the mental states of perpetrators, their justifications, their beliefs, their feelings, and their illusions. In this sense, Truth Commissions are more flexible instruments, especially for minor perpetrators, than courts in order to understand the past: contradictory meanings, feelings and thoughts, can arise and find a place to be acknowledged by perpetrators and the general public, and where confrontation with victims takes place, they can even be negotiated. On the other hand, Truth Commissions can be a source of suffering for victims if a complementary action by the courts is not enforced at the same time, and the Truth Commission becomes a quicker way to prematurely close the door on past abuses and grant extensive amnesty. Juan Méndez[14] reminds us that we need to be careful to counter attempts to disguise impunity with fanciful adjectives. If restorative justice is a valuable concept that has its place in a transitional justice policy, the term is often used to advocate some alternative to criminal justice, honest truth telling and the full investigation of abuses. When used in such a way, it is no more than an attempt to justify or disguise impunity (Méndez, 2005).

On the contrary, national and international courts are the places deputed to reveal the 'truth *on* perpetrators'. With their mandate to investigate and try offenders, courts are in charge of giving back to perpetrators, and to society at large, that part of truth that perpetrators refuse to acknowledge and to admit. Indeed, not all of them are willing to disclose their (mis-)deeds, especially those higher up in the military hierarchy, or those more responsible for the political design of massive human rights abuses. On the other hand, recognition of this part of truth is equally important for dismantling impunity, seeking to apply the established law, and for putting in place measures for the non-repetition of abuses in the future (Yav Katshung, 2005).

One possible solution is to see them as complementary, although certain technical and substantial issues in this perspective arise. For example, in the relationship between Truth Commissions and courts, the *issue of confidentiality* is crucial both for self-incriminating evidence and for testimonies of potential crimes committed by commanders or other individuals. This creates a dilemma: central to the mandate of the Truth and Reconciliation Commissions is that perpetrators tell their stories publicly, although these commissions may also need to guarantee confidentiality in order to encourage perpetrators to acknowledge that their actions may have been criminal in nature (Schabas and Darcy, 2004). Some commissions do not involve specific provisions to solve this issue. For example, South African legislation specified that self-incriminating evidence presented to the Truth and Reconciliation Commission, set up after the end of Apartheid, could not be used in criminal prosecutions before the courts in South Africa. Thus, a dilemma pertains to the question as to whether an international tribunal can use information from a TRC.

The relationship between TRCs and tribunals is, in practice, far from easy, such that these questions cannot to be solved smoothly.

The truth of victims and their reparation: restorative justice and procedural justice

Recent research has found that public truth-telling in post-conflict settings can simultaneously have a negative impact on some victims, while having positive effects on others. Findings from these studies illustrate that truth-telling can result in negative consequences including re-victimization/re-traumatization, disappointment or dissatisfaction, frustration, increased symptoms of post-traumatic stress disorder and insecurity (Brounéus, 2010). At the same time, some small-N studies conducted within the same settings show that truth-telling may be beneficial for victims by offering them a sense of relief, providing them with new information, confronting perpetrators to achieve a degree of closure, and receiving recognition, including the possibility of being provided with reparations or assistance (Brounéus, 2008; Byrne, 2004; Clark, 2010; Hamber et al., 2000; Kent, 2012; Laplante and Theidon, 2007; Rimé et al., 2011; Stanley, 2009). It is not clear the reasons why truth-telling processes are experienced in such vastly different ways by victims.

Guthrey (2015) has investigated the intersection between restorative justice and procedural justice, and their effects on victims. *Restorative justice* relates to repairing harm that results from past crimes by attempting to facilitate healing at the victim, offender and community levels through a participatory process (d'Estrée, 2006; Doak and O'Mahony, 2006; Rugge and Scott, 2009; van Camp and Wemmers, 2013). *Procedural justice*, on the other hand, refers to the perceived fairness of a justice or decision-making process (Folger, 1977; Lind and Tyler, 1988; Thibaut and Walker, 1975; Tyler, 1994).

Scholars point to many possible therapeutic benefits of justice for victims of violence, particularly in relation to *voice*, which is believed to promote a sense of satisfaction, acknowledgment, reduction of uncertainty, empowerment and healing for individuals (d'Estrée, 2006; Folger, 1977; Herman, 2003; Laxminarayan, 2012; Lind and Tyler, 1988; Tyler et al., 1985; van Camp and Wemmers, 2013; Wemmers and Cyr, 2006).

According to procedural justice scholars, *voice* is the ability of an individual to express their views and opinions in a justice or decision-making process (Folger, 1977; Lind and Tyler, 1988). Guthrey approaches the concept of *voice* as a multi-dimensional concept, in which the telling of one's experiences is as important as *being heard*. This interaction between *telling* and *being heard* can result in the feeling that one's suffering has been acknowledged and recognized by others (d'Estée, 2006; van Camp and Wemmers, 2013), an outcome that is considered to be a crucial component of the healing process, that is, another way to conceptualize the beneficial effect of recognition in the social domain. As already mentioned, a primary characteristic of victimization is that it establishes an imbalanced power relationship between the perpetrators of harm and the one who is abused, essentially empowering the torturers, while usurping power and dignity from the tortured (Agger and Jensen, 1996; Mollica, 1988). Giving *voice* may help victims to overcome disempowerment and marginalization or victimization because,

> Voice can be seen as power, status, self-worth, identity and even existence. Denial of voice can threaten perceptions of fairness, sense of legitimacy of authorities and systems and ultimately can pose even an existential threat. People may react to denial of voice with non-compliance, passivity, frustration, agitation and violence. Provision of voice is essential for a sense of justice, community restoration and healing.
>
> (d'Estée, 2006: 118)

Healing is here understood as restoring one's capacity to resume the course of one's life, in which the personal past, 'whether it be political commitment, personal relationships, work, and social connections', may become meaningful to the present and the future (Cienfuegos and Monelli, 1983: 44).

The process of giving testimony can allow victims an opportunity to restore the control that was lost as a result of being victimized, by letting others know what happened to them in the past (French, 2009). It may be an opportunity to restore a meaningful and crucial connection between the past and the present and the future, and to weave the threads of the personal and social history at the point where they were traumatically cut. Indeed, giving public testimony can be beneficial for victims by allowing them to contribute to the documented history of past violence in their country (McKinney 2008; Stauffer, 2013). Witnessing in the context of public hearings, also allows individuals to transmit the knowledge of historical reality to others, which may help to halt future conflict and repression (McKinney, 2008). Therefore, the public construction of the narrative truth of the past may not only contribute to healing, but also may result in a sense of safety from future abuses. Being provided with an opportunity to tell one's story can be affirming and empowering. Indeed, whether in private or public interviews, Truth Commissions can provide a way for victims to have some degree of control over the narrative of their traumatic experiences within these processes (Aldana, 2006: 111). This feeling of empowerment may also increase a victim's sense of dignity as the 'restoration of dignity is not simply a function of restored voice, but of a voice in control' (Ross, 2003: 336). This feature, which is considered to be characteristic of Truth Commissions, may be an area of criticism in trials. In most criminal trials, the presentation of testimony serves another function, that of adjudicating a case by determining guilt or innocence. It is something different from witnessing, which does not necessarily offer a chance for the potentially cathartic and empowering experience of storytelling (O'Connell, 2005). However, even in Truth Commissions, the healing potential of truth-telling may be curtailed when victims' ability to share their stories is limited, they experience too much distress related to giving testimony, or their testimonies are met with negative responses from community members. For example, Truth Commissions, are not often capable of hearing public testimony from everyone who may wish to give it, as only those who are chosen to give testimony will be able to share their experiences; thus, those who are not selected to testify may continue to feel marginalized and insignificant. In addition, there may be practical reasons that preclude victims from having the ability to tell their stories. For example, some victims may actually be too traumatized to tell their stories, even years after the events have occurred (Stanley, 2009). In addition, sharing traumatic experiences in public may also be detrimental to victims because of the social stigmatization that can result from publicly telling their traumatic stories (particularly for women who speak about sexual violence), which has been reported in a number of countries, such as Nepal, Rwanda, Sierra Leone and Timor-Leste (Aguirre and Pietropaoli, 2008; Allden, 2007; Brounéus, 2008; Kendall and Staggs, 2005). Although some victims may experience a sense of catharsis immediately after giving testimony, sharing their stories can have long-term negative effects on victims, related to either personal emotional suffering or social ostracization from their family or community. Some Truth Commissions, such as that in Sierra Leone, have instituted various options to increase the comfort of victims who wish to give testimony, including offering victims the choice of testifying in public or in private hearings, which record witnesses' testimony, while preserving their anonymity (Nowrojee, 2005).

A key issue about Truth Commissions is the fact that, in general, Commissions only have the authority to make recommendations to Parliament about the need for long-term financial and other symbolic forms of reparation for victims, as they are not accorded the authority to hand them out. For this reason, the Commissions have to rely on the political good-will of the respective government. This turns out to be one of the most serious weaknesses inherent in the functioning of these Commissions. In addition, Truth Commissions generally have the power to grant amnesty to offenders. As a result, there may be a sense of resentment among victims that the Truth Commission concerned was biased in favour of the perpetrators. This happened in South Africa, where the plight of victims in the country's truth and reconciliation process created a perception in the victims that the new government was unwilling to acknowledge the pain and suffering they endured. This perception was deepened by the fact that, while most amnesty applicants received legal assistance from the state, victims received poor, if any, legal advice. This had a profoundly disempowering impact on those affected, most of whom struggled to follow the appeals procedure, which had many legal technicalities. Many frustrated victims have since made strong statements that there can be no reconciliation without justice (Maepa, 2005).

Reparations and 'truth' must go hand in hand because, without this link, any form of reparation runs the danger of being seen by survivors as a governmental strategy to prematurely close the book on the past, and leave its secrets hidden. 'Reparations without truth make survivors feel that reparations are being used to buy their silence and put a stop to their continuing quest for truth and justice' (Hamber and Wilson, 2002: 46).

Reflections on 'shared truths'

The discourse about 'truth' is infused with misconceptions. Part of these misconceptions derive from the fact that the majority of Truth Commissions are governmental, in that they are typically set up by the 'transitional governments' of newly established fragile democracies, in order to attempt a formal account of the violence, crimes, and civil and human rights abuses of previous regimes (Avruch, 2010; Avruch and Vejarano, 2001). However, these commissions have demonstrated great diversity and functioned in diverse socio-political settings, with varying levels of international, governmental and popular support. The most critical points seem to involve the conflation of individual and collective dimensions about 'truth', a controversial conception of collective memory, and confusion about issues around healing, reconciliation and forgiveness.

One of the most problematic points is that sharing facts is not necessarily conducive to 'shared truths'. Maybe the question about 'shared truth' is more quantitative than qualitative in nature: that is, to what extent can social actors involved in past abuses recognize the other party's truth (Thomas, 2010)? The issue of the complexity and multiplicity of truth is a central one, linking the problematic demands of justice and the hopes for reconciliation. It is the arena in which parties' competing versions of history and politics of memory play themselves out. Thus, the question becomes about the extent to which Truth Commissions may contribute to opening up those *in-between spaces* in society, where, although contested and problematic, survivors, perpetrators and bystanders can begin to reclaim their history and articulate their individual narratives in a recognizing and valadating relationship (Hamber and Wilson, 2002). Benjamin (2004) suggests that recognition is mutual, a two-way road: truth, as officially recognized knowledge of horrible past events, needs the truth of perpetrators and victims to be mutually acknowledged. For this space to be created, tensions between opposing social forces must both exist there and be *contained*.

The question about 'what restores the truth' may be considered to be the same as the question about 'what restores subjectivity' (Avruch, 2010). The essential condition for this to happen is a framework of safe-enough grounding in some workable future, the wind of hope blowing forward, because an honest connection with the past is pursued. Truth as contradictory and conflicting testimony to one's experience, can only emerge if protective social boundaries through political and legal instruments are set up. Such boundaries may take different forms according to the historical and political climate. But a set of basic conditions of justice is required. Provided that this can be guaranteed, can truth have a repairing potential, while restoring trust and vision of a possible future.

Truth is an open space, not a solid set of facts. It needs responsibilities to be ascertained, but also a shared and never-complete narrative about events in construction. Truth, like memory, is something workable, which, to a certain extent, is subject to change and re-evaluation, although it cannot be reversed.

In relational thinking, an important sign of a re-opening of *states of thirdness* is the capacity to hear multiple inner voices, without losing the ability to feel one.

This standard may also be considered with regard to truth: the ability to work through multiple truths without losing the sense of what happened. This delicate balance between unity and multiplicity may be 'shared truth'.

Mutuality is a movement towards the wholeness of self and society, the space to recognize the other in one's own experience, without losing a sense of the difference among diverse social actions and the importance that responsibility be appropriately attributed.

Notes

1 See www.ohchr.org/EN/ProfessionalInterest/Pages/RemedyAndReparation.aspx.
2 Inter-American Court of Human Rights, *Loayza-Tamayo vs. Peru (Reparations and Costs)*, Judgment of 27-11-1998, Series C No. 42, §148.
3 *Chorzow Factory Case*, PCIJ, Series A, No. 17, 1928, pp. 47–8.
4 Articles 34, 35, 36 of International Law Commission on Responsibility of States for Internationally Wrongful Acts.
5 Article 9(5) of the International Covenant on Civil and Political Rights and Article 5(5) of the European Convention on Human Rights mention an 'enforceable right to compensation'. Article 14(1) of the United Nations Convention Against Torture, similar to Article 19 of the Declaration on the Protection of All Persons from Enforced Disappearances, refers to 'an enforceable right to fair and adequate compensation, including the means for as full rehabilitation as possible'. Article 9 of the Inter-American Convention to Prevent and Punish Torture provides that, 'the States Parties undertake to incorporate into their national laws regulations guaranteeing suitable compensation for victims of torture'. Protocol I (Additional) to the Geneva Conventions of 1949 provides in Article 91 that: 'A Party to the conflict which violates the provisions of the Conventions or of this Protocol shall, if the case demands, be liable to pay compensation. It shall be responsible for all acts committed by persons forming part of its armed forces'. Equally the Statutes of the ICTR and ICTY refer to the right of compensation (Article 106); the Rome Statute contains elaborate provisions on reparations to victims, including compensation (Article 75) as do a number of instruments regulating the laws and customs of war. The UN Basic Principles and Guidelines on the Right to a Remedy and Reparation state that compensation should be provided for any economically assessable damage, as appropriate and proportional to the gravity of violation and the circumstances of each case, resulting from gross violation of international humanitarian law, such as: a) a physical or mental harm; b) lost opportunities, including employment, education and social benefits; c) material damages and loss of earnings, including loss of earning potential; d) moral damage; and e) costs required for legal or expert assistance, medicine and medical services, and psychological and social service.
6 The Conference on Jewish Material Claims Against Germany is an umbrella organization (founded in New York in 1951) composed of national and international Jewish organizations, which represents the Diaspora Jews in the West. Its aims are to obtain funds for the relief, rehabilitation and resettlement of Jewish victims of Nazi persecution and to obtain indemnification for injuries inflicted and restitution for properties confiscated by the Nazis.
7 See resolution by the UN Commission on Human Rights, UN Doc. E/CN.4/RES/2001/70, 25 April 2001, para.8.
8 For example, *Aksoy vs. Turkey*. App. No. 21987/93, Judgment of 18 December 1996 para 113; *Aydin vs. Turkey*, App. No. 23178/94, Judgment of 25 September 1997; *Selmouni vs. France*, App. No. 25803/92, Judgment of 28 July 1999.
9 Resolution on the Guidelines and Measures for the Prohibition and Prevention of Torture, Cruel, Inhuman or Degrading Treatment or Punishment in Africa (Robben Island Guidelines).

10 See for example the UN Convention on the Rights of the Child U.N. Doc. A/44/49 (1989), entered into force 2 September 1990, and its Optional Protocol U.N. Doc. A/54/49, Vol. III (2000), entered into force 12 February 2002; UN Convention Against Torture U.N. Doc. A/39/51 (1984)], entered into force 26 June 1987; Declaration on the Protection of All Persons from Enforced Disappearances GA Res. 47/133 of 18 December 1992; Declaration on the Elimination of Violence against Women GA Res. 48/104 of 20 December 1993.
11 For example, *Chumbipuma Aguirre et al. vs. Peru* (*Barrios Altos Case*), Series C No. 87, Reparations, Judgment of 30 November 2001, para. 40.
12 For instance, in Guatemala the Historical Clarification Commission was created out of the United Nations negotiated peace accords; in Argentina an equivalent body was called National Commission on the Disappearance of Persons; in Uruguay it was known as Commission for Peace.
13 Examples of this approach include the National Commission on Disappearance of Persons in Argentina, the National Commission for Truth and Reconciliation in Chile, the Commission on the Truth for El Salvador, and the Truth and Reconciliation Commission for South Africa.
14 He was appointed UN Special Rapporteur on Torture for the years 2010-2016.

References

African Commission on Human and Peoples' Rights, Guidelines and Measures for the Prohibition and Prevention of Torture, Cruel, Inhuman or Degrading Treatment or Punishment in Africa (Robben Island Guidelines). 32nd Session, Banjul, The Gambia, 17–23 October 2002. Available at: www.achpr.org/sessions/32nd/resolutions/61/ (accessed 15 April 2015).

Agger, I. and Jensen, S.B. (1996) *Trauma and Healing Under State Terrorism*. London: Zed Books.

Aguirre, D. and Pietropaoli, I. (2008) 'Gender equality, development and transitional justice: the case of Nepal'. *International Journal of Transitional Justice*, 2(3): 356–77. doi:10.1093/ijtj/ijn027.

Aldana, R. (2006) 'A victim-centered reflection on truth commissions and prosecutions as a response to mass atrocities'. *Journal of Human Rights*, 5(1): 107–26. doi:10.1080/14754830500485916.

Allden, S. (2007) 'Internalising the culture of human rights: securing women's rights in post-conflict East Timor'. *Asia Pacific Journal on Human Rights and the Law*, 8(1): 1–23. doi:10.1163/157181507782200240.

Allen, E. 'Chain of command: can torture in Iraq be linked to the White House?' *The Financial Times*, June 17, 2004, p. 21.

Ambos, K. (2002) 'Superior responsibility'. In Cassese A., Gaeta P. and Jones, J. (Eds.), *The Rome Statute of the International Criminal Court: A Commentary*, Volume 1. Oxford: Oxford University Press, 2002, pp. 823–72.

Antkowiak, T. (2008) 'Remedial approaches to human rights violations: The Inter-American Court of Human Rights and beyond'. *Columbia Journal of Transnational Law*, 46(2): 351–406. Available at: http://digitalcommons.law.seattleu.edu/faculty/313 (accessed 17 July 2015).

Arcel, L.T., Christiansen, M. and Roque, E. (2000) 'Reparation for victims of torture: some definitions and questions'. *Torture*, 10 (3): 89–91.

Arendt, H. (1963) *Eichmann in Jerusalem: A Report on the Banality of Evil*. New York: Penguin Books, 1977.

Auckerman, M. J. (2002) 'Extraordinary evil, ordinary crime: a framework for understanding transitional justice'. *Harvard Human Rights Journal*, 15: 39–98.

Avruch, K. (2010) 'Truth and reconciliation commissions: problems in transitional justice and the reconstruction of identity'. *Transcultural Psychiatry*, 47(1) (February): 33–49. doi:10.1177/1363461510362043.

Avruch, K. and Vejarano, B. (2001) 'Truth and Reconciliation Commissions: a review essay and annotated bibliography'. *Social Justice*, 2(1–2): 47–108.

Bantekas, I. (1999) 'The contemporary law of superior responsibility'. *The American Journal of International Law*, 93(3) (July): 573–95.

Bantekas, I. (2000) 'The interests of states versus the doctrine of superior responsibility'. *International Review of the Red Cross*, 82(838): 391–402. doi:10.1017/5156077550017556x.

Benjamin, J. (1990) 'An outline of intersubjectivity: the development of recognition.' *Psychoanalytic Psychology*, 7: 33–46. Reprinted as 'Recognition and destruction': an outline of intersubjectivity', in Mitchell, S.A. and Aron L. (Eds.) (1999) *Relational Psychoanalysis: The Emergence of a Tradition*. Hillsdale, NJ and London: The Analytic Press, pp. 181–210.

Benjamin, J. (2004) 'Beyond doer and done to: an intersubjective view of thirdness'. *Psychoanalytic Quarterly*, 73: 5–46. Reprinted in Aron, L. and Harris, A. (Eds) (2012) *Relational Psychoanalysis, Vol. 4 Expansion of Theory*. New York and London: Routledge, pp. 91–130.

Benjamin, J. (2007) 'Intersubjectivity, thirdness and mutual recognition'. Talk given at the Institute for Contemporary Psychoanalysis, Los Angeles, CA.

Bonafé, B. (2007) 'Finding a proper role for command responsibility'. *Journal of International Criminal Justice*, 5(3) (July): 599–618. doi:10.1093/jicj/mqm030.

Bromberg, P.M. (1993) 'Shadow and substance: a relational perspective on clinical process'. *Psychoanalytic Psychology*, 10(2): 147–68. doi:10.1037/h0079464.

Bromberg, P. M. (1998) *Standing in the Spaces*. Hillsdale, NJ: Analytic Press.

Brounéus, K. (2008) 'Truth-telling as a talking cure? Insecurity and retraumatization in the Rwandan Gacaca courts.' *Security Dialogue*, 2008, 39(1): 55–76. doi:10.1177/0967010607086823.

Brounéus, K. (2010) 'The trauma of truth telling: effects of witnessing in the Rwandan gacaca courts on psychological health'. *Journal of Conflict Resolution*, 54(3): 408–37. doi:10.1177/0022002709360322

Byrne, C.C. (2004) 'Benefit or burden: victims' reflections on TRC participation'. *Peace and Conflict: Journal of Peace Psychology*, 10(3): 237–56. doi:10.1207/s15327949pac1003_2.

Carmichael, K., McKay, F. and Dishington, B. (1996) 'The need for REDRESS: why seek a remedy? Reparation as rehabilitation'. *Torture*, 6(1): 7–9.

Cassese, A. and Gaeta, P. (2013) *Cassese's International Criminal Law*. Revised by Antonio Cassese, Paola Gaeta, Laurel Baig, Mary Fan, Christopher Gosnell and Alex Whiting, 3rd edition, Oxford: Oxford University Press.

Chanbonpin, K.D. (2011) 'We don't want dollars, just change': Narrative counter-terrorism strategy, an inclusive model for social healing, and the truth about torture commission. *North-Western University Journal of Law and Social Policy*, 6(1) (Winter): 1–46. Available at: https://ssrn.com/abstract=1594269 (accessed 5 January 2017)

Chapman, A.R. and Ball, P. (2001) 'The truth of Truth Commissions: comparative lessons from Haiti, South Africa, and Guatemala'. *Human Rights Quarterly*, 23(1):1–43. doi:10.1353/hrq.2001.0005

Cienfuegos, A.J. and Monelli, C. (1983) 'The testimony of political repression as a therapeutic instrument'. *American Journal of Orthopsychiatry*, 53(1): 43–51. doi:10.1111/j.1939-0025.1983.tb03348.x

Clark, P. (2010) *The Gacaca Courts, Post-Genocide Justice and Reconciliation in Rwanda: Justice Without Lawyers*. Cambridge: Cambridge University Press.

Council of Europe, European Convention for the Prevention of Torture and Inhuman or Degrading Treatment or Punishment, European Treaties Series, ETS No. 126. Adopted in Strasbourg on 26 November 1987, entered into force 1 February 1989 in accordance with article 19. Text amended according to the provisions of Protocols No. 1 (ETS No. 151) and No. 2 (ETS No. 152), entered into force on 1 March 2002.

Crawford, J., Pellet, A. and Olleon, S. (Eds.) (2010) *The Law of International Responsibility*. Oxford: Oxford University Press.

Cryer, R., Friman, H., Robinson, D. and Wilmshurst, E. (2010) *An Introduction to International Criminal Law and Procedure*. Second edition, Cambridge: Cambridge University Press.

d'Estrée, T.P. (2006) 'The role of "voice" in intergroup conflict de-escalation and resolution'. In Fitzduff, M. and Stout, C.E. (Eds.), *The Psychology of Resolving Global Conflicts: From War to Peace*. Westport, CT: Praeger Security International, pp. 103–21.

Dinstein, Y. (2012) *The Defense of 'Obedience to Superior Orders' in International Law*. Oxford: Oxford University Press.

Doak, J. and O'Mahony, D. (2006) 'The vengeful victim? Assessing the attitudes of victims participating in restorative youth conferencing'. *International Review of Victimology*, 13(2): 157–77. doi:10.1177/026975800601300202

Echeverria, G. (2006) 'Redressing torture: a genealogy of remedies and enforcement'. *Torture*, 16(3): 152–81.

Folger, R. (1977) 'Distributive and procedural justice: combined impact of voice and improvement on experienced inequity'. *Journal of Personality and Social Psychology*, 35(2): 108–19. doi:10.1037/0022-3514.35.2.108.

French, B.M. (2009) 'Technologies of telling: discourse, transparency, and erasure in Guatemalan truth commission testimony'. *Journal of Human Rights*, 8(1): 92–109. doi:10.1080/14754830902717734.

Gillard, E.C. (2003) 'Reparation for violations of international humanitarian law'. *RICR*, September 2003, 85(851): 529–53.

Gómez Isa, F. (2013) 'Justice, truth and reparation in the Colombian peace process'. Norwegian Peacebuilding Resource Center, April 2013. Available at: https://www.files.ethz.ch/isn/163462/5e7c839d7cf77846086b6065c72d13c5.pdf (accessed 30 September 2015).

Gonzalez, E. and Varney, H. (2013) 'Truth seeking: elements of creating an effective Truth Commission'. Available at: www.ictj.org/sites/default/files/ICTJ-Book-Truth-Seeking-2013-English.pdf (accessed 1 November 2015).

Gordon, N. (1995) 'Compensation suits as an instrument in the rehabilitation of tortured people'. In Gordon, N. and Marton, R. (Eds.), *Torture: Human Rights, Medical Ethics and the Case of Israel*. London: Zed Books.

Guthrey, H.L. (2015) *Victim Healing and Truth Commissions. Transforming Pain Through Voice in Solomon-Islands and Timor-Leste*. Switzerland: Springer International Publishing.

Hamber, B. and Wilson, R.A. (2002) 'Symbolic closure through memory, reparation and revenge in post-conflict societies'. *Journal of Human Rights*, 1 (1) (March): 35–53. doi: 10.1080/14754830110111553

Hamber, B., Nageng, D. and O'Malley, G. (2000) ' "Telling it like it is . . . ": Understanding the truth and reconciliation commission from the perspective of survivors'. *Psychology in Society*, 26(1): 18–42.

Hayner, P.B. (1997) 'International guidelines for the creation and operation of truth commissions: a preliminary proposal'. *Law and Contemporary Problems*, 59(4): 173–80.

Hayner, P.B. (2011) *Unspeakable truths: Transitional Justice and the Challenge of Truth Commissions*. New York: Routledge.

Hendin, S.E. (2003) 'Command responsibility and superior orders in the twentieth century – a century of evolution'. *Murdoch University Electronic Journal of Law*, 10(1) (March).

Available at: www.austlii.edu.au/au/journals/MurUEJL/2003/4.html (accessed 24 October 2015).
Herman, J.L. (2003). 'The mental health of crime victims: impact of legal intervention'. *Journal of Traumatic Stress*, 16(2): 159–66. doi:10.1023/A:1022847223135.
Human Rights Watch, 'U.S.: Rumsfeld potentially liable for torture. Defense Secretary Allegedly Involved in Abusive Interrogation', 13 April 2006. Available at: www.hrw.org/news/2006/04/13/us-rumsfeld-potentially-liable-torture. (accessed 13 March 2014).
Humphrey, M. (2003) 'From victim to victimhood: truth commissions and trials as rituals of political transition and individual healing'. *The Australian Journal of Anthropology*, 14(2): 171–87. doi:10.1111/j.1835-9310.2003.tb00229.x.
Insco, J. (2003) 'Defence of superior orders before military commissions'. *Duke Journal of Comparative and International Law*, 13 (Spring): 389–418.
Jung, C.G. (1920) 'The psychological foundations of belief in spirits'. *Collected Works of C.G. Jung*, vol. 8, Read, H. Fordham M. and Adler G. (Eds.), translated by R. Hull, Princeton, NJ: Princeton University Press/Bollingen Series XX (thereafter, *CW*).
Jung, C.G. (1928) 'The relations between the ego and the unconscious'. In *CW*, vol. 7.
Jung, C.G. (1934) 'A review of the complex theory'. In *CW*, vol. 8.
Kendall, S. and Staggs, M. (2005) *Silencing Sexual Violence: Recent Developments in the CDF Case at the Special Court for Sierra Leone*. Berkeley, CA: UC Berkeley War Crimes Studies Center.
Kent, L. (2012). *The Dynamics of Transitional Justice: International Models and Local Realities in East Timor*. New York: Routledge.
Kilpatrick, D.G. and Ross, M. (2001) 'Torture and human rights violations. Public policy and the law'. In Gerrity, E., Keane, T.M. and Tuma, F. (Eds.), *The Mental Health Consequences of Torture*. New York: Plenum, pp. 317–31.
Knoops, G.G.J. (2006) 'Truth and reconciliation commission models and international tribunals: a comparison'. Paper presented at the Symposium 'The Right to Self-Determination in International Law', 29 September – 1 October 2006. Available at: www.unpo.org/downloads/ProfKnoops.pdf (accessed 11 September, 2014).
Kristof, N.D. (2008) 'The Truth Commission', *New York Times*, 6 July.
Lael, R. (1982) *The Yamashita Precedent: War Crimes and Command Responsibility*. Rowman and Littlefield Publishers.
Laplante, L.J. and Theidon, K. (2007) 'Truth with consequences: justice and reparations in post-Truth Commission Peru'. *Human Rights Quarterly*, 29(1) (Febuary): 228–50. Available at: www.jstor.org/stable/20072794 (accessed 28 September 2015).
Laub, D. and Auerhahn, N.C. (1993) 'Knowing and not knowing massive psychic trauma: forms of traumatic memory'. *The International Journal of Psychoanalysis*, 74(2): 287–302.
Laxminarayan, M. (2012) 'Procedural justice and psychological effects of criminal proceedings: the moderating effect of offense type'. *Social Justice Research*, 25(4): 390–405. doi:10.1007/s11211-012-0167-6.
Levi, P. (1947) *If This is a Man*. London: Abacus, 1991.
Levine, E. (2005) 'Command responsibility: the mens rea requirement'. *Global Policy Forum*, (February). Available at www.globalpolicy.org/component/content/article/163/28306.html (accessed 16 June 2012).
Lifton, R.J. (1986) *The Nazi Doctors: Medical Killing and the Psychology of Genocide*. New York: Basic Books, 1986.
Lind, E. and Tyler, T. (1988) *The Social Psychology of Procedural Justice*. New York: Springer.
Maepa, T. (Ed.) (2005) 'Beyond retribution: prospects for restorative justice in South Africa'. *ISS Monograph* no. 111, February. Pretoria, South Africa: Institute for Security Studies,

with the Restorative Justice Center. Available at: www.issafrica.org/uploads/Mono111. pdf (accessed 30 December 2014).
Magarell, L. (2007) 'Reparations in theory and practice'. ICTJ, Reparative Justice Series. Available at: www.swisspeace.ch/typo3/fileadmin/user_upload/Media/Topics/Dealing_ with_the_Past/Resources/ICTJ_Reparations_in_Theory_and_Practice.pdf (accessed 6 July 2011).
Markham, M. (2011) 'The evolution of command responsibility in international humanitarian law'. *Penn State Journal of International Affairs*, (Fall): 50–7.
Martinez, J.S. (2007) 'Understanding mens rea in command responsibility: from Yamashita to Blaškić and beyond'. *Journal of International Criminal Justice*, 5(3): 638–64. doi:10.1093/jicj/mqm031
McFarlane, A. (1996) 'Attitudes to victims: issues for medicine, the law and society'. In Chris Sumner *et al.* (Eds.), *International Victimology: Selected Papers from the 8th International Symposium*. Australian Institute of Criminology, Canberra, pp. 259–75.
McKinney, K. (2008) ' "Breaking the conspiracy of silence": testimony, traumatic memory, and psychotherapy with survivors of political violence'. *Ethos*, 35(3): 265–99. doi: 10. 1525/eth.2007.35.3.265
Meloni, C. (2010) *Command Responsibility in International Criminal Law*. The Hague: T.M.C. Asser Press.
Méndez, J.E. (2005, April 1) 'How to take forward a transitional justice and human security agenda: policy implications for the international community', Cape Town.
Mettraux, G. (2009) *The Law of Command Responsibility*. Oxford: Oxford University Press.
Mignone, E.F. (1992) 'The experience of Argentina'. In Netherlands Institute of Human Rights (Ed.), *Seminar on the Right to Restitution, Compensation and Rehabilitation for Victims of Gross Violations of Human Rights and Fundamental Freedoms*, SIM Special No.12.
Mitchell, A.D. (2000) 'Failure to halt, prevent or punish: the doctrine of command responsibility for war crimes'. *Sidney Law Review*, 22(3): 381–410.
Mollica, R. (1988) 'The trauma story: the psychiatric care of refugee survivors of violence and torture'. In Ochberg, F.M. (Ed.), *Post-Traumatic Therapy and Victims of Violence*. New York: Brunner/Mazel, pp. 295–314.
Muddel, K. (2009) 'Limitations and opportunities of reparations for women's empowerment' (2009) ICTJ Briefing. Available at: http://ictj.org/publication/limitations-and-opportunities-reparations-womens-empowerment (accessed 6 July 2011).
Nowrojee, B. (2005) 'Making the invisible war crime visible: post-conflict justice for Sierra Leone's rape victims'. *Harvard Human Rights Journal*, 18 (Spring): 85–105.
O'Connell, J. (2005) 'Gambling with the psyche: does prosecuting human rights violators console their victims?' *Harvard International Law Journal*, 46(2): 295–345. Available at: http://scholarship.law.berkeley.edu/facpubs/1036 (accessed 20 December 2016).
Office of the High Commissioner for Human Rights (2008) 'Rule-of-law tools for post-conflict states. Reparations programmes'. United Nations Publication. Available at: www.ohchr.org/Documents/Publications/ReparationsProgrammes.pdf (accessed 6 July 2011).
Organization of American States, Inter-American Convention to Prevent and Punish Torture. Adopted at Cartagena de Indias, Colombia, on 9 December 1985, at the fifteenth regular session of the General Assembly. Entered into force on 28 February 1987. OAS Treaty Series, No. 67. Available at: www.refworld.org/docid/3ae6b3620.html (accessed 3 January 2017).
Pokempner, D. (2005) 'Command responsibility for torture'. In Roth, K., Worden, M. and Bernstein A.D. (Eds.), *Torture: Does it Make us Safer? Is it Ever Ok? A Human Rights Perspective*. New York: New Press and Human Rights Watch, pp. 158–72.

Rombout, H. and Vandeginste, S. (2003) 'Reparation for victims of gross and systematic human rights violations: the notion of victim'. *Third World Legal Studies*, 16(5): 89:114.

REDRESS (2003) *Reparation. A Sourcebook for Victims of Torture and Other Violation of Human Rights and International Humanitarian Law*. London: The Redress Trust. Available at: www.redress.org/downloads/reparation/SourceBook.pdf (accessed 4 October 2015).

REDRESS (2006a) *Implementing Victims' Rights. A Handbook on the Basic Principles and Guidelines on the Right to a Remedy and Reparation*. London: The Redress Trust. Available at: www.redress.org/downloads/publications/Reparation%20Principles.pdf (accessed 10 November 2016.

REDRESS (2006b) *Enforcement of Awards for Victims of Torture and Other International Crimes*. London: The Redress Trust. Available at: www.redress.org/downloads/publications/master_enforcement%2030%20May%202006.pdf (accessed 4 October 2015).

Reisman, W.M. (1999) 'Compensation for human rights violations: the practice of the past decade in the Americas'. In Randelzhofer, A. and Tomuschat, C. (Eds.), *State Responsibility and the Individual: Reparation in Instances of Grave Violations of Human Rights*. The Hague, London and Boston: Martinus Nijhoff, pp. 63–108.

Rimé, B., Kanyangara, P., Yzerbyt, V. and Paez, D. (2011) 'The impact of Gacaca tribunals in Rwanda: psychosocial effects of participation in a truth and reconciliation process after a genocide'. *European Journal of Social Psychology*, 41(6): 695–706. doi:10.1002/ejsp.822.

Rodriguez-Pinzon, D. and Martin, C. (2006) *The Prohibition of Torture and Ill-treatment in the Inter-American Human Rights System*. OMCT Handbook Series, Vol. 2. Geneva, Switzerland.

Ross, F. (2003) 'On having voice and being heard: some after-effects of testifying before the South African Truth and Reconciliation Commission'. *Anthropological Theory*, 3(3): 325–41. doi:10.1177/14634996030033005.

Rugge, T. and Scott, T.L. (2009) *Restorative Justice's Impact on Participants' Psychological and Physical Health*. Ottawa: Public Safety Canada.

Sandoval, C. and Duttwiler, M., (2010) 'Redressing non-pecuniary damages of torture survivors: the practice of the Inter-American Court of Human Rights'. In Gilbert, G., Hampson, F. and Sandoval, C. (Eds.), *The Delivery of Human Rights: Essays in Honour of Professor Sir Nigel Rodley*. London: Routledge, pp. 114–36.

Schabas, W.A. and Darcy, S. (2004) *Truth Commissions and Courts: The Tension Between Criminal Justice and the Search for Truth*. Dordrecht, The Netherlands: Kluwer Academic Publishers.

Senese, S. (2006) 'Argentina. Tortura e dittature militari in American Latina negli anni '70: la dottrina della sicurezza nazionale'. In Bimbi, L. and Tognoni, G. (Eds.), *La Tortura Oggi nel Mondo*. Roma: Fondazione Internazionale Lelio Basso, pp. 63–72.

Sengheiser, J. (2008) 'Command responsibility for omission and detainee abuse in the "war on terror"'. *Thomas Jefferson Law Review*, 30(2) (Spring): 693–722.

Shelton, D. (2005) *Remedies in International Human Rights Law*. Second edition. Oxford: Oxford University Press.

Stanley, E. (2009) *Torture, Truth and Justice: The Case of Timor Leste*. New York: Routledge.

Stauffer, J. (2013) 'Speaking truth to reconciliation: political transition, recovery, and the work of time'. *Humanity: An International Journal of Human Rights, Humanitarianism, and Development*, 4(1): 27–48. doi:10.1353/hum.2013.0007.

Streichler, S. (2010) 'The illusion of accountability: the idea of an American Truth Commission on torture'. *Global Dialogue*, 12(1) (Winter/Spring 2010). Available at: www.worlddialogue.org/content.php?id=455 (accessed 1 November 2015).

Stryszak, M. (2002) 'Command responsibility: how much should a commander be expected to know?' (United States Air Force Academy) *Journal of Legal Studies*, 27: 27–81.

Suchkova, M. (2011) 'The importance of a participatory reparations process and its relationship to the principles of reparation'. Essex Transitional Justice Network, Reparation Unit, Briefing Paper No. 5, Published in August 2011, Ed. Clara Sandoval. Available at: www.essex.ac.uk/tjn/research/reparations.shtm (accessed 7 February 2014).

Sveaass, N. (1994) 'The psychological effects of impunity'. In Navik, N.J., Nygård, M., Sveaass, N. and Fannemel, E. (Eds.) *Pain and survival: Human Rights Violations and Health*. Scandinavian University Press, Oslo, pp. 211–20.

Sveaass, N. and Lavik, N.J. (2000) 'Psychological aspects of human rights violations: the importance of justice and reconciliation'. *Nordic Journal of International Law*, 69 (1): 35–52. doi:10.1163/15718100020296170.

Thibaut, J. and Walker, L. (1975) *Procedural Justice: A Psychological Analysis*. Hillsdale, MI: L. Erlbaum Associates.

Thomas, N.K. (2010) 'Whose truth?: Inevitable tensions in testimony and the search for repair'. In Harris, A. and Botticelli, S. (Eds.), *First Do No Harm: The Paradoxical Encounter of Psychoanalysis, Warmaking and Resistance*. New York: Routledge Press.

Tyler, T. (1994) 'Psychological models of the justice motive: antecedents of distributive and procedural justice'. *Journal of Personality and Social Psychology*, 67(5): 850–63.

Tyler, T., Rasinski, K. and Spodick, N. (1985) 'Influence of voice on satisfaction with leaders: exploring the meaning of process control'. *Journal of Personality and Social Psychology*, 48(1) (January): 72–81. doi:10.1037/0022-3514.48.1.72.

United Nations, Basic Principles and Guidelines on the Right to a Remedy and Reparation for Victims of Gross Violations of International Human Rights Law and Serious Violations of International Humanitarian Law. Adopted by General Assembly resolution 60/147 of 21 March 2006. Available at: www.refworld.org/docid/4721cb942.html (accessed 25 February 2015).

United Nations, Convention against Torture and Other Cruel, Inhuman or Degrading Treatment or Punishment. Adopted and opened for signature, ratification and accession by General Assembly resolution 39/46 of 10 December 1984, entered into force on 26 June 1987. Available at: www.ohchr.org/EN/ProfessionalInterest/Pages/CAT.aspx (accessed 14 September 2015).

United Nations, Convention on the Rights of the Child. Adopted and opened for signature, ratification and accession by General Assembly resolution 44/25 of 20 November 1989, entered into force 2 September 1990, in accordance with article 49. Available at: www.ohchr.org/en/professionalinterest/pages/crc.aspx (accessed 18 January 2016).

United Nations, Declaration of Basic Principles of Justice for Victims of Crime and Abuse of Power. Adopted by the General Assembly on 29 November 1985 with resolution 40/34. Available at: www.un.org/documents/ga/res/40/a40r034.htm (accessed 15 November, 2015).

United Nations, Declaration on the Elimination of Violence against Women. Adopted without vote by the UN General Assembly in its resolution 48/104 of 20 December 1993. Available at www.un.org/documents/ga/res/48/a48r104.htm (accessed 7 December 2015).

United Nations, Declaration on the Protection of All Persons from Enforced Disappearance. Adopted by the UN General Assembly on 20 December 2006, opened for signature on 6 February 2007 and entered into force on 23 December 2010. Available at: www.ohchr.org/EN/HRBodies/CED/Pages/ConventionCED.aspx (accessed 21 January 2015).

United Nations, International Covenant on Civil and Political Rights. Adopted by the UN General Assembly on 16 December 1966, entered into force on 23 March 1976. Available at: www.ohchr.org/en/professionalinterest/pages/ccpr.aspx (accessed 18 January, 2016).

United Nations High Commissioner for Human Rights, Istanbul Protocol: Manual of the Effective Investigation and Documentation of Torture and Other Cruel, Inhuman and Degrading Treatment or Punishment, Professional Training Series no. 8/Rev. 1, New York, Geneva, 2004.

United Nations Treaty Collection, Optional Protocol to the Convention Against Torture and Other Cruel, Inhuman or Degrading Treatment or Punishment, G.A. res. A/RES/57/199. Adopted by the UN General Assembly on 18 December 2002, entered into force 22 June 2006, in accordance with article 28(1). Available at: https://treaties.un.org/Pages/ViewDetails.aspx?src=IND&mtdsg_no=IV-9-b&chapter=4&lang=en (accessed 18 May 2015).

van Boven, T. 'Study concerning the right to restitution, compensation and rehabilitation for victims of gross violations of human rights and fundamental freedoms. Final Report'. UN Doc. E/CN.4/Sub.2/1993.

van Boven, T. (2010) 'The United Nations Basic Principles and Guidelines on the Right to a Remedy and Reparation for Victims of Gross Violations of International Human Rights Law and Serious Violations of International Humanitarian Law'. *United Nations Audiovisual Library of International Law*, 2010. Available at: http://legal.un.org/avl/pdf/ha/ga_60-147/ga_60-147_e.pdf (accessed 14 January 2015)

van Camp, T. and Wemmers, J. (2013) 'Victim satisfaction with restorative justice: more than simply procedural justice'. *International Review of Victimology*, 19(2): 117–43. doi: 10.1177/0269758012472764.

van Sliedregt, E. (2012) *Individual Criminal Responsibility in International Law*. Oxford: Oxford University Press.

Verbitsky, H. (1996) *The Flight: Confessions of An Argentine Dirty Warrior*. New York: The New York Press.

Wemmers J.A. and Cyr, K. (2006) 'What fairness means to crime victims: a social psychological perspective on victim-offender mediation'. *Applied Psychology in Criminal Justice*, 2(2): 102–28.

Werle, G. (2009) *Principles of International Criminal Law*. Second edition, The Hague: TMC Asser.

Winnicott, D.W. (1963) 'The development of the capacity for concern'. *Bulletin of the Menninger Clinic*, 27: 167–76.

Wise, M.Z. (1993) 'Reparations'. *The Atlantic Monthly* (October 1993), 272 (4): 32–5. Available at: www.theatlantic.com/past/docs/unbound/flashbks/nazigold/wise.htm (accessed 30 January 2016).

Yav Katshung, J. (2005) 'The relationship between International Criminal Court and truth commissions: some thoughts on how to build a bridge across retributive and restorative justices'. Center for Human Rights and Democracy Studies, Lubumbashi. Available at: www.iccnow.org/documents/InterestofJustice_JosephYav_May05.pdf (accessed 2 November 2015).

Zedner, L. (1994) 'Reparation and retribution: are they reconcilable?'. *The Modern Law Review*, 57(2): 228–50.

INDEX

Please note that page numbers relating to Notes contain the letter 'n' followed by the note number

abaissement du niveau mental 117–18
abductions 73
Abed, R. T. 153
abjection (Kristeva) 141, 142
absence 162, 167
absolute defences 215
absolute pain 24
Abu Ghraib prison 24, 69, 75n3, 196
action, and involvement 40
act utilitarianism 207, 208
adoptions 26
Adversity Activated Development (AAD) 63, 182, 183
affect 167
affective impulses, alterations in regulation of 56
affectivity and boundaries of self 173
affect-mirroring 122
affinity groups 44
after-effects of torture 8, 56–7; bodily 8, 52–3; interpersonal 176; intrapsychic 176
aggressiveness 47, 53, 60, 111, 114, 150, 173, 179
Akhtar, S. 173
alchemy 118, 120, 121
Algerian War 16, 18, 19, 22, 24, 65, 140
alienation 65
Alleg, H. 12, 140
Allen, J. 198–9

Allen, J. G. 58
allocation of knowledge 218
Allodi, F. 49
alpha function (Bion) 103, 122, 139
Altman, N. 207
altruism 73–4
America *see* United States (US)
American Psychological Association 71
American Relational Psychoanalysis *see* Relational Psychoanalysis, American
Améry, J. 8, 176
Amnesty International xii, 17, 40, 51, 69, 70, 183
amnesty laws 216
Analytical Psychology 116–21; and Relational Psychoanalysis xiv, xv, 93–6
ancient Greeks, function of torture in 10, 19
an-other subjectivity 219
anti-Semitism 25
Anzieu, D. 142
Apartheid 19, 140, 231
Arcel, L. T. 222
'archetypal radiation' (Papadopoulos) 148
archetypes 98, 117, 127n1, 128n2, 155; unipolar 148, 163
Arendt, H. 32, 34, 40
Argentina: Dirty War *see* Dirty War (1974–1983), Argentina; 'double discourse' of junta 72–3; 'Due

Obedience Law' (1987) 216; ESMA flights 49–50; kidnappings 23, 26, 75n5, 216; persecutory anxiety 101, 102, 164; renewal and transformation 26; rhetoric 140; self-inflated representation 18, 149; torture 179
Aristotle 10
Armenians 19, 25, 73
Army (Freud) 138
Aronson, E. 44
Arrigo, J. M. 201, 204
Aryan ideology 17–18, 25
assaultive projective identification 169–70, 174, 176–7
associative processes 98
asylum-seeking 51
asymmetrical relationships 58
atomic bombs 196, 197
attachment 57–60, 61
attention, alterations in 56
attunement 116, 122; privation of attuned holding 104–5
Auerhahn, N. C. 179, 181, 217
Auschwitz death camp 39–40
'Auschwitz self' (Lifton) 44
authoritarianism, F-scale 36
authority principle 38
'autistic-contiguous' mode (Ogden) 106, 141
aversion to strangers 150
avoidance 54, 156, 179, 180
Azo of Bologna 11

Balint, M. 97
Bantekas, I. 214, 215
Baranger, W. 147
Barnett, J. 152
Bar-On, D. 163
basanos (search for truth) 10
Basic Principles and Guidelines on the Right to a Remedy and Reparation for Victims of Gross Violations of International Human Rights Law and Serious Violations of International Humanitarian Law, UN 226
Basoğlu, M. 182
Beauvoir, S. de 113
'behavioural change technology' (Singer) 170
behavioural re-enactments 59
belief, and knowledge 73, 202, 203
Benasayag, M. 179
Benjamin, J. 113–16, 122, 123, 151, 156, 157, 172, 218, 235; *Bonds of Love* 113; *one in the third* 116, 123; *shared intersubjective third* 115; *third in the one* 123; *thirdness* 115; *see also* Benjamin, J.
Bentham, J. 144, 151, 197–8; *see also* Panopticon (Bentham)
beta elements (Bion) 103, 128, 178
Bettelheim, B. 40
better world ideology 25–6
Big Brother society 64
binary thinking (us/them) 22, 25, 64, 152
biological rhythms 177
Bion, W. R. 102–3, 108, 110; alpha function 103, 122, 139; beta elements 103, 128, 178; 'nameless' terror 139; *rêverie* (Bion) 103, 117–18; 'reversal of alpha-function' 139
biphasic development 105
BISCUITS (Behavioural Science Consultation Teams) 70
blackwhite 152, 157n3
Blass, T. 25
'blood money' 223
'blue lit stage' (Chile) 157
Bocer (seventeenth-century civil lawyer) 11
bodily after-effects 8, 52–3, 176
body–mind dichotomy 8
Bonds of Love (Benjamin) 113
Boulanger, G. 178
boundaries 114, 150, 162, 177, 205, 218; bodily 140, 143, 177; of child 123; of endangered ego 126; group 139–43; limited 200; national 75n1; negotiating 142; permeable 173; physical and mental 9, 176; psychic 118, 177; of self 173, 174; social 235; systemic 75n1
Bowlby, J. 57
brainwashing 62
Branche, R. 177
Brazil 33, 50
breaking the prisoner 59, 177
Brecher, B. 204, 206
bridging, empathic relationships 121
British Object Relations Theory *see* Object Relations Theory (British)
Britos, D. 70
Bromberg, P. M. 97–8, 111–12; 'standing in the spaces' 112, 122
Bufacchi, V. 201
burden of guilt 51, 60
bureaucratic perpetrators 167–8
bureaucratic specialization 39, 48
burnout 49
Bush, G. W. 16, 228

bystanders 63–74; 'bystander state' 66, 162; concepts/definitions 64; denial 64–5; external 74; and genocide 65–6; internal 66–74; knowledge 66, 165; 'missing witness' (absence) 162, 167; passive opposition 66, 72–3; passive support 66; and perpetrators 68, 162–4; silent acquiescence 64; and victims 66, 164–7

Calley, W. 216
Card, C. 205
Carmichael, K. 226
Casebeer, W. 207
Castresana, C. 205
catastrophic threats 139, 197, 203
Central America, counterinsurgency warfare in 17
certainty of knowledge 206
Cheney, R. B. ('Dick') 196, 208n1
Chicago police 38
children: adoption of from disappeared parents 26; construction of reality 172; consumed by the father 155; idealised attachments 58; relationship with mother 122; transmission of trauma 60, 182
Chile 157
Chilean Medical Association 68–9
China 62; Chinese Cultural Revolution 171
choosiness and entitlement 17
chosen glories (Volkan) 17
chronic pain 52–3
Chronos (Saturn) 155
Church 138
CIA 70–1
'cinema room' (South Vietnam) 157
citizens 10, 19
civil suits 226
'closed system superego' (Novick and Novick) 174–5
coerced confessions 205
coercion 5, 9, 43, 69, 168, 170, 171, 172
cognitive dedifferentiation 180
cognitive neutralization techniques 64
Cohen, S. 64–8
Cold War 18, 71, 72
collective identity 161, 163
collective modes of denial 167
Colman, W. 128n1, 155
commanders 50, 213–14, 217, 231
command responsibility doctrine 212–15, 217

Commentary to the Secret of the Golden Flower (Jung) 118
Commission on Human Rights (OHCHR) 223
Committee Against Torture (CAT), UN 6
common paranoid-schizoid mode 154
communism 25–6, 72
community 163–4
compartmentalization 39–40
compensation 222–3
complementary relations 115, 118
Complex PTSD (C-PTSD) 56–7
concentration camps 67; survivors 32
conception of self 96
Conference on Jewish Material Claims against Germany 236n6
confessions 11, 171; coerced 205
confidentiality 231
conflicts of identity 175
'confusion of tongues' (Ferenczi) 172
coniunctio oppositorum 118, 119, 120, 122
Conroy, J. 37–8, 45, 46, 168
conscious knowledge 217
consequentialist fallacies 201
constant observation 162
constant visibility 151, 165
constructive knowledge 213
contagion 95, 143, 145; panic of 144
containment 110, 111, 122, 164, 184; emotional 103, 125, 143, 161, 162, 183
continuous traumatic stress 163
contradictory beliefs 64
control over troops 213, 217
Convention on the Rights of the Child (UN) 219, 237n10
conviction rates 204
counterinsurgency warfare 17, 22, 24
counterproductive torture 204
counter-terrorism 17, 20
Crelinsten, R. D. 11–12, 26, 41, 43, 45, 64, 68, 74
crimes of obedience 33, 215–17
criminal liability xvi, 200, 211, 214, 226
criminal suspects 51
Critical Discourse Analysis 21
cruel, inhuman or degrading treatment (CIDT) 5, 6
culpability 11, 215, 217; *see also mens rea* (culpable state of mind)
cultural differences 54
cultural superiority 17–18, 149
cultural ties 177

cultural transformation 61
cultures of fear 72
customary law 213, 214, 217

damaged self-concept 54
damages of torture 220–7
Danielian, A. 25
Darley, J. M. 64
Dawson, T. 95
death camps 67
death flights (ESMA) 50
decentred unity 97, 124
Declaration of Basic Principles of Justice for Victims of Crime and Abuse of Power (UN, 1985) 219, 224
declaration of the wrongfulness 223
Declaration of Tokyo (WMA 1975) 70
Declaration on the Protection of All Persons from Being Subjected to Torture or Other Cruel, Inhuman and Degrading Treatment or Punishment, UN 6
deductive fallacies 201
defect of symbolization 179
defence mechanisms 39, 93, 97, 108, 125, 136, 162, 164, 166, 175
defenders of the state 22
dehumanization of torturers 49
dehumanization of victims 20, 47, 49
de-individuation 44, 145
delusions of unity 136, 152
'democratic culture of denial' (Cohen) 67–8
democratic societies 17
denial 64–5, 167, 217; and splitting 152, 164, 165, 206
Denmark 73
dependence/dependency 59, 71, 111, 113, 115
depersonalization 54, 56, 118, 180–1
deportation 52, 73
depression 53–4, 55, 57
depressive position 101, 102, 108–9, 122
derealization 180
Dershowitz, A. 197, 198, 199, 204
desaparecidos 73
de-skilling 201
D'Estrée, T. P. 232
destruction, role of 114
destruction of self 53
destruction of trust 153
de-subjectification of victims 177
devalued people 19
de Zulueta, F. 60

difference, and identity xv, xvi, 122, 123, 126, 136, 142, 156, 161
difference in relations xv, 122
'dirty hands' 199, 204, 207
Dirty War (1974–1983), Argentina 18, 23, 40, 50, 64, 75n5, 154; primary strategy 154–5
disappearances 23, 26, 73
disavowal 152, 162, 164, 166
Discipline and Punish (Foucault) 11
discontinuity of self 97
disorientation 37
dissidents 19–20
dissociation 39, 40, 127, 151, 169, 171, 175, 180, 184n2, 218; and continuity 96–100, 162; and depersonalization 54, 56; as ego function 98; healthy and pathological 99; paradoxical multiple self states 93, 94, 95; physical and psychological consequences of torture 54, 56, 58; *Reflective Triangles* 122, 124, 125; *in-between spaces* 111, 112, 116, 117
distress 35, 40, 49, 53, 54, 103, 222, 223, 225, 233; in infants 110, 111, 122; psychological 50
doctors 8, 68–72, 74, 163; Nazi Germany 39, 50, 175; *see also* physicians
doer/done-to mode (Benjamin) 115
domination 10, 113–14, 156, 171; and love 113; and submission 114
Dorfman, A. 149
double reality 25
doublethink (Orwell) 64, 152, 158n3, 165
doubling (Lifton) 39–40, 44, 175, 217
dread 101, 136, 138, 141; formless 140, 143; nameless 103, 139–43, 170, 179; unbearable 142
'dry narratives' 177
dual loyalty 69
DuBois, P. 10
Dutton, D. G. 57–8
Duttwiler, M. 220
duty 41

early infancy theorists 164
economic superiority 17
ego 98, 99, 119, 122, 123, 124, 166
ego ideal 137, 138, 149, 150, 151, 174
'ego-skin' (Anzieu) 142
Eichmann, A. 32, 34, 39, 40, 48, 216
Eichmann in Jerusalem (Arendt) 34
Einsatzgruppen (Nazi killing units) 67
electric shock experiments 34, 38
emergency situations 20–1, 22

emotional deprivation 58
emotional inaccessibility 181
emotional numbing 54, 180
emotional rationale of torture xvi, 206
emotional state of collective terror 139
emotions *see* hate/hatred; love; rage
'enactment' (Bromberg) 111–2
endless war 165
enemies of the state 22, 33
'enhanced interrogation' 65, 70–1
enigmatic experience 53
ESA (Greek Military Police) 43
Escuela de Mecànica de la Armada (ESMA) 49–50, 75n5
ethical dilemmas 163
European Convention on the Prevention of Torture 223, 224
European Court of Human Rights (ECHR) 223
euthanasia programmes 66
evasive thinking 72
evil 139, 149, 173, 175, 196, 202, 206, 207; and anti-Semitism 25; defences 39; good and evil 39, 118, 163; individuation of 207; inner 171; lesser of two evils 197, 198; overcoming difficulties in performing 41, 47–9; problem of xiv, 31, 32–3; pure 101, 148
experience: centers of 124; enigmatic 53; historical mode 105, 106, 108–9; lived 108; presymbolic 115; relational 112; rhythmic 115–16; sensory 106; split-self experience 109; splitting 107; of time 178
external bystanders 74
'extra-legal' areas 196–7
extraordinary powers 20–2

Fairbairn, W. R. D. 97, 172
false arrests 205
fascists 140, 149, 154, 157n2
Faulkner, W. 60
fear xii, 98, 162, 164, 174, 175, 208, 229; and bystanders 68, 73; collective 137, 138; cultures of 72; in infants 103, 105; Monolithic Societal States 139, 140, 141; Paradoxical Multiple Self States and Monolithic Self States 122, 126; and perpetrators 37, 40; torture, arguments for and against 204, 206; torturous societies 20, 22, 23; of trauma 111; victims of torture, 58, 59, 61
female torturers 75n3
Ferenczi, S. 172

fictionality of torture 157
'field of forces' 33, 148
fight or flight reaction 59
Final Solution 67
Fisler, R. 177–8
'five techniques' (combination of tortures) 37
flashbacks 54, 59
Fonagy, P. 166–7, 172; *mentalization* 109–10, 122; psychological self 110; *reflective function* xv, 97, 109–10, 111, 122, 127n1
force 5, 6
forces within/between individuals 114
foreclosed spaces 94, 227
foreshortened future 54
former Yugoslavia (ICTY) 6, 212
formless dread 140, 143
Foucault, M. xv, 23, 143–5; *Discipline and Punish* 11; leper model 153
fragmented societies 167
France 16, 18, 24, 140
Frankl, V. 62
free human agency 213
Freud, S.: on Army 138; on Church 138; on group psychology 96, 166; *Group Psychology and the Analysis of the Ego* xv, 137, 150; and Jung 128n3; 'On narcissism' 137; post-Freudian psychoanalysis 95; 'primary groups' 137; psychoanalytic tradition 94, 95; 'taboo of virginity' 150; on trauma 59; *Verleugnung* (disavowal) 166
F-scale of authoritarianism 36

General Security Service (GSS, Israel) 200
genocide: Armenians 25, 73; and bystanders 65–6; Holocaust 73
George, S. K. 53
Geras, N. 65
Germany *see* Nazi Germany
Ghent, E. 114
Giannoni, M. 95, 128n1
Gibson, J. T. 45
God 151–2
Golston, J. C. 169
Gordon, N. 149, 226
government power 23
Gramsci, A. xi
Grand, S. 178
Graziano, F. 149, 154, 155–6
Great Britain 17, 21, 37, 196; *see also* Northern Ireland
Greece 43

groupal self 142
group conflict 42, 65
group identity 44, 153
group psychology 96, 137–9, 166
Group Psychology and the Analysis of the Ego (Freud) xv, 137, 150
groups: boundaries 139–43; controlling individuals 146; illusionary knowledge 157; large group dynamics xv, 135, 136; narcissism 150; obedience to authority 35–7
Guantánamo Bay 70, 196, 228
Guerre Moderne (Trinquier) 24
guerre révolutionnaire 18
guilt feelings 51, 60
Gur-Aye, M. 200, 205
Guthrey, H. L. 232

Hamburg Declaration (WMA 1997) 70
Hamilton, V. L. 33
Haritos-Fatouros, M. 33, 43–4, 45
hate/hatred 41, 63, 64, 126, 142, 147, 170, 173–4; infant development 106–7, 173–4; self-hatred 56, 175
Havel, V. 72
healing processes 120, 227, 232, 233
hearings, public 229, 233
Hegel, G. W. F. 218
hegemonic ideologies 163, 164
Heinz, W. S. 21, 32
Herman, J. L. 58–9
Hilberg, R. 48
historical mode of experience 105, 106, 108–9
Hitler, A. 17, 25
Hofstadter, N. 7
Hollander, N. C. 23, 164
Holocaust 32, 34, 48, 62, 73; as Final Solution 67; *see also* Auschwitz death camp; concentration camps; Jewish people; Nazi Germany
Holtz, T. H. 182
Horwitz, G. J. 67
hostility 36, 42, 150, 173
Huggins, M. 33, 44–5, 48, 50, 75n1
Human Rights Foundation of Turkey 70
human rights treaty bodies 6, 7, 212, 213
human rights violations 16, 222
human subjectivity 218
human ties 174
Hussein, S. 23
Hutus (Rwanda) 67
hyperarousal 54
hyper-masculinity 41

idealization 58, 155, 175
identity: civilian 45; collapse of 124; collective 161, 163; conflicts of 175; and difference xv, xvi, 122, 123, 126, 136, 142, 156, 161; with ego 123; group 44, 153; homogeneous 127; individual 163; loss 117; narcissistic 150, 151; partial 117; personal 97, 104; political 18; positive 18; pure 218; re-shaping of 45–7; with the shadow 118; stable 99; unconscious 117; of victims 169, 176, 180
ideological mental state 153
ideological movements 40
ideological persuasion 42, 149
ideological thinking 206
ideological zeal 216
ideologization process 49
ideology: Aryan 17–18, 25, 140; better world 25–6; bystanders 64; definition 35, 146–7; hegemonic ideologies 163, 164; illusion of omniscience 149, 152; internalizing 32–3, 47, 64; justifying torture 26, 33; nationalistic 25–6; 'new man' 26; of parents and leaders 165; 'social emergency state' 64; and utopian visions 165
If This Is a Man (Levi) 227
Ignatieff, M. 149–50
illusionary knowledge 157
illusion of omniscience 149, 152
illusion of oneness 143
illusion of safety 153
imminence of danger 196, 197, 201, 202, 206
immoral torture 199
impunity 183
in-between spaces xvi, 135, 157, 235; social reflective in-between spaces 157; Paradoxical Multiple Self States and Monolithic Self States 93–4, 116, 125, 127; permissibility of torture 217, 218, 219; *Reflective Triangle* 161, 162, 177
independence: and dependence 113; medical 69; psychological 105
Indifferent, The (Gramsci) xi
individuality 45, 58, 100
individuals: controlled within groups 146; dynamics between 114
individuation 118, 119, 142; de-individuation 44, 145; of evil 207
Indochina 24
indoctrination 45, 171
"I-ness" (Ogden) 99, 106, 107, 108

infant development 100–11; anxieties 172; hate 106–7, 173–4; idealised attachments 58; narcissism 137; parents 172; ruthless love 173; splitting 101, 102, 103; *states of twoness/thirdness* 101–2; *see also* mother and baby interactions
informers 72, 153
initiation processes 43–5
'innerism' 65
innocence 199
'innocents' and 'guilty' 19–20
institutional colonization 168
institutional torture 37–8, 203, 204, 207–8
insurgents 19–20
intelligence gathering xiii, 204, 205
intense pain 5, 11, 53, 176
interactions, between mother and baby 122, 151, 173
Inter-American Convention to Prevent and Punish Torture (1985) 6, 7
Inter-American Court of Human Rights 220, 224
intergenerational effects 60, 182
internal bystanders 66–74
internal fragmentation 39
internalization 110, 151, 172, 173; of ideology 32–3, 47, 64
internal objects/subjects 93, 94, 99, 171
internal Panopticon 171
internal struggles 175
internal war 22
international condemnation 74
international courts 6, 212, 217, 229–32
International Covenant on Civil and Political Rights 219
International Criminal Court (ICC) 6, 7, 212, 213
International Criminal Tribunal for Rwanda (ICTR) 6, 212
International Criminal Tribunal for the former Yugoslavia (ICTY) 6, 212
international law xiv, xvii, 198, 201, 212, 214, 215, 217, 218, 221; torture in 3–7
International Law Commission 201, 236n4
interpersonal after-effects 176
interpreting subjects 106–8, 109, 147
interrogation manuals 11–12, 17, 176
interrogations: 'in-depth' 70; doctors' role 70; enhanced methods 65, 70–1; justification 65, 198, 202–3; Northern Ireland 37; Palestinians 21; special procedure 65; and the truth 11; using 'moderate physical pressure' 21, 65
intersubjectivity 123, 166, 218–19
interviews 50
intimacy 58
intrapsychic after-effects 176
intrusive memories 54
investigations 4, 38, 228, 231; psychoanalytic xiii
invisibility *see* visibility/invisibility
invisible enemies 24
Iran 151–2
Iraq 23
Irish Republican Army (IRA) 17, 37
irresolvable paradox of self 98, 124
ISIS (Islamic State of Iraq and Syria) 10
Islamic fundamentalism 10; *see also* ISIS (Islamic State of Iraq and Syria)
isolation of victims 58, 152
Israel: cultural superiority 17–18, 149; democratic culture of denial 67–8; Penal Law article 34(1) 200; Supreme Court judgement 200; treatment of Palestinians 17, 21, 37–8
Istanbul Protocol (OHCHR, 2004) 52, 54, 70, 224

Jackson, R. 21
Janet, P. 59
Japan 196
Jaranson, J. 10
Jewish people 19, 25, 67, 73, 149; *see also* anti-Semitism; concentration camps; Holocaust; Nazi Germany
Jongman, B. 16
judicial processes 223
judicial torture 11
Jung, C. G. 94, 95, 98–100, 148, 206; complexes, theory of 98, 99; *possession by the shadow* 118; 'psychological complexes' 98, 117; *Psychology and Alchemy* 99–100; 'splinter psyches' 98, 122; tension of opposites 123; transcendent function 119, 122, 123, 124
jus cogens (peremptory norm) 3
Just and Unjust Wars (Walzer) 196
'just' compensation 222
justice: procedural 232; restorative 230, 231, 232
justification of torture 20, 26, 33, 65
'just satisfaction' (ECHR) 223
just wars 196
'just world thinking' 64, 66

Kalsched, D. E. 95
Keen, Sam 32
Kelman, H. C. 9, 17, 19, 20, 22, 33, 48
KESA (Centre for Military Police Training, Greece) 43
Khmer Rouge (S-21, Tuol Sleng) 11–12
kidnappings 17, 23, 24, 26, 51, 170, 176; Argentina 23, 26, 75n5, 216
Kira, I. 62
Klein, M. 101–2, 106–7; 'part-object' 101, 102, 106, 109
'knowing and not knowing' (Laub and Auerhahn) 167, 179, 217
knowledge: actual and constructive 213; allocation of 218; and belief 73, 202, 203; bystanders 66, 165; certainty of 206; conscious 217; of crimes 217; denial 217; displaced 181; duty of 214; of extermination policy 67; good and evil 118; guilty 202; illusionary 157; levels of 213; and negligence 214; of pain-inflicting techniques 9; preformed 139, 143, 154, 164; public 223; and responsibility 217–19; self-knowledge 100, 119, 120; status of 12, 149, 152, 162, 165, 206, 207; subjective 216; ticking-time bomb scenarios 203; of torture xii, 3, 68, 69; and trauma 179; unconscious 218; of violence 67
Korean War 62
Koru, F. E. 7
Kristeva, J. 141–2
KURBAK Counterintelligence Interrogation manual (CIA 1963) 176

Laing, R. D. 97
Landau Report (1987) 21, 65
Laqueur, W. 67
large group dynamics xv, 135, 136
Latané, B. 64
Latin America 21, 24, 72, 164
Laub, D. 167, 179
Lavranos, A. 51
Law of Command Responsibility (Mettraux) 213
Lazar, R. 155, 173–4
Lazreg, M. 15, 18, 22
learned helplessness 44
legal doctrines 218
legal/illegal orders 215–16
legal restitution 221
legitimacy of torture 20, 48, 195–200
leper model (Foucault) 143, 153
Levi, P. 32, 227

Levin, M. 197
liberal democracies 38
liberal ideology of torture 202
'Libertad' prison (Uruguay) 70
'life force' (Winnicott) 173
life plan 62, 220–1
Lifton, R. J. 25, 50, 62, 69, 163, 171; doubling 39–40, 44, 175, 217
'living with the lie' (Havel) 72
logical error 203
logotherapy (Frankl) 62
loss of self 53
love: and domination 113; and hate 107, 147, 173; parental 173, 174
loyalties 58, 176; dual 69; Hitler, loyalty to 40
Luban, D. 202

Makiya, K. 23
manifest illegality principle 216, 217, 218
manipulation of pain and stress 8
manoevre of closure (Kristeva) 141
Marks, J. H. 22
Martinez, J. S. 214
Marton, R. 149
Marxian totalitarian system 72
massive psychic trauma 177
material restitution 221
Matthews, R. 202–3, 204, 207
Mauthausen Concentration Camp 67
May, L. 200–1
McFarlane, A. 178, 226
Me, You and Other xv, 94, 124, 156, 161, 184
mechanisms: coping 62; defence 39, 93, 97, 108, 125, 136, 162, 164, 166, 175; mechanism of power 145; of pain 8; projective 123
medical assessments 52, 225
medical independence 69
Melzack, R. 8
Méndez, J. 231
mens rea (culpable state of mind) xvi, 212–19; *see also* culpability
mental health, of perpetrators 32
mental health professionals 163
mentalization (Fonagy) 109–10, 122
mental states 93, 156, 165; of children 110; collective 148; containment 110; culpable 213; denial 64; ideological 153; *Monolithic Self State* 127; putative 110; shifting 121–2; *Splintered Reflective Triangle* 125; temporary 121; of terror 154; of *thirdness* 112, 113, 116; of

torturers 231; traumatic 60; of *twoness* 112, 113, 116, 147–8
mental suffering 5, 222
Mettreaux, G. 213
Miles, S. H. 68
Milgram, S. 34–6, 47, 48, 168
military dictatorships 24
military necessity 200–1
military officers 21, 32, 214, 216
Miller, A. 182
Millet, K. 8–9, 15–16, 46, 140, 151–2
Mills, J. 44
mind control 170–1
minorities 19, 51
mirroring 110, 111, 124, 161, 165, 167, 172; affect-mirroring 122
mistreatment 47, 174
mistrust 62
Mitchell, S. 96–7
model of control (plague) 144
model of exclusion (leper) 144
model of mind 100
monetary compensation 222
monolithic, meaning 136, 168
monolithic mode of governance 16
monolithic power 151
Monolithic Self States (MSS) xv, 93, 135, 168; and *Paradoxical Multiple Self States (PMSS)* 121–7
monolithic selves 165, 182
Monolithic Societal States(MSoS) xv, 136, 137, 139, 152, 206, 217, 227
monotheism 151, 175
morality 163
moral psychology 41
moral restraints 41
moral superiority 17
mother and baby interactions 122, 151, 173; *see also* infant development
multidisciplinary therapeutic approaches 53
multiple inner voices 235–6
multiple personalities 40
multiple truths 236
multiplicity of self xv, 97, 99, 111
mutuality 236
mutual recognition 113, 115, 123, 136, 151, 161, 162, 180
mutual regulation 115, 116
mythical and heroic past 17

nameless dread 103, 139–43, 170, 179
narcissism: expressions of 155; Freud on 150; groupal 150; infantile/primary 137; of minor differences 149, 150; social 149–50
narcissistic identity 150, 151
national courts 229–32
nationalistic ideology 25–6
national security legislation 21–2
Nazi Germany: Aryan ideology 17–18, 25, 140; Denmark 73; doctors 39, 50, 175; and education 26; *Einsatzgruppen* 67; guards as sadists 32; and legitimacy of torture 196; loyalty to the Führer 40; propaganda 20, 25, 26; *see also* concentration camps; Holocaust; Jewish people
necessity defence 21, 196–7, 200, 201, 206
negative intimacy 182
Neumann, E. 155
neuropsychological studies 177–8
neurotic denial of reality 166
'new man' ideologies 26
nightmares 59
9/11 attacks 17, 21, 22, 196
Nineteen Eighty-Four (Orwell) 64, 151, 165, 171, 179–80
nociceptive pain 52
non-citizens 10
non-democratic societies 16
non-pecuniary harm 220
non-state actors 15
non-Western cultures 54
Northern Ireland 17, 37, 70; *see also* Great Britain
not-knowing 65
Novick, J. and Novick, K. K. 174–5
Nuremberg defendants 32

obedience to authority 33–8; groups 35–7; individual level 34–5; societal 37–8; suffering of the victim 47; torturers 42, 43; unthinkable violence 168
Obedience to Authority (Milgram) 34
objective hatred (Winnicott) 173
object-presenting 104–5
object relations 110, 112, 164, 180
Object Relations Theory (British) xv, 94, 96, 101–8
object usage 123, 218
Occupied Territories 21
offenders, as defenders of the state 22
Office of the High Commissioner for Human Rights (OHCHR), Interpretation of Torture in the Light of the Practice and Jurisprudence of International Bodies 5

254 Index

Ogden, T. H. 105–9, 147–8; 'autistic-contiguous' mode 106, 141; "I-ness" 99, 106, 107, 108; paranoid-schizoid mode 94, 105, 106–8, 147–8, 152, 154, 162, 206
OHCHR *see* Office of the High Commissioner for Human Rights (OHCHR)
omissions 5, 7, 212, 214
omnipotence 106, 114, 155, 174, 195, 206–7; fantasies xvi; in infants 104, 107, 109
omniscience, illusion of 149, 152
one in the third (Benjamin) 116, 123
oneness 141; illusion of 143
one-sidedness 125
only following orders 215, 216
'On narcissism' (Freud) 137
'open system superego' (Novick and Novick) 174
Operation Condor 24
Optional Protocol to Convention against Torture 224
orders, only following 215, 216
Ortiz, Dianna 180
Orwell, G.: *blackwhite* 152, 157n3; coercion and mind control 171; *doublethink* 64, 152, 158n3, 165; mentality supporting war 153; *Nineteen Eighty-Four* 64, 151, 165, 171, 179–80; terror reconstructing society 26; traumatic bondage 179–80; unidirectional control 151
Other/Otherness 124, 141, 142, 153; unconscious 'otherness' 143, 219
other within (Kristeva) 141, 142

pain: absolute 24; acute and chronic 52; complex structure 8; intense 5, 11, 53, 176; manipulation of 8; maximization of 8; physical 11, 51, 172, 176; power of torturers 23–4; psychic 140; psychological 51, 172; psychotic states 37; relationship with torture 5; torturers desensitized to 47; and the truth 11; unsharable 53; utilitarianism 195; victims' feelings for perpetrator 58, 172
Painter, S. 57–8
Palestinians 17, 21, 37–8
Panopticon (Bentham) xv, 128n3, 144–55, 162, 165, 175; internal 171
Papadopoulos, R. K. 55, 61, 63, 140, 148, 163

Paradoxical Multiple Self States (PMSS) xv, 93, 165; and *Monolithic Self States (MSS)* 121–7
paradox of the multiple self: theories of Bromberg 97–8; theories of Jung 98–100; theories of Mitchell 96–7
paranoid-schizoid mode (Ogden) 94, 105, 106–8, 147–8, 152, 154, 162, 206; common 154
paranoid-schizoid position 101, 109, 125, 178; *see also* states of twoness
paranoid-schizoid states 151
parents 26, 165, 172, 182; parental love 173, 174; *see also* mother and baby interactions
Parry, J. T. 10, 12
participation mystique (Jung) 116–18
participatory reparations processes 226
partitioning 143, 145, 149
'part-object' (Klein) 101, 102, 106, 109
part-object relatedness 106, 109
passive bystanders 66, 72–3
passive opposition 66, 72–3
passive support 66, 68–72
Paxton, R. O. 140, 154, 157n2
pecuniary damages 220
perceived threats 20–1
perceptions 178
permission 9
perpetrators; *see also* torturers
persecutory anxiety 101, 102, 164
personal autonomy, ceding of 34
personal trust, erosion of 51
Peters, E. 9, 11, 20
Philippines 157
physical deprivation 37
physical harm 52–3, 220
physical pain 11, 51, 172, 176
physicians 52, 68–70; *see also* doctors
Physicians for Human Rights USA 70
physiological stress reactions 53–4
piecemeal processes 48
plague-stricken towns 145
pleasure (utilitarianism) 195
pluralism/pluralist societies 16–17
police officers 40
'Political action: The problem of dirty hands' (Walzer) 199
political-institutional conditions 21
political leaders xvi, 176, 211, 212, 214, 215
political opposition 51
political upheavals 148

positioning 148
positive psychology movement 61
positive responses 61–3, 182–4
possession by the shadow (Jung) 118
post-Freudian psychoanalysis 95
post-traumatic condition 177, 180
post-traumatic growth 62
post-traumatic personalities 169, 201
Post-Traumatic Stress Disorder (PTSD) 49, 53, 54, 55–7, 60, 177, 180; Complex PTSD (C-PTSD) 56–7
'potential space' (Winnicott) 105, 122, 126, 172
power 148–52; government 23; mechanism of 145; monolithic 151; obedience to authority 36; political systems 151; spectacle of 23–4; of torturers/torturous 16–18, 23–4; unverifiable 151; visible 151
power asymmetry 19
power differentials 58
power relationships 15–16
Powers of Horror (Kristeva) 141–2
POWs (prisoners of war) 62
Prelinger, E. 181
primacy of the "race" 154
'primary groups' (Freud) 137
primary narcissism 137
'primitive agonies' (Winnicott) 104, 140
prisons/prisoners: breaking the prisoner 59, 177; female prisoners 141; prison dynamics studies 35–7; prisoners of war (POWs) 62; student-prisoners 35–6; *see also specific prisons, such as Abu Ghraib prison*
privacy 96, 177
private violence 9
privation of attuned holding 104–5
procedural justice 232
production of torturers 41, 49
'production room' (Philippines) 157
professionalism 48–9
professions 68–72
projection, impulses in 101
projective identification 102–3, 108, 112, 117, 121–2, 147, 155, 162, 169, 174, 182, 227; assaultive 169–70, 174, 176–7; in torture 176–7
prolonged stress 59
propaganda 20, 25, 26
proportional force 5, 205
prosecutions 212, 215, 229, 230, 231
protector–protected relationships 207
pro-torture arguments xvi, 195, 196, 206

psychiatric epidemiological instruments 54, 55
psychiatrists 70–1
psychic body 177
'psychic envelope' (Anzieu) 142
psychic pain 140
psychic trauma 177
psychoanalytic investigation xiii
psychoanalytic issues 95
psychobiological systems 57
psychological abuse 169
'psychological complexes' (Jung) 98, 117
psychological consequences 52–61
psychological development 105
psychological distress 50
Psychological Ethics and National Security task force (PENS, APA) 71
psychological pain 51, 172
psychological renewal 61
psychological reorganization 40
psychological self (Fonagy) 110
psychological stress reactions 54
psychological warfare 71
psychologists 8, 68, 70–1
Psychology and Alchemy (Jung) 99–100
psychosocial activities 225
psychotic denial of reality 166
psychotic states 37
public acknowledgement of violations 223
public character of torture 9–10, 23
public hearings 229, 233
public language of counter-terrorism 21
public officials 6–7
public terror 72–3
punishment of the guilty 20
purity of race 25, 140, 149, 151
purpose of torture 7, 11–12, 33

Question, The (Alleg) 140
Quiroga, J. 10

racial differences 150
racial purity 25, 140, 149, 151
racist accounts 140
rage 173–4
re-attachment to communities 60–1
recognition, other and self 123
reconciliation processes 229, 234
recruitment 42–3
re-enactment behaviours 59
re-experiencing trauma 54, 59
reflective function (Fonagy) xv, 97, 109–10, 111, 122, 127n1

Reflective Triangle xv, xvi, 94, 99, 121–5, 142, 165, 183, 184; *see also Splintered Reflective Triangle*
'regression to the Father' (Stein) 175
rehabilitation 224–5
re-integration within communities 60–1
Rejali, D. 204, 205
relational perspectives 166, 235–6
Relational Psychoanalysis (American) xiii, 93, 94, 100, 111–16; and Analytical Psychology xv, 95, 96
relational-transferential factors 170
religious fundamentalism 175; *see also* ISIS (Islamic State of Iraq and Syria)
relocating victims 51–2
renewing society 26
reorganization of self 168–75
reparations: compensation 222–3; eligibility for 220–1; forms 221–4; full reparation 221; international law 219; interrogations 221; local ownership 226; participatory processes 226; rehabilitation 224–5; restitution 221–2; as therapy 226–7
repression 64
repugnance to torture 47
reputation, damage to 220
rescuers 73–4
reshaping identities 44, 45–7
resilience 61–2, 182
resistance 12
respondeat superior 215
responses to torture 56, 61–3
responsibility 48; command 213; for crimes of obedience 215–17; diffusion of 64; and knowledge 217–19
restitutio in integrum 221, 227
restitution 221–2, 224
restorative justice 230, 231, 232
retaliatory cycles 114–15, 156
rêverie (Bion) 103, 117–18
'reversal of alpha-function' (Bion) 139
'revolutionary war' 24
rhythmicity 106, 115–16
Robben Island Guidelines 224
Robin, M. 22, 24
Rodley, N. 5, 7
role of destruction (Winnicott) 114
Romans 19
Rome Statute (ICC) 6, 7, 212, 213, 236n5
Rorschach test data 32
Rosarium Philosophorum 120
Rosenman, S. 169–70, 180–1, 183
Ross, F. 233

'rotten war' 24
routinization 47–8
rule utilitarianism 207, 208
Russell Tribunal II on Latin America 21
Rwanda 67, 73, 212, 234

S-21 Interrogator's Manual (Khmer Rouge) 11–12
sacrifice 143, 152, 157, 174, 199, 200; of complexity 148; of individuality 181; material 156; narrative of 154; self-sacrifice xvi, 45, 148, 154, 155, 195, 204, 207
sadistic behaviour 32, 36
safety, illusion of 153
salutogenic effects 62
Samuels, A. 120–1, 128n1
Sandoval, C. 220
Sartre, J. P. 12, 19, 140, 199
satisfaction 223, 224
Saturn (Chronos) 155
scapegoats 64
Scarry, E. 11, 23, 157, 176
schemata of self 97, 98
Schmid, A. P. 43, 45
School of Americas (US Army) 17
Schwager, E. 164, 165, 167, 168, 176, 181
Schwartz-Salant, N. 121
Scilingo, A. 49–50, 175–6
Searles, H. F. 97
secret display 23
secret torture 38
security reasons paradigm 22
seen/being seen dyad 151
segregating races 140
self 93–134; decentred unity 97, 124; deprived of meanings and reality 165; discontinuity of 97; dissociation *see* dissociation; essence 166; fear and control 162; individuality 45, 58, 100, 156–7, 181; irresolvable paradox of 98, 124; loss and destruction through pain 53; monolithic 165, 182; multiplicity of xv, 97, 99; and object differentiation 174; one-sidedness (Jung) 125; overarching personality structure (Jung) 99; paradoxical multiplicity 96; polarized 'I-dentification' 126; recognition of other 123; schemata 97, 98; shattered 176; *see also Monolithic Self States (MSS); Paradoxical Multiple Self States (PMSS);* paradox of the multiple self
self and society 65, 135, 227, 236

Index

self-as-object 107, 182
self-betrayal 59, 171
self-censorship 73
self-concept, damaged 54
self-defence 21, 205
self-enhancers 63
self-hatred 56, 175
self-image 25, 39
self-incriminating evidence 231
self-inflated representation 18, 149
self-perception, alterations in 56
self-regulation 116, 123, 174
self-sacrifice xvi, 45, 148, 154, 155, 195, 204, 207
Senese, S. 21–2
senex archetype 155
Sengheiser, J. 212, 213–14
sensory deprivation 58
sentience 195
separations 25, 39, 51–2
severe stress 59
severe superego 150
shameful obsequiousness 25
shared illusions 48
shared intersubjective third (Benjamin) 115
shared truths xvii, 235–6
shattered self 176
Shelton, D. 225
Sherman, N. 49
'should have known' principle 217
Shue, H. 199, 205
Sierra Leone TRC 234
silent acquiescence 64
'simple negligence' standard 214
simultaneous therapy 227
Singer, M. 170
Sironi, F. 44, 177
situationalist interpretations, of experiments 36
slaves 10–11, 19
social denial 64–5
'social emergency state' 64
social environment of fear and control 162
social isolation 58
social narcissism 149–50
social reality 64
social reflective in-between spaces 157
social stigmatization 234
socio-cultural contexts 9–10, 54
soldiers 40, 41, 203
Soldz, S. 70
solitary acts of torture 198, 211
somatic sensations 178, 179
somatization 57

South Africa 163; Apartheid 19, 140, 231; Truth and Reconciliation Commissions (TRC) 231, 237n13
South America 24
South Vietnam 157
space in-between (Winnicott) 104, 105, 112; absence of 125, 126
'speaking with double heart' (Schwager) 176
special state powers 21
special units 45
spectacle of power 23–4
spectacular torture 23
Spitz, S. 53
Splintered Reflective Triangle xv, xvi, 125–7, 136, 146, 153, 161–210; *see also* *Reflective Triangle*
'splinter psyches' (Jung) 98, 122
split moralities 163
split-self experience 109
splitting 25, 26, 44, 58, 106–7, 108, 127, 147, 152, 162, 164, 165, 173, 206, 217; and denial 152, 164, 165, 206; infant development 101, 102, 103
'standing in the spaces' (Bromberg) 112, 122
Stanford University experiment 35
state: defenders of 22; enemies of 22, 33; exclusion from 20; non-state actors 15; special powers 21; state terror 72–3, 153, 164
state of 'voyeur' (Boulanger) 178
state of 'witness' (Boulanger) 178
state protection 20–2
states of thirdness xv, 93, 94, 100–21, 124, 217–19, 235; infant development 101–2
states of twoness xv, xvi, 93, 100–21, 127, 135, 137, 138, 147–8, 152, 161–3, 165, 182, 218; infant development 101–2; *see also* paranoid-schizoid position
Staub, E. 16, 18, 19, 42, 66, 74
Steel, Z. 56
Stein, R. 151, 170, 175
Stockholm syndrome 172
Straker, G. 163
stress 8, 178; continuous traumatic 163; extreme stressors 54, 55; manipulation of 8; in new cadets 44; physiological reactions 53–4; prolonged 59; psychological reactions 54; severe 59; *see also* Post-Traumatic Stress Disorder (PTSD); trauma
strict liability 213, 214
student-prisoners 35–6

sub-human 18–20
sub-humans 25, 139
subject-in-process (Kristeva) 141
subjectivity 123, 141, 156–7, 181, 218, 219; human 218; an-other subjectivity 219; *see also* intersubjectivity
submission 41, 114–16, 156, 171
subordinates 136, 138, 146, 162, 212–14, 216, 218
subordinate-superordinate relationships 34, 213
subversives 19, 25
Suedfeld, P. 62
Sullivan, H. S. 97
Summers, F. 71
superego 105, 137; 'closed' and 'open' systems 174–5; severe 150
superiority core belief 17–18
superior responsibility doctrine 214, 217, 218
supreme emergency 195, 196, 197, 200–1, 206
surrender 113–16, 115
survivors: guilt of 51; psychological symptoms 53; relationships 181, 225; and restitution 221–2
suspects 203
suspension of opposites 120
Sussman, D. 59, 61
symbolization 94, 108–10, 122, 124, 125, 157, 161, 162, 165, 166, 180; defect of 179

'taboo of virginity' (Freud) 150
Tarantelli, C. B. 177
targets of torture 33
technical personnel 8
technology, torture as 176
telling and being heard interaction 232
tension of opposites (Jung) 123
terror: emotional climate 206; etymological origin *tromos* 140; ideology and utopian visions 165; 'nameless' (Bion) 139; state terror 72–3, 153, 164; and torture 22; torturous societies 139
terrorists xiii, 19–20, 24, 43
terrorscopic vision 22
testimony 10–11, 46, 52, 69, 230, 231; public 233, 234; truth as contradictory and conflicting testimony 235
theory of complexes (Jung) 98, 99
thinking and meaning 178
third in the one (Benjamin) 116, 123
thirdness (Benjamin) 115

Third Reich 25
thought reform 171
threat 21, 197, 202
Tibetan nuns 182
ticking-time bomb scenarios 197–8, 199, 201–4, 206
tissue damage 52
tissue of the body/mind (trauma) 177
titrosko (to rub in, trauma) 63
Todorov, T. 39, 63
tolerance of others 62
torment 11; collusion with tormentor 59; physical and psychological 8–9, 12
torture: arguments against 200–5; definition 12; extreme stressors 54, 55; 'five techniques' 37; in literature 8–12; nature of 5–6; physical and psychological consequences 52–61; physical and psychological torment 8–9, 9, 12; projective identification in 176–7; public character 9–10, 23; as punishment of the guilty 20; purpose 7, 11–12, 33; socio-political contexts 9–10; spectacular 23; through generations 60–1; widespread practice 22
Torture and the Ticking Bomb (Brecher) 204
Torture and Truth (DuBois) 10
Torture in 2014 (Amnesty International) xii
torture of the truth (Foucault) 11
torture policies 203
torture rooms 157
torturers 31–51; aim to shatter personalities 179; bureaucratic perpetrators 167–8; bystanders and perpetrators 68, 162–4; desensitized to pain 47; disobeying orders 205; female 75n3; future of 49–51, 175–6; learning sessions 174; made and not born 41; mental health of perpetrators 32; obedience to authority 42, 43; police officers 40; production of 41, 49; PTSD 49; public officials 6–7; recruitment and selection 42–3; socio-economic class 42; soldiers 40, 41; training 41–9, 168–75
'torture warrants' (Dershowitz) 197
torturous power 16–18
torturous societies 15–30; delusions of unity 136, 152; distinguishing 'innocents' from 'guilty' 19–20; features 20–6, 139; multiple separations 25; panic of contagion 144; rigid political/cultural contexts 136; social organism injured through trauma 142; two-dimensional reality 153

totalitarian systems: action as involvement 40; archetypes 155; bystanders 67; Marxian 72; *monolithic* mode of governance 16; 'new man' 26; separations 39
totally aversive pain 53
training manuals 17, 217
training of torturers 41–9, 168–75
trance states 170
transcendent function (Jung) 119, 122, 123, 124
transformation of society 26
transitional object theory (Winnicott) 105, 123, 172
transitional phenomena theory (Winnicot) 105
trauma: cognitive changes 163; disruption of illusion of 'integration' 98; effects 63; etymology 63; experience of time 178; 'just' compensation 222; 'knowing and not knowing' (Laub and Auerhahn) 167, 179; meaning 177; psychic 177; re-experiencing 54, 59; and rehabilitation 225; social organism injured through 142; transmission of 60; *see also* Post-Traumatic Stress Disorder (PTSD)
Trauma Grid (Papadopoulos) 63
traumatic bonding 57–60, 179–81, 182
traumatic initiation 44
traumatic memories 178
traumatogenic political environments 164
treatment of trauma 60–1
Trinquier, R. 24
tromos (terror/trembling) 140
troops, control over 213, 217
trust: destruction of 153; mistrust 62; personal trust, erosion of 51; public truth-telling 231
truth 10–12, 227–36; and interrogations 11; multiple truths 236; shared truths xvii, 235–6; as testimony 235
Truth and Reconciliation Commissions (TRC) xvii, 229, 231; in South Africa 230, 237n13
Truth Commissions (TC): and courts 229–32; definitions/aims 228–9; mandates 229; mixed success rates 228; public hearings 229; role 228; and torture 228
Turkey 25, 182
turning 'a blind eye' 65, 69
turning points 40
Tutsis (Rwanda) 67

Twin Towers collapse (9/11) 17, 21, 22, 196
two-in-one (Kristeva) 141
twoness 118, 125, 162; mental states of 112, 113, 116, 147–8; unconscious 148; *see also states of twoness*
tyranny of powers 155

Ulpian (Roman lawyer) 11
unbearable dread 142
unconscious (Mitchell) 96
unconscious complexes (Young-Eisendrath) 117
unconscious identity 117
unconscious knowledge 218
unconscious mind (Hollander) 164
unconscious 'otherness' 143, 219
unconscious twoness 148
UN Convention against Torture and Other Cruel, Inhuman or Degrading Treatment or Punishment (UNCAT, 1984) 17; Article 1 4, 6; Article 2 4; Article 4(1) 211; Article 14 219; CAT Committee 6, 224; Optional Protocol 224
Understanding Torture (Parry) 9–10
Understanding Torture (Wisnewski) xii–xiii
unio oppositorum 119
unipolar archetypes (Papadopoulos) 148, 163
unitary selfhood 97, 98
unitary Westphalian state 15
United States (US) 16, 17, 21, 24, 62, 196, 228; Central America 17; Cold War 71; Latin America 21, 24, 72, 164; South America 24; Vietnam War 62, 71; *see also* Central America, counterinsurgency warfare in
unity: decentred 97, 124; delusions of 136, 152; monolithic 152; and multiplicity 236; sense of 206
Universal Declaration of Human Rights (UN) xii
Unspeakable Acts, Ordinary People (Conroy) 37–8
unthinkable violence 168
unverifiable power 151
Uruguay 70, 237n12
us/them binary thinking 22, 25, 64, 152
utilitarianism 195, 206
utopian visions 165

van Boven, T. 222
van der Kolk, B. A. 58, 177–8

Varvin, S. 178, 179
Verbitsky, H. 49, 175–6
Verleugnung (disavowal, Freud) 166
vertical desire 175
verticalization of difference 175
'vertical mystical homoeros' (Stein) 175
victims: after-affects 176; and bystanders 66, 164–7; collusion with tormentor 59; contact with attackers 182; dehumanization of 20, 47, 49; dependence 59; de-subjectification 177; domination of 10; feelings for perpetrators 58, 172; giving testimony 233, 234; guilt and shame of surviving 51; identity 169, 176, 180; isolation 58, 152; minority groups 19, 51; public truth-telling 231; relocating 51–2; severing bonds to family 59; sympathy towards perpetrator 172; *see also* Basic Principles and Guidelines on the Right to a Remedy and Reparation for Victims of Gross Violations of International Human Rights Law and Serious Violations of International Humanitarian Law, UN; Declaration of Basic Principles of Justice for Victims of Crime and Abuse of Power (UN, 1985); testimony
Vidal-Naquet, P. 16
Videla, J. R. 26, 154
Vienna Convention on the Law of Treaties 3
Vietnam War 62, 71
Viñar, M. xi–xii
violations 55, 70, 198, 214, 224; of human rights xii, 15, 16, 219, 220, 221, 222, 223, 225, 229, 230; of international criminal law 219; of national security 22
violence 163
visibility/invisibility: constant visibility 151, 165; invisibility 144; invisible enemies 24; power 151

visible power 151
vision of suffering 23–4
voice 232–3; multiple inner voices 235–6
Volkan, V. 17
'voyeur,' state of (Boulanger) 178
vulnerability 18

Waldheim, K. 216
Wall, P. D. 8
Walzer, M. 196, 199
'war on terror' 17, 21, 22, 24, 70–1
Warrior's Honour (Igantieff) 149
Weisaeth, L. 178
Weltanschauung 149
Western psycho-diagnostic categories 54
Westphalian sovereignty principle 15
whole-object relatedness 109
Wiesel, E. 62
wilful blindness 214
Winnicott, D. W. 96–7, 104–5, 115, 120, 165, 218; 'life force' 173; objective hatred 173; 'potential space' 105, 122, 126, 172; 'primitive agonies' 104, 140; role of destruction 114; *space in-between* 104, 105, 112, 125, 126; transitional object theory 105, 123, 172; transitional phenomena theory 105
Wise, M. Z. 223
Wisnewski, J. J. 201, 203–4, 205
'witness,' state of (Boulanger) 178
witnessing 150, 233; 'missing witness' (absence) 162, 167; state of 'witness' (Boulanger) 178
World Federation of Mental Health 32
World Medical Association (WMA) 70

Yale University 34
Yawar, A. 51
Young-Eisendrath, P. 95, 117

Zedner, L. 225
Zimbardo, P. 35–7, 168